Sources of World Civilization

Sources of World Civilization

Volume II
Connections and Conflict

THIRD EDITION

Edited by

OLIVER A. JOHNSON
University of California Riverside

JAMES L. HALVERSON
Judson College

Upper Saddle River, New Jersey 07458

Library of Congress Cataloging-in-Publication Data

Sources of world civilization / Oliver A. Johnson, James L. Halverson.   -- 3rd ed.
    p. cm.
    Contents: v. l. Before 1500 -- v. 2. Since 1500.
    ISBN 0-13-182483-X (v. 1) -- ISBN 0-13-183505-X (v. 2)
    1. Civilization -- History -- Sources. I. Johnson, Oliver A. II. Halverson,
    James L.

CB69.S68 2004
909--dc21

                                                    2003048687

Acquisitions Editor: Charles Cavaliere
Editor-in-Chief: Charlyce Jones Owen
Associate Editor: Emsal Hasan
Editorial Assistant: Adrienne Paul
Marketing Manager: Heather Shelstad
Marketing Assistant: Jennifer Bryant
Production Editor: Laura A. Lawrie
Manufacturing Buyer: Tricia Kenny
Cover Design: Kiwi Design

Cover Illustration: Two platforms, one
for the Christians, the other for Muslims,
at the opening of the Suez Canal.
Courtesy of the Library of Congress.
Composition: This book was set in
10/12 Palatino by Integra
Printer/Binder: The interior was
printed by Courier Companies, Inc.
The cover was printed by Coral Graphics.

Credits and acknowledgments borrowed from other sources and reproduced, with
permission, in this textbook appear on appropriate page within text.

Pearson Education LTD.
Pearson Education Singapore, Pte. Ltd.
Pearson Education Canada, Ltd.
Pearson Education—Japan

Pearson Education Australia PTY, Limited
Pearson Education North Asia, Ltd.
Pearson Educación de Mexico, S.A. de C.V.
Pearson Education Malaysia, Pte. Ltd.

10 9 8 7 6 5 4 3 2 1
ISBN 0-13-183505-X

CONTENTS

THE MODERN ERA   111

PREFACE

Those familiar with previous editions of this book will immediately notice some significant changes. First, the number of selections has been greatly reduced. Second, sources from Western civilization are less predominant. Finally, study questions have been added before each selection and at the end of each major section of the book. These changes reflect my desire to update the book and at the same time remain true to the vision of previous editions. For this edition, the total length of the book needed to be reduced, while the geographic scope needed to be widened. This could have been done by either shortening the selections or by eliminating entire selections. I chose to keep the selections relatively long. There are other world history readers on the market that include a great number of brief excerpts. I have found this to be bewildering to my own students. Thus, this edition continues to affirm that any document significant enough to be included in an anthology such as this deserves to be excerpted in such a way that it retains some of its integrity and meaning. To make room for a broader scope of sources, I eliminated many of the documents pertaining to Western civilization. Even so, there is still a bias toward Western sources in this volume. As in previous editions, the assumption is that North American college students not only should be introduced to a variety of world cultures but also should dig more deeply into the origins of the culture in which they find themselves.

Acknowledgments

There are, as always, many people to thank at the end of a project like this. I would not have been involved in this project if the editors at Prentice Hall had not asked me. Nor could this project have gone forward had Dr. Johnson's estate not trusted me with making changes to the previous edition. Reviewers of the second edition, Nupur Chaudhuri (Texas Southern University), John Lyons (Joliet Junior College), Kurt J. Peterson (North Park University), and Robert Walker (Jackson State University), provided valuable insights into how this book might be improved. This project would have gone on much longer and been much less pleasant without the help of my assistant, Kelley Burke. Judson College greatly facilitated my work by awarding me a Surbeck Research Grant and relieving me of some of my faculty duties. My children, C.J., Tommy, and Anna, were constant sources of rejuvenation. But all this would have been for naught without the encouragement, patience, and support of my wife, Terri.

GENERAL INTRODUCTION

The purpose of this book is to introduce students to the history of world civilization through the documents that have formed and shaped that civilization. One word in the title of the book needs explanation. Our use of the singular "civilization," rather than "civilizations," is not meant to be question-begging. We are not implying by its use that world history is the story of a single civilization or even that the myriad societies that have occupied various parts of the world during the past five thousand years have much more in common than the shared humanity of their people. Our intent, rather, is the much more modest one of simply indicating that the book is concerned with the history of people who have lived together in organized and stable societies.

An attempt might be made to give the term "civilization" in the history of the world some substantive, positive content by selecting a central theme to serve as an overarching principle capable of uniting the various historical societies into a single world civilization. Such a theme could be used as an organizing device for these documents, giving this book a coherence and unity that it may seem to lack. But any such principle, whether chosen from politics, religion, economics, philosophy, or another field, would distort history by reducing the variety and complexity of historical societies into artificial and unreal unity. Although there are continuities in history and similarities among cultures that need to be recognized, there also are discontinuities and diversities as well. However convenient it might be for us to try, we cannot fit world history into a straitjacket. Although we have not found a central thread from which to hang the selections in this book, we have not chosen them arbitrarily. Instead, we have adopted three general criteria to guide the selection of documents: (1) that the document be of major significance, shaping the history of an important society or succession of societies through time; (2) that the document give us substantial insights into the nature of the society from which it sprang, either at a given period in its history or over a long period of time; and (3) that the document be intrinsically interesting. Almost all of the selections in this book satisfy one of the first two criteria; those that satisfy the third may appear (at least to students) to be fewer in number.

Even with the help of our criteria, the process of selecting the documents to include in this book has been difficult. It would be unrealistic to assume that all (or even much) of the significant literature of the societies of the world throughout history can be encapsulated within less than a hundred documents. Of necessity, innumerable items, some arguably as worthy of inclusion as those selected, have not been chosen. Readers of this book will, on occasion, undoubtedly question some of the decisions we have made, preferring other selections to those contained here. It is our hope, however, that readers will recognize that none of these decisions was made arbitrarily but all with consideration and with careful weighing of the alternative possibilities.

One way in which we might have eased the task of selection would have been through the inclusion of a much larger number of selections in the book. But, because of constraints on the length of the book, any increase in the number of selections would have necessitated a decrease in their average length. In deciding against this procedure, we have been guided by educational principles. We are convinced that to gain the fullest possible understanding of history through reading of original source materials, students must have these materials presented to them at length and in detail. Short extracts excerpted from the original sources too often fail to provide a reader with anything more than a superficial and fragmented acquaintance with the society under study. If a document chosen for inclusion satisfies our criteria for selection, it should yield an understanding of the society from which it sprang that justifies its being reproduced in its entirety or, where that is not possible, at sufficient length so that contribution to the history of that society is rendered clear.

Although its various introductions contain a considerable amount of historical information, this book is not designed to be a history of world civilization. The function of the introductory materials is, rather, to provide a background framework in which to exhibit the source documents themselves. Or, to reverse the metaphor, the book can be viewed as a gallery filled with documents that illuminate the societies of which they are a product. To anyone who wishes a full understanding of the course of world civilization, we recommend the study of the documents included in this book be supplemented by a reading of a standard work on the history of civilization.

Sources of World Civilization

THE AGE OF ENCOUNTERS

The European voyages of exploration (and often conquest) mark a new state of affairs in world history, but they are part of trend toward worldwide cultural and commercial contact that had begun several hundred years before. Commercial connections throughout Eurasia (Asia, Europe, and North Africa) had existed in ancient times, although the various civilizations rarely had direct contact with each other. The spread of Muslim civilization into southern Europe, sub-Saharan Africa, and Central Asia extended the reach and volume of trade in the Eastern Hemisphere. More important, the Mongol conquest of a vast Asian empire in the thirteenth century in which trade was encouraged and cultural and religious conflict was suppressed created a context in which international trade thrived and direct contact between distant civilizations could occur. The collapse of Mongol hegemony and the rise of conservative Muslim regimes in North Africa and Western Asia in the fourteenth and fifteenth century changed the nature of international trade. Europe was especially hurt by these developments. The need of European merchants for safe and inexpensive access to the goods of East and Southeast Asia coincided very well with the attitudes of the political and military elites of Europe. It is no accident that the royal families of Portugal and the recently joined Castile and Aragon (Spain) sponsored the first European voyages to bypass Muslim territories. The nobility of Castile, Aragon, and Portugal had been in a war (in their minds, a Crusade) with Muslim princes over the Iberian Peninsula for centuries. The last Muslim kingdom, Granada, was finally conquered in 1492. Many Portuguese and Spanish elites saw the voyages of exploration as a continuation of their Crusade. By finding direct sea routes to sub-Saharan Africa and Asia, Spain and Portugal could both increase revenues and do economic damage to their Muslim enemies.

The first areas of European maritime expansion were the West African Coast and the islands of the tropical Atlantic. Although both Spain and Portugal would participate in the early stages of this venture, Portugal would eventually force the Spanish out of West Africa. By 1488, the Portuguese had found the southern tip of Africa and began sailing in the Indian Ocean. Here they found an already established maritime trade network that extended from East Africa to the Spice Islands of Southeast Asia and on into the Pacific north to the Chinese coast and Japan. Far from dominating the Indian Ocean trade, the Portuguese instead found their niches and prospered. This itself was no small achievement. Portugal was small nation competing in a trade network that included China and the major

Muslim empires. In many ways, these other societies were far more advanced than Portugal. The Portuguese could compete because of slightly superior military technology (improvements on technology they had borrowed from Asian civilizations) and a willingness to take enormous risks. Instead of shipping all the goods back to Portugal, the Portuguese became valued in the Indian Ocean as transporters of goods from one point to another within the Indian Ocean. Where they found indigenous societies that could be dominated, they established fortified ports for resupply and access to inland goods. When they encountered powerful societies, such as China or unified Japan, they submitted to local restrictions.

Shut out of West Africa and the southern route to Asia, the Spanish supported Christopher Columbus in his attempt to find a western route to Asia. Whereas the Portuguese explorers initiated the first sustained, direct contact between Europe and Asia, the voyages of Columbus had wholly unintended, albeit equally monumental, consequences. Before then, the people of the Eastern and Western Hemispheres had gone their ways, each civilization unaware of the existence of the other. After his discovery of the lands beyond the Atlantic, and the further discoveries of the explorers who followed in his wake, the two hemispheres were gradually brought into ever-increasing contact with each other. The Europeans encountered a number of advanced civilizations in the Western Hemisphere. For example, when Cortez and his troops arrived in the Aztec capital, now Mexico City, they found a metropolis larger than any city in Europe at that time. Nevertheless, the result of the intermingling of cultures that followed was the gradual (but never complete) Europeanization of the Western Hemisphere. At the same time that immigrants arrived from the Eastern Hemisphere in increasing numbers, the indigenous population went into decline. Some became victims of the warfare that broke out as the new arrivals invaded the land, but the greater number died from imported diseases against which they had little natural immunity. By the twentieth century, much of the original population, particularly in North America, had disappeared, while in South America, although the loss was much less, many had intermarried with outsiders. Most, but by no means all, of the immigrants to the Americas were Europeans. Another large group consisted of Africans, who were forcibly brought to the Western Hemisphere through the slave trade, which was carried on for over three hundred years.

Europeanization of the Western Hemisphere was not simply cultural but political as well. As they settled into the lands they had invaded, the conquerors turned these into colonies of their homelands. All the maritime powers in Europe participated in this process. Through an act of the pope, Portugal was given Brazil. Spain, however, was the most successful colonizer, taking over the remainder of South America, Central America, and some of North America. The vast bulk of North America was divided up between the British and French, while the Dutch gained land in the

Caribbean. Although most of these colonial divisions were made by agreements between European powers (the local inhabitants not being consulted), clashes of interest resulted in warfare.

While these events were going on in other parts of the world, Europe was witnessing fundamental and unsettling internal changes. Although the news of contact with distant civilizations and the discovery of new worlds was greeted with excitement in Europe, it was overshadowed by religious conflict. For centuries, Western European Christianity had increasingly centered on the Bishop of Rome, commonly known as the Pope. Europeans who did not assent to the prescribed doctrines or participate in the regular ritual life of the official church were marginalized and often persecuted. For various complex reasons, in the sixteenth century a number of northern European territories officially broke from the Roman church while significant minorities in southern and eastern Europe dissented from the allegiance to Rome imposed by the political elites. This event is commonly known as the Reformation, and those who rejected the Roman church are known as Protestants. There had always been some criticism and dissatisfaction with the Roman church among both elite and common Europeans, but the Reformation created a permanent religious division in a civilization that defined itself primarily in religious terms. The Protestant Reformation has its origins in the theology of a northern German theology professor and monk named Martin Luther. A staunchly pro-Roman conservative theologian in his early years, by 1517 Martin Luther began questioning the truth and legitimacy of papal claims to authority. The new technology of the printing press allowed his ideas to spread quickly. Soon there were "Lutheran" sympathizers throughout the intellectual classes of Europe. The Reformation also found support among urban merchant elites and nobility who wished to subvert the authority of the European royal families whose legitimacy rested on their adherence to Roman Christianity. While Luther produced the formative ideas of the Reformation, other reformers such as John Calvin provided systematic coherence to the intellectual foundations of the movement and implemented Protestant reforms in various territories. Roman Christianity responded by eliminating some of the abuses that had given the Protestant Reformers an easy target. But the essential characteristics of Roman Christianity were preserved. A new order of priests, the Jesuits, was formed to reconvert Protestants to Roman Christianity. The competition between the two forms of European Christianity spilled over into the concurrent voyages of exploration. Roman Catholic countries such as Spain, Portugal, and France supported Franciscan and Jesuit missionaries in Asia and the Americas, while Protestant missionaries accompanied English and Dutch explorers.

Of less immediate impact than the voyages of exploration or the Reformation, but of equal long-term significance, was the "new science" being developed in European universities in the sixteenth and seventeenth centuries. Those discoveries, which are now part of our intellectual heritage, need not be rehearsed. But something should be said of the methodology and goals the scientists developed to make these discoveries possible. First was the development of a scientific method that emphasized an appeal to empirical evidence. No theory could be seriously entertained unless the scientist was able to produce evidence in its favor to the qualified investigator. This requirement is a commonplace now, but it is a result mainly of the success of science itself. When Isaac Newton said, "I fashion no hypotheses," he was in fact confirming this because he meant that he put forward no explanation of nature unless he could support it by empirical evidence. Even more important was the new goal of science. In most societies science was a branch of philosophy. For instance, the Greeks were almost totally uninterested in the practical application of scientific knowledge. Francis Bacon, seeing the stunning explanatory power of the new scientific method, proposed that science should be devoted to the pursuit of material progress. The new scientific methods and the new goals of science would eventually lead to the technological advances that shape the modern world. It also would radically change the dynamics of world power. Technological sophistication is the primary condition for power and wealth in the modern world. For instance, in the seventeenth century, a united Japan was able to eject the Portuguese who were only marginally superior in their military technology. Two hundred years later, American gunboats would appear in Tokyo Bay that were the technological equivalent of spaceships to the culturally isolated Japanese.

Christopher Columbus

It is easily forgotten that when Christopher Columbus (1451–1506) set sail across the "Western Ocean" with his three tiny ships on August 3, 1492, he was bound not for a new world but for "the Indies" (India, China, and the islands of East Asia). His venture was a prosaic even though a hazardous one. He hoped to discover a sea route that would make trade with the East—with its highly desired silks, rugs, jewelry, drugs, and spices—easier than the long and arduous caravan treks across Asia. According to Columbus's (mis)calculations, his destination could be reached by sailing some three thousand miles due west around the world. As it turned out, this was the distance to the islands of the Western Hemisphere that he encountered.

In 1484, Columbus had submitted his proposal of reaching the East by sailing west to the king of Portugal, hoping to receive financial support for the project. But the Portuguese were already deeply committed to an attempt to reach the same destination by sailing south around Africa and thence east to India and beyond, so Columbus's appeal was rejected. From there he went to Spain and after two years of effort he gained an audience with King Ferdinand and Queen Isabella. After six more years in negotiations, the monarchs finally agreed to underwrite the venture, and Columbus set off on his epochal voyage. The crossing of the Atlantic, from the Canary Islands (the last port of call on the European side) to an island in the Bahamas group (northeast of Cuba), where Columbus landed on October 12 and took possession in the name of Ferdinand and Isabella, took thirty-six days.

Over a period of twelve years Columbus made four voyages, exploring many of the Caribbean islands and establishing several colonies. His voyages took him to the mainland of South and Central America as well. And although he heard tales of a great ocean farther to the west, he never realized that the lands he had reached belonged not to the Orient but to another continent.

The two selections that follow consist of the initial entry in a journal Columbus kept of his first voyage and a letter he wrote as he neared the end of that voyage, describing some of what he had seen and done. Of special interest is his description of the people who lived on the Caribbean islands, particularly his account of their character, style of life, and reception of the Europeans.

1.   Which aspects of the land and people most interested Columbus?

2.   Describe Columbus's attitude toward the Native Americans he
      encountered.

Journal and Letter

Prologue

Because, most Christian and very exalted and very excellent and very powerful Princes, King and Queen of the Spains and of the Islands of the Sea, our
Lords, in this present year of 1492 after your Highnesses had made an end to
the war of the Moors, who were reigning in Europe, and having finished the
war in the very great city of Granada, where in this present year on the 2nd
day of the month of January, I saw the Royal banners of your Highnesses
placed by force of arms on the towers of the Alhambra, which is the fortress
of the said City: and I saw the Moorish King come out to the gates of the City
and kiss the Royal hands of your Highnesses, and the hands of the Prince, my
Lord: and then in that present month, because of the information which I had
given your Highnesses about the lands of India, and about a Prince who is
called Great Khan, which means in our Romance language, King of Kings,—
how he and his predecessors had many times sent to Rome to beg for men
learned in our Holy Faith that they might be instructed therein, and that the
Holy Father had never furnished them, and so, many people believing in
idolatries and receiving among themselves sects of perdition, were lost:—
your Highnesses, as Catholic Christians and Princes, loving the Holy
Christian faith and the spreading of it, and enemies of the sect of Mahomet
and of all idolatries and heresies, decided to send me, Christopher Columbus,
to the said regions of India, to see the said Princes and the peoples and lands,
and learn of their disposition, and of everything, and the measures which
could be taken for their conversion to our Holy Faith: and you ordered that I
should not go to the east by land, by which it is customary to go, but by way
of the west, whence until to-day we do not know certainly that any one has
gone. So that, after having banished all the Jews from all your Kingdoms and
realms, in the same month of January, your Highnesses ordered me to go with
a sufficient fleet to the said regions of India: and for that purpose granted me
great favours and ennobled me, that from then henceforward I might entitle
myself *Don* and should be High Admiral of the Ocean-Sea [Atlantic—*Ed.*]
and Viceroy and perpetual Governor of all the islands and continental land
which I might discover and acquire, and which from now henceforward

Trans. J. B. Thacher.

might be discovered and acquired in the Ocean-Sea, and that my eldest son should succeed in the same manner, and thus from generation to generation for ever after: and I started from the city of Granada on Saturday, the 12th day of the month of May in the same year 1492: I came to the village of Palos, which is a sea-port, where I fitted out three vessels, very suitable for a similar undertaking: and I left the said port, well supplied with a large quantity of provisions and with many seamen, on the 3rd day of the month of August in the said year on a Friday at the half hour before sunrise, and took my way to the Canary Islands of your Highnesses, which are in the said Ocean-Sea, in order to set out on my voyage from there and sail until I arrived at the Indies, and make known the message of your Highnesses to those Princes, and fulfil the commands which had thus been given me: and for this purpose, I decided to write everything I might do and see and which might take place on this voyage, very punctually from day to day, as will be seen henceforth. Also, Lords and Princes, besides describing each night what takes place during the day, and during the day, the sailings of the night, I propose to make a new chart for navigation, on which I will locate all the sea and the lands of the Ocean-Sea, in their proper places, under their winds; and further, to compose a book and show everything by means of drawing, by the latitude from the equator and by longitude from the west, and above all, it is fitting that I forget sleep, and study the navigation diligently, in order to thus fulfil these duties, which will be a great labour.

Letter

Sir:

As I know that you will have pleasure of the great victory which our Lord hath given me in my voyage, I write you this, by which you shall know that, in twenty days I passed over to the Indies with the fleet which the most illustrious King and Queen, our Lords, gave me: where I found very many islands peopled with inhabitants beyond number. And, of them all, I have taken possession for their Highnesses, with proclamation and the royal standard displayed; and I was not gainsaid. On the first which I found, I put the name San Salvador, in commemoration of His high Majesty, who marvellously hath given all this: the Indians call it Guanahani. The second I named the Island of Santa Maria de Concepcion, the third Ferrandina, the fourth Isabella, the fifth La Isla Juana [Cuba]; and so for each one a new name. When I reached Juana, I followed its coast west-wardly, and found it so large that I thought it might be the mainland province of Cathay. And as I did not thus find any towns and villages on the sea-coast, save small hamlets with the people whereof I could not get speech, because they all fled away forthwith, I went on farther in the same direction, thinking I should not miss

of great cities or towns. And at the end of many leagues, seeing that there
was no change, and that the coast was bearing me northwards, whereunto
my desire was contrary since the winter was already confronting us, I
formed the purpose of making from thence to the South, and as the wind
also blew against me, I determined not to wait for other weather and turned
back as far as a port agreed upon; from which I sent two men into the country to learn if there were a king, or any great cities. They travelled for three
days, and found interminable small villages and a numberless population,
but nought of ruling authority; wherefore they returned. I understood sufficiently from other Indians whom I had already taken, that this land, in its
continuousness, was an island; and so I followed its coast eastwardly for a
hundred and seven leagues as far as where it terminated; from which headland I saw another island to the east, ten or eight leagues distant from this,
to which I at once gave the name La Spañola. And I proceeded thither, and
followed the northern coast, as with La Juana, eastwardly for a hundred and
seventy-eight great leagues in a direct easterly course, as with La Juana. The
which, and all the others, are very large to an excessive degree, and this
extremely so. In it, there are many havens on the seacoast, incomparable
with any others that I know in Christendom, and plenty of rivers so good
and great that it is a marvel. The lands thereof are high, and in it are very
many ranges of hills, and most lofty mountains incomparably beyond the
Island of Centrefrei; all most beautiful in a thousand shapes, and all accessible, and full of trees of a thousand kinds, so lofty that they seem to reach the
sky. And I am assured that they never lose their foliage; as may be imagined,
since I saw them as green and as beautiful as they are in Spain during May.
And some of them were in flower, some in fruit, some in another stage
according to their kind. And the nightingale was singing, and other birds of a
thousand sorts, in the month of November, round about the way that I was
going. There are palm-trees of six or eight species, wondrous to see for their
beautiful variety; but so are the other trees, and fruits, and plants therein.
There are wonderful pinegroves, and very large plains of verdure, and there
is honey, and many kinds of birds, and many various fruits. In the earth
there are many mines of metals; and there is a population of incalculable
number. Spañola is a marvel; the mountains and hills, and plains and fields,
and land, so beautiful and rich for planting and sowing, for breeding cattle
of all sorts, for building of towns and villages. There could be no believing,
without seeing, such harbours as are here, as well as the many and great
rivers, and excellent waters, most of which contain gold. In the trees and
fruits and plants, there are great differences from those of Juana. In this,
there are many spiceries, and great mines of gold and other metals. The
people of this island, and of all the others that I have found and seen or not
seen, all go naked, men and women, just as their mothers bring them
forth; although some women cover a single place with the leaf of a plant, or
a cotton something which they make for that purpose. They have no iron or

steel, nor any weapons; nor are they fit there-unto; not because they be not a well-formed people and of fair stature, but that they are most wondrously timorous. They have no other weapons than the stems of reeds in their seeding state, on the end of which they fix little sharpened stakes. Even these, they dare not use; for many times has it happened that I sent two or three men ashore to some village to parley, and countless numbers of them sallied forth, but as soon as they saw those approach, they fled away in such wise that even a father would not wait for his son. And this was not because any hurt had ever been done to any of them:—on the contrary, at every headland where I have gone and been able to hold speech with them, I gave them of everything which I had, as well cloth as many other things, without accepting aught therefor; but such they are, incurably timid. It is true that since they have become more assured, and are losing that terror, they are artless and generous with what they have, to such a degree as no one would believe but he who had seen it. Of anything they have, if it be asked for, they never say no, but do rather invite the person to accept it, and show as much lovingness as though they would give their hearts. And whether it be a thing of value, or one of little worth, they are straightways content with whatsoever trifle of whatsoever kind may be given them in return for it. I forbade that anything so worthless as fragments of broken platters, and pieces of broken glass, and strap-buckles, should be given them; although when they were able to get such things they seemed to think they had the best jewel in the world, for it was the hap of a sailor to get, in exchange for a strap, gold to the weight of two and a half castellanos, and others much more for other things of far less value; while for new blancas they gave every thing they had, even though it were the worth of two or three gold castellanos, or one or two arrobas of spun cotton. They took even pieces of broken barrelhoops, and gave whatever they had, like senseless brutes; insomuch that it seemed to me ill. I forbade it, and I gave gratuitously a thousand useful things that I carried, in order that they may conceive affection, and furthermore may be made Christians; for they are inclined to the love and service of their Highnesses and of all the Castilian nation, and they strive to combine in giving us things which they have in abundance, and of which we are in need. And they know no sect, or idolatry; save that they all believe that power and goodness are in the sky, and they believed very firmly that I, with these ships and crew, came from the sky; and in such opinion, they received me at every place where I landed, after they had lost their terror. And this comes not because they are ignorant; on the contrary, they are men of very subtle wit, who navigate all those seas, and who give a marvellously good account of everything—but because they never saw men wearing clothes or the like of our ships. And as soon as I arrived in the Indies, in the first island that I found, I took some of them by force, to the intent that they should learn our speech and give me information of what there was in those parts. And so it was, that very soon they understood us and we them, what by speech or what by signs; and those Indians have been of much service. To this day I carry them with me who are still of the opinion that I come from heaven, as appears from much conversation which they have had with me. And they were the first to proclaim it wherever I arrived; and the others went running from house to house and to the neighbouring villages, with loud cries of "Come! come to see the people from heaven!" Then, as soon as their minds were reassured about us, every one came, men as well as women, so that there remained none behind, big or little; and they all brought something to eat and drink, which they gave with wondrous lovingness. They have in all the islands very many canoes, after the manner of rowing-galleys, some larger, some smaller; and a good many are larger than a galley of eighteen benches. They are not so wide, because they are made of a single log of timber, but a galley could not keep up with them in rowing, for their motion is a thing beyond belief. And with these, they navigate through all those islands which are numberless, and ply their traffic. I have seen some of those canoes with seventy and eighty men in them, each one with his oar. In all those islands, I saw not much diversity in the looks of the people, or in their manners and language; but they all understand each other, which is a thing of singular towardness for what I hope their Highnesses will determine, as to making them conversant with our holy faith, unto which they are well disposed. I have already told how I had gone a hundred and seven leagues, in a straight line from West to East, along the seacoast of the Island of Juana; according to which itinerary, I can declare that that island is larger than England and Scotland combined; as, over and above those hundred and seven leagues, there remains for me, on the western side, two provinces whereto I did not go—one of which they call Anan, where the people are born with tails—which provinces cannot be less in length than fifty or sixty leagues, according to what may be understood from the Indians with me, who know all the islands. This other, Española, has a greater circumference than the whole of Spain from Colibre in Catalunya, by the sea-coast, as far as Fuente Ravia in Biscay; since, along one of its four sides, I went for a hundred and eighty-eight great leagues in a straight line from West to East. This is a land to be desired,—and once seen, never to be relinquished—in which—although, indeed, I have taken possession of them all for their Highnesses, and all are more richly endowed than I have skill and power to say, and I hold them all in the name of their Highnesses who can dispose thereof as much and as completely as of the kingdoms of Castile—in this Española, in the place most suitable and best for its proximity to the gold mines, and for traffic with the continent, as well on this side as on the further side of the Great Can, where there will be great commerce and profit, I took possession of a large town which I named the city of Navidad. And I have made fortifications there, and a fort which by this time will have been completely finished and I have left therein men enough for such a purpose, with arms and artillery, and provisions for more than a year, and a boat, and a man who is master of all sea-craft for making others; and great friendship with the King of that land, to such a degree that he prided himself on calling and holding me as his brother. And even though his mind might change towards attacking those men, neither he nor his people know what arms are, and go naked. As I have already said, they are the most timorous creatures there are in the world, so that the men who remain there are alone sufficient to destroy all that land, and the island is without personal danger for them if they know how to behave themselves. It seems to me that in all those islands, the men are all content with a single wife; and to their chief or king they give as many as twenty. The women, it appears to me, do more work than the men. Nor have I been able to learn whether they held personal property, for it seemed to me that whatever one had, they all took shares of, especially of eatable things. Down to the present, I have not found in those islands any monstrous men, as many expected, but on the contrary all the people are very comely; nor are they black like those in Guinea, but have flowing hair; and they are not begotten where there is an excessive violence of the rays of the sun. It is true that the sun is there very strong, notwithstanding that it is twenty-six degrees distant from the equinoctial line. In those islands, where there are lofty mountains, the cold was very keen there, this winter; but they endure it by being accustomed thereto, and by the help of the meats which they eat with many and inordinately hot spices. Thus I have not found, nor had any information of monsters, except of an island which is here the second in the approach to the Indies, which is inhabited by a people whom, in all the islands, they regard as very ferocious, who eat human flesh. These have many canoes with which they run through all the islands of India, and plunder and take as much as they can. They are no more illshapen than the others, but have the custom of wearing their hair long, like women; and they use bows and arrows of the same reedstems, with a point of wood at the top, for lack of iron which they have not. Amongst those other tribes who are excessively cowardly, these are ferocious; but I hold them as nothing more than the others. These are they who have to do with the women of Matremonio—which is the first island that is encountered in the passage from Spain to the Indies—in which there are no men. Those women practise no female usages, but have bows and arrows of reeds such as above mentioned; and they arm and cover themselves with plates of copper of which they have much. In another island, which they assure me is larger than Española, the people have no hair. In this, there is incalculable gold; and concerning these and the rest I bring Indians with me as witnesses. And in conclusion, to speak only of what has been done in this voyage, which has been so hastily performed, their Highnesses may see that I shall give them as much gold as they may need, with very little aid which their Highnesses will give me; spices and cotton at once, as much as their Highnesses will order to be shipped, and as much as they shall order to be shipped of mastic—which till now has never been found except in Greece, in the island of Xio, and the Seignory sells it for what it likes; and aloe-wood as much as they shall order to be shipped; and slaves as many as they shall order to be shipped—and these shall be from idolaters. And I believe that I have discovered rhubarb and cinnamon, and I shall find that the men whom I am leaving there will have discovered a thousand other things of value; as I made no delay at any point, so long as the wind gave me an opportunity of sailing, except only in the town of Navidad till I had left things safely arranged and well established. And in truth I should have done much more if the ships had served me as well as might reasonably have been expected. This is enough; and thanks to eternal God our Lord who gives to all those who walk. His way, victory over things which seem impossible; and this was signally one such, for although men have talked or written of those lands, it was all by conjecture, without confirmation from eyesight, importing just so much that the hearers for the most part listened and judged that there was more fable in it than anything actual, however trifling. Since thus our Redeemer has given to our most illustrious King and Queen, and to their famous kingdoms, this victory in so high a matter, Christendom should take gladness therein and make great festivals, and give solemn thanks to the Holy Trinity for the great exaltation they shall have by the conversion of so many peoples to our Holy faith; and next for the temporal benefit which will bring hither refreshment and profit, not only to Spain, but to all Christians. This briefly, in accordance with the facts. Dated on the caravel, off the Canary Islands, the 15 February of the year 1493.

     At your command,

The Admiral

Bernal Díaz del Castillo

Bernal Díaz del Castillo, the author of the selection that follows, was born in the Spanish town of Medina del Campo in the year of Columbus's epochal voyage, 1492. Like many of his contemporaries, he was excited by the tales that soon began to circulate through Spain of the gold to be had in the lands recently discovered beyond the great "Western Ocean," so he decided to seek his fortune there. He left his home in 1514, crossing first to Cuba, where he spent about three years, before going on two exploratory trips farther west. In 1519 he joined the historic expedition of the *conquistador* Hernando Cortés (1485–1547) that was to lead to the subjugation of Mexico and part of Central America and the annexation of these lands to the Spanish crown. Except for two trips he made back to his native land in later years, Bernal Díaz remained in the Western Hemisphere for the remainder of his long life, dying in Guatemala around the year 1581. He wrote his book, which he called *The True History of the Conquest of New Spain*, in his old age, many years after the events he describes in it.

According to Bernal Díaz's account, Cortés, after landing on the east coast of what is now Mexico and burning his ships (so he could not retreat), marched with a small band of soldiers, fighting his way inland and arriving at the capital city of the Aztec civilization, Tenochtitlán (or Mexico City), in November 1519. There he was received by the great *cacique* (king) Montezuma. The selection that follows begins with the meeting between these two warriors. Its central figure, however, is the Aztec, Montezuma. Bernal Díaz describes his person at some length, as well as his family and court. He gives a detailed account of the personal and physical environment in which the Aztec chief lived, from the architecture of his palaces to the contents of his storehouses to the ritual surrounding his meals. The selection ends with a more general description of the society and commerce of Mexico City, in particular its great marketplace. It is obvious from his comments that Bernal Díaz was greatly impressed by many of the sights he beheld in this strange land and realized that in some ways its civilization equaled or even surpassed that of his native Spain.

1. What impresses Diaz most about Aztec civilization? What is he most critical of?

2. How are the Aztecs different from the Caribbean people Columbus encountered?

The Conquest of New Spain

About the Great and Solemn Reception which the Great Montezuma Gave Cortés and all of us at the Entering of the Great City of Mexico

EARLY next day we left Iztapalapa with a large escort of those great Caciques whom I have already mentioned. We proceeded along the Causeway which is here eight paces in width and runs so straight to the City of Mexico that it does not seem to me to turn either much or little, but, broad as it is, it was so crowded with people that there was hardly room for them all, some of them going to and others returning from Mexico, besides those who had come out to see us, so that we were hardly able to pass by the crowds of them that came; and the towers and cues were full of people as well as the canoes from all parts of the lake. It was not to be wondered at, for they had never before seen horses or men such as we are.

Gazing on such wonderful sights, we did not know what to say, or whether what appeared before us was real, for on one side, on the land, there were great cities, and in the lake ever so many more, and the lake itself was crowded with canoes, and in the Causeway were many bridges at intervals, and in front of us stood the great City of Mexico, and we,—we did not even number four hundred soldiers! and we well remembered the words and warnings given us by the people of Huexotzingo and Tlaxcala and Tlamanalco, and the many other warnings that had been given that we should beware of entering Mexico, where they would kill us, as soon as they had us inside.

Let the curious readers consider whether there is not much to ponder over in this that I am writing. What men have there been in the world who have shown such daring? But let us get on, and march along the Causeway. When we arrived where another small causeway branches off (leading to Coyoacan, which is another city) where there were some buildings like towers, which are their oratories, many more chieftains and Caciques approached clad in very rich mantles, the brilliant liveries of one chieftain differing from those of another, and the causeways were crowded with them. The Great Montezuma had sent these great Caciques in advance to receive us, and when they came before Cortés they bade us welcome in their language, and as a sign of peace, they touched their hands against the ground, and kissed the ground with the hand.

There we halted for a good while, and Cacamatzin, the Lord of Texcoco, and the Lord of Iztapalapa and the Lord of Tacuba and the Lord of Coyoacan went on in advance to meet the Great Montezuma, who was

Trans. A. P. Maudslay.

approaching in a rich litter accompanied by other great Lords and Caciques, who owned vassals. When we arrived near to Mexico, where there were some other small towers, the Great Montezuma got down from his litter, and those great Caciques supported him with their arms beneath a marvellously rich canopy of green coloured feathers with much gold and silver embroidery and with pearls and chalchihuites suspended from a sort of bordering, which was wonderful to look at. The Great Montezuma was richly attired according to his usage, and he was shod with sandals. For so they call what they wear on their feet, the soles were of gold and the upper part adorned with precious stones. The four Chieftains who supported his arms were also richly clothed according to their usage, in garments which were apparently held ready for them on the road to enable them to accompany their prince, for they did not appear in such attire when they came to receive us. Besides these four Chieftains, there were four other great Caciques, who supported the canopy over their heads, and many other Lords who walked before the Great Montezuma, sweeping the ground where he would tread and spreading cloths on it, so that he should not tread on the earth. Not one of these chieftains dared even to think of looking him in the face, but kept their eyes lowered with great reverence, except those four relations, his nephews, who supported him with their arms.

When Cortés was told that the Great Montezuma was approaching, and he saw him coming, he dismounted from his horse, and when he was near Montezuma, they simultaneously paid great reverence to one another. Montezuma bade him welcome and our Cortés replied through Doña Marina wishing him very good health. And it seems to me that Cortés, through Doña Marina, offered him his right hand, and Montezuma did not wish to take it, but he did give his hand to Cortés and then Cortés brought out a necklace which he had ready at hand, made of glass stones, which I have already said are called Margaritas, which have within them many patterns of diverse colours, these were strung on a cord of gold and with musk so that it should have a sweet scent, and he placed it round the neck of the Great Montezuma and when he had so placed it he was going to embrace him, and those great Princes who accompained Montezuma held back Cortés by the arm so that he should not embrace him, for they considered it an indignity.

Then Cortés through the mouth of Doña Marina told him that now his heart rejoiced at having seen such a great Prince, and that he took it as a great honour that he had come in person to meet him and had frequently shown him such favour.

Then Montezuma spoke other words of politeness to him, and told two of his nephews who supported his arms, the Lord of Texcoco and the Lord of Coyoacan, to go with us and show us to our quarters, and Montezuma with his other two relations, the Lord of Cuitlahuac and the Lord of Tacuba who accompanied him, returned to the city, and all those grand companies of Caciques and chieftains who had come with him returned in his train. As they turned back after their Prince we stood watching them and observed how they all marched with their eyes fixed on the ground without looking at him, keeping close to the wall, following him with great reverence. Thus space was made for us to enter the streets of Mexico, without being so much crowded. But who could now count the multitude of men and women and boys who were in the streets and on the azoteas, and in canoes on the canals, who had come out to see us.

• • •

They took us to lodge in some large houses, where there were apartments for all of us, for they had belonged to the father of the Great Montezuma, who was named Axayaca, and at that time Montezuma kept there the great oratories for his idols, and a secret chamber where he kept bars and jewels of gold, which was the treasure that he had inherited from his father Axayaca, and he never disturbed it. They took us to lodge in that house, because they called us Teules, and took us for such, so that we should be with the Idols or Teules which were kept there. However, for one reason or another, it was there they took us, where there were great halls and chambers canopied with the cloth of the country for our Captain, and for every one of us beds of matting with canopies above, and no better bed is given, however great the chief may be, for they are not used. And all these palaces were coated with shining cement and swept and garlanded.

As soon as we arrived and entered into the great court, the Great Montezuma took our Captain by the hand, for he was there awaiting him, and led him to the apartment and saloon where he was to lodge, which was very richly adorned according to their usage, and he had at hand a very rich necklace made of golden crabs, a marvellous piece of work, and Montezuma himself placed it round the neck of our Captain Cortés, and greatly astonished his own Captains by the great honour that he was bestowing on him. When the necklace had been fastened, Cortés thanked Montezuma through our interpreters, and Montezuma replied—"Malinche you and your brethren are in your own house, rest awhile," and then he went to his palaces which were not far away, and we divided our lodgings by companies, and placed the artillery pointing in a convenient direction, and the order which we had to keep was clearly explained to us, and that we were to be much on the alert, both the cavalry and all of us soldiers. A sumptuous dinner was provided for us according to their use and custom, and we ate it at once. So this was our lucky and daring entry into the great city of Tenochtitlan Mexico on the 8th day of November the year of our Savior Jesus Christ 1519.

• • •

How on the Following Day our Captain Cortés went to See the Great Montezuma, and About a certain Conversation that Took Place

THE next day Cortés decided to go to Montezuma's palace, and he first sent to find out what he intended doing and to let him know that we were coming. He took with him four captains, namely Pedro de Alvarado, Juan Velásquez de Leon, Diego de Ordás, and Gonzalo de Sandoval, and five of us soldiers also went with him.

When Montezuma knew of our coming he advanced to the middle of the hall to receive us, accompanied by many of his nephews, for no other chiefs were permitted to enter or hold communication with Montezuma where he then was, unless it were on important business. Cortés and he paid the greatest reverence to each other and then they took one another by the hand and Montezuma made him sit down on his couch on his right hand, and he also bade all of us to be seated on seats which he ordered to be brought.

Then Cortés began to make an explanation through our interpreters Doña Marina and Aguilar, and said that he and all of us were rested, and that in coming to see and converse with such a great Prince as he was, we had completed the journey and fulfilled the command which our great King and Prince had laid on us. But what he chiefly came to say on behalf of our Lord God had already been brought to his [Montezuma's] knowledge through his ambassadors, Tendile, Pitalpitoque and Quintalbor, at the time when he did us the favour to send the golden sun and moon to the sand dunes; for we told them then that we were Christians and worshipped one true and only God, named Jesus Christ, who suffered death and passion to save us, and we told them that a cross (when they asked us why we worshipped it) was a sign of the other Cross on which our Lord God was crucified for our salvation, and that the death and passion which He suffered was for the salvation of the whole human race, which was lost, and that this our God rose on the third day and is now in heaven, and it is He who made the heavens and the earth, the sea and the sands, and created all the things there are in the world, and He sends the rain and the dew, and nothing happens in the world without His holy will. That we believe in Him and worship Him, but that those whom they look upon as gods are not so, but are devils, which are evil things, and if their looks are bad their deeds are worse, and they could see that they were evil and of little worth, for where we had set up crosses such as those his ambassadors had seen, they dared not appear before them, through fear of them, and that as time went on they would notice this.

The favour he now begged of him was his attention to the words that he now wished to tell him; then he explained to him very clearly about the creation of the world, and how we are all brothers, sons of one father and one mother who were called Adam and Eve, and how such a brother as our great Emperor, grieving for the perdition of so many souls, such as those which their idols were leading to Hell, where they burn in living flames, had sent us, so that after what he [Montezuma] had now heard he would put a stop to it and they would no longer adore these Idols or sacrifice Indian men and women to them, for we were all brethren, nor should they commit sodomy or thefts. He also told them that, in course of time, our Lord and King would send some men who among us lead very holy lives, much better than we do, who will explain to them all about it, for at present we merely came to give them due warning, and so he prayed him to do what he was asked and carry it into effect.

As Montezuma appeared to wish to reply, Cortés broke off his argument, and to all of us who were with him he said: "With this we have done our duty considering it is the first attempt."

Montezuma replied—"Señor Malinche, I have understood your words and arguments very well before now, from what you said to my servants at the sand dunes, this about three Gods and the Cross, and all those things that you have preached in the towns through which you have come. We have not made any answer to it because here throughout all time we have worshipped our own gods, and thought they were good, as no doubt yours are, so do not trouble to speak to us any more about them at present. Regarding the creation of the world, we have held the same belief for ages past, and for this reason we take it for certain that you are those whom our ancestors predicted would come from the direction of the sunrise. As for your great King, I feel that I am indebted to him, and I will give him of what I possess."

• • •

While this conversation was going on, Montezuma secretly sent a great Cacique, one of his nephews who was in his company, to order his stewards to bring certain pieces of gold, which it seems must have been put apart to give to Cortés, and ten loads of fine cloth, which he apportioned, the gold and mantles between Cortés and the four captains, and to each of us soldiers he gave two golden necklaces, each necklace being worth ten pesos, and two loads of mantles. The gold that he then gave us was worth in all more than a thousand pesos and he gave it all cheerfully and with the air of a great and valiant prince. As it was now past midday, so as not to appear importunate, Cortés said to him: "Señor Montezuma, you always have the habit of heaping load upon load in every day conferring favours on us, and it is already your dinner time." Montezuma replied that he thanked us for coming to see him, and then we took our leave with the greatest courtesy and we went to our lodgings.

And as we went along we spoke of the good manners and breeding which he showed in everything, and that we should show him in all ways the greatest respect, doffing our quilted caps when we passed before him, and this we always did, but let us leave this subject here, and pass on.

Of the Manner and Appearance of the Great Montezuma and What a Great Prince He Was

THE Great Montezuma was about forty years old, of good height and well proportioned, slender, and spare of flesh, not very swarthy, but of the natural colour and shade of an Indian. He did not wear his hair long, but so as just to cover his ears, his scanty black beard was well shaped and thin. His face was somewhat long, but cheerful, and he had good eyes and showed in his appearance and manner both tenderness and, when necessary, gravity. He was very neat and clean and bathed once every day in the afternoon. He had many women as mistresses, daughters of Chieftains, and he had two great Cacicas as his legitimate wives, and when he had intercourse with them it was so secretly that no one knew anything about it, except some of his servants. He was free from unnatural offences. The clothes that he wore one day, he did not put on again until four days later. He had over two hundred chieftains in his guard, in other rooms close to his own, not that all were meant to converse with him, but only one or another, and when they went to speak to him they were obliged to take off their rich mantles and put on others of little worth, but they had to be clean, and they had to enter barefoot with their eyes lowered to the ground, and not to look up in his face. And they made him three obeisances, and said: "Lord, my Lord, my Great Lord," before they came up to him, and then they made their report and with a few words he dismissed them, and on taking leave they did not turn their backs, but kept their faces toward him with their eyes to the ground, and they did not turn their backs until they left the room. I noticed another thing, that when other great chiefs came from distant lands about disputes or business, when they reached the apartments of the Great Montezuma, they had to come barefoot and with poor mantles, and they might not enter directly into the Palace, but had to loiter about a little on one side of the Palace door, for to enter hurriedly was considered to be disrespectful.

For each meal, over thirty different dishes were prepared by his cooks according to their ways and usage, and they placed small pottery brasiers beneath the dishes so that they should not get cold. They prepared more than three hundred plates of the food that Montezuma was going to eat, and more than a thousand for the guard. When he was going to eat, Montezuma would sometimes go out with his chiefs and stewards, and they would point out to him which dish was best, and of what birds and other things it was composed, and as they advised him, so he would eat, but it was not often that he would go out to see the food, and then merely as a pastime.

I have heard it said that they were wont to cook for him the flesh of young boys, but as he had such a variety of dishes, made of so many things, we could not succeed in seeing if they were of human flesh or of other things, for they daily cooked fowls, turkeys, pheasants, native partridges, quail, tame and wild ducks, venison, wild boar, reed birds, pigeons, hares and rabbits, and many sorts of birds and other things which are bred in this country, and they are so numerous that I cannot finish naming them in a hurry; so we had no insight into it, but I know for certain that after our Captain censured the sacrifice of human beings, and the eating of their flesh, he ordered that such food should not be prepared for him thenceforth.

Let us cease speaking of this and return to the way things were served to him at meal times. It was in this way: if it was cold they made up a large fire of live coals of a firewood made from the bark of trees which did not give off any smoke, and the scent of the bark from which the fire was made was very fragrant, and so that it should not give off more heat than he required, they placed in front of it a sort of screen adorned with figures of idols worked in gold. He was seated on a low stool, soft and richly worked, and the table, which was also low, was made in the same style as the seats, and on it they placed the table cloths of white cloth and some rather long napkins of the same material. Four very beautiful cleanly women brought water for his hands in a sort of deep basin which they call "xicales," and they held others like plates below to catch the water, and they brought him towels. And two other women brought him tortilla bread, and as soon as he began to eat they placed before him a sort of wooden screen painted over with gold, so that no one should watch him eating. Then the four women stood aside, and four great chieftains who were old men came and stood beside them, and with these Montezuma now and then conversed, and asked them questions, and as a great favour he would give to each of these elders a dish of what to him tasted best. They say that these elders were his near relations, and were his counsellors and judges of law suits, and the dishes and food which Montezuma gave them they ate standing up with much reverence and without looking at his face. He was served on Cholula earthenware either red or black. While he was at his meal the men of his guard who were in the rooms near to that of Montezuma, never dreamed of making any noise or speaking aloud. They brought him fruit of all the different kinds that the land produced, but he ate very little of it. From time to time they brought him, in cupshaped vessels of pure gold, a certain drink made from cacao which they said he took when he was going to visit his wives, and at the time he took no heed of it, but what I did see was that they brought over fifty great jugs of good cacao frothed up, and he drank of that, and the women served this drink to him with great reverence.

Sometimes at meal-times there were present some very ugly humpbacks, very small of stature and their bodies almost broken in half, who are their jesters, and other Indians, who must have been buffoons, who told him witty sayings, and others who sang and danced, for Montezuma was fond of pleasure and song, and to these he ordered to be given what was left of the food and the jugs of cacao. Then the same four women removed the table cloths, and with much ceremony they brought water for his hands. And Montezuma talked with those four old chieftains about things that interested him, and they took leave of him with the great reverence in which they held him, and he remained to repose.

As soon as the Great Montezuma had dined, all the men of the Guard had their meal and as many more of the other house servants, and it seems to me that they brought out over a thousand dishes of the food of which I have spoken, and then over two thousand jugs of cacao all frothed up, as they make it in Mexico, and a limitless quantity of fruit, so that with his women and female servants and bread makers and cacao makers his expenses must have been very great.

Let us cease talking about the expenses and the food for his household and let us speak of the Stewards and the Treasurers and the stores and pantries and of those who had charge of the houses where the maize was stored. I say that there would be so much to write about, each thing by itself, that I should not know where to begin, but we stood astonished at the excellent arrangements and the great abundance of provisions that he had in all, but I must add what I had forgotten, for it is as well to go back and relate it, and that is, that while Montezuma was at table eating as I have described, there were waiting on him two other graceful women to bring him tortillas, kneaded with eggs and other sustaining ingredients, and these tortillas were very white, and they were brought on plates covered with clean napkins, and they also brought him another kind of bread, like long balls kneaded with other kinds of sustaining food, and "pan pachol" for so they call it in this country, which is a sort of wafer. There were also placed on the table three tubes much painted and gilded, which held *liquidambar* mixed with certain herbs which they call *tabaco*, and when he had finished eating, after they had danced before him and sung and the table was removed, he inhaled the smoke from one of those tubes, but he took very little of it and with that he fell asleep.

• • •

Montezuma had two houses full of every sort of arms, many of them richly adorned with gold and precious stones. There were shields great and small, and a sort of broadswords, and others like two handed swords set with stone knives which cut much better than our swords, and lances longer than ours are, with a fathom of blade with many knives set in it, which even when they are driven into a buckler or shield do not come out, in fact they cut like razors so that they can shave their heads with them. There were very good bows and arrows and double-pointed lances and others with one point, as well as their throwing sticks, and many slings and round stones shaped by hand, and some sort of artful shields which are so made that they can be rolled up, so as not to be in the way when they are not fighting, and when they are needed for fighting they let them fall down, and they cover the body from top to toe. There was also much quilted cotton armour, richly ornamented on the outside with many coloured feathers, used as devices and distinguishing marks, and there were casques or helmets made of wood and bone, also highly decorated with feathers on the outside, and there were other arms of other makes which, so as to avoid prolixity, I will not describe, and there were artisans who were skilled in such things and worked at them, and stewards who had charge of the arms.

Let us leave this and go on to another great house, where they keep many Idols, and they say that they are their fierce gods, and with them many kinds of carnivorous beasts of prey, tigers and two kinds of lions, and animals something like wolves which in this country they call jackals and foxes, and other smaller carnivorous animals, and all these carnivores they feed with flesh, and the greater number of them breed in the house. They give them as food deer and fowls, dogs and other things which they are used to hunt, and I have heard it said that they feed them on the bodies of the Indians who have been sacrificed. It is in this way: you have already heard me say that when they sacrifice a wretched Indian they saw open the chest with stone knives and hasten to tear out the palpitating heart and blood, and offer it to their Idols in whose name the sacrifice is made. Then they cut off the thighs, arms and head and eat the former at feasts and banquets, and the head they hang up on some beams, and the body of the man sacrificed is not eaten but given to these fierce animals. They also have in that cursed house many vipers and poisonous snakes which carry on their tails things that sound like bells. These are the worst vipers of all, and they keep them in jars and great pottery vessels with many feathers, and there they lay their eggs and rear their young, and they give them to eat the bodies of the Indians who have been sacrificed, and the flesh of dogs which they are in the habit of breeding.

● ● ●

Let us go on and speak of the skilled workmen he [Montezuma] employed in every craft that was practised among them. We will begin with lapidaries and workers in gold and silver and all the hollow work, which even the great goldsmiths in Spain were forced to admire, and of these there were a great number of the best in a town named Atzcapotzalco, a league from Mexico. Then for working precious stones and chalchihuites, which are like emeralds, there were other great artists. Let us go on to the great craftsmen in feather work, and painters and sculptors who were most refined; from what we see of their work today we can form a judgment of what they did then, for there are three Indians today in the City of Mexico named Marcos de Aquino, Juan de la Cruz and El Crespillo, so skilful in their work as sculptors and painters, that had they lived in the days of the ancient and famous Apelles, or of Michael Angelo Buonarotti, in our times, they would be placed in the same company. Let us go on to the Indian women who did the weaving and the washing, who made such an immense quantity of fine fabrics with wonderful feather work designs; the greater part of it was brought daily from some towns of the province on the north coast near Vera Cruz called Cotaxtla, close by San Juan de Ulua, where we disembarked when we came with Cortés.

In the house of the Great Montezuma himself, all the daughters of chieftains whom he had as mistresses always wore beautiful things, and there were many daughters of Mexican citizens who lived in retirement and wished to appear to be like nuns, who also did weaving but it was wholly of feather work. These nuns had their houses near the great Cue of Huichilobos and out of devotion to it, or to another idol, that of a woman who was said to be their mediatrix in the matter of marriage, their fathers placed them in that religious retirement until they married, and they were [only] taken out thence to be married.

Let us go on and tell about the great number of dancers kept by the Great Montezuma for his amusement, and others who used stilts on their feet, and others who flew when they danced up in the air, and others like Merry-Andrews, and I may say that there was a district full of these people who had no other occupation. Let us go on and speak of the workmen that he had as stone cutters, masons and carpenters, all of whom attended to the work of his houses, I say that he had as many as he wished for. We must not forget the gardens of flowers and sweet-scented trees, and the many kinds that there were of them, and the arrangement of them and the walks, and the ponds and tanks of fresh water where the water entered at one end and flowed out at the other; and the baths which he had there, and the variety of small birds that nested in the branches, and the medicinal and useful herbs that were in the gardens. It was a wonder to see, and to take care of it there were many gardeners. Everything was made in masonry and well cemented, baths and walks and closets, and apartments like summer houses where they danced and sang. There was as much to be seen in these gardens as there was everywhere else, and we could not tire of witnessing his great power. Thus as a consequence of so many crafts being practised among them, a large number of skilled Indians were employed.

• • •

How our Captain went out to See the City of Mexico and Tlaltelolco, Which is the Great Market Place and the Great Cue of Huichilobos, and What else Happened

As we had already been four days in Mexico and neither the Captain nor any of us had left our lodgings except to go to the houses and gardens, Cortés said to us that it would be well to go to the great Plaza and see the great

Temple of Huichilobos, and that he wished to consult the Great Montezuma and have his approval. For this purpose he sent Jerónimo de Aguilar and the Doña Marina as messengers, and with them went our Captain's small page named Orteguilla, who already understood something of the language. When Montezuma knew his wishes he sent to say that we were welcome to go; on the other hand, as he was afraid that we might do some dishonour to his Idols, he determined to go with us himself with many of his chieftains. He came out from his Palace in his rich litter, but when half the distance had been traversed and he was near some oratories, he stepped out of the litter, for he thought it a great affront to his idols to go to their house and temple in that manner. Some of the great chieftains supported him with their arms, and the tribal lords went in front of him carrying two staves like sceptres held on high, which was the sign that the Great Montezuma was coming. (When he went in his litter he carried a wand half of gold and half of wood, which was held up like a wand of justice). So he went on and ascended the great Cue accompanied by many priests, and he began to burn incense and perform other ceremonies to Huichilobos.

Let us leave Montezuma, who had gone ahead as I have said, and return to Cortés and our captains and soldiers, who according to our custom both night and day were armed, and as Montezuma was used to see us so armed when we went to visit him, he did not look upon it as anything new. I say this because our Captain and all those who had horses went to Tlaltelolco on horseback, and nearly all of us soldiers were fully equipped, and many Caciques whom Montezuma had sent for that purpose went in our company. When we arrived at the great market place, called Tlaltelolco, we were astounded at the number of people and the quantity of merchandise that it contained, and at the good order and control that was maintained, for we had never seen such a thing before. The chieftains who accompanied us acted as guides. Each kind of merchandise was kept by itself and had its fixed place marked out. Let us begin with the dealers in gold, silver, and precious stones, feathers, mantles, and embroidered goods. Then there were other wares consisting of Indian slaves both men and women; and I say that they bring as many of them to that great market for sale as the Portuguese bring negroes from Guinea; and they brought them along tied to long poles, with collars round their necks so that they could not escape, and others they left free. Next there were other traders who sold great pieces of cloth and cotton, and articles of twisted thread, and there were *cacahuateros* who sold cacao. In this way one could see every sort of merchandise that is to be found in the whole of New Spain, placed in arrangement in the same manner as they do in my own country, which is Medina del Campo, where they hold the fairs, where each line of booths has its particular kind of merchandise, and so it is in this great market. There were those who sold cloths of henequen and ropes and the *cotaras* with which they are shod, which are made from the same plant, and sweet cooked roots, and other tubers which they get from this plant, all were kept in one part of the market in the place assigned to them. In another part there were skins of tigers and lions, of otters and jackals, deer and other animals and badgers and mountain cats, some tanned and others untanned, and other classes of merchandise.

Let us go on and speak of those who sold beans and sage and other vegetables and herbs in another part, and to those who sold fowls, cocks with wattles, rabbits, hares, deer, mallards, young dogs and other things of that sort in their part of the market, and let us also mention the fruiterers, and the women who sold cooked food, dough and tripe in their own part of the market; then every sort of pottery made in a thousand different forms from great water jars to little jugs, these also had a place to themselves; then those who sold honey and honey paste and other dainties like nut paste, and those who sold lumber, boards, cradles, beams, blocks and benches, each article by itself, and the vendors of *ocote* firewood, and other things of a similar nature. I must furthermore mention, asking your pardon, that they also sold many canoes full of human excrement, and these were kept in the creeks near the market, and this they use to make salt or for tanning skins, for without it they say that they cannot be well prepared. I know well that some gentlemen laugh at this, but I say that it is so, and I may add that on all the roads it is a usual thing to have places made of reeds or straw or grass, so that they may be screened from the passers by, into these they retire when they wish to purge their bowels so that even that filth should not be lost. But why do I waste so many words in recounting what they sell in that great market, for I shall never finish if I tell it all in detail. Paper, which in this country is called *Amal*, and reeds scented with *liquidambar*, and full of tobacco, and yellow ointments and things of that sort are sold by themselves, and much cochineal is sold under the arcades which are in that great market place, and there are many vendors of herbs and other sorts of trades. There are also buildings where three magistrates sit in judgment, and there are executive officers like *Alguacils* who inspect the merchandise. I am forgetting those who sell salt, and those who make the stone knives, and how they split them off the stone itself; and the fisherwomen and others who sell some small cakes made from a sort of ooze which they get out of the great lake, which curdles, and from this they make a bread having a flavour something like cheese. There are for sale axes of brass and copper and tin, and gourds and gaily painted jars made of wood. I could wish that I had finished telling of all the things which are sold there, but they are so numerous and of such different quality and the great market place with its surrounding arcades was so crowded with people, that one would not have been able to see and inquire about it all in two days.

Then we went to the great Cue, and when we were already approaching its great courts, before leaving the market place itself, there were many more merchants, who, as I was told, brought gold for sale in grains, just as it is taken from the mines. The gold is placed in thin quills of the geese of the country, white quills, so that the gold can be seen through, and according to the length and thickness of the quills they arrange their accounts with one another, how much so many mantles or so many gourds full of cacao were worth, or how many slaves, or whatever other thing they were exchanging.

Cahuilla

The Cahuilla are a group of native Americans whose territory occupies a region of low desert and nearby mountain valleys of Southern California, including the site now occupied by the city of Palm Springs. They are subdivided into three closely related clans known as the desert, pass, and mountain Cahuilla. All are part of the great Shoshonean linguistic family whose territory once covered much of the United States west of the Rocky Mountains. The origin of the name Cahuilla is obscure, but it may have been given to these people by early Spanish explorers.

The Cahuilla held their most important ritual ceremony—the mourning for the dead—normally, but not always, annually. This ceremony was spread over an entire week and comemorated the members of the clan who had died since the previous ceremony. Although their bodies had been cremated at the time of death and their homes burned shortly thereafter, a central feature of the mourning ceremony was the burning of effigies of the departed. Once this had been done the dead were not to be spoken of again but to be forgotten.

Most of the ceremonial week was devoted to singing and chanting, with much repetition, the creation myth, which appears in the following selection. Although no attempt will be made here to interpret the myth in detail (something the reader may wish to do), a few general remarks can be made about it. First, it reveals the Cahuillas' interest in metaphysical issues, in particular the creation of the world and of humankind. Second, it addresses the universal problem of death and raises questions about the reality and nature of immortality. Third, it describes (indirectly) a number of features of the life of the people, including the ritual of the mourning ceremony itself.

The creation myth was shared by all the Cahuilla, but with some minor variations in details. The version appearing in the selection is one that was sung during a mourning ceremony that occurred in Palm Springs in 1925, presided over by the ceremonial chief, Alejo Potencio, and recorded through an interpreter by the anthropologist, William Strong. Since the time of the myth's origin is not known, its inclusion in this part is, of necessity, somewhat arbitrary. To ease its comprehension, some of the terms from the original language appearing in it have been deleted or replaced by their English equivalents.

1.　According to this story, what is man's place in the world? What is his relationship to the gods? To animals?

2.　What aspects of their world were the Cahuilla most interested in explaining? How do they explain these things? What does this tell us about their society?

Palm Springs Cahuilla Creation Myth

In the beginning there was nothing but darkness. At times it was lighter but with no moon or stars. One was called female, the other male. Sounds, humming or thunder, were heard at times. Red, white, blue, and brown colors came all twisting to one point in the darkness. These were acting all together—twisting. These came together in one point to produce. This ball shook and whirled all together into one substance, which became two embryos wrapped in this placenta. This was formed in space and darkness. These were born prematurely, everything stopped for they were stillborn.

　　Then again all the lights whirled together, joined, and produced. This time the embryos grew fully—the children inside talked to one another. They asked each other, "What are we? We are eskwatkwatwiteem, and estanamawitum," for at that time they did not know themselves. While they were in this sack they rolled back and forth; they stretched their arms and knees to make a hole so they could get out. Then they named themselves Mukat and Temaiyauit.

　　First their heads came out; they called themselves teimuluka; both heads came out at once. Then came out their shoulders, ribs, waist, thighs, knees, and ankles. Thus they came out of their house into the darkness, but they were unable to see one another in the dark space. As they sat in the dark Temaiyauit said, "I am older than you, for I first heard the darkness making sounds." Mukat answered, "No! I am the older for I heard it first." Thus they began to quarrel. Then Temaiyauit said, "What can we do to eat our smoke and blow—aaah! away the dark?" Mukat answered, "Why do you say you are older than I am? Take the pipe from your heart, out of your mouth." So Mukat took from his heart the black pipe, and Temaiyauit took from his heart the white pipe.

　　Temaiyauit asked Mukat, "What will we smoke in it?" Mukat answered, "Why do you say you are older than I am? We can draw from our hearts tobacco. Then we can eat and smoke it in our pipe." He drew black

Strong, William D., *Aboriginal Society in Southern California*, University of California Publications in American Archaeology and Ethnology, Vol. 26 (Berkeley: University of California Press, 1929). Courtesy of University of California Press.

tobacco from his heart, and Temaiyauit drew white tobacco from his heart. Their pipes were solid, and Temaiyauit asked Mukat, "How can we open up our pipes to eat and smoke tobacco?" Mukat answered, "Why do you say you are older than I, if you do not know that with our whiskers we can bore a hole through which to draw smoke?" Then the hole was too big and the tobacco would not stay, but from their hearts they drew out white and black materials and made it smaller. All was settled, but they had no fire.

Then Temaiyauit asked Mukat, "How can we light our tobacco to eat and smoke it?" and Mukat answered, "You still say you are older than I am and yet do not know how to light your pipe! We can draw from our heart the sun from which we can light our pipe." Then he began to draw the sun; from his mouth it came, but it slipped through his hands to his feet. Both tried to catch it, but it was too fast and got away and disappeared. It was lost in the darkness.

Then Mukat drew out from his heart the West Light, and Temaiyauit drew from his heart the East Light. With these Mukat lit his pipe. When he smoked the smoke drifted up and formed clouds. He blew it out in spreading puffs, and said, "This is to eat our hearts and kill our hearts!"

To find out who was the oldest he held up his pipe, saying, "I am holding it down." Temaiyauit said, "Where are you?" looking on the ground. Temaiyauit tried to find it below, but Mukat cheated him holding it up in the air. At last he reached it. Mukat said, "You claim you are older but you are not old enough to know this!" Temaiyauit smoked until he had had enough, then he said, "I am holding it up," but he held it on the ground. But Mukat knew where it was, and right away reached and took it. This proved Mukat was the oldest.

Then they smoked, and Temaiyauit asked Mukat what they should do next. Mukat answered, "We can draw from our heart the center pole of the world," and from their hearts they both drew it. "Lift it up, stand it up, your center pole of the world, our center pole of the world. Make it stand, your heart of the world, our heart of the world," they said. They put it into the air but it would not stand. They then drew from their hearts all kinds of snakes to hold the center pole of the world. These they told to hold it but they could not. Then they put two huge rocks together to hold it but still it moved.

Then from their hearts they drew all kinds of web-spinning spiders, and these ran their webs from the top of the pole in all directions, and at last the center pole of the world stood firm.

Both said, "It is all still, our heart of the world, your heart of the world," and they began to climb up it, saying, "We, Mukat and Temaiyauit, are climbing up!" Still farther up they sing, "Mukat, Temaiyauit, going up, up, farther up we are going!" Halfway up the center pole they sing again, and still singing they come nearly to the top, always calling themselves by name. Then, still calling their names, they reach the top, and sing,

"We, Mukat and Temaiyauit, are sitting on the top, on the point of the center pole of the world." From the top they looked down and saw clouds of smoke rolling up from the place whence they had come.

Temaiyauit asked where the smoke came from. Mukat answered, "It is settling in the place where we were lying and comes from our afterbirth. It is black blood, red blood, fresh blood, smallpox, colds and sore throat, cramps in the back, boils, mumps, hives and itches, inflamed and sore eyes, blindness, acute body pains, palsy and twitching, consumption, venereal diseases, rheumatism, emaciation, swelling of the body, and all other sicknesses." All these were the clouds of smoke coming from the place where they came into being. Then Mukat said, "We will give power to man or woman, so that each sickness can be cured by someone that has power. These will be the doctors."

Mukat was on the west side of the center pole of the world and Temaiyauit on the east side. Mukat asked Temaiyauit, "Which direction shall be the oldest?" Temaiyauit answered, "We will name that direction where you are now." Mukat then said, "I am older than you, so first of the directions is the west, then the north, south, and east." Thus it is that when people come into the ceremonial house they blow west, north, south, and east.

Temaiyauit said, "How can we make the earth?" Mukat answered, "You see I am older than you, for we can draw the earth from our heart." And he drew black earth from his heart, and Temaiyauit drew white earth from his. This earth they put on top of the center pole of the world but it rolled off and was lost. From their hearts they drew all black and all white spiders, who spread webs in all directions. So for a second time they drew black and white earth from their hearts and placed it on the top. To spread this earth they drew forth from their hearts all the kinds of ants who spread out the earth on all sides. To make it faster they drew out two whirlwinds that rapidly completed the spreading out of the black and white earth. Thus was the whole earth made, but it moved and would not stay still. The ants were too light, they could not hold it steady. From their hearts Mukat and Temaiyauit drew the ocean and placed it all around the world, and likewise they drew out the two water demons, and placed them in the ocean. All water creatures they put into the ocean, and last of all they drew the sacred seaweed mat, and sacred dancing feathers of the doctors, the water apron and water tail and placed these in the ocean. Thus by their combined weight the last quivers of the earth were stilled, and it was flat as a table.

From their hearts again they drew the sky but it swayed and flapped in the wind. They blew their saliva to the sky and thus made the stars which held the sky in place. Then they put the two whirlwinds at the edge of the earth, and they held the bottom of the sky firmly in place.

The creators determined to make creatures for the earth. Temaiyauit drew coyote from his heart for he was the first assistant. Mukat drew the horned owl, who could see in the darkness, from his heart. Mukat had black mud and Temaiyauit white mud to make creatures from, and they each commenced to make the body of a man. Mukat worked slowly and carefully, modeling a fine body such as men have now. Temaiyauit worked rapidly making a rude body with a belly on both sides, eyes on both sides, and hands like the paws of a dog. The creators worked in the darkness, and the horned owl sat watching them. When a body was finished the owl would say, "M-M-M! It is finished," and coyote would come and put it away, putting those created by Mukat in one place, and those by Temaiyauit in another. The latter worked three times as fast as the former, and had a great number of crude bodies finished, compared to the few good bodies made by Mukat. All this took a long, long time.

Finally Mukat stopped and drew the moon from his heart and it became faintly light so they could see their creatures. Mukat looked at those made by Temaiyauit and said, "No wonder you have finished them so quickly, you are not doing good work!" Temaiyauit wished to know why, and Mukat said, "They have two faces, eyes all around, bellies on both sides, feet pointing both ways and hands like a dog's paws!" Temaiyauit answered, "That is right, it is good, but your work is not good. One face and all parts on one side are not right for they cannot see behind. Mine can see coming and going. Open fingers will let food slip through, mine will hold anything." Mukat replied, "Yes, but they can draw their hands together and hold anything. Your creatures cannot carry anything for they have no back or shoulders. They cannot hold an arrow to the bow or draw it back, for they are like a dog." "But," said Temaiyauit, "there will be no shooting." "Yes, there will be, later on," said Mukat.

"But there will be no death," said Temaiyauit. Mukat answered, "Yes, there will be death." "Then," said Temaiyauit, "if they die, they shall come back." "If they come back they shall smell like dead things," answered Mukat. Temaiyauit said, "Then they can wash with white clay, and smoke their bodies with burning salt grass and willow and become clean and good smelling." "If they do this the world will be too small," answered Mukat. Temaiyauit said, "We can then spread it wider." "Yes, but there will not be enough food for all of them," answered Mukat. "They can eat earth," said Temaiyauit. "But they will then eat up all the earth," answered Mukat. Temaiyauit replied, "No, for by our power it will be swelling again." This was the end of the dispute.

Temaiyauit was angry because he always lost in every dispute. He said, "I will go to the bottom of the earth, whence I came, and take all my creatures with me, the earth, sky and all my other creations." Mukat answered, "You can take yours but all mine will stay." Then Temaiyauit blew, and his breath opened the earth. His creatures went down with him, all save the moon, the palm, coyote, the wood duck, and a few others. He tried to take earth and sky with him; a fierce wind blew and the earth shook all over, while the sky bent and swayed. Mukat put one knee on the ground, held one hand on all his creatures, and with the other held up the sky. He cried, "hi! hi! hi! hi!" which is the way all people do now when the earthquake comes. In the struggle all the mountains and canyons appeared on the earth's surface, stream beds were formed, and water came out and filled them. At last Temaiyauit disappeared below, all became quiet, and the earth stopped shaking, but its rough uneven surface remains until today.

Then all Mukat's creatures became alive. While it was still dark the white people had stolen away to the north, during the time Mukat held up the sky. The sun suddenly appeared, and all Mukat's creatures were so frightened they began to chatter like blackbirds each in a different language. Mukat could not understand any of these, but hearing one man speak the Cahuilla language he pressed him to his side, and let the others run around. This man was the ancestor of the Cahuilla people, and now lives in the abode of the sun, moon, and evening star. Thus only the Cahuillas speak the original language. Among these creatures was one with red hair and a white clean face; he was cranky and crying, always running about. Mukat saw this, and he took a long and a short stick. The first he put between the creature's legs like a horse, the second he put in his hand like a whip. Then the creature ran back and forth, going farther and farther away, until at last he disappeared into the north where all his party had gone before. Then Mukat put all his creatures into the ceremonial house for it was night. Far away to the north they saw a light, and all the creatures asked Mukat, "What is that light in the north which we see now?" "Yes," he replied, "those are your older brothers and your younger brothers, your older sisters and your younger sisters. They went away at night. They did not hear me, they did not ask me. They are devils! They have four names."

When the sun arose in the east the dog was talking, but then he became dumb. He knows everything in his heart, but he cannot say one word. The sun came up very hot. Some of Mukat's children were burned black, some were burned red (well done, well cooked), but in the north where the white people were, it was cold, and they remained raw and white.

The moon was the only woman among all Mukat's creatures. Every morning she would go away from the ceremonial house to a clean sandy place, where with woven grass string she showed all the creatures how to make cat's cradles. Then she would put one group of people on one side and say, "You are coyote people," and the others she would call wildcat people. She told the coyote people to sing against the wildcat people as though they were singing enemy songs. Then the wildcat people would begin to dance; then they would do it the other way around. This was a game. She told them to build a little brush house and put one creature in the house to be chief. Then she told another group to come from far away singing and dancing to the house. This was the way they should do later through all the generations to come. She also taught them to run, jump, wrestle, throw balls of mud at one another, and to flip pebbles at one another from their finger tips. Certain ones she picked out and said, "You are women. You must grind, and feed these others, who are men, that come dancing to the house."

At sunset they would return to the ceremonial house, dancing as they came. Among them was one called tevienikieteumelmii, who always kicked the rattlesnake when he came in. The latter could not play with the other creatures because he could not walk. Mukat took pity on the rattlesnake and gave him a cactus thorn in his mouth as a fang. When all the other creatures were gone, Mukat took his ceremonial staff and told the snake to bite it. This the rattlesnake did, but his fang broke off. Then Mukat pulled out a black whisker and put it in as a fang, but it broke off. So he pulled out a gray whisker, and with this fang the rattlesnake bit through the ceremonial staff and blood came out of it. Mukat told the snake to bite his enemy and then crawl away to the mountain and stay in his hole. All was ready. When all the creatures came back from their playground tevienikieteumelmii laughed and kicked the snake, which bit him. Tevienikieteumelmii died at once, and the snake crawled away to his hole in the mountain, where he has always stayed since, rattling and biting, as the enemy of all Mukat's creatures.

Mukat told the moon to have his creatures make bows of wood and arrows of reeds, with no points on them, and to have them stand in two lines and shoot at each other with these arrows. Then Mukat told them to sharpen the points of the arrows. He then told them to make rock arrow straighten-ers and to make arrows of arrow-weed about two feet long, with stone arrow-points. These they were to shoot with short, strong, sycamore bows. He told them to stand in two lines and shoot at one another, but they were afraid because it looked dangerous. Then the fireball demon said, "It is noth-ing. You cannot die from this," and he stuck an arrow through his body, pulling it out the other side. Then the hummingbird put a quiver on his back, and all shot at him, but they could not hit him for he was too small. He dodged each arrow, and said, "See, it is nothing!" The Arkansas kingbird and then the butterfly did the same, and each said, "See, it is nothing!" So did the crow and the poor will, and they both dodged. Then the vulture tried it but he was too slow; they hit him, and he disappeared. Then the cony wanted to fight them all, and he cried, "Hurry up! Hurry up!" All the crea-tures began to shoot each other, hunting through the tall grass. Mukat laughed, and said, "Now they are beginning to kill one another." They shot until both sides were nearly all killed. Then the remainder saw their dead comrades and began to cry loudly.

Mukat looked at the dead people whose bodies were quivering and shaking. Their spirits arose, but their bodies were dead, and the spirits did not know where to go. They looked toward the west, and it seemed to be all clear for them. They went flying to the west. But when they got there there was no gate, they had to stop and come back crying to their bodies. Then toward the north they did the same thing, and to the south, but in vain. They flew to the sky but again in vain. Finally they went to the east where Temaiyauit was. He answered them. "Yes," he said, "You are something. You are great devils. This is what I told Mukat, that you would die and come back to life, but he always pushed away my word. Thus we created two kinds of clay and two herbs to brush the body and make it clean. Go back again to earth as great devils." Hearing this they all hung their heads, and crying and wailing they came back to where their bodies lay. Among the creatures left alive was muntukwut, who was a powerful shaman. He took pity on the dead spirits and with his ceremonial staff bored a hole in the earth, opening the gate of the abode of the dead. When they saw this gate was opened all went below sounding their heart, sounding their body, making great breathings, fading away with noise, disappearing forever. To this place go all the spirits of the dead. This is the way Mukat tricked and joked with his people.

All the people who were left on earth were very sad, but their teacher, the moon, was still with them. The moon was a naked, white, and beautifully formed woman. She slept apart from all the other creatures. One night Mukat, who had often watched her, leaned above her and touched her as he passed. Next morning the moon was weak, sleepy, and sore; she felt very sad. She planned to go away somewhere, but before going she spoke to all Mukat's creatures, saying, "I am going away, but must go to the place where you used to play. Go there and play as before. In the evening you will see me in the west, then you must say ha! ha! ha! ha! and run to the water to bathe. Remember this always." Then she disappeared and no one saw or knew what became of her. In a short while they saw the new moon rise in the west, and they cried, "ha! ha! ha! ha!" as she had told them and ran to bathe.

Some of his creatures now began to plan how they could stop their creator Mukat from playing more evil tricks on them. They knew that he had told the rattlesnake to kill them, that he had told them to kill one another with arrows, and lastly, that he had mistreated the moon and caused her to leave. So while they were all in the place where the moon had taught them to play they planned to get rid of Mukat. Then the flicker cried, "pium" which meant, "Don't talk so much but go and poison him." All agreed to this, so they planned to watch him at night time. They came into the house dancing, and told a little lizard that hides in cracks in the wood to watch the creator; for the lizard alone was not afraid to watch Mukat at night. He hid in a crack in the center post while all the others were dancing around it. All night he stayed there, watching.

At midnight, all were asleep as Mukat had commanded them, save the little lizard who kept watch. Mukat got up, took his pipe, lit it and smoked, blowing clouds of smoke over all his creatures to make them sleep soundly. Three times he blew smoke over them. Then he set his pipe down, and taking his ceremonial staff stood up. All the floor of the ceremonial house was covered with his creatures. First he stepped at their feet, then between their legs, then next to their arms, then above their heads, and so walked out. All this time the lizard was watching.

Mukat went at once to the ocean, where two logs crossed above the water, and here defecated. Lizard saw him do this, and heard the noise when this kwaimuitei hit the water. Three times Mukat did this, and each time it was followed by a sound like thunder in the ocean. Then Mukat returned into the house, stepping in the same places that he had coming out, but he did not see the lizard who was watching. In the dawn all the creatures awoke, danced around the center post, and the lizard joined them. They all went out to their sandy playground, dancing. There the lizard told them all that he had seen that night.

So they planned to poison Mukat through his own excrement, and they told the water skipper to stay below the place where the creator sat at night when he came down to the ocean. He tried to do this, but the great waves washed him away. Then another small water creature attempted it, but failed. Finally, the blue frog tried it, and stayed in spite of the ocean's attempt to drive him away. Here he stayed until midnight, when the creator came out as he always did. His first kwaimuitei hit the water and splashed but there was no sound like thunder in the ocean, for the frog had taken it before it hit bottom. Then Mukat was very frightened, and with his ceremonial staff felt down in the water to see what was beneath him. He scratched the frog's back leaving three white marks there. Half of the kwaimuitei was left in the water and all the water creatures scattered it over the great ocean. Half of it was brought to land, and all the land creatures one by one scattered it over the earth. Thus it could not be put together again and Mukat could not be made well. Mukat sang to himself, "I felt sick in that water. My body became cold, swollen and weak. Either this water or my house makes me sick." All his creatures stayed in the ceremonial house watching him. Coyote was his nurse, and tended Mukat. He dug a hole in the ground, made a fire in it, and then put the creator in, covering him up. Day and night he did this for Mukat, and thus he learned all of Mukat's songs. The others slept all night so they did not learn Mukat's songs.

Mukat grew sicker and sicker, and he called the horse fly to suck blood. This was the first time this was ever done. It did him no good. Then he called the sow bugs and the dragon flies to doctor him. These two failed, so he tried the water snake, the gopher snake, the red racer, and the king snake, all of whom failed. All of these had only pretended to help him for they all wanted Mukat to die.

Then he told his creatures to tell the west wind, that belonged to him, to come and help him. The west wind came, like a hurricane, with a great dust storm. Mukat was afraid, but the west wind went into his body, and for a while he was better, but it was too strong; he was being blown away. He told the white-throated swift, which he named wind meeter, to go meet the west wind and tell it to go away for he was afraid. This same thing happened with the north, south, and east winds in succession.

Then he said, "All my creatures have tried to cure me but I am no better. I know now that I am about to die. Perhaps I shall die in the dark of the moon, or in the faint light of the new moon, or during the young crescent moon, or during the older crescent moon, or in the first week of the new moon, or when the moon has a cloudy ring around it, or during the clear half-moon, or when the half-moon has its rim parallel to the earth, or during the full moon when its spots show clearly, or when the full moon comes from the east and is red, or when it begins to wane and one side is flattened, or when it has half disappeared, or during the last dying moon."

All the time Mukat was sick coyote tended him. When he spat coyote would pretend to take it away, but he would really swallow it, and thus make Mukat sicker and sicker. Coyote helped Mukat move from one side to another, from his face to his back, and helped him to sit up. When Mukat was too weak to spit coyote would lick the saliva off with his tongue. When coyote was away Mukat called all his creatures, and said, "My hands are growing cold, my heart is growing cold, I shall die soon. When I die coyote will try to eat me, for he is planning to do this while you sleep. Therefore, when I am dead tell coyote to go after the eastern fire which I drew from my heart to light my pipe. When he is gone have bear and skunk gather all kinds of wood, dig a hole, and prepare to burn my body. Take the palm and with a drill make fire." When the palm, who was a woman, heard this she began to cry and complain that it was unfair to select her from among all the other creatures. But Mukat continued, "The fly will bore for fire with a drill. Then you can burn me with my creature the fire." That night Mukat made all his creatures sleep, even coyote, and then he died.

In the morning coyote woke up. He felt Mukat's heart and knew that he was dead. He said, "I think it is all over with our creator!" All the other creatures woke up, saying, "He is dead! Our father, your father, is dead!" Then they all cried that there was nothing with which to burn their father, and they asked coyote, because he ran fast, to go after the east light. Coyote went away to the east after the fire. When he was out of sight they prepared the pit, gathered all kinds of wood, and catching the palm tree they threw her down and held her although she tried to escape. The fly took a stick and started to make fire, twirling it between his hands. First came water, then blood, and then fire. With this they kindled the fire, dragged the body of Mukat to the pile, and put it on the burning wood. It burned.

They all stood in a close circle around the fire. Meanwhile coyote went toward the eastern edge of the world and tried to catch the fire, but it always ran just ahead of him. Finally he looked back and saw the smoke of Mukat's body burning. "I thought that might be the way!" he said, and he came back running very fast. All the people saw him coming, and shouted, "Here comes coyote! Do not let him in to the fire where Mukat is burning." "Turn around my brothers and sisters," said coyote, "I am full of tears. Let me in! Let me in! I too want to see my father." But they would not let him through. All of Mukat's body save the heart was burned. Then coyote said, "I will fly over you," and he jumped over their heads into the fire. All Mukat's creatures pressed the creator's heart into the flames with their sticks, but coyote reached it and scattered blood and fire, so that the people were burnt and pushed back. Then coyote ran out with the heart.

To the east he ran, carrying the heart. All the good runners, mountain lion, wolf, gray fox and kit fox, followed him, but could not catch him. Then he called each by name, and said, "Stay away! Why do you, my brothers, pursue me?" Then he talked to the heart of the creator, saying, "I am carrying you upon the earth, to the edge of the world, to the point of earth and sky, to the bottom of the sky, to the bottom of the world." All things tried to frighten him as he ran, but he said, "I am not afraid of you!" Then he swallowed the heart. He at once became very sick; he became emaciated and his ribs showed.

Some of Mukat's creatures who had gone away in search of food for their sick creator returned too late, and found the body of their father in ashes. Among these were suuwit, elelelic, witctcuic, tuivonpic, the jaguar, and the marsh hawk. They all cried loudly, and rolled in the ashes. Last of all returned the buzzard, who was slow and returned late. He did not cry, he became dumb, took the skin off his head, and with a stick bored a hole through his beak. After that he was always quiet, he could only hiss.

Then in the place where Mukat was burned there began to grow all kinds of strange plants, but no one knew what they were. They were afraid to go near the place for a hot wind always blew there. One, a great shaman, said, "Why do you not go and ask our father what they are?" No one else would go so he followed the spirit of Mukat. By the aid of his ceremonial staff he followed the trail of Mukat's spirit although whirlwinds had hidden the trail. In one place were thickets of prickly cactus and clumps of interlaced thorny vines, but at the touch of his ceremonial staff they opened up for him to pass. Far away on the horizon he saw a bright glow where the spirit of Mukat was leaning against a rock. The creator's spirit spoke, "Who are you, that follows and makes me move on when I am lying still?" When the creator's spirit spoke the shaman was dumb and could not answer, though Mukat asked him several times. Finally he was able to speak: "Yes, I am that one who disturbs you while you rest, but we, your creatures, do not know what the strange things are that grow where your body was burned." Mukat's spirit answered him, "Yes, that was the last thing I wanted to tell you, but you killed me before I could do so." Then he continued, "You need not be afraid of these things. They are from my body." He asked the shaman to describe them and when he had finished the spirit of Mukat said, "That big tree is tobacco. It is my heart. It can be cleaned with white clay, and smoked in the big house to drive away evil spirits. The vines with yellow squashes are from my stomach, watermelons are from the pupil of my eye, corn is from my teeth, wheat is my lice eggs, beans are from my semen, and all other vegetables are from other parts of my body."

Then he said, "I am in that big house. My spirit is there, my saliva is there. You can move the big house away and always live there." They did this and all Mukat's creatures stayed in the house weeping for their father. Then they began to wonder how they could make the image of their father. Meanwhile coyote was far away, being very sick. At last he took some wet short reeds, rolled them into a ball, and swallowed it. Then he vomited up all kinds of disease from his heart. Thus he got well. From far away he heard the people in the big house talking, planning to kill him when he came back. So coyote came near them and they saw him. He talked gently to them from far away and they listened. He said, "I have heard you wondering how to make our father's image. I will show you." And he gathered all kinds of flowers saying, "With these we can make the image of our father." He was joking with them, making them forget their anger. He brought many kinds of flowers, but by the next morning they would all be dead. All this time he was planning what he should do. At last he remembered that he must go to the ocean and get seaweed matting, water tail, and water apron. So he told the people he was going after these things.

Then he went to the ocean which was far away. That evening he slept at the edge of the earth, and woke up very early thinking it was dawn. He called aloud, asking it not to become light right away. Then he began to sing because the surf was pounding in so hard that he could not go into it. He sang asking the ocean to stop pounding for a little while. Then he went into the water, and got those three things with which to make the image of Mukat. These three things he brought back to the big house.

Then he began to make the image of his father. All Mukat's creatures were crying, and they sang songs as each part of the seaweed matting was cut and wrapped. Thus the image was made. They sang a song about moving it, standing it up, carrying it to the fire, placing it on the pile, lighting the fire, the smoking, the burning, the crumbling of the last ashes, the last of the burning. Then, covering the ashes with dirt, they sang the last song. All was over.

Olaudah Equiano

The early European explorers of the Western Hemisphere were soon followed by colonists, who quickly came to recognize the vast wealth of these untapped lands. Not only gold, silver, and precious stones could be found there but also the land itself produced highly desired crops, such as sugar, tobacco, tea, and coffee. So land was cleared and farms were developed. Because most of the farming was labor-intensive and because the local populations were often decimated by diseases brought in from Europe, it became necessary to search elsewhere for farm laborers. The result was the slave trade.

Most slaves were brought from Africa, in a trade that began in the sixteenth century and did not end until the middle of the nineteenth century. They came mainly from West Africa, the majority of them being prisoners captured in wars among various local tribes. Some, however, were simply kidnapped from their villages by professional thieves and then sold to slavetraders. The major European powers established trading posts along the Atlantic coast, where they purchased slaves from the interior and then transported them for sale across the ocean. One can only estimate the total number of slaves imported into the Americas during these centuries, but the best estimates place the figure in excess of ten million. Also, approximately three times this number never completed the journey across the Atlantic but perished en route to their destinations. Although the slaves were consigned to areas throughout the Western Hemisphere, only a small portion of them, perhaps five percent, came to the United States. The vast bulk ended in the Caribbean Islands and on the mainland of Latin America, particularly in Brazil.

One of the millions of victims of the slave trade was Olaudah Equiano. But he was more fortunate than most of the others. Born in a part of west-central Africa near the lower Niger River in 1745, he was kidnapped at the age of eleven and eventually sold to British slavers who transported him to Barbados in the West Indies. Soon afterward he was moved to Virginia where he was bought by a British naval officer who took him to England. He served in the British navy during the Seven Years' War and at its end was returned to the West Indies where he was bought by a Quaker merchant-trader from Philadelphia, who employed him on one of his ships. There he was able to earn enough money to buy his freedom in 1766. Thereafter he migrated to London but spent a number of years as a sailor, visiting many parts of the world. Later in life he became an active participant in the British antislavery movement. His autobiography, which he wrote at the request of friends, was published in 1789. Equiano's curious alternative name, with its royal connotations, was given him by the British naval officer who purchased him in Virginia.

The following selection is taken from the first two chapters of Equiano's memoirs. Its importance lies not only in its vivid description of the conditions under which he, and those like him, were shipped across the ocean and sold at auction in the slave market but also, in contrast, of his account of his early life and experiences in his homeland before his abduction.

---

1. What do we learn about West African society in the nineteenth century form this document?

2. How did African slavery differ from European slavery? Does such a distinction matter?

The Life of Gustavus Vassa*

That part of Africa known by the name of Guinea, to which the trade for slaves is carried on, extends along the coast above 3,400 miles, from Senegal to Angola, and includes a variety of kingdoms. Of these the most considerable is the kingdom of Benin, both as to extent and wealth, the richness and cultivation of the soil, the power of its king, and the number and warlike disposition of the inhabitants. It is situated nearly under the line, and extends along the coast above 170 miles, but runs back into the interior part of Africa, to a distance hitherto, I believe, unexplored by any traveller and seems only terminated at length by the empire of Abyssinia, near 1,500 miles from its beginning. This kingdom is divided into many provinces or districts, in one of the most remote and fertile of which I was born, in the year 1745, situated in a charming fruitful vale named Essaka. The distance of this province from the capital of Benin and the sea coast must be very considerable for I had never heard of white men or Europeans, nor of the sea; and our subjection to the king of Benin was little more than nominal for every transaction of the government, as far as my slender observation extended, was conducted by the chiefs or elders of the place.

The manners and government of a people who have little commerce with other countries are generally very simple and the history of what passes in one family or village may serve as a specimen of the whole

---

*Another name of Olaudah Equiano—*Ed.*
Published in London in 1789. Minor changes have been made in spelling and punctuation.

nation. My father was one of those elders or chiefs I have spoken of and was styled Embrenché, a term, as I remember, importing the highest distinction, and signifying in our language a mark of grandeur. This mark is conferred on the person entitled to it by cutting the skin across at the top of the forehead and drawing it down to the eye-brows and while it is in this situation applying a warm hand and rubbing it until it shrinks up into a thick weal across the lower part of the forehead. Most of the judges and senators were thus marked; my father had long borne it; I had seen it conferred on one of my brothers and I also was destined to receive it by my parents.

Those Embrenché, or chief men, decided disputes and punished crimes, for which purpose they always assembled together. The proceedings were generally short and in most cases the law of retaliation prevailed. I remember a man was brought before my father and the other judges for kidnapping a boy and, although he was the son of a chief or senator, he was condemned to make recompense by a man and woman slave.

Adultery, however, was sometimes punished with slavery or death, a punishment which I believe is inflicted on it throughout most of the nations of Africa, so sacred among them is the honour of the marriage bed and so jealous are they of the fidelity of their wives. Of this I recollect an instance. A woman was convicted before the judges of adultery and was delivered over, as the custom was, to her husband to be punished. Accordingly he determined to put her to death, but it being found, just before her execution, that she had an infant at her breast and no woman being prevailed on to perform the part of a nurse, she was spared on account of the child. The men, however, do not preserve the same constancy to their wives which they expect from them, for they indulge in a plurality, though seldom in more than two.

Their mode of marriage is thus: Both parties are usually betrothed when young by their parents (though I have known the males to betroth themselves). On this occasion a feast is prepared and the bride and bridegroom stand up in the midst of all their friends, who are assembled for the purpose, while he declares she is thenceforth to be looked upon as his wife, and that no person is to pay any addresses to her. This is also immediately proclaimed in the vicinity, on which the bride retires from the assembly. Some time after she is brought home to her husband and then another feast is made, to which the relations of both parties are invited. Her parents then deliver her to the bridegroom, accompanied with a number of blessings, and at the same time they tie around her waist a cotton string, of the thickness of a goose quill, which none but married women are permitted to wear. She is now considered as completely his wife and at this time the dowry is given to the new married pair, which generally consists of portions of land, slaves, and cattle, household goods, and implements of husbandry. These are offered by the friends of both parties, besides which the parents of the bridegroom present gifts to those of the bride, whose property she is looked upon before marriage, but after it she is esteemed the sole property of the husband. The ceremony being now ended, the festival begins, which is celebrated with bonfires and loud acclamations of joy, accompanied with music and dancing.

We are almost a nation of dancers, musicians, and poets. Thus every great event, such as a triumphant return from battle, or other cause of public rejoicing, is celebrated in public dances, which are accompanied with songs and music suited to the occasion. The assembly is separated into four divisions, which dance either apart or in succession, and each with a character peculiar to itself. The first division contains the married men, who in their dances frequently exhibit feats of arms and the representation of a battle. To these succeed the married women, who dance in the second division. The young men occupy the third and the maidens the fourth. Each represents some interesting scene of real life, such as a great achievement, domestic employment, a pathetic story, or some rural sport and, as the subject is generally founded on some recent event, it is therefore ever new. This gives our dances a spirit and variety which I have scarcely seen elsewhere. We have many musical instruments, particularly drums of different kinds, a piece of music which resembles a guitar, and another much like a stickado. These last are chiefly used by betrothed virgins, who play on them on all grand festivals.

As our manners are simple, our luxuries are few. The dress of both sexes are nearly the same. It generally consists of a long piece of calico, or muslin, wrapped loosely round the body, somewhat in the form of a Highland plaid. This is usually dyed blue, which is our favourite colour. It is extracted from a berry and is brighter and richer than any I have seen in Europe. Besides this, our women of distinction wear golden ornaments, which they dispose with some profusion on their arms and legs. When our women are not employed with the men in tillage their usual occupation is spinning and weaving cotton, which they afterwards dye and make into garments. They also manufacture earthen vessels, of which we have many kinds. Among the rest tobacco pipes, made after the same fashion and used in the same manner, as those in Turkey.

Our manner of living is entirely plain, for as yet the natives are unacquainted with those refinements in cookery which debauch the taste—bullocks, goats, and poultry supply the greatest part of their food. These constitute likewise the principal wealth of the country and the chief articles of its commerce. The flesh is usually stewed in a pan. To make it savory we sometimes use also pepper and other spices and we have salt made of wood-ashes. Our vegetables are mostly plantains, eadas, yams, beans, and Indian corn. The head of the family usually eats alone, his wives and slaves have also their separate tables. Before we taste food we always wash our hands; indeed our cleanliness on all occasions is extreme, but on this it is an indispensible ceremony. After washing, libation is made by pouring out a small portion of the drink on the floor, and tossing a small quantity of the food in a certain place, for the spirits of departed relations, which the natives suppose to preside over their conduct and guard them from evil. They are totally unacquainted with strong or spiritous liquors and their principal beverage is palm wine. This is got from a tree of that name, by tapping it at the top and fastening a large gourd to it, and sometimes one tree will yield three or four gallons in a night. When just drawn it is of a most delicious sweetness but in a few days it acquires a tartish and most spiritous flavour, though I never saw anyone intoxicated by it. The same tree also produces nuts and oil. Our principal luxury is in perfumes; one sort of these is an odoriferous wood of delicious fragrance, the other a kind of earth, a small portion of which thrown into the fire diffuses a most powerful odour. We beat this wood into powder and mix it with palm oil, with which both men and women perfume themselves.

In our buildings we study convenience rather than ornament. Each master of a family has a large square piece of ground, surrounded with a moat or fence or inclosed with a wall made of red earth tempered, which, when dry, is as hard as brick. Within this are his houses to accommodate his family and slaves, which, if numerous, frequently present the appearance of a village. In the middle stands the principal building, appropriated to the sole use of the master, and consisting of two apartments, in one of which he sits in the day with his family; the other is left apart for the reception of his friends. He has besides these a distinct apartment in which he sleeps, together with his male children. On each side are the apartments of his wives, who have also their separate day and night houses. The habitations of the slaves and their families are distributed throughout the rest of the inclosure. These houses never exceed one story in height; they are always built of wood, or stakes driven into the ground, crossed with wattles and neatly plastered within and without. The roof is thatched with reeds. Our day houses are left open at the sides but those in which we sleep are always covered and plastered in the inside with a composition mixed with cow-dung, to keep off the different insects which annoy us during the night. The walls and floors also of these are generally covered with mats. Our beds consist of a platform, raised three or four feet from the ground, on which are laid skins and different parts of a spungy tree called plantain. Our covering is calico, or muslin, the same as our dress. The usual seats are a few logs of wood but we have benches, which are generally perfumed, to accommodate strangers; these compose the greater part of our household furniture. Houses so constructed and furnished require but little skill to erect them. Every man is a sufficient architect for the purpose. The whole neighborhood afford their unanimous assistance in building them and, in return, receive and expect no other recompense than a feast.

As we live in a country where nature is prodigal of her favors our wants are few, and easily supplied; of course we have few manufactures. They consist for the most part of calicoes, earthen ware, ornaments, and instruments of war and husbandry. But these make no part of our commerce, the principal articles of which, as I have observed, are provisions. In such a state money is of little use; however, we have some small pieces of coin, if I may call them such. They are made something like an anchor but I do not remember either their value or denomination. We have also markets, at which I have been frequently with my mother. These are sometimes visited by stout, mahogany-coloured men from the southwest of us; we call them *Oye-Eboe,* which term signifies red men living at a distance. They generally bring us fire-arms, gun-powder, hats, beads, and dried fish. The last we esteemed a great rarity, as our waters were only brooks and springs. These articles they barter with us for odoriferous woods and earth, and our salt of wood-ashes. They always carry slaves through our land but the strictest account is exacted of their manner of procuring them before they are suffered to pass. Sometimes indeed we sold slaves to them but they were only prisoners of war, or such among us as had been convicted of kidnapping, or adultery, and some other crimes which we esteemed heinous. This practice of kidnapping induces me to think that, notwithstanding all our strictness, their principal business among us was to trepan our people. I remember too they carried great sacks along with them which, not long after, I had an opportunity of fatally seeing applied to that infamous purpose.

Our land is uncommonly rich and fruitful and produces all kinds of vegetables in great abundance. We have plenty of Indian corn, and vast quantities of cotton and tobacco. Our pine apples grow without culture; they are about the size of the largest sugar-loaf, and finely flavoured. We have also spices of different kinds, particularly of pepper, and a variety of delicious fruits which I have never seen in Europe, together with gums of various kinds and honey in abundance. All our industry is exerted to improve those blessings of nature. Agriculture is our chief employment and every one, even the children and women, are engaged in it. Thus we are all habituated to labour from our earliest years. Every one contributes something to the common stock and, as we are unacquainted with idleness, we have no beggars. The benefits of such a mode of living are obvious. The West India planters prefer the slaves of Benin or Eboe to those of any other part of Guinea, for their hardiness, intelligence, integrity, and zeal. Those benefits are felt by us in the general healthiness of the people and in their vigor and activity; I might add too in their comeliness. Deformity is indeed unknown among us, I mean that of shape. Numbers of the natives of Eboe, now in London, might be brought in support of this assertion for, in regard to complexion, ideas of beauty are wholly relative. I remember while in Africa to have seen three negro children who were tawny, and another quite white, who were universally regarded by myself and the natives in general, as far as related to their complexions, as deformed. Our women too were, in my eyes at least, uncommonly graceful, alert, and modest to a degree of bashfulness; nor do I remember to have ever heard of an instance of incontinence among them before marriage. They are also remarkably cheerful. Indeed cheerfulness and affability are two of the leading characteristics of our nation.

Our tillage is exercised in a large plain or common, some hours walk from our dwellings, and all the neighbors resort thither in a body. They use no beasts of husbandry and their only instruments are hoes, axes, shovels, and beaks, or pointed iron, to dig with. Sometimes we are visited by locusts which come in large clouds so as to darken the air and destroy our harvest. This however happens rarely, but when it does a famine is produced by it. I remember an instance or two wherein this happened.

This common is oftimes the theater of war and therefore when our people go out to till their land they not only go in a body but generally take their arms with them for fear of a surprise, and when they apprehend an invasion they guard the avenues to their dwellings by driving sticks into the ground which are so sharp at one end as to pierce the foot and are generally dipt in poison. From what I can recollect of these battles, they appear to have been irruptions of one little state or district on the other, to obtain prisoners or booty. Perhaps they were incited to this by those traders who brought the European goods I mentioned among us. Such a mode of obtaining slaves in Africa is common and I believe more are procured this way, and by kidnapping, than any other. When a trader wants slaves he applies to a chief for them and tempts him with his wares. It is not extraordinary if on this occasion he yields to the temptation with as little firmness, and accepts the price of his fellow creatures' liberty with as little reluctance, as the enlightened merchant. Accordingly, he falls on his neighbors and a desperate battle ensues. If he prevails and takes prisoners he gratifies his avarice by selling them but if his party be vanquished and he falls into the hands of the enemy he is put to death; for, as he has been known to foment their quarrels, it is thought dangerous to let him survive and no ransom can save him, though all other prisoners may be redeemed. We have fire-arms, bows and arrows, broad two-edged swords and javelins; we have shields also, which cover a man from head to foot. All are taught the use of these weapons. Even our women are warriors and march boldly out to fight along with the men. Our whole district is a kind of militia. On a certain signal given, such as the firing of a gun at night, they all rise in arms and rush upon their enemy. It is perhaps something remarkable that, when our people march to the field, a red flag or banner is borne before them.

I was once a witness to a battle in our common. We had been all at work in it one day as usual, when our people were suddenly attacked. I climbed a tree at some distance, from which I beheld the fight. There were many women as well as men on both sides; among others my mother was there, and armed with a broad sword. After fighting for a considerable time with great fury, and many had been killed, our people obtained the victory and took their enemy's Chief prisoner. He was carried off in great triumph and, though he offered a large ransom for his life, he was put to death. A virgin of note among our enemies had been slain in the battle, and her arm was exposed in our market-place, where our trophies were always exhibited. The spoils were divided according to the merit of the warriors.

Those prisoners which were not sold or redeemed we kept as slaves but how different was their condition from that of the slaves in the West Indies! With us they do no more work than other members of the community, even their master. Their food, clothing, and lodging were nearly the same as theirs, except that they were not permitted to eat with those who were free born, and there were scarce any other difference between them than a superior degree of importance which the head of a family possesses in our state and that authority which, as such, he exercises over every part of his household. Some of these slaves have even slaves under them as their own property and for their own use.

As to religion, the natives believe that there is one Creator of all things, and that he lives in the sun and is girded round with a belt; that he may never eat or drink, but according to some he smokes a pipe, which is our own favorite luxury. They believe he governs events, especially our deaths or captivity but, as for the doctrine of eternity, I do not remember to have ever heard of it; some however believe in the transmigration of souls to a certain degree. Those spirits which are not transmigrated, such as their dear friends or relations, they believe always attend them and guard them from the bad spirits of their foes. For this reason they always, before eating, as I have observed, put some small portion of the meat, and pour some of their drink, on the ground for them, and they often make oblations of the blood of beasts or fowls at their graves.

•••

My father, besides many slaves, had a numerous family, of which seven lived to grow up, including myself and a sister, who was the only daughter. As I was the youngest of the sons, I became, of course, the greatest favourite with my mother, and was always with her, and she used to take particular pains to form my mind. I was trained up from my earliest years in the arts of agriculture and war; my daily exercise was shooting and throwing javelins and my mother adorned me with emblems, after the manner of our greatest warriors. In this way I grew up till I was turned the age of eleven, when an end was put to my happiness in the following manner: Generally, when the grown people in the neighbourhood were gone far in the fields to labour, the children assembled together in some of the neighbours' premises to play, and commonly some of us used to get up a tree to look out for any assailant or kidnapper that might come upon us, for they sometimes took these opportunities of our parents' absence to attack and carry off as many as they could seize. One day, as I was watching at the top of a tree in our yard, I saw one of those people come into the yard of our next neighbour but one, to kidnap, there being many stout young people in it. Immediately on this I gave the alarm of the rogue and he was surrounded by the stoutest of them, who entangled him with cords, so that he could not escape till some of the grown people came and secured him.

But, alas! ere long it was my fate to be thus attacked, and to be carried off, when none of the grown people were nigh. One day, when all our people were gone out to their works as usual, and only I and my dear sister were left to mind the house, two men and a woman got over our walls and in a moment seized us both and, without giving us time to cry out, or make resistance, they stopped our mouths, tied our hands, and ran off with us into the nearest wood, and continued to carry us as far as they could, till night came on, when we reached a small house, where the robbers halted for refreshment and spent the night. We were then unbound but were unable to take any food and being quite overpowered by fatigue and grief our only relief was some slumber, which allayed our misfortune for a short time. The next morning we left the house and continued travelling all the day. For a long time we had kept the woods but at last we came into a road which I believed I knew. I had now some hopes of being delivered for we had advanced but a little way before I discovered some people at a distance, on which I began to cry out for their assistance; but my cries had no other effect than to make them tie me faster and stop my mouth, and then they put me into a large sack. They also stopped my sister's mouth and tied her hands and in this manner we proceeded till we were out of the sight of these people.

When we went to rest the following night they offered us some victuals but we refused them, and the only comfort we had was in being in one another's arms all that night and bathing each other with our tears. But, alas! we were soon deprived of even the smallest comfort of weeping together. The next day proved a day of greater sorrow than I had yet experienced for my sister and I were then separated, while we lay clasped in each other's arms. It was in vain that we besought them not to part us; she was torn from me and immediately carried away while I was left in a state of distraction not to be described.

● ● ●

Thus I continued to travel, sometimes by land, sometimes by water, through different countries, and various nations till, at the end of six or seven months after I had been kidnapped, I arrived at the sea coast. It would be tedious and uninteresting to relate all the incidents which befel me during this journey, and which I have not yet forgotten, of the various lands I passed through, and the manners and customs of all the different people among whom I lived. I shall therefore only observe that, in all the places where I was the soil was exceedingly rich, the pomkins, eadas, plantains, yams, Ec. Ec. were in great abundance, and of incredible size. There were also large quantities of different gums, though not used for any purpose, and every where a great deal of tobacco. The cotton even grew quite wild and there was plenty of red wood. I saw no mechanics whatever in all the way, except such as I have mentioned. The chief employment in all these countries was agriculture and both the males and females, as with us, were brought up to it, and trained in the arts of war.

The first object which saluted my eyes when I arrived on the coast was the sea, and a slave-ship, which was then riding at anchor and waiting for its cargo. These filled me with astonishment, which was soon converted into terror, which I am yet at a loss to describe, nor the then feelings of my mind. When I was carried on board I was immediately handled, and tossed up, to see if I were sound, by some of the crew, and I was now persuaded that I had got into a world of bad spirits and that they were going to kill me. Their complexions too differing so much from ours, their long hair, and the language they spoke, which was very different from any I had ever heard, united to confirm me in this belief. Indeed, such were the horrors of my views and fears at the moment that, if ten thousand worlds had been my own, I would have freely parted with them all to have exchanged my condition with that of the meanest slave in my own country. When I looked round the ship too and saw a large furnace or copper boiling, and a multitude of black people of every description chained together, every one of their countenances expressing dejection and sorrow, I no longer doubted of my fate and, quite overpowered with horror and anguish, I fell motionless on the deck and fainted.

When I recovered a little I found some black people about me, who I believed were some of those who brought me on board and had been receiving their pay; they talked to me in order to cheer me, but all in vain. I asked them if we were not to be eaten by those white men with horrible looks, red faces, and long hair. They told me I was not, and one of the crew brought me a small portion of spiritous liquor in a wine glass but, being afraid of him, I would not take it out of his hand. One of the blacks therefore took it from him and gave it to me and I took a little down my palate which, instead of reviving me, as they thought it would, threw me into the greatest consternation at the strange feeling it produced, having never tasted any such liquor before. Soon after this the blacks who brought me on board went off and left me abandoned to despair. I now saw myself deprived of all chance of returning to my native country, or even the least glimpse of hope of gaining the shore, which I now considered as friendly, and even wished for my former slavery, in preference to my present situation, which was filled with horrors of every kind, still heightened by my ignorance of what I was to undergo. I was not long suffered to indulge my grief; I was soon put down under the decks and there I received such a salutation in my nostrils as I had never experienced in my life, so that with the loathsomeness of the stench, and crying together, I became so sick and low that I was not able to eat, nor had I the least desire to taste any thing. I now wished for the last friend, Death, to relieve me, but soon, to my grief, two of the white men offered me eatables and, on my refusing to eat, one of them held me fast by the hands and laid me across, I think, the windlass and tied my feet, while the other flogged me severely. I had never experienced any thing of this kind before and although not being used to the water I naturally feared that element the first time I saw it, yet, nevertheless, could I have got over the nettings, I would have jumped over the side, but I could not and, besides, the crew used to watch us very closely who were not chained down to the decks, lest we should leap into the water, and I have seen some of these poor African prisoners most severely cut for attempting to do so and hourly whipped for not eating. This indeed was often the case with myself.

In a little time after, amongst the poor chained men, I found some of my own nation, which in a small degree gave ease to my mind. I inquired of them what was to be done with us. They gave me to understand we were to be carried to these white people's country to work for them. I then was a little revived and thought, if it were no worse than working, my situation was not so desperate, but still I feared I should be put to death. The white people looked and acted, as I thought, in so savage a manner, for I had never seen among any people such instances of brutal cruelty, and this not only shewn towards us blacks, but also to some of the whites themselves. One white man in particular I saw, when we were permitted to be on deck, flogged so unmercifully with a large rope near the foremast that he died in consequence of it, and they tossed him over the side as they would have done a brute. This made me fear these people the more and I expected nothing less than to be treated in the same manner. I could not help expressing my fears and apprehensions to some of my countrymen. I asked them if these people had no country but lived in this hollow place the ship. They told me they did not but came from a distant one. "Then," said I, "how comes it in all our country we never heard of them?" They told me, because they lived so very far off. I then asked, Where were their women? Had they any like themselves? I was told they had. "And why," said I, "do we not see them?" They answered, because they were left behind. I asked how the vessel could go. They told me they could not tell but that there were cloth put upon the masts by the help of the ropes I saw and then the vessel went on, and the white men had some spell or magic they put in the water when they liked in order to stop the vessel. I was exceedingly amazed at this account and really thought they were spirits. I therefore wished much to be from amongst them for I expected they would sacrifice me, but my wishes were vain for we were so quartered that it was impossible for any of us to make our escape.

While we staid on the coast I was mostly on deck and one day, to my great astonishment, I saw one of these vessels coming in with the sails up. As soon as the whites saw it they gave a great shout, at which we were amazed, and the more so as the vessel appeared larger by approaching nearer. At last she came to an anchor in my sight and when the anchor was let go I and my countrymen who saw it were lost in astonishment to observe the vessel stop and were now convinced it was done by magic. Soon after the other ship got her boats out and they came on board of us and the people of both ships seemed very glad to see each other. Several of the strangers also shook hands with us black people and made motions with their hands signifying, I suppose, we were to go to their country, but we did not understand them. At last, when the ship we were in had got in all her cargo, they made ready with many fearful noises, and we were all put under deck so that we could not see how they managed the vessel. But this disappointment was the least of my sorrow. The stench of the hold while we were on the coast was so intolerably loathsome that it was too dangerous to remain there for any time and some of us had been permitted to stay on the deck for the fresh air, but now that the whole ship's cargo were confined together it became absolutely pestilential. The closeness of the place and the heat of the climate, added to the number in the ship, which was so crowded that each had scarcely room to turn himself, almost suffocated us. This produced copious perspiration so that the air soon became unfit for respiration, from a variety of loathsome smells, and brought on a sickness amongst the slaves of which many died, thus falling victims to the improvident avarice, as I may call it, of their purchasers. This wretched situation was again aggravated by the galling of the chains, now become insupportable, and the filth of the necessary tubs, into which the children often fell and were almost suffocated. The shrieks of the women and the groans of the dying rendered the whole a scene of horror almost inconceiveable. Happily perhaps for myself I was soon reduced so low here that it was thought necessary to keep me almost always on deck, and from my extreme youth I was not put in fetters. In this situation I expected every hour to share the fate of my companions, some of whom were almost daily brought upon deck at the point of death, which I began to hope would soon put an end to my miseries. Often did I think many of the inhabitants of the deep much more happy than myself. I envied them the freedom they enjoyed and as often wished I could change my condition for theirs. Every circumstance I met with served only to render my state more painful and heighten my apprehensions and my opinion of the cruelty of the whites. One day they had taken a number of fishes and when they had killed and satisfied themselves with as many as they thought fit, to our astonishment who were on the deck, rather than give any of them to us to eat, as we expected, they tossed the remaining fish into the sea again, although we begged and prayed for some as well as we could, but in vain, and some of my countrymen, being pressed by hunger, took an opportunity, when they thought no one saw them, of trying to get a little privately but they were discovered and the attempt procured them some very severe floggings.

One day, when we had a smooth sea and moderate wind, two of my wearied countrymen, who were chained together (I was near them at the time), preferring death to such a life of misery, somehow made through the nettings and jumped into the sea. Immediately another quite dejected fellow who, on account of his illness, was suffered to be out of irons also followed their example and I believe many more would very soon have done the same, if they had not been prevented by the ship's crew, who were instantly alarmed. Those of us that were the most active were, in a moment, put down under the deck and there was such a noise and confusion amongst the people of the ship as I never heard before, to stop her, and get the boat out to go after the slaves. However, two of the wretches were drowned but they got the other and afterwards flogged him unmercifully, for thus attempting to prefer death to slavery. In this manner we continued to undergo more hardships than I can now relate, hardships which are inseparable from this accursed trade. Many a time we were near suffocation, from the want of fresh air, which we were often without for whole days together. This, and the stench of the necessary tubs, carried off many. During our passage I first saw flying fishes, which surprised me very much. They used frequently to fly across the ship and many of them fell on the deck. I also now first saw the use of the quadrant. I had often with astonishment seen the mariners make observations with it and I could not think what it meant. They at last took notice of my surprise and one of them, willing to increase it as well as to gratify my curiosity, made me one day look through it. The clouds appeared to me to be land, which disappeared as they passed along. This heightened my wonder and I was now more persuaded than ever that I was in another world and that every thing about me was magic.

At last, we came in sight of the island of Barbadoes, at which the whites on board gave a great shout and made many signs of joy to us. We did not know what to think of this but, as the vessel drew nearer, we plainly saw the harbour, and other ships of different kinds and sizes, and we soon anchored amongst them off Bridge Town. Many merchants and planters now came on board, though it was in the evening. They put us in separate parcels and examined us attentively. They also made us jump, and pointed to the land, signifying we were to go there. We thought by this we should be eaten by these ugly men, as they appeared to us, and when, soon after we were all put down under the deck again, there was much dread and trembling among us, and nothing but bitter cries to be heard all the night from these apprehensions, insomuch that at last the white people got some old slaves from the land to pacify us. They told us we were not to be eaten, but to work, and were soon to go on land, where we should see many of our country people. This report eased us much and sure enough, soon after we landed, there came to us Africans of all languages. We were conducted immediately to the merchant's yard, where we were all pent up together like so many sheep in a fold, without regard to sex or age. As every object was new to me, every thing I saw filled me with surprise. What struck me first was that the houses were built with bricks, in stories, and in every other respect different from those I have seen in Africa, but I was still more astonished on seeing people on horseback. I did not know what this could mean and indeed I thought these people were full of nothing but magical arts. While I was in this aston-ishment one of my fellow prisoners spoke to a countryman of his about the horses who said they were the same kind they had in their country. I under-stood them, though they were from a distant part of Africa, and I thought it odd I had not seen any horses there but afterwards, when I came to converse with different Africans I found they had many horses amongst them, and much larger than those I then saw.

We were not many days in the merchant's custody before we were sold after their usual manner, which is this: On a signal given (as the beat of a drum), the buyers rush at once into the yard where the slaves are confined and make choice of that parcel they like best. The noise and clamour with which this is attended, and the eagerness visible in the countenances of the buyers, serve not a little to increase the apprehension of the terrified Africans, who may well be supposed to consider them as the ministers of that destruction to which they think themselves devoted. In this manner, without scruple, are relations and friends separated, most of them never to see each other again.

The Portuguese in Asia

Throughout the fifteenth century, Portuguese sailors had been exploring the South Atlantic and the west coast of Africa. Their immediate goal was not a southern route to Asia, but direct commercial contact with the wealthy empire of Mali. By 1498, the Portuguese had sailed around the southern tip of Africa and reached India. This changed the focus of Portuguese expansion to the Indian Ocean and the spice trade. Spices from Southeast Asia had become valuable commodities in Europe. They were not only used to enhance a bland diet but also as preservatives and medicine. Since Muslim rulers controlled the overland routes to Asia there were also religious motives behind the Portuguese voyages. Bypassing Muslim middlemen would both increase profits and hurt the longtime enemies of Iberian (Spanish and Portuguese) Christians.

Even more significant than the voyages to the Indian Ocean was the Portuguese success against Muslim and Chinese warships once they arrived. Although the Portuguese and Spanish had borrowed the technologies to build seafaring ships from Muslim and Chinese examples, they quickly adapted them into vessels superior to those of the older and historically more advanced cultures. But even with technical superiority on the seas, Portugal could not establish a colonial empire in Asia to match the Spanish one in the Americas. Portugal was far too small and the Asian civilizations still too large and powerful to conquer and colonize. Instead, the Portuguese conquered and fortified a chain of towns on the coasts of Africa, South Asia, and Southeast Asia.

The following selection is an account of a speech made by Alfonso de Albuquerque, Portuguese viceroy of the Indies, to his troops before assaulting the city of Malacca. In 1510, Albuquerque had conquered the Indian coastal city of Goa. The next step was to secure passage to and from the Spice Islands through the Straits of Malacca. The Straits cut a narrow passage between the Malay Peninsula and the island of Sumatra. In 1511, on his second attempt, Albuquerque conquered the city of Malacca for Portugal.

---

1. What are the Portuguese goals in South and Southeast Asia?

2. Which aspects of this speech do you think evoked the strongest responses from the men? Why?

Sirs, you will have no difficulty in remembering that when we decided upon attacking this city, it was with the determination of building a fortress within it, for so it appeared to all to be necessary, and after having captured it I was unwilling to let slip the possession of it, yet, because ye all advised me to do so, I left it, and withdrew; but being ready, as you see, to put my hands upon it again once more, I learned that you had already changed your opinion: now this cannot be because the Moors have destroyed the best part of us, but on account of my sins, which merit the failure of accomplishing this undertaking in the way that I had desired. And, inasmuch as my will and determination is, as long as I am Governor of India, neither to fight nor to hazard men on land, except in those parts wherein I must build a fortress to maintain them, as I have already told you before this, I desire you earnestly, of your goodness, although you all have already agreed upon what is to be done, to freely give me again your opinions in writing as to what I ought to do; for inasmuch as I have to give an account of these matters and a justification of my proceedings to the King D. Manuel, our Lord, I am unwilling to be left alone to bear the blame of them; and although there be many reasons which I could allege in favour of our taking this city and building a fortress therein to maintain possession of it, two only will I mention to you, on this occasion, as tending to point out wherefore you ought not to turn back from what you have agreed upon.

The first is the great service which we shall perform to Our Lord in casting the Moors out of this country, and quenching the fire of this sect of Mafamede so that it may never burst out again hereafter; and I am so sanguine as to hope for this from our undertaking, that if we can only achieve the task before us, it will result in the Moors resigning India altogether to our rule, for the greater part of them—or perhaps all of them—live upon the trade of this country and are become great and rich, and lords of extensive treasures. It is, too, well worthy of belief that as the King of Malaca, who has already once been discomfited and had proof of our strength, with no hope of obtaining any succour from any other quarter—sixteen days having already elapsed since this took place—makes no endeavour to negotiate with us for the security of his estate. Our Lord is blinding his judgement and hardening his heart, and desires the completion of this affair of Malaca: for when we were committing ourselves to the business of cruising in the Straits (of the Red Sea) where the King of Portugal had often ordered me to go (for it was there that His Highness considered we could cut down the commerce which the Moors of Cairo, of Méca, and of Judá, carry on with these parts), Our Lord for his service thought right to lead us hither, for when Malaca is taken the places on the Straits must be shut up, and they will never more be able to introduce their spiceries into those places.

And the other reason is the additional service which we shall render to the King D. Manuel in taking this city, because it is the headquarters of all the spiceries and drugs which the Moors carry every year hence to the Straits without our being able to prevent them from so doing; but if we deprive them of this their ancient market there, there does not remain for them a single port, nor a single situation, so commodious in the whole of these parts, where they can carry on their trade in these things. For after we were in possession of the pepper of Malabar, never more did any reach Cairo, except that which the Moors carried thither from these parts, and forty or fifty ships, which sail hence every year laden with all sorts of spiceries bound to Méca, cannot be stopped without great expence and large fleets, which must necessarily cruise about continually in the offing of Cape Comorim; and the pepper of Malabar, of which they may hope to get some portion because they have the King of Calicut on their side, is in our hands, under the eyes of the Governor of India, from whom the Moors cannot carry off so much with impunity as they hope to do; and I hold it as very certain that if we take this trade of Malaca away out of their hands, Cairo and Méca are entirely ruined, and to Venice will no spiceries be conveyed except that which her merchants go and buy in Portugal.

But if you are of opinion that, because Malaca is a large city and very populous, it will give us much trouble to maintain possession of it, no such doubts as these ought to arise, for when once the city is gained, all the rest of the Kingdom is of so little account that the King has not a single place left where he can rally his forces; and if you dread lest by taking the city we be involved in great expenses, and on account of the season of the year there be no place where our men and our Fleet can be recruited, I trust in God's mercy that when Malaca is held in subjection to our dominion by a strong fortress, provided that the Kings of Portugal appoint thereto those who are well experienced as Governors and Managers of the Revenues, the taxes of the land will pay all the expenses which may arise in the administration of the city; and if the merchants who are wont to resort thither—accustomed as they are to live under the tyrannical yoke of the Malays—experience a taste of our just dealing, truthfulness, frankness, and mildness, and come to know of the instructions of the King D. Manuel, our Lord, wherein he commands that all his subjects in these parts be very well treated, I venture to affirm that they will all return and take up their abode in the city again, yea, and build the walls of their houses with gold; and all these matters which here I lay before you may be secured to us by this half-turn of the key, which is that we build a fortress in this city of Malaca and sustain it, and that this land be brought under the dominion of the Portuguese, and the King D. Manuel be styled true king thereof, and therefore I desire you of your kindness to consider seriously the enterprise that ye have in hand, and not to leave it to fall to the ground.

Japan Encounters the West

The Portuguese reached Japan in 1543. The Japanese were curious and eager to interact with the Westerners at first. Japanese ships already dominated an active Asian trade network centered on the East China Sea and began vigorous interaction with Portuguese, Spanish, and Dutch merchants. Along with the merchants came Christian missionaries. Japan has a long history of intellectual and religious openness. In addition to native Shinto beliefs, various forms of Buddhism were well established in Japan and Confucian philosophy was influential among the educated. Christianity became very popular in the western regions of Japan in the century after contact with the West.

By 1638, however, missionaries had been expelled, foreign merchants were virtually banned, and Japanese were prohibited from leaving. There are several reasons for this abrupt turn of events. First, European explorers arrived in Japan during a time of civil war among powerful landlords called *daimyo*. Over time, European were seen as supporting certain factions in return for the opportunity to spread Christianity in territories of those *daimyo*. Once Japan was unified by Toyotomi Hideyoshi and his successors, the Tokugawas, European influence became even more suspect. Japanese Christians were suspected of having loyalties to religious leaders outside Japan. After the Spanish conquered the Philippines, the Tokugawas worried that European merchants and missionaries were merely the vanguard of a conquering force. Finally, the new regime desired a monopoly on international trade. First missionaries were expelled, then Christianity was suppressed, and eventually all contact with the West was broken off, with the exception of one Dutch merchant vessel a year.

The first two documents, from 1587, show the growing suspicion of Christian missionaries by Hideyoshi. At this point, Europeans are still allowed to trade, but not spread their religion. The second set of documents date from 1638 to 1640 and represent the final stages of the Closing of Japan, including the killing of Portuguese envoys from Macao, a trading colony on the south China coast.

---

1. Why do Hideyoshi and the Tokugawas want to suppress Christianity?

2. How do the documents generally depict Europeans?

Limitation on the Propagation of Christianity, 1587

1.   Whether one desires to become a follower of the padre is up to that person's own conscience.

2.   If one receives a province, a district, or a village as his fief, and forces farmers in his domain who are properly registered under certain temples to become followers of the padre against their wishes, then he has committed a most unreasonable illegal act.

3.   When a vassal (*kyūnin*) receives a grant of a province or a district, he must consider it as a property entrusted to him on a temporary basis. A vassal may be moved from one place to another, but farmers remain in the same place. Thus if an unreasonable illegal act is committed [as described above], the vassal will be called upon to account for his culpable offense. The intent of this provision must be observed.

4.   Anyone whose fief is over 200 *chō* and who can expect two to three thousand *kan* of rice harvest each year must receive permission from the authorities before becoming a follower of the padre.

5.   Anyone whose fief is smaller than the one described above may, as his conscience dictates, select for himself from between eight or nine religions.

6.   If a *daimyō* who has a fief over a province, a district or a village, forces his retainers to become followers of the padre, he is committing a crime worse than the followers of Honganji who assembled in their temple [to engage in the Ikkō riot]. This will have an adverse effect on [the welfare of] the nation. Anyone who cannot use good judgment in this matter will be punished.

Expulsion of Missionaries, 1587

1.   Japan is the country of gods, but has been receiving false teachings from Christian countries. this cannot be tolerated any further.

2.   The [missionaries] approach people in provinces and districts to make them their followers, and let them destroy shrines and temples. This is an unheard of outrage. When a vassal receives a province, a district, a village, or another form of fief, he must consider it as a property entrusted to him on a temporary basis. He must follow the laws of this country, and abide by their intent. However, some vassals illegally [commend part of their fiefs to the church]. This is a culpable offense.

3.   The padres, by their special knowledge [in the sciences and medicine], feel that they can at will entice people to become their believers. In so doing they commit the illegal act of destroying the teachings of Buddha prevailing in Japan. These padres cannot be permitted to remain in Japan. They

must prepare to leave the country within twenty days of the issuance of this notice. However, the vassals must not make unreasonable demands on the padres, which shall be treated as a culpable offense.

4. The black [Portuguese and Spanish] ships come to Japan to engage in trade. Thus the matter is a separate one. They can continue to engage in trade.

5. Hereafter, anyone who does not hinder the teachings of Buddha, whether he be a merchant or not, may come and go freely from Christian countries to Japan.

This is our wish, and so ordered.

Fifteenth year of Tenshō [1587], sixth month, 19th day.

The Edict of 1635 Ordering the Closing of Japan: Addressed to the Joint Bugyō of Nagasaki

1. Japanese ships are strictly forbidden to leave for foreign countries.

2. No Japanese is permitted to go abroad. If there is anyone who attempts to do so secretly, he must be executed. The ship so involved must be impounded and its owner arrested, and the matter must be reported to the higher authority.

3. If any Japanese returns from overseas after residing there, he must be put to death.

4. If there is any place where the teachings of padres (Christianity) is practiced, the two of you must order a thorough investigation.

5. Any informer revealing the whereabouts of the followers of padres (Christians) must be rewarded accordingly. If anyone reveals the whereabouts of a high ranking padre, he must be given one hundred pieces of silver. For those of lower ranks, depending on the deed, the reward must be set accordingly.

6. If a foreign ship has an objection [to the measures adopted] and it becomes necessary to report the matter to Edo, you may ask the Ōmura domain to provide ships to guard the foreign ship, as was done previously.

7. If there are any Southern Barbarians (Westerners) who propagate the teachings of padres, or otherwise commit crimes, they may be incarcerated in the prison maintained by the Ōmura domain, as was done previously.

8. All incoming ships must be carefully searched for the followers of padres.

9. No single trading city [see 12 below] shall be permitted to purchase all the merchandise brought by foreign ships.

10. Samurai are not permitted to purchase any goods originating from foreign ships directly from Chinese merchants in Nagasaki.

11.   After a list of merchandise brought by foreign ships is sent to Edo, as before you may order that commercial dealings may take place without waiting for a reply from Edo.

12.   After settling the price, all white yarns (raw silk) brought by foreign ships shall be allocated to the five trading cities and other quarters as stipulated.

13.   After settling the price of white yarns (raw silk), other merchandise [brought by foreign ships] may be traded freely between the [licensed] dealers. However, in view of the fact that Chinese ships are small and cannot bring large consignments, you may issue orders of sale at your discretion. Additionally, payment for goods purchased must be made within twenty days after the price is set.

14.   The date of departure homeward of foreign ships shall not be later than the twentieth day of the ninth month. Any ships arriving in Japan later than usual shall depart within fifty days of their arrival. As to the departure of Chinese ships, you may use your discretion to order their departure after the departure of the Portuguese *galeota* (galleon).

15.   The goods brought by foreign ships which remained unsold may not be deposited or accepted for deposit.

16.   The arrival in Nagasaki of representatives of the five trading cities shall not be later than the fifth day of the seventh month. Anyone arriving later than that date shall lose the quota assigned to his city.

17.   Ships arriving in Hirado must sell their raw silk at the price set in Nagasaki, and are not permitted to engage in business transactions until after the price is established in Nagasaki.

You are hereby required to act in accordance with the provisions set above. It is so ordered.

Kaga no-kami Hotta Masamori et al., seals.

To: Sakakibara Hida no-kami, Sengoku Yamoto no-kami Completion of the Exclusion, 1639

1.   The matter relating to the proscription of Christianity is known [to the Portuguese]. However, heretofore thay have secretly transported those who are going to propagate that religion.

2.   If those who believe in that religion band together in an attempt to do evil things, they must be subjected to punishment.

3.   While those who believe in the preaching of padres are in hiding, there are incidents in which that country (Portugal) has sent gifts to them for their sustenance.

In view of the above, hereafter entry by the Portuguese *galeota* is forbidden. If they insist on coming [to Japan], the ships must be destroyed and anyone aboard those ships must be beheaded. We have received the above order and are thus transmitting it to you accordingly.

The above concerns our disposition with regard to the *galeota*.

Memorandum

With regard to those who believe in Christianity, you are aware that there is a proscription, and thus knowing, you are not permitted to let padres and those who believe in their preaching to come aboard your ships. If there is any violation, all of you who are aboard will be considered culpable. If there is anyone who hides the fact that he is a Christian and boards your ship, you may report it to us. A substantial reward will be given to you for this information.

This memorandum is to be given to those who come on Chinese ships. (A similar note to the Dutch ships.)

The Fate of the Embassy from Macao, 1640, by Antonio Cardim, S.J.

Because many serious crimes have been committed over a number of years by the propagation of the Christian religion in defiance of his decree, the *shōgun* last year forbade under grave penalties all voyages from Macao to Japan, laying down that if any ship were to come to Japan despite this prohibition, the vessel would be burnt and the sailors and merchants executed. This edict was promulgated both summarily and in detail. Nevertheless, these men have blatantly violated the aforesaid decree by their voyage and are seriously at fault. Furthermore, in spite of their assertion that on no account will they send hereafter ministers of the Christian religion to Japan, the ambassadorial letters from Macao are silent on this point. Since, therefore, the *shōgun* has prohibited such voyages on account of the Christian religion and since no mention of this matter is made in these letters, it is quite evident that the entire legation is but a pretence. For this reason, all who have come hither in this ship are to pay the extreme penalty.

It has accordingly been decided that the ship shall be consumed by flames and that the principal ambassadors shall be put to death along with their companions so that nothing may remain of this harbinger of evil. Thus the example which the *shōgun* has made of them will be noticed abroad in Macao and the home country; as a consequence, all will learn to respect the rights of Princes and Kings. We nevertheless desire that the rabble among the crew be spared and sent back to Macao. But should any other ship come hither by force of adverse circumstances or for any other reason whatsoever, let it be known that, in whatsoever port it may call, one and all will be put to death.

Given on the 3rd day of the 6th moon of the 17th year of the Kanei era, that is, the 25th day of July in the year 1640.

At the same time they also asked what they would say about this punishment to foreign peoples in the Orient and even in Europe, if by chance they should go thither. They replied that they would tell the truth; to wit, that the *shōgun* of Japan had put the Portuguese ambassadors to death and had set fire to their ship because they professed the Christian religion and had disobeyed his edict, and that they, to the number of thirteen, had been spared this punishment and sent back so that they could recount what had happened; but they added that the kings and all the peoples of the world would most certainly condemn what had been done as a crime against international law.

They were then taken thence to the mount of execution in order to identify the heads of the executed men, which they found affixed to boards in three groups. The heads of the ambassadors were set apart from the rest; they did not appear pale or washed out, but rather the freshness and beauty of their features well indicated their fate. Now they were set up near a large pole, from the top of which hung the Tyrant's proclamation. Not far away they espied a house wherein the corpses had been buried and cairns of immense stones had been set up over them; thus if at any time the Japanese should be silent about these men, the very stones would speak.

Inscribed on a pole which emerged from the midst of these stones was the name of the legation and the reason for the executions; it was indeed their monument for posterity and an everlasting trophy of their glory. With unfeeling barbarity the Tyrant had added this inscription: *A similar penalty will be suffered by all those who henceforward come to these shores from Portugal, whether they be sailors, whether they come by error or whether they be driven hither by storm. Even more, if the King of Portugal, or Shaka, or even the GOD of the Christians were to come, they would all pay the very same penalty.*

Martin Luther

The theory that all events are interrelated receives dramatic confirmation in the relationship between the Renaissance and the Reformation. To raise money to build St. Peter's Cathedral in Rome, the greatest monument of Renaissance art, Pope Leo X authorized the granting of papal indulgences in return for suitable donations to the church. In 1517, one of the papal agents, a Dominican friar named John Tetzel, appeared in central Germany to grant these indulgences. Martin Luther (1483–1546), a professor at the University of Wittenberg, responded by posting on the door of the Castle Church a list of Ninety-Five Theses, in which he attacked the entire theory and practice of indulgences. Luther's act, in turn, set in motion a series of events that resulted finally in the Protestant Reformation.

Although Tetzel's activities had set him off, Luther based his opposition to the church on grounds far deeper than the problem of indulgences. Basically, the question centered on the salvation of people's souls. From his studies of St. Paul and St. Augustine, Luther, who was himself a Catholic monk, became convinced that, since all people are utterly condemned and lost as a result of original sin, it is impossible for them to achieve salvation by any works of their own. Rather, salvation is the free gift of God's grace through faith. This doctrine of justification by faith rather than by works undercut the position of the Catholic Church, which maintained that since the works necessary to salvation (such as the sacraments) could be performed only with the aid of the priesthood, the church provided the sole means to salvation. In place of the priestly hierarchy, Luther substituted the notion of the priesthood of all believers, an idea that was to become a cornerstone of Protestantism. In the selection that follows he defends his "heretical" views, largely through a vigorous attack on both the theology and the practices of the church.

---

1. According to Luther, what authority do political leaders have to enact religious reform?

2. What role do the Christian Scriptures play in Luther's argument?

An Open Letter to the Christian Nobility of the German Nation Concerning the Reform of the Christian Estate, 1520

To His Most Illustrious and Mighty Imperial Majesty, and to the Christian Nobility of the German Nation

Doctor Martin Luther

Grace and power from God, Most illustrious Majesty, and most gracious and dear Lords.

It is not out of sheer forwardness or rashness that I, a single, poor man, have undertaken to address your worships. The distress and oppression which weigh down all the Estate of Christendom, especially of Germany, and which move not me alone, but everyone to cry out time and again, and to pray for help, have forced me even now to cry aloud that God may inspire some one with His Spirit to lend this suffering nation a helping hand. Ofttimes the councils have made some pretence at reformation, but their attempts have been cleverly hindered by the guile of certain men and things have gone from bad to worse. I now intend, by the help of God, to throw some light upon the wiles and wickedness of these men, to the end that when they are known, they may not henceforth be so hurtful and so great a hindrance. God has given us a noble youth to be our head and thereby has awakened great hopes of good in many hearts; wherefore it is meet that we should do our part and profitably use this time of grace.

In this whole matter the first and most important thing is that we take earnest heed not to enter on it trusting in great might or in human reason, even though all power in the world were ours; for God cannot and will not suffer a good work to be begun with trust in our own power or reason. Such works He crushes ruthlessly to earth, as it is written in the xxxiii Psalm, "There is no king saved by the multitude of an host: a mighty man is not delivered by much strength." On this account, I fear, it came to pass of old that the good Emperors Frederick I and II, and many other German emperors were shamefully oppressed and trodden under foot by the popes, although all the world feared them. It may be that they relied on their own might more than on God, and therefore they had to fall. In our own times, too, what was it that raised the blood-thirsty Julius II to such heights? Nothing else, I fear, except that France, the Germans, and Venice relied upon themselves. The children of Benjamin slew forty-two thousand Israelites because the latter relied on their own strength.

Trans. C. M. Jacobs.

That it may not so fare with us and our noble young Emperor Charles, we must be sure that in this matter we are dealing not with men, but with the princes of hell, who can fill the world with war and bloodshed, but whom war and bloodshed do not overcome. We must go at this work despairing of physical force and humbly trusting God; we must seek God's help with earnest prayer, and fix our minds on nothing else than the misery and distress of suffering Christendom, without regard to the deserts of evil men. Otherwise we may start the game with great prospect of success, but when we get well into it the evil spirits will stir up such confusion that the whole world will swim in blood, and yet nothing will come of it. Let us act wisely, therefore, and in the fear of God. The more force we use, the greater our disaster if we do not act humbly and in God's fear. The popes and the Romans have hitherto been able, by the devil's help, to set kings at odds with one another, and they may well be able to do it again, if we proceed by our own might and cunning, without God's help.

I. The Three Walls of the Romanists

The Romanists, with great adroitness, have built three walls about them, behind which they have hitherto defended themselves in such wise that no one has been able to reform them; and this has been the cause of terrible corruption throughout all Christendom.

First, when pressed by the temporal power, they have made decrees and said that the temporal power has no jurisdiction over them, but, on the other hand, that the spiritual is above the temporal power. Second, when the attempt is made to reprove them out of the Scriptures, they raise the objection that the interpretation of the Scriptures belongs to no one except the pope. Third, if threatened with a council, they answer with the fable that no one can call a council but the pope.

In this wise they have slyly stolen from us our three rods, that they may go unpunished, and have ensconced themselves within the safe stronghold of these three walls, that they may practise all the knavery and wickedness which we now see. Even when they have been compelled to hold a council they have weakened its power in advance by previously binding the princes with an oath to let them remain as they are. Moreover, they have given the pope full authority over all the decisions of the council, so that it is all one whether there are many councils—except that they deceive us with puppet-shows and sham-battles. So terribly do they fear for their skin in a really free council! And they have intimidated kings and princes by making them believe it would be an offence against God not to obey them in all these knavish, crafty deceptions.

Now God help us, and give us one of the trumpets with which the walls of Jericho were overthrown, that we may blow down these walls of straw and paper, and may set free the Christian rods for the punishment of sin, bringing to light the craft and deceit of the devil, to the end that through punishment we may reform ourselves, and once more attain God's favor.

Against the first wall we will direct our first attack.

It is pure invention that pope, bishops, priests, and monks are to be called the "spiritual estate"; princes, lords, artisans, and farmers the "temporal estate." That is indeed a fine bit of lying and hypocrisy. Yet no one should be frightened by it; and for this reason—*viz.*, that all Christians are truly of the "spiritual estate," and there is among them no difference at all but that of office, as Paul says in I Corinthians xii, "We are all one body, yet every member has its own work, whereby it serves every other, all because we have one baptism, one Gospel, one faith, and are all alike Christians"; for baptism, Gospel and faith alone make us "spiritual" and a Christian people.

But that a pope or a bishop anoints, confers, tonsures, ordains, consecrates, or prescribes dress unlike that of the laity,—this may make hypocrites, and graven images, but it never makes a Christian or "spiritual" man. Through baptism all of us are consecrated to the priesthood, as St. Peter says in I Peter ii, "Ye are a royal priesthood, a priestly kingdom," and the book of Revelation says, "Thou hast made us by Thy blood to be priests and kings." For if we had no higher consecration than pope or bishop gives, the consecration by pope or bishop would never make a priest, nor might anyone either say mass or preach a sermon or give absolution. Therefore when the bishop consecrates it is the same thing as if he, in the place and stead of the whole congregation, all of whom have like power, were to take one out of their number and charge him to use this power for the others; just as though ten brothers, all king's sons and equal heirs, were to choose one of themselves to rule the inheritance for them all,—they would all be kings and equal in power, though one of them would be charged with the duty of ruling.

To make it still clearer. If a little group of pious Christian laymen were taken captive and set down in a wilderness, and had among them no priest consecrated by a bishop, and if there in the wilderness they were to agree in choosing one of themselves, married or unmarried, and were to charge him with the office of baptising, saying mass, absolving, and preaching, such a man would be as truly a priest as though all bishops and popes had consecrated him. That is why in cases of necessity any one can baptise and give absolution, which would be impossible unless we were all priests. This great grace and power of baptism and of the Christian Estate they have well-nigh destroyed and caused us to forget through the canon law. It was in the manner aforesaid that Christians in olden days chose from their number bishops and priests, who were afterwards confirmed by other bishops, without all the show which now obtains. It was thus that Sts. Augustine, Ambrose, and Cyprian became bishops.

Since, then, the temporal authorities are baptised with the same baptism and have the same faith and Gospel as we, we must grant that they are priests and bishops, and count their office one which has a proper and a useful place in the Christian community. For whoever comes out of the water of baptism can boast that he is already consecrated priest, bishop, and pope, though it is not seemly that every one should exercise the office. Nay, just because we are all in like manner priests, no one must put himself forward and undertake, without our consent and election, to do what is in the power of all of us. For what is common to all, no one dare take upon himself without the will and the commands of the community; and should it happen that one chosen for such an office were deposed for malfeasance, he would then be just what he was before he held office. Therefore a priest in Christendom is nothing else than an office-holder. While he is in office, he has precedence; when deposed, he is a peasant or a townsman like the rest. Beyond all doubt, then, a priest is no longer a priest when he is deposed. But now they have invented *characters indelebiles*, and prate that a deposed priest is nevertheless something different from a mere layman. They even dream that a priest can never become a layman, or be anything else than a priest. All this is mere talk and man-made law.

From all this it follows that there is really no difference between laymen and priests, princes and bishops, "spirituals" and "temporals," as they call them, except that of office and work, but not of "estate"; for they are all of the same estate,—true priests, bishops, and popes,—though they are not all engaged in the same work, just as all priests and monks have not the same work. This is the teaching of St. Paul in Romans xii and I Corinthians xii, and of St. Peter in I Peter ii, as I have said above, *viz.*, that we are all one body of Christ, the Head, all members one of another. Christ has not two different bodies, one "temporal," the other "spiritual." He is one Head, and He has one Body.

Therefore, just as those who are now called "spiritual"—priests, bishops or popes—are neither different from other Christians nor superior to them, except that they are charged with the administration of the Word of God and the sacraments, which is their work and office, so it is with the temporal authorities,—they bear sword and rod with which to punish the evil and to protect the good. A cobbler, a smith, a farmer, each has the work and office of his trade, and yet they are all alike consecrated priests and bishops, and every one by means of his own work or office must benefit and serve every other, that in this way many kinds of work may be done for the bodily and spiritual welfare of the community, even as all the members of the body serve one another.

See, now, how Christian is the decree which says that the temporal power is not above the "spiritual estate" and may not punish it. That is as much as to say that the hand shall lend no aid when the eye is suffering. Is it not unnatural, not to say unchristian, that one member should not help another and prevent its destruction? Verily, the more honorable the member, the more should the others help. I say then, since the temporal power is ordained of God to punish evildoers and to protect them that do well, it should therefore be left free to perform its office without hindrance through the whole body of Christendom without respect of persons, whether it affect pope, bishops, priests, monks, nuns or anybody else. For if the mere fact that the temporal power has a smaller place among the Christian offices than has the office of preachers or confessors, or of the clergy, then the tailors, cobblers, masons, carpenters, potboys, tapsters, farmers, and all the secular tradesmen, should also be prevented from providing pope, bishops, priests and monks with shoes, clothing, houses, meat and drink, and from paying them tribute. But if these laymen are allowed to do their work unhindered, what do the Roman scribes mean by their laws, with which they withdraw themselves from the jurisdiction of the temporal Christian power, only so that they may be free to do evil and to fulfill what St. Peter has said: "There shall be false teachers among you, and through covetousness shall they with feigned words make merchandise of you."

On this account the Christian temporal power should exercise its office without let or hindrance, regardless whether it be pope, bishop, or priest whom it affects; whoever is guilty, let him suffer. All that the canon law has said to the contrary is sheer invention of Roman presumption. For thus saith St. Paul to all Christians: "Let every soul (I take that to mean the pope's soul also) be subject unto the higher powers; for they bear not the sword in vain, but are the ministers of God for the punishment of evildoers, and for the praise of them that do well." St. Peter also says: "Submit yourselves unto every ordinance of man for the Lord's sake, for so is the will of God." He has also prophesied that such men shall come as will despise the temporal authorities, and this has come to pass through the canon law.

So then, I think this first paper-wall is overthrown, since the temporal power has become a member of the body of Christendom, and is of the "spiritual estate," though its work is of a temporal nature. Therefore its work should extend freely and without hindrance to all the members of the whole body; it should punish and use force whenever guilt deserves or necessity demands, without regard to pope, bishops, and priests,—let them hurl threats and bans as much as they will.

This is why guilty priests, if they are surrendered to the temporal law, are first deprived of their priestly dignities, which would not be right unless the temporal sword had previously had authority over them by divine right.

Again, it is intolerable that in the canon law so much importance is attached to the freedom, life, and property of the clergy, as though the laity were not also as spiritual and as good Christians as they, or did not belong to the Church. Why are your life and limb, your property and honor so free, and mine not? We are all alike Christians, and have baptism, faith, Spirit, and all things alike. If a priest is killed, the land is laid under interdict,—why not when a peasant is killed? Whence comes this great distinction between those who are equally Christians? Only from human laws and inventions!

Moreover, it can be no good spirit who has invented such exceptions and granted to sin such license and impunity. For if we are bound to strive against the works and words of the evil spirit, and to drive him out in whatever way we can, as Christ commands and His Apostles, ought we, then, to suffer it in silence when the pope or his satellites are bent on devilish words and works? Ought we for the sake of men to allow the suppression of divine commandments and truths which we have sworn in baptism to support with life and limb? Of a truth we should then have to answer for all the souls that would thereby be abandoned and led astray.

It must therefore have been the very prince of devils who said what is written in the canon law: "If the pope were so scandalously bad as to lead souls in crowds to the devil, yet he could not be deposed." On this accursed and devilish foundation they build at Rome, and think that we should let all the world go to the devil, rather than resist their knavery. If the fact that one man is set over others were sufficient reason why he should escape punishment, then no Christian could punish another, since Christ commands the lowliest and the least.

Where sin is, there is no escape from punishment; as St. Gregory also writes that we are indeed all equal, but guilt puts us in subjection one to another. Now we see how they whom God and the Apostles have made subject to the temporal sword deal with Christendom, depriving it of its liberty by their own wickedness, without warrant of Scripture. It is to be feared that this is a game of Antichrist or a sign that he is close at hand.

The second wall is still more flimsy and worthless. They wish to be the only Masters of the Holy Scriptures, even though in all their lives they learn nothing from them. They assume for themselves sole authority, and with insolent juggling of words they would persuade us that the pope, whether he be a bad man or a good man, cannot err in matters of faith; and yet they cannot prove a single letter of it. Hence it comes that so many heretical and unchristian, nay, even unnatural ordinances have a place in the canon law, of which, however, there is no present need to speak. For since they think that the Holy Spirit never leaves them, be they ever so unlearned and wicked, they make bold to decree whatever they will. And if it were true, where would be the need or use of the Holy Scriptures? Let us burn them, and be satisfied with the unlearned lords at Rome, who are possessed of the Holy Spirit,—although He can possess only pious hearts! Unless I had read it myself, I could not have believed that the devil would make such clumsy pretensions at Rome, and find a following.

But, not to fight them with mere words, we will quote the Scriptures. St. Paul says in I Corinthians xiv: "If to anyone something better is revealed, though he be sitting and listening to another in God's Word, then the first, who is speaking, shall hold his peace and give place." What would be the use of this commandment, if we were only to believe him who does the talking or who has the highest seat? Christ also says in John vi, that all Christians shall be taught of God. Thus it may well happen that the pope and his followers are wicked men, and no true Christians, not taught of God, not having true understanding. On the other hand, an ordinary man may have true understanding; why then should we not follow him? Has not the pope erred many times? Who would help Christendom when the pope errs, if we were not to believe another, who had the Scriptures on his side, more than the pope?

Therefore it is a wickedly invented fable, and they cannot produce a letter in defence of it, that the interpretation of Scripture or the confirmation of its interpretation belongs to the pope alone. They have themselves usurped this power; and although they allege that this power was given to Peter when the keys were given to him, it is plain enough that the keys were not given to Peter alone, but to the whole community. Moreover, the keys were not ordained for doctrine or government, but only for the binding and loosing of sin, and whatever further power of the keys they arrogate to themselves is mere invention. But Christ's word to Peter, "I have prayed for thee that thy faith fail not," cannot be applied to the pope, since the majority of the popes have been without faith, as they must themselves confess. Besides, it is not only for Peter that Christ prayed, but also for all Apostles and Christians, as he says in John xvii: "Father, I pray for those whom Thou has given Me, and not for these only, but for all who believe on Me through their word." Is not this clear enough?

Only think of it yourself! They must confess that there are pious Christians among us, who have the true faith, Spirit, understanding, word, and mind of Christ. Why, then, should we reject their word and understanding and follow the pope, who has neither faith nor Spirit? That would be to deny the whole faith and the Christian Church. Moreover, it is not the pope alone who is always in the right, if the article of the Creed is correct: "I believe in one holy Christian Church"; otherwise the prayer must run: "I believe in the pope at Rome," and so reduce the Christian Church to one man,—which would be nothing else than a devilish and hellish error.

Besides, if we are all priests, as was said above, and all have one faith, one Gospel, one sacrament, why should we not also have the power to test and judge what is correct or incorrect in matters of faith? What becomes of the words of Paul in I Corinthians ii: "He that is spiritual judgeth all things, yet he himself is judged of no man," and II Corinthians iv: "We have all the same Spirit of faith"? Why, then, should not we perceive what squares with faith and what does not, as well as does an unbelieving pope?

All these and many other texts should make us bold and free, and we should not allow the Spirit of liberty, as Paul calls Him, to be frightened off by the fabrications of the popes, but we ought to go boldly forward to test all that they do or leave undone, according to our interpretation of the

Scriptures, which rests on faith, and compel them to follow not their own interpretation, but the one that is better. In the olden days Abraham had to listen to his Sarah, although she was in more complete subjection to him than we are to anyone on earth. Balaam's ass, also, was wiser than the prophet himself. If God then spoke by an ass against a prophet, why should He not be able even now to speak by a righteous man against the pope? In like manner St. Paul rebukes St. Peter as a man in error. Therefore it behooves every Christian to espouse the cause of the faith, to understand and defend it, and to rebuke all errors.

The third wall falls of itself when the first two are down. For when the pope acts contrary to the Scriptures, it is our duty to stand by the Scriptures, to reprove him, and to constrain him, according to the word of Christ in Matthew xviii: "If thy brother sin against thee, go and tell it him between thee and him alone; if he hear thee not, then take with thee one or two more; if he hear them not, tell it to the Church; if he hear not the Church, consider him a heathen." Here every member is commanded to care for every other. How much rather should we do this when the member that does evil is a ruling member, and by his evil-doing is the cause of much harm and offence to the rest! But if I am to accuse him before the Church, I must bring the Church together.

They have no basis in Scripture for their contention that it belongs to the pope alone to call a council or confirm its actions; for this is based merely upon their own laws, which are valid only in so far as they are not injurious to Christendom or contrary to the laws of God. When the Pope deserves punishment, such laws go out of force, since it is injurious to Christendom not to punish him by means of a council.

Thus we read in Acts xv that it was not St. Peter who called the Apostolic Council, but the Apostles and elders. If, then, that right had belonged to St. Peter alone, the council would not have been a Christian council, but an heretical *conciliabulum*. Even the Council of Nicaea—the most famous of all—was neither called nor confirmed by the Bishop of Rome, but by the Emperor Constantine, and many other emperors after him did the like, yet these councils were the most Christian of all. But if the pope alone had the right to call councils, then all these councils must have been heretical. Moreover, if I consider the councils which the pope has created, I find that they have done nothing of special importance.

Therefore, when necessity demands, and the pope is an offence to Christendom, the first man who is able should, as a faithful member of the whole body, do what he can to bring about a truly free council. No one can do this so well as the temporal authorities, especially since now they also are fellow-Christians, fellow-priests, "fellow-spirituals," fellow-lords over all things, and whenever it is needful or profitable, they should give free course to the office and work in which God has put them above every man. Would it not be an unnatural thing, if a fire broke out in a city, and every body were to stand by and let it burn on and on and consume everything that could burn, for the sole reason that nobody had the authority of the burgomaster, or because, perhaps, the fire broke out in the burgomaster's house? In such case is it not the duty of every citizen to arouse and call the rest? How much more should this be done in the spiritual city of Christ, if a fire of offence breaks out, whether in the papal government, or anywhere else? In the same way, if the enemy attacks a city, he who first rouses the others deserves honour and thanks; why then should he not deserve honour who makes known the presence of the enemy from hell, and awakens the Christians, and calls them together?

But all their boasts of an authority which dare not be opposed amount to nothing after all. No one in Christendom has authority to do injury, or to forbid the resisting of injury. There is no authority in the Church save for edification. Therefore, if the pope were to use his authority to prevent the calling of a free council, and thus became a hindrance to the edification of the Church, we should have regard neither for him nor for his authority; and if he were to hurl his bans and thunderbolts, we should despise his conduct as that of a madman, and relying on God, hurl back the ban on him, and coerce him as best we could. For this presumptuous authority of his is nothing; he has no such authority; and he is quickly overthrown by a text of Scripture; for Paul says to the Corinthians: "God has given us authority not for the destruction, but for the edification of Christendom." Who is ready to overleap this text? It is only the power of the devil and of Antichrist which resists the things that serve for the edification of Christendom; it is, therefore, in no wise to be obeyed, but is to be opposed with life and goods and all our strength.

Even though a miracle were to be done in the pope's behalf against the temporal powers, or though someone were to be stricken with a plague—which they boast has sometimes happened—it should be considered only the work of the devil, because of the weakness of our faith in God. Christ Himself prophesied in Matthew xxiv: "There shall come in My Name false Christs and false prophets, and do signs and wonders, so as to deceive even the elect," and Paul says in II Thessalonians ii, that Antichrist shall, through the power of Satan, be mighty in lying wonders.

Let us, therefore, hold fast to this: No Christian authority can do anything against Christ; as St. Paul says, "We can do nothing against Christ, but for Christ." Whatever does aught against Christ is the power of Antichrist and of the devil, even though it were to rain and hail wonders and plagues. Wonders and plagues prove nothing, especially in these evil times, for which all the Scriptures prophesy false wonders. Therefore we must cling with firm faith to the words of God, and then the devil will cease from wonders.

Thus I hope that the false, lying terror with which the Romans have this long time made our conscience timid and stupid, has been allayed. They, like all of us, are subject to the temporal sword; they have no power to interpret the Scriptures by mere authority, without learning; they have no authority to prevent a council or, in sheer wantonness, to pledge it, bind it, or take away its liberty; but if they do this, they are in truth in the communion of Antichrist and of the devil, and have nothing at all of Christ except the name.

II. Abuses to be Discussed in Councils

We shall now look at the matters which should be discussed in the councils, and with which popes, cardinals, bishops, and all the scholars ought properly to be occupied day and night if they love Christ and His Church. But if they neglect this duty, then let the laity and the temporal authorities see to it, regardless of bans and thunders; for an unjust ban is better than ten just releases, and an unjust release worse than ten just bans. Let us, therefore, awake, dear Germans, and fear God rather than men, that we may not share the fate of all the poor souls who are so lamentably lost through the shameful and devilish rule of the Romans, in which the devil daily takes a larger and larger place—if indeed, it were possible that such a hellish rule could grow worse, a thing I can neither conceive nor believe.

1.   It is a horrible and frightful thing that the ruler of Christendom, who boasts himself vicar of Christ and successor of St. Peter, lives in such wordly splendor that in this regard no king nor emperor can equal or approach him, and that he who claims the title of "most holy" and "most spiritual" is more worldly than the world itself. He wears a triple crown, when the greatest kings wear but a single crown; if that is like the poverty of Christ and of St. Peter, then it is a new kind of likeness. When a word is said against it, they cry out "Heresy!" but that is because they do not wish to hear how unchristian and ungodly such a practice is. I think, however, that if the pope were with tears to pray to God he would have to lay aside these crowns, for our God can suffer no pride, and his office is nothing else than this,—daily to weep and pray for Christendom, and to set an example of all humility.

However that may be, this splendour of his is an offence, and the pope is bound on his soul's salvation to lay it aside, because St. Paul says, "Abstain from all outward shows, which give offence," and in Rom. xii, "We should provide good, not only in the sight of God, but also in the sight of all men." An ordinary bishop's crown would be enough for the pope; he should be greater than others in wisdom and holiness, and leave the crown of pride to Antichrist, as did his predecessors several centuries ago. They say he is a lord of the world; that is a lie; for Christ, Whose vicar and officer he boasts himself to be, said before Pilate, "My kingdom is not of this world," and no vicar's rule can go beyond his lord's. Moreover, he is not the vicar of the glorified, but of the crucified Christ, as Paul says, "I was willing to know nothing among you save Christ, and Him only as the Crucified"; and in Philippians ii, "So think of yourselves as ye see in Christ. Who emptied Himself and took upon Him the appearance of a servant"; and again in I Corinthians i, "We preach Christ, the Crucified." Now they make the pope a vicar of the glorified Christ in heaven, and some of them have allowed the devil to rule them so completely that they have maintained that the pope is above the angels in heaven and has authority over them. These are indeed the very works of the very Antichrist.

2.   What is the use in Christendom of these people who are called the cardinals? I shall tell you. Italy and Germany have many rich monasteries, foundations, benefices, and livings. No better way has been discovered to bring all these to Rome than by creating cardinals and giving them the bishoprics, monasteries, and prelacies, and so overthrowing the worship of God. For this reason we now see Italy a very wilderness—monasteries in ruins, bishoprics devoured, the prelacies and the revenues of all the churches drawn to Rome, cities decayed, land and people laid waste, because there is no more worship or preaching. Why? The cardinals must have the income. No Turk could have so devastated Italy and suppressed the worship of God.

Now that Italy is sucked dry, they come into Germany, and begin oh so gently. But let us beware, or Germany will soon become like Italy. Already we have some cardinals; what the Romans seek by that the "drunken Germans" are not to understand until we have not a bishopric, a monastery, a living, a benefice, a *heller* or a *pfennig* left. Antichrist must take the treasures of the earth, as it was prophesied. So it goes on. They skim the cream off the bishoprics, monasteries, and benefices, and because they do not yet venture to turn them all to shameful use, as they have done in Italy, they only practise for the present the sacred trickery of coupling together ten or twenty prelacies and taking a yearly portion from each of them, so as to make a tidy sum after all. The priory of Würzburg yields a thousand *gulden*; that of Bamberg, something; Mainz, Trier and the others, something more; and so from one to ten thousand *gulden* might be got together, in order that a cardinal might live at Rome like a rich king.

"After they are used to this, we will create thirty or forty cardinals in a day, and give to one Mount St. Michael at Bamberg and the bishopric of Würzburg to boot, hang on to these a few rich livings, until churches and cities are waste, and after that we will say, 'We are Christ's vicars and shepherds of Christ's sheep; the mad, drunken Germans must put up with it.'"

I advise, however, that the number of cardinals be reduced, or that the pope be made to keep them at his own expense. Twelve of them would be more than enough, and each of them might have an income of a thousand *gulden* a year. How comes it that we Germans must put up with such robbery and such extortion of our property, at the hands of the pope? If the Kingdom of France has prevented it, why do we Germans let them make such fools and apes of us? It would all be more bearable if in this way they only stole our property; but they lay waste the churches and rob Christ's sheep of their pious shepherds, and destroy the worship and the Word of God. Even if there were not a single cardinal, the Church would not go under. As it is they do nothing for the good of Christendom; they only wrangle about the incomes of bishoprics and prelacies, and that any robber could do.

3. If ninety-nine parts of the papal court were done away and only the hundredth part allowed to remain, it would still be large enough to give decisions in matters of faith. Now, however, there is such a swarm of vermin yonder in Rome, all boasting that they are "papal," that there was nothing like it in Babylon. There are more than three thousand papal secretaries alone; who will count the other offices, when they are so many that they scarcely can be counted? And they all lie in wait for the prebends and benefices of Germany as wolves lie in wait for the sheep. I believe that Germany now gives much more to the pope at Rome than it gave in former times to the emperors. Indeed, some estimate that every year more than three hundred thousand *gulden* find their way from Germany to Rome, quite uselessly and fruitlessly; we get nothing for it but scorn and contempt. And yet we wonder that princes, nobles, cities, endowments, land, and people are impoverished! We should rather wonder that we still have anything to eat!

John Calvin

The success of Protestantism as an international reform movement was due largely to the work of a younger contemporary of Martin Luther, the Frenchman John Calvin. Born Jean Cauvin in Picardy in 1509, Calvin went to Paris in 1523 to study first for a clerical and later for a legal career. While there he became acquainted with writings of Luther, which were beginning to circulate through France at the time. His growing sympathy for the German "heresies" brought him to the attention of the authorities and he was forced to flee the country. He finally settled in the small city of Geneva, Switzerland. There he initiated one of the most remarkable social and political experiments of modern times. Under his leadership Geneva was organized as a theocratic state. The clergy assumed control not only of the political affairs of the city but of the moral life of its citizens as well. In his attempts to realize a society of saints, Calvin systematically set about to banish gaiety, frivolity, and sin from the city. Although he was unusually successful, and Geneva became a city of piety and sobriety, Calvin was never fully satisfied. Sin, he discovered, could not be eradicated completely but would periodically rear its ugly head in the midst of his saintly society.

From Geneva, which came to be known as the Protestant Rome, Calvinism spread throughout most of Europe, into Germany, Poland, Bohemia, Hungary, and the Low Countries. The French Huguenots were Calvinists, as were the Scottish Presbyterians and the English Puritans, who brought both the religious doctrines and the theocratic social organization of Calvin across the Atlantic to the colony of Massachusetts.

Calvin was not only a religious and social reformer but also one of the greatest of all Christian theologians. In his *Institutes of the Christian Religion* (1536), which he first published at the age of twenty-seven, he reiterated and defended the Augustinian doctrine of original sin, with its implied notions of election, faith, and grace. On the subject of predestination, about which most theologians had spoken in muted tones, Calvin was quite explicit. God in his omnipotence has decreed from all eternity the ultimate destiny of every individual soul. We, guilty sinners, can do nothing to alter this divine decree; all that rests with us is to praise God's infinite grace if he has elected us for salvation or to accept his just condemnation if he has damned us to hell.

The selection from the *Institutes* that follows outlines the main features of Calvin's theology.

1. How does Calvin depict the human condition?

2. What role does predestination play in his theology?

Institutes of the Christian Religion

Discussion of Human Nature as Created, of the Faculties of the Soul, of the Image of God, of Free Will, and of the Original Integrity of Man's Nature

We must now speak of the creation of man: not only because among all God's works here is the noblest and most remarkable example of his justice, wisdom, and goodness; but because, as we said at the beginning, we cannot have a clear and complete knowledge of God unless it is accompanied by a corresponding knowledge of ourselves. This knowledge of ourselves is twofold: namely, to know what we were like when we were first created and what our condition became after the fall of Adam. While it would be of little benefit to understand our creation unless we recognized in this sad ruin what our nature in its corruption and deformity is like, we shall nevertheless be content for the moment with the description of our originally upright nature. And to be sure, before we come to the miserable condition of man to which he is now subjected, it is worth-while to know what he was like when first created. Now we must guard against singling out only those natural evils of man, lest we seem to attribute them to the Author of nature. For in this excuse, impiety thinks it has sufficient defense, if it is able to claim that whatever defects it possesses have in some way proceeded from God. It does not hesitate, if it is reproved, to contend with God himself, and to impute to him the fault of which it is deservedly accused. And those who wish to seem to speak more reverently of the Godhead still willingly blame their depravity on nature, not realizing that they also, although more obscurely, insult God. For if any defect were proved to inhere in nature, this would bring reproach upon him.

Since, then, we see the flesh panting for every subterfuge by which it thinks that the blame for its own evils may in any way be diverted from itself to another, we must diligently oppose this evil intent. Therefore we must so deal with the calamity of mankind that we may cut off every shift, and may vindicate God's justice from every accusation. Afterward, in the proper place, we shall see how far away men are from the purity that was bestowed upon Adam. . . .

In this integrity man by free will had the power, if he so willed, to attain eternal life. Here it would be out of place to raise the question of God's secret predestination because our present subject is not what can happen or not, but what man's nature was like. Therefore Adam could have stood if he wished, seeing that he fell solely by his own will. But it was because his will was capable of being bent to one side or the other, and was not given the constancy to persevere, that he fell so easily. Yet his choice of good and evil was free, and not that alone, but the highest rectitude was in his mind and will, and all the organic parts were rightly composed to obedience, until in destroying himself he corrupted his own blessings.

Hence the great obscurity faced by the philosophers, for they were seeking in a ruin for a building, and in scattered fragments from a well-knit structure. They held this principle, that man would not be a rational animal unless he possessed free choice of good and evil; also it entered their minds that the distinction between virtues and vices would be obliterated if man did not order his life by his own planning. Well reasoned so far—if there had been no change in man. But since this was hidden from them, it is no wonder they mix up heaven and earth! They, as professed disciples of Christ, are obviously playing the fool when, by compromising between the opinions of the philosophers and heavenly doctrine, so that these touch neither heaven nor earth, in man—who is lost and sunk down into spiritual destruction—they will seek after free choice. But these matters will be better dealt with in their proper place. Now we need bear only this in mind: man was far different at the first creation from his whole posterity, who, deriving their origin from him in his corrupted state, have contracted from him a hereditary taint. For, the individual parts of his soul were formed to uprightness, the soundness of his mind stood firm, and his will was free to choose the good. If anyone objects that his will was placed in an insecure position because its power was weak, his status should have availed to remove any excuse; nor was it reasonable for God to be constrained by the necessity of making a man who either could not or would not sin at all. Such a nature would, indeed, have been more excellent. But to quarrel with God on this precise point, as if he ought to have conferred this upon man, is more than iniquitous, inasmuch as it was in his own choice to give whatever he pleased. But the reason he did not sustain man by the virtue of perseverance lies hidden in his plan; sobriety is for us the part of wisdom. Man, indeed, received the ability provided he exercised the will; but he did not have the will to use his ability, for this exercising of the will would have been followed by the perseverence. Yet he is not excusable, for he received so much that he voluntarily brought about his own destruction; indeed, no necessity was imposed upon God of giving man

other than a mediocre and even transitory will, that from man's Fall he
might gather occasion for his own glory.

· · ·

By the Fall and Revolt of Adam the Whole Human Race Was Delivered to the Curse, and Degenerated from Its Original Condition; the Doctrine of Original Sin

With good reason the ancient proverb strongly recommended knowledge of
self to man. For if it is considered disgraceful for us not to know all that per-
tains to the business of human life, even more detestable is our ignorance of
ourselves, by which, when making decisions in necessary matters, we miserably deceive and even blind ourselves!

But since this precept is so valuable, we ought more diligently to avoid
applying it perversely. This, we observe, has happened to certain philosophers, who, while urging man to know himself, propose the goal of recognizing his own worth and excellence. And they would have him contemplate
in himself nothing but what swells him with empty assurance and puffs him
up with pride.

But knowledge of ourselves lies first in considering what we were
given at creation and how generously God continues his favor toward us, in
order to know how great our natural excellence would be if only it had
remained unblemished; yet at the same time to bear in mind that there is in
us nothing of our own, but that we hold on sufferance whatever God has
bestowed upon us. Hence we are ever dependent on him. Secondly, to call to
mind our miserable condition after Adam's fall; the awareness of which,
when all our boasting and self-assurance are laid low, should truly humble
us and overwhelm us with shame. In the beginning God fashioned us after
his image that he might arouse our minds both to zeal for virtue and to
meditation upon eternal life. Thus, in order that the great nobility of our race
(which distinguishes us from brute beasts) may not be buried beneath our
own dullness of wit, it behooves us to recognize that we have been endowed
with reason and understanding so that, by leading a holy and upright life,
we may press on to the appointed goal of blessed immortality.

But that primal worthiness cannot come to mind without the sorry spec-
tacle of our foulness and dishonour presenting itself by way of contrast, since
in the person of the first man we have fallen from our original condition. From
this source arise abhorrence and displeasure with ourselves, as well as true
humility; and thence is kindled a new zeal to seek God, in whom each of us
may recover those good things which we have utterly and completely lost. . . .

Because what God so severely punished must have been no light sin
but a detestable crime, we must consider what kind of sin there was in

Adam's desertion that enkindled God's fearful vengeance against the whole of mankind. To regard Adam's sin as gluttonous intemperance (a common notion) is childish. As if the sum and head of all virtues lay in abstaining solely from one fruit, when all sorts of desirable delights abounded everywhere; and not only abundance but also magnificent variety was at hand in that blessed fruitfulness of earth!

We ought therefore to look more deeply. Adam was denied the tree of the knowledge of good and evil to test his obedience and prove that he was willingly under God's command. The very name of the tree shows the sole purpose of the precept was to keep him content with his lot and to prevent him from becoming puffed up with wicked lust. But the promise by which he was bidden to hope for eternal life so long as he ate from the tree of life, and conversely, the terrible threat of death once he tasted of the tree of knowledge of good and evil, served to prove and exercise his faith. Hence it is not hard to deduce by what means Adam provoked God's wrath upon himself. Indeed, Augustine speaks rightly when he declares that pride was the beginning of all evils. For if ambition had not raised man higher than was meet and right, he could have remained in his original state.

But we must take a fuller definition from the nature of the temptation which Moses describes. Since the woman through unfaithfulness was led away from God's Word by the serpent's deceit, it is already clear that disobedience was the beginning of the Fall. This Paul also confirms, teaching that all were lost through the disobedience of one man. Yet it is at the same time to be noted that the first man revolted from God's authority, not only because he was seized by Satan's blandishments, but also because, contemptuous of truth, he turned aside to falsehood. And surely, once we hold God's Word in contempt, we shake off all reverence for him. For, unless we listen attentively to him, his majesty will not dwell among us, nor his worship remain perfect. Unfaithfulness, then, was the root of the Fall. But thereafter ambition and pride, together with ungratefulness, arose, because Adam by seeking more than was granted him shamefully spurned God's great bounty, which had been lavished upon him. To have been made in the likeness of God seemed a small matter to a son of earth unless he also attained equality with God—a monstrous wickedness! If apostasy, by which man withdraws from the authority of his Maker— indeed insolently shakes off his yoke—is a foul and detestable offense, it is vain to extenuate Adam's sin. Yet it was not simply apostasy, but was joined with vile reproaches against God. These assented to Satan's slanders, which accused God of falsehood and envy and ill will. Lastly, faithlessness opened the door to ambition, and ambition was indeed the mother of obstinate disobedience; as a result, men, having cast off the fear of God, threw themselves wherever lust carried them. Hence Bernard rightly teaches that the door of salvation is opened to us when we receive the gospel today with our ears, even as death was then admitted by those same windows when they were opened to Satan. For Adam would never have dared oppose God's authority unless he had disbelieved in God's Word. Here, indeed, was the best bridle to control all passions: the thought that nothing is better than to practice righteousness by obeying God's commandments; then, that the ultimate goal of the happy life is to be loved by him. Therefore Adam, carried away by the devil's blasphemies, as far as he was able extinguished the whole glory of God.

As it was the spiritual life of Adam to remain united and bound to his Maker, so estrangement from him was the death of his soul. Nor it is any wonder that he consigned his race to ruin by his rebellion when he perverted to the whole order of nature in heaven and on earth. "All creatures," says Paul, "are groaning, subject to corruption, not of their own will." If the cause is sought, there is no doubt that they are bearing part of the punishment deserved by man, for whose use they were created. Since, therefore, the curse, which goes about through all the regions of the world, flowed hither and yon from Adam's guilt, it is not unreasonable if it is spread to all his offspring. Therefore, after the heavenly image was obliterated in him, he was not the only one to suffer this punishment—that, in place of wisdom, virtue, holiness, truth, and justice, with which adornments he had been clad, there came forth the most filthy plagues, blindness, impotence, impurity, vanity, and injustice—but he also entangled and immersed his offspring in the same miseries.

This is the inherited corruption, which the church fathers termed "original sin," meaning by the word "sin" the depravation of a nature previously good and pure. There was much contention over this matter, inasmuch as nothing is farther from the usual view than for all to be made guilty by the guilt of one, and thus for sin to be made common. This seems to be the reason why the most ancient doctors of the church touched upon this subject so obscurely. At least they explained it less clearly than was fitting. Yet this timidity could not prevent Pelagius from rising up with the profane fiction that Adam sinned only to his own loss without harming his posterity. Through this subtlety Satan attempted to cover up the disease and thus to render it incurable. But when it was shown by the clear testimony of Scripture that sin was transmitted from the first man to all his posterity, Pelagius quibbled that it was transmitted through imitation, not propagation. Therefore, good men (and Augustine above the rest) labored to show us that we are corrupted not by derived wickedness, but that we bear inborn defect from our mother's womb. . . .

So that these remarks may not be made concerning an uncertain and unknown matter, let us define original sin. It is not my intention to investigate the several definitions proposed by various writers, but simply to bring forward the one that appears to me most in accordance with truth. Original sin, therefore, seems to be a hereditary depravity and corruption of our nature, diffused into all parts of the soul, which first makes us liable to God's wrath, then also brings forth in us those works which Scripture calls "works of the flesh." And that is properly what Paul often calls sin. The works that come forth from it—such as adulteries, fornications, thefts, hatreds, murders, carousings—he accordingly calls "fruit of sin," although they are also commonly called "sins" in Scripture, and even by Paul himself.

We must, therefore, distinctly note these two things. First, we are so vitiated and perverted in every part of our nature that by this great corruption we stand justly condemned and convicted before God, to whom nothing is acceptable but righteousness, innocence, and purity. And this is not liability for another's transgression. For, since it is said that we became subject to God's judgment through Adam's sin, we are to understand it not as if we, guiltless and undeserving, bore the guilt of his offense but in the sense that, since we through his transgression have become entangled in the curse, he is said to have made us guilty. Yet not only has punishment fallen upon us from Adam, but a contagion imparted by him resides in us, which justly deserves punishment. For this reason, Augustine, though he often calls sin "another's" to show more clearly that it is distributed among us through propagation, nevertheless declares at the same time that it is peculiar to each. And the apostle himself most eloquently testifies that "death has spread to all because all have sinned." That is, they have been enveloped in original sin and defiled by its stains. For that reason, even infants themselves, while they carry their condemnation along with them from the mother's womb, are guilty not of another's fault but of their own. For, even though the fruits of their iniquity have not yet come forth, they have the seed enclosed within them. Indeed, their whole nature is a seed of sin; hence it can be only hateful and abhorrent to God. From this it follows that it is rightly considered sin in God's sight, for without guilt there would be no accusation.

Then comes the second consideration: that this perversity never ceases in us, but continually bears new fruits—the works of the flesh that we have already described—just as a burning furnace gives forth flame and sparks, or water ceaselessly bubbles up from a spring. Thus those who have defined original sin as "the lack of the original righteousness, which ought to reside in us," although they comprehend in this definition the whole meaning of the term, have still not expressed effectively enough its power and energy. For our nature is not only destitute and empty of good, but so fertile and fruitful of every evil that it cannot be idle. . . .

Man Has Now Been Deprived of Freedom of Choice and Bound Over to Miserable Servitude

We have now seen that the domination of sin, from the time it held the first man bound to itself, not only ranges among all mankind, but also completely occupies individual souls. It remains for us to investigate more closely whether we have been deprived of all freedom since we have been reduced to this servitude; and, if any particle of it still survives, how far its power extends. But in order that the truth of this question may be more readily apparent to us, I shall presently set a goal to which the whole argument should be directed. The best way to avoid error will be to consider the perils that threaten man on both sides. (1) When man is denied all uprightness, he immediately takes occasion for complacency from the fact; and, because he is said to have no ability to pursue righteousness on his own, he holds all such pursuit to be of no consequence, as if it did not pertain to him at all. (2) Nothing, however slight, can be credited to man without depriving God of his honour, and without man himself falling into ruin through brazen confidence. Augustine points out both these precipices.

Here, then, is the course that we must follow if we are to avoid crashing upon these rocks: when man has been taught that no good thing remains in his power, and that he is hedged about on all sides by most miserable necessity, in spite of this he should nevertheless be instructed to aspire to a good of which he is empty, to a freedom of which he has been deprived. In fact, he may thus be more sharply aroused from inactivity than if he were supposed that he was endowed with the highest virtues. Everyone sees how necessary this second point is. I observe that too many persons have doubts about the first point. For since this is an undoubted fact, that nothing of his own ought to be taken away from man, it ought to be clearly evident how important it is for him to be barred from false boasting. At the time when man was distinguished with the noblest marks of honor through God's beneficence, not even then was he permitted to boast about himself. How much more ought he now to humble himself, cast down as he has been—due to his own ungratefulness—from the loftiest glory into extreme disgrace! At that time, I say, when he has been advanced to the highest degree or honor, Scripture attributed nothing else to him than that he had been created in the image of God, thus suggesting that man was blessed, not because of his own actions, but by participation of God. What, therefore, now remains for man, bare and destitute of all glory, but to recognize God for whose beneficence he could not be grateful when he abounded with the riches of this grace; and at least, by confessing his own poverty, to glorify him in whom he did not previously glory in recognition of his own blessings?

Also, it is no less to our advantage than pertinent to God's glory that we be deprived of all credit for our wisdom and virtue. Thus those who bestow upon us anything beyond the truth add sacrilege to our ruin. When we are taught to wage our own war, we are but borne aloft on a reed stick, only to fall as soon as it breaks! Yet we flatter our strength unduly when we compare it even to a reed stick! For whatever vain men devise and babble concerning these matters is but smoke. . . .

If this be admitted, it will be indisputable that free will is not sufficient to enable man to do good works, unless he be helped by grace, indeed by special grace, which only the elect receive through regeneration. For I do not tarry over those fanatics who babble that grace is equally and indiscriminately distributed. But it has not yet been demonstrated whether man has been wholly deprived of all power to do good, or still has some power, though meager and weak; a power, indeed, that can do nothing of itself, but with the help of grace also does its part. The Master of the Sentences meant to settle this point when he taught: "We need two kinds of grace to render us capable of good works." He calls the first kind "operating," which ensures that we effectively will to do good. The second he calls "cooperating," which follows the good will as a help. The thing that displeases me about this division is that, while he attributes the effective desire for good to the grace of God, yet he hints that man by his very own nature somehow seeks after the good—though ineffectively. Thus Bernard declares the good will is God's work, yet concedes to man that of his own impulse he seeks this sort of good will. But this is far from Augustine's thought, from whom Peter Lombard pretended to have taken this distinction. The ambiguity in the second part offends me, for it has given rise to a perverted interpretation. They thought we cooperate with the assisting grace of God, because it is our right either to render it ineffectual by spurning the first grace, or to confirm it by obediently following it. This the author of the work *The Calling of the Gentiles* expresses as follows: "Those who employ the judgment of reason are free to forsake grace, so that not to have forsaken it is a meritorious act; and what could not be done without the co-operation of the Spirit is counted meritorious for those whose own will could not have accomplished it." I chose to note these two points in passing that you, my reader, may see how far I disagree with the sounder Schoolmen. I differ with the more recent Sophists to an even greater extent, as they are farther removed from antiquity. However, we at least understand from this division in what way they grant free will to man. For Lombard finally declares that we have free will, not in that we are equally capable of doing or thinking good and evil, but merely that we are freed from compulsion. According to Lombard, this freedom is not hindered, even if we be wicked and slaves of sin, and can do nothing but sin.

Man will then be spoken of as having this sort of free decision, not because he has free choice equally of good and evil, but because he acts wickedly by will, not by compulsion. Well put, indeed, but what purpose is served by labeling with a proud name such a slight thing? A noble freedom, indeed—for man not to be forced to serve sin, yet to be such a willing slave that his will is bound by the fetters of sin!

$$\bullet\ \bullet\ \bullet$$

Eternal Election, by Which God Has Predestined Some to Salvation, Others to Destruction

In actual fact, the covenant of life is not preached equally among all men, and among those to whom it is preached, it does not gain the same acceptance either constantly or in equal degree. In this diversity the wonderful depth of God's judgment is made known. For there is no doubt that this variety also serves the decision of God's eternal election. If it is plain that it comes to pass by God's bidding that salvation is freely offered to some while others are barred from access to it, at once great and difficult questions spring up, explicable only when reverent minds regard as settled what they may suitably hold concerning election and predestination. A baffling question this seems to many. For they think nothing more inconsistent than that out of the common multitude of men some should be predestined to salvation, others to destruction. But how mistakenly they entangle themselves will become clear in the following discussion. Besides, in the very darkness that frightens them not only is the usefulness of this doctrine made known but also its very sweet fruit. We shall never be clearly persuaded, as we ought to be, that our salvation flows from the wellspring of God's free mercy until we come to know his eternal election, which illuminates God's grace by this contrast: that he does not indiscriminately adopt all into the hope of salvation but gives to some what he denies to others.

How much the ignorance of this principle detracts from God's glory, how much it takes away from true humility, is well known. Yet Paul denies that this which needs so much to be known can be known unless God, utterly disregarding works, chooses those whom he has decreed within himself. "At the present time," he says, "a remnant has been saved according to the election of grace. But if it is by grace, it is no more of works; otherwise grace would no more be grace. But if it is of works, it is no more of grace; otherwise work would not be work." If—to make it clear that our salvation comes about solely from God's mere generosity—we must be called back to the course of election, those who wish to get rid of all this are obscuring as maliciously as they can what ought to have been gloriously and vociferously proclaimed, and they tear humility up by the very roots. Paul clearly testifies that, when the salvation of a remnant of the people is ascribed to the election of grace, then only is it acknowledged that God of his mere good pleasure preserves whom he will, and moreover that he pays no reward, since he can owe none.

They who shut the gates that no one may dare seek a taste of this doctrine wrong men no less than God. For neither will anything else suffice to make us humble as we ought to be nor shall we otherwise sincerely feel how much we are obliged to God. And as Christ teaches, here is our only ground for firmness and confidence: in order to free us of all fear and render us victorious amid so many dangers, snares, and mortal struggles, he promises that whatever the Father has entrusted into his keeping will be safe. From this we infer that all those who do not know that they are God's own will be miserable through constant fear. Hence, those who by being blind to the three benefits we have noted would wish the foundation of our salvation to be removed from our midst, very badly serve the interests of themselves and of all other believers. How is it that the church becomes manifest to us from this, when, as Bernard rightly teaches, "it could not otherwise be found or recognized among creatures, since it lies marvelously hidden . . . both within the bosom of a blessed predestination and within the mass of a miserable condemnation?"

But before I enter into the matter itself, I need to mention by way of preface two kinds of men.

Human curiosity renders the discussion of predestination, already somewhat difficult of itself, very confusing and even dangerous. No restraints can hold it back from wandering in forbidden bypaths and thrusting upward to the heights. If allowed, it will leave no secret to God that it will not search out and unravel. Since we see so many on all sides rushing into this audacity and impudence, among them certain men not otherwise bad, they should in due season be reminded of the measure of this duty in this regard.

First, then, let them remember that when they inquire into predestination they are penetrating the sacred precincts of divine wisdom. If anyone with carefree assurance breaks into this place, he will not succeed in satisfying his curiosity and he will enter a labyrinth from which he can find no exit. For it is not right for man unrestrainedly to search out things that the Lord has willed to be hid in himself, and to unfold from eternity itself the sublimest wisdom, which he would have us revere but not understand that through this also he should fill us with wonder. He has set forth by his Word the secrets of his will that he has decided to reveal to us. These he decided to reveal in so far as he foresaw that they would concern us and benefit us. . . .

Profane men, I admit, in the matter of predestination abruptly seize upon something to carp, rail, bark, or scoff at. But if their shamelessness deters us, we shall have to keep secret the chief doctrines of the faith, almost none of which they or their like leave untouched by blasphemy. An obstinate person would be no less insolently puffed up on hearing that within the essence of God there are three Persons than if he were told that God foresaw what would happen to man when he created him. And they will not refrain from guffaws when they are informed that but little more than five thousand years have passed since the creation of the universe, for they ask why God's power was idle and asleep for so long. Nothing, in short, can be brought forth that they do not assail with their mockery. Should we, to silence these blasphemies, forbear to speak of the deity of Son and Spirit? Must we pass over in silence the creation of the universe? No! God's truth is so powerful, both in this respect and in every other, that it has nothing to fear from the evil-speaking of wicked men.

So Augustine stoutly maintains in his little treatise *The Gift of Perseverance*. For we see that the false apostles could not make Paul ashamed by defaming and accusing his true doctrine. They say that this whole discussion is dangerous for godly minds—because it hinders exhortations, because it shakes faith, because it disturbs and terrifies the heart itself—but this is nonsense! Augustine admits that for these reasons he was frequently charged with preaching predestination too freely, but, as it was easy for him, he overwhelmingly refuted the charge. We, moreover, because many and various absurdities are obtruded at this point, have preferred to dispose of each in its own place. I desire only to have them generally admit that we should not investigate what the Lord has left hidden in secret, that we should not neglect what he has brought into the open, so that we may not be convicted of excessive curiosity on the one hand, or of excessive ingratitude on the other. For Augustine also skillfully expressed this idea; we can safely follow Scripture, which proceeds at the pace of a mother stooping to her child, so to speak, so as not to leave us behind in our weakness. But for those who are so cautious or fearful that they desire to bury predestination in order not to disturb weak souls—with what color will they cloak their arrogance when they accuse God indirectly of stupid thoughtlessness, as if he had not foreseen the peril that they feel they have wisely met? Whoever, then, heaps odium upon the doctrine of predestination openly reproaches God, as if he had unadvisedly let slip something hurtful to the church.

No one who wishes to be thought religious dares simply deny predestination, by which God adopts some to hope of life, and sentences others to eternal death. But our opponents, especially those who make foreknowledge its cause, envelop it in numerous petty objections. We, indeed, place both doctrines in God, but we say that subjecting one to the other is absurd.

When we attribute foreknowledge to God, we mean that all things always were, and perpetually remain, under his eyes, so that to his knowledge there is nothing future or past, but all things are present. And they are present in such a way that he not only conceives them through ideas, as we have before us those things which our minds remember, but he truly looks upon them and discerns them as things placed before him. And this foreknowledge is extended throughout the universe to every creature. We call predestination

God's eternal decree, by which he determined with himself what he willed to become of each man. For all are not created in equal condition; rather, eternal life is foreordained for some, eternal damnation for others. Therefore, as any man has been created to one or the other of these ends, we speak of him as predestined to life or to death. . . .

As Scripture, then, clearly shows, we say that God once established by his eternal and unchangeable plan those whom he long before determined once for all to receive into salvation, and those whom, on the other hand, he would devote to destruction. We assert that, with respect to the elect, this plan was founded upon his freely given mercy, without regard to human worth; but by his just and irreprehensible but incomprehensible judgment he has barred the door of life to those whom he has given over to damnation. Now among the elect we regard the call as a testimony of election. Then we hold justification another sign of its manifestation, until they come into the glory in which the fulfillment of that election lies. But as the Lord seals his elect by call and justification, so, by shutting off the reprobate from knowledge of his name or from the sanctification of his Spirit, he, as it were, reveals by these marks what sort of judgment awaits them.

The Catholic Reformation

The Catholic Reformation expressed itself in three main institutions: the Society of Jesus (usually called the Jesuits), the Inquisition (or Holy Office), and the Council of Trent. The Society of Jesus was founded by St. Ignatius of Loyola (1491–1556), an unlettered Spanish soldier who, as the result of a religious experience he underwent after being wounded in battle, resolved to become a "soldier of Christ." Once he had recovered, he set about educating himself, starting with elementary school and continuing through the University of Paris, where he began organizing the Jesuit order. Loyola's new society was established along military lines: An iron discipline demanded that each member show complete obedience to his immediate superiors and ultimately to his supreme commander, the pope. During the religious conflicts of the sixteenth and seventeenth centuries the Jesuits were always to be found on the side of the papal forces, in opposition primarily to the Protestants but to Catholic liberals as well.

The Inquisition was an old organization developed by the Dominican order in the thirteenth century primarily to combat the Albigensian heresy in southern France. It gained its greatest strength, however, in Spain. There it was used, particularly under the leadership of Torquemada, as the prime agent of persecution of the Moors and the Jews. After the Reformation the Inquisition joined forces with the Jesuits to combat the "Protestant heresy."

The Council of Trent, called originally by Pope Paul III in 1545, met at irregular intervals over a period of nearly twenty years under three different popes in the northern Italian city of Trent. Although the council reaffirmed the central doctrines of the Catholic church against what it considered to be the heretical views of Protestantism, it also called for the elimination of abuses that had crept into the church. The selection that follows includes some of the more important decrees, concerning both doctrine and practice, adopted by the council.

---

1. What aspects of the Reformation did the Council of Trent reject?

2. What are the sacraments? What role do they play in Tridentine Roman Catholicism?

The Canons and Decrees of the Council of Trent

Decree Touching the Opening of the Council

Doth it please you,—unto the praise and glory of the holy and undivided Trinity, Father, and Son, and Holy Ghost; for the increase and exaltation of the Christian faith and religion; for the extirpation of heresies; for the peace and union of the Church; for the reformation of the Clergy and Christian people; for the depression and extinction of the enemies of the Christian name,—to decree and declare that the sacred and general council of Trent do begin, and hath begun?

They answered: It pleaseth us.

Decree Concerning the Canonical Scriptures

The sacred and holy, œcumenical, and general Synod of Trent,—lawfully assembled in the Holy Ghost, the same three legates of the Apostolic See presiding therein,—keeping this always in view, that, errors being removed, the purity itself of the Gospel be preserved in the Church; which [Gospel], before promised through the prophets in the holy Scriptures, our Lord Jesus Christ, the Son of God, first promulgated with His own mouth, and then commanded to be preached by His Apostles to every creature, as the fountain of all, both saving truth, and moral discipline; and seeing clearly that this truth and books, and the unwritten traditions which, received by the Apostles from the mouth of Christ himself, or from the Apostles themselves, the Holy Ghost dictating, have come down even unto us, transmitted as it were from hand to hand; [the Synod] following the examples of the orthodox Fathers, receives and venerates with an equal affection of piety, and reverence, all the books both of the Old and the New Testament—seeing that one God is the author of both—as also the said traditions, as well those appertaining to faith as to morals, as having been dictated, either by Christ's own word of mouth, or by the Holy Ghost, and preserved in the Catholic Church by a continuous succession.

Decree Concerning the Edition, and the Use, of the Sacred Books

Moreover, the same sacred and holy Synod,—considering that no small utility may accrue to the Church of God, if it be made known which out of all the Latin editions, now in circulation, of the sacred books, is to be held as authen-

Trans. J. Waterworth.

tic,—ordains and declares, that the said old and vulgate edition, which, by the lengthened usage of so many ages, has been approved of in the Church, be, in public lectures, disputations, sermons and expositions, held as authentic; and that no one is to dare, or presume to reject it under any pretext whatever.

Furthermore, in order to restrain petulant spirits, It decrees, that no one, relying on his own skill, shall,—in matters of faith, and of morals pertaining to the edification of Christian doctrine,—wresting the sacred Scripture to his own senses, presume to interpret the said sacred Scripture contrary to that sense which holy mother Church,—whose it is to judge of the true sense and interpretation of the holy Scriptures,—hath held and doth hold;—or even contrary to the unanimous consent of the Fathers; even though such interpretations were never [intended] to be at any time published. . . .

Decree Concerning Original Sin

That our Catholic *faith, without which it is impossible to please God*, may, errors being purged away, continue in its own perfect and spotless integrity, and that the Christian people may not *be carried about with every wind of doctrine*; whereas that old serpent, the perpetual enemy of mankind, amongst the very many evils with which the Church of God is in these our times troubled, has also stirred up not only new, but even old, dissensions touching original sin, and the remedy thereof; the sacred and holy, œcumenical and general Synod of Trent,— lawfully assembled in the Holy See presiding therein,—wishing now to come to the reclaiming of the erring, and the confirming of the wavering—following the testimonies of the sacred Scriptures, of the holy Fathers, or the most approved councils, and the judgment and consent of the Church itself, ordains, confesses, and declares these things touching the said original sin:

1.   If any one does not confess that the first man, Adam, when he had transgressed the commandment of God in Paradise, immediately lost the holiness and justice wherein he had been constituted; and that he incurred, through the offense of that prevarication, the wrath and indignation of God, and consequently death, with which God had previously threatened him, and, together with death, captivity under his power who thenceforth *had the empire of death, that is to say, the devil*, and that the entire Adam, through that offence of prevarication, was changed, in body and soul, for the worse; let him be anathema.

2.   If any one asserts, that the prevarication of Adam injured himself alone, and not his posterity; and that the holiness and justice, received of God, which he lost, he lost for himself alone, and not for us also; or that he, being defiled by the sin of disobedience, has only transfused death, and pains of the body, into the whole human race, but not sin also, which is the death of the soul; let him be anathema:—whereas he contradicts the apostle

who says; *By one man sin entered into the world, and by sin death, and so death passed upon all men, in whom all have sinned.*

3.   If any one asserts, that this sin of Adam,—which in its origin is one, and being transfused into all by propagation, not by imitation, is in each one as his own,—is taken away either by the powers of human nature, or by any other remedy than the merit of the *one mediator, our Lord Jesus Christ, who had reconciled us to God in his own blood, made unto us justice, sanctification, and redemption*; or if he denies that the said merit of Jesus Christ is applied, both to adults and to infants, by the sacrament of baptism rightly administered in the form of the Church; let him be anathema: *For there is no other name under heaven given to men, whereby we must be saved.* Whence that voice; *Behold the lamb of God, behold him who taketh away the sins of the world*; and that other; *As many as have been baptized, have put on Christ.*

• • •

That a Rash Presumptuousness in the Matter of Predestination Is to Be Avoided

No one, moreover, so long as he is in this mortal life, ought so far to presume as regards the secret mystery of divine predestination, as to determine for certain that he is assuredly in the number of the predestinate; as if it were true, that he that is justified, either cannot sin any more, or, if he do sin, that he ought to promise himself an assured repentance; for except by special revelation, it cannot be known whom God hath chosen unto Himself.

• • •

On the Sacraments in General

CANON I

If any one saith, that the sacraments of the New Law were not all instituted by Jesus Christ, our Lord; or, that they are more, or less, than seven, to wit, Baptism, Confirmation, the Eucharist, Penance, Extreme Unction, Order, and Matrimony; or even that any one of these seven is not truly and properly a sacrament; let him be anathema.

CANON II

If any one saith, that these said sacraments of the New Law do not differ from the sacraments of the Old Law, save that the ceremonies are different, and different the outward rites; let him be anathema.

CANON III

If any one saith, that these seven sacraments are in such wise equal to each other, as that one is not in any way more worthy than another; let him be anathema.

CANON IV

If any one saith, that the sacraments of the New Law are not necessary unto salvation, but superfluous; and that, without them, or without the desire thereof, men obtain of God, through faith alone, the grace of justification;— though all [the sacraments] are not indeed necessary for every individual; let him be anathema.

CANON V

If any one saith, that these sacraments were instituted for the sake of nourishing faith alone; let him be anathema.

CANON VI

If any one saith, that the sacraments of the New Law do not contain the grace which they signify; or, that they do not confer that grace on those who do not place an obstacle thereunto; as though they were merely outward signs of grace or justice received through faith, and certain marks of the Christian profession, whereby believers are distinguished amongst men from unbelievers; let him be anathema.

CANON VII

If any one saith, that grace, as far as God's part is concerned, is not given through the said sacraments, always, and to all men, even though they receive them rightly, but [only] sometimes, and to some persons; let him be anathema.

CANON VIII

If any one saith, that by the said sacraments of the New Law grace is not conferred through the act performed, but that faith alone in the divine promise suffices for the obtaining of grace; let him be anathema.

CANON IX

If any one saith, that, in the three sacraments, Baptism, to wit, Confirmation, and Order, there is not imprinted in the soul a character, that is, a certain spiritual and indelible sign, on account of which they cannot be repeated; let him be anathema.

CANON X

If any one saith, that all Christians have power to administer the word, and all the sacraments; let him be anathema.

CANON XI

If any one saith, that, in ministers, when they effect, and confer the sacraments, there is not required the intention at least of doing what the Church does; let him be anathema.

CANON XII

If any one saith, that a minister, being in mortal sin,—if so be that he observe all the essentials which belong to the effecting, or conferring of, the sacrament,—neither effects, nor confers the sacrament; let him be anathema.

CANON XIII

If any one saith, that the received and approved rites of the Catholic Church, wont to be used in the solemn administration of the sacraments, may be condemned, or without sin be omitted at pleasure by the ministers, or be changed, by every pastor of the churches, into other new ones; let him be anathema.

● ● ●

On the Real Presence of Our Lord Jesus Christ in the Most Holy Sacrament of the Eucharist

In the first place, the holy Synod teaches, and openly and simply professes, that, in the august sacrament of the holy Eucharist, after the consecration of the bread and wine, our Lord Jesus Christ, true God and man, is truly, really, and substantially contained under the species of those sensible things. For neither are these things mutually repugnant,—that our Saviour Himself always sitteth at the right hand of the Father in heaven, according to the natural mode of existing, and that, nevertheless, He be, in many other places, sacramentally present to us in his own substance, by a manner of existing, which, though we can scarcely express it in words, yet can we, by the understanding illuminated by faith, conceive, and we ought most firmly to believe, to be possible unto God: for thus all our forefathers, as many as were in the true Church of Christ, who have treated of his most holy Sacrament have most openly professed, that our Redeemer instituted this so admirable a sacrament at the last supper, when, after the blessing of the bread and wine, He testified, in express and clear words, that He gave them His own very Body, and His own Blood; words which,—recorded by the holy Evangelists, and afterwards repeated by Saint Paul, whereas they carry with them that proper and most manifest meaning in which they were understood by the Fathers,—it is indeed a crime the most unworthy that they should be wrested, by certain contentious and wicked men, to fictitious and imaginary tropes, whereby the verity of the flesh and blood of Christ is denied, contrary to the universal sense of the Church, which, as *the pillar and ground of truth*, has detested, as satanical, these inventions devised by impious men; she recognising, with a mind ever grateful and unforgetting, this most excellent benefit of Christ.

• • •

On the Most Holy Sacrament of the Eucharist

CANON I

If any one denieth, that, in the sacrament of the most holy Eucharist, are contained truly, really, and substantially, the body and blood together with the soul and divinity of our Lord Jesus Christ, and consequently the whole Christ; but saith that He is only therein as in a sign, or in figure, or virtue; let him be anathema.

CANON II

If any one saith, that, in the sacred and holy sacrament of the Eucharist, the substance of the bread and wine remains conjointly with the body and blood of our Lord Jesus Christ, and denieth that wonderful and singular conversion of the whole substance of the bread into the Body, and of the whole substance of the wine into the Blood—the species only of the bread and wine remaining which—conversion indeed the Catholic Church most aptly calls Transubstantiation; let him be anathema.

• • •

CANON IX

If any one denieth, that all and each of Christ's faithful of both sexes are bound, when they have attained to years of discretion, to communicate every year, at least at Easter, in accordance with the precept of the holy Mother Church; let him be anathema.

•••

CANON XI

If any one saith, that faith alone is a sufficient preparation for receiving the sacrament of the most holy Eucharist; let him be anathema. And for fear lest so great a sacrament may be received unworthily, and so unto death and condemnation, this holy Synod ordains and declares, that sacramental confession, when a confessor may be had, is of necessity to be made beforehand, by those whose conscience is burthened with mortal sin, how contrite evensoever they may think themselves. But if any one shall presume to teach, preach, or obstinately to assert, or even in public disputation to defend the contrary, he shall be thereupon excommunicated.

•••

On the Ecclesiastical Hierarchy, and on Ordination

But, forasmuch as in the sacrament of Order, as also in Baptism, and Confirmation, a character is imprinted, which can neither be effaced nor taken away; the holy Synod with reason condemns the opinion of those, who assert that the priests of the New Testament have only a temporary power; and that those who have once been rightly ordained, can again become laymen, if they do not exercise the ministry of the word of God. And if any one affirm, that all Christians indiscriminately are priests of the New Testament, or that they are all mutually endowed with an equal spiritual power, he clearly does nothing but confound the ecclesiastical hierarchy, which is *as an army set in array*; as if, contrary to the doctrine of blessed Paul, *all* were *apostles, all prophets, all evangelists, all pastors, all doctors*. Wherefore, the holy Synod declares that, besides the other ecclesiastical degrees, bishops, who have succeeded to the place of the apostles, principally belong to this hierarchical order; that they are *placed*, as the same apostle says *by the Holy Ghost, to rule the Church of God*; that they are superior to priests; administer the sacrament of Confirmation; ordain the ministers of the Church; and that they can perform very many other things; over which functions others of an inferior order have no power. Furthermore, the sacred and holy Synod teaches, that, in the ordination of bishops, priests, and of the other orders, neither the consent, nor vocation, nor authority, whether of the people, or of any civil power or magistrate whatsoever, is required in such wise as that, without this, the ordination is invalid; yea rather doth It decree, that all those who, being only called and instituted by the people, or by the civil power and magistrate, ascend to the exercise of these ministrations, and those who of their own rashness assume them to themselves, are not ministers of the Church, but are to be looked upon as *thieves and robbers, who have not entered by the door*. These are the things which it hath seemed good to the sacred Synod to teach the faithful of Christ, in general terms, touching the sacrament of Order.

• • •

On the Sacrament of Matrimony

CANON IX

If anyone saith, that clerics constituted in sacred orders or Regulars, who have solemnly professed chastity, are able to contract marriage, and that being contracted it is valid, notwithstanding the ecclesiastical law, or vow; and that the contrary is nothing else than to condemn marriage; and, that all who do not feel that they have the gift of chastity, even though they have made a vow thereof, may contract marriage; let him be anathema; seeing that God refuses not that gift to those who ask for it rightly, neither does *He suffer us to be tempted above that which we are able.*

CANON X

If any one saith, that the marriage state is to be placed above the state of virginity, or of celibacy, and that it is not better and more blessed to remain in virginity, or in celibacy, than to be united in matrimony; let him be anathema.

• • •

On the Invocation, Veneration, and Relics, of Saints, and on Sacred Images

The holy Synod enjoins on all bishops, and others who sustain the office and charge of teaching, that, agreeably to the usage of the Catholic and Apostolic Church, received from the primitive times of the Christian religion, and agreeably to the consent of the holy Fathers, and to the decrees of sacred Councils, they especially instruct the faithful diligently concerning the intercession and invocation of saints; the honour [paid] to relics; and the legitimate use of images: teaching them, that the saints, who reign together with Christ, offer up their own prayers to God for men; that it is good and useful suppliantly to invoke them, and to have recourse to their prayers, aid, [and] help for obtaining benefits from God, through His Son, Jesus Christ our Lord, who is our alone Redeemer and Saviour; but that they think impiously, who deny that the saints, who enjoy eternal happiness in heaven, are to be invocated; or who assert either that they do not pray for men; or, that the invocation of them to pray for each of us even in particular, is idolatry: or that it is repugnant to the word of God; and is opposed to the honour of the *one mediator of God and men, Christ Jesus*; or, that it is foolish to supplicate, vocally, or mentally, those who reign in heaven. Also, that the holy bodies of holy martyrs, and of others now living with Christ—which bodies were the living members of Christ, and *the temple of the Holy Ghost*, and which are by Him to be raised unto eternal life, and to be glorified—are to be venerated by the faithful; through which [bodies] many benefits are bestowed by God on men; so that they who affirm that veneration and honour are not due to the relics of saints; or, that these, and other sacred monuments, are uselessly honoured by the faithful; and that the places dedicated to the memories of the saints are in vain visited with the view of obtaining their aid; are wholly to be condemned, as the Church has already long since condemned, and now also condemns them.

Moreover, that the images of Christ, of the Virgin Mother of God, and of the other saints, are to be had and retained particularly in temples, and that due honour and veneration are to be given them; not that any divinity, or virtue, is believed to be in them, on account of which they are to be worshipped; or that anything is to be asked of them; or, that trust is to be reposed in images, as was of old done by the Gentiles who placed their hope in idols; but because the honour which is shown them is referred to the prototypes which those images represent; in such wise that by the images which we kiss, and before which we uncover the head, and prostrate ourselves, we adore Christ; and we venerate the saints, whose similitude they bear: as by the decrees of Councils, and especially of the second Synod of Nicaea, has been defined against the opponents of images.

• • •

Cardinals and All Prelates of the Churches Shall Be Content with Modest Furniture and a Frugal Table: They Shall Not Enrich Their Relatives or Domestics Out of the Property of the Church

It is to be wished, that those who undertake the office of a bishop should understand what their portion is; and comprehend that they are called, not to their own convenience, not to riches or luxury, but to labours and cares for the glory of God. For it is not to be doubted, that the rest of the faithful also will be more easily excited to religion and innocence, if they shall see those who are set over them, not fixing their thoughts on the things of this world, but on the salvation of souls, and on their heavenly country. Wherefore the holy Synod, being minded that these things are of the greatest importance toward restoring ecclesiastical discipline, admonishes all bishops, that, often meditating thereon, they show themselves conformable to their office, by their actual deeds, and the actions of their lives; which is a kind of perpetual sermon; but above all that they so order their whole conversation, as that others may thence be able to derive examples of frugality, modesty, continency, and of that holy humility which so much recommends us to God.

Wherefore, after the example of our fathers in the Council of Carthage, it not only orders that bishops be content with modest furniture, and a frugal table and diet, but that they also give heed that in the rest of their manner of living, and in their whole house, there be nothing seen that is alien from this holy institution, and which does not manifest simplicity, zeal toward God, and a contempt of vanities. Also, it wholly forbids them to strive to enrich their own kindred or domestics out of the revenues of the church: seeing that even the canons of the Apostles forbid them to give to their kindred the property of the church, which belongs to God: but if their kindred be poor, let them distribute to them thereof as poor, but not misapply, or waste, it for their sakes: yea, the holy Synod with the utmost earnestness, admonishes them completely to lay aside all this human and carnal affection toward brothers, nephews, and kindred, which is the seed-plot of many evils in the Church. And what has been said of bishops, the same is not only to be observed by all who hold ecclesiastical benefices, whether Secular or Regular, each according to the nature of his rank, but the Synod decrees that it also regards the cardinals of the holy Roman Church; for whereas, upon their advice to the most holy Roman Pontiff, the administration of the universal Church depends, it would seem to be a shame, if they did not at the same time shine so pre-eminent in virtue and in the discipline of their lives, as deservedly to draw upon themselves the eyes of all men.

$$\bullet\bullet\bullet$$

Decree Concerning Indulgences

Whereas the power of conferring Indulgences was granted by Christ to the Church; and she has, even in the most ancient times, used the said power, delivered unto her of God; the sacred holy Synod teaches, and enjoins, that the use of Indulgences, for the Christian people most salutary, and approved of by the authority of sacred Councils, is to be retained in the Church; and It condemns with anathema those who either assert, that they are useless; or who deny that there is in the Church the power of granting them. In granting them, however, It desires that, in accordance with the ancient and approved custom in the Church, moderation be observed; lest, by excessive facility, ecclesiastical discipline be enervated. And being desirous that the abuses which have crept therein, and by occasion of which this honourable name of Indulgences is blasphemed by heretics, be amended and corrected, It ordains generally by this decree, that all evil gains for the obtaining thereof,—whence a most prolific cause of abuses amongst the Christian people has been derived,—be wholly abolished. But as regards the other abuses which have proceeded from superstition, ignorance, irreverence, or from whatsoever other source, since, by reason of the manifold corruptions in the places and provinces where the said abuses are committed, they cannot conveniently be specially prohibited; it commands all bishops, diligently to collect, each in his own church, all abuses of this nature, and to report them in the first provincial Synod; that, after having been reviewed by the opinions of the other bishops also, they may forthwith be referred to the Sovereign Roman Pontiff, by whose authority and prudence that which may be expedient for the universal Church will be ordained; that thus the gift of holy Indulgences may be dispensed to all the faithful, piously, holily, and incorruptly.

Francis Bacon

Francis Bacon (1561–1626) was a prophet of the scientific revolution of the seventeenth century—a revolution that transformed the foundations of thought and ushered in the Age of Science. Like the prophets of the Old Testament, Bacon concentrated first on the evils around him. Although for him these evils were intellectual rather than moral or religious, he couched his criticism of the science of his day in biblical terms. The leading thinkers of his age, he argued, had wandered from the path of truth into the worship of idols. In the selection that follows he lists four such idols, to which he gives the picturesque titles of idols of the Tribe, the Cave, the Market-place, and the Theatre. To avoid falling prey to these idols, people must turn their backs on scholastic philosophy and develop a new science based on a true knowledge of the workings of nature. Such knowledge, Bacon held, was to be derived from careful and continued observation of specific natural occurrences. This observational method, which he called *induction*, is explained and illustrated in his major work, the *Instauratio Magna* (Great Renewal). In his opinion, this treatise represented a "total reconstruction of the sciences, arts, and all human knowledge."

Although he was a prophet of the new science, Bacon himself did not fully grasp the nature of the method that men like Galileo and Newton were to employ in their work. His concept of induction fails to take adequate account of two other basic elements of the modern scientific method—the formulation of hypotheses and the deduction and verification of their consequences.

Living at the height of the English Renaissance (which followed by a hundred years the Italian Renaissance), Bacon exemplified many of the attitudes found in previous Renaissance writers: the rejection of the medieval worldview as pernicious error, the somewhat naive optimism about his ability to take the whole of human knowledge as his sphere of activity, and the faith that he stood on the threshold of a new intellectual era. Finally, in his assertion that "knowledge is power" Bacon repeated a central concept of Machiavelli—but with a significant difference. Machiavelli was concerned with the power that a prince could wield over his subjects, but Bacon was concerned with the power, derived from scientific understanding, that all humans could wield over nature.

The following selection is from *Novum Organum* (the New Organon written in 1620), which forms a part of *Instauratio Magna*.

1. In your own words, what are the four idols referred to in this selection?

2. According to Bacon, how should science be done?

Novum Organum

Aphorisms Concerning the Interpretation of Nature and the Kingdom of Man

I. Man, being the servant and interpreter of Nature, can do and understand so much and so much only as he has observed in fact or in thought in the course of nature: beyond this he neither knows anything nor can do anything.

II. Neither the naked hand nor the understanding left to itself can effect much. It is by instruments and helps that the work is done, which are as much wanted for the understanding as for the hand. And as the instruments of the hand either give motion or guide it, so the instruments of the mind supply either suggestions for the understanding or cautions.

III. Human knowledge and human power meet in one; for where the cause is not known the effect cannot be produced. Nature to be commanded must be obeyed; and that which in contemplation is as the cause is in operation as the rule.

IV. Towards the effecting of works, all that man can do is to put together or put asunder natural bodies. The rest is done by nature working within.

• • •

VI. It would be an unsound fancy and self-contradictory to expect that things which have never yet been done can be done except by means which have never yet been tried.

• • •

XI. As the sciences which we now have do not help us in finding out new works, so neither does the logic which we now have help us in finding out new sciences.

XII. The logic now in use serves rather to fix and give stability to the errors which have their foundations in commonly received notions than to help the search after truth. So it does more harm than good.

• • •

Trans. J. Spedding.

XVIII.   The discoveries which have hitherto been made in the sciences are such as lie close to vulgar notions, scarcely beneath the surface. In order to penetrate into the inner and further recesses of nature, it is necessary that both notions and axioms be derived from things by a more sure and guarded way; and that a method of intellectual operation be introduced altogether better and more certain.

XIX.   There are and can be only two ways of searching into and discovering truth. The one flies from the senses and particulars to the most general axioms, and from these principles, the truth of which it takes for settled and immovable, proceeds to judgment and to the discovery of middle axioms. And this way is now in fashion. The other derives axioms from the senses and particulars, rising by a gradual and unbroken ascent, so that it arrives at the most general axioms last of all. This is the true way, but as yet untried.

• • •

XXII.   Both ways set out from the senses and particulars, and rest in the highest generalities; but the difference between them is infinite. For the one just glances at experiment and particulars in passing, the other dwells duly and orderly among them. The one, again, begins at once by establishing certain abstract and useless generalities, the other rises by gradual steps to that which is prior and better known in the order of nature.

• • •

XXXI.   It is idle to expect any great advancement in science from the superinducing and engrafting of new things upon old. We must begin anew from the very foundations, unless we would revolve forever in a circle with mean and contemptible progress.

• • •

XXXV.   It was said by Borgia of the expedition of the French into Italy, that they came with chalk in their hands to mark out their lodgings, not with arms to force their way in. I in like manner would have my doctrine enter quietly into the minds that are fit and capable of receiving it; for confutations cannot be employed, when the difference is upon first principles and very notions and even upon forms of demonstration.

XXXVI.   One method of delivery alone remains to us; which is simply this: we must lead men to the particulars themselves, and their series and order; while men on their side must force themselves for awhile to lay their notions by and begin to familiarize themselves with facts.

XXXVII.   The doctrine of those who have denied that certainty could be attained at all, has some agreement with my way of proceeding at the first setting out; but they end in being infinitely separated and opposed. For the holders of that doctrine assert simply that nothing can be known; I also assert that not much can be known in nature by the way which is now in use. But then they go on to destroy the authority of the senses and understanding; whereas I proceed to devise and supply helps for the same.

XXXVIII. The idols and false notions which are now in possession of the human understanding, and have taken deep root therein, not only so beset men's minds that truth can hardly find entrance, but even after entrance is obtained, they will again in the very instauration of the science meet and trouble us, unless men being forewarned of the danger fortify themselves as far as may be against their assaults.

XXXIX. There are four classes of Idols which beset men's minds. To these for distinction's sake I have assigned names, calling the first class *Idols of the Tribe*; the second, *Idols of the Cave*; the third, *Idols of the Marketplace*; the fourth, *Idols of the Theatre*.

XL. The formation of ideas and axioms by true induction is no doubt the proper remedy to be applied for the keeping off and clearing away of idols. To point them out, however, is of great use; for the doctrine of Idols is to the Interpretation of Nature what the doctrine of the refutation of Sophisms is to common Logic.

XLI. The Idols of the Tribe have their foundation in human nature itself, and in the tribe or race of men. For it is a false assertion that the sense of man is the measure of things. On the contrary, all perceptions as well of the sense as of the mind are according to the measure of the universe. And the human understanding is like a false mirror, which, receiving rays irregularly, distorts and discolours the nature of things by mingling its own nature with it.

XLII. The Idols of the Cave are the idols of the individual man. For every one (besides the errors common to human nature in general) has a cave or den of his own, which refracts and discolors the light of nature; owing either to his own proper and peculiar nature; or to his education and conversation with others; or to the reading of books, and the authority of those whom he esteems and admires; or to the differences of impressions, accordingly as they take place in a mind preoccupied and predisposed or in a mind indifferent and settled; or the like. So that the spirit of man (according as it is meted out to different individuals) is in fact a thing variable and full of perturbation, and governed as it were by chance. Whence it was observed by Heraclitus[1] that men look for sciences in their own lesser worlds, and not in the greater or common world.

XLIII. There are also Idols formed by the intercourse and association of men with each other, which I call Idols of the Marketplace, on account of the commerce and consort of men there. For it is by discourse that men associate; and words are imposed according to the apprehension of the vulgar.

---

[1] Ancient Greek philosopher—*Ed.*

And therefore the ill and unfit choice of words wonderfully obstructs the understanding. Nor do the definitions or explanations wherewith in some things learned men are wont to guard and defend themselves, by any means set the matter right. But words plainly force and overrule the understanding, and throw all into confusion, and lead men away into numberless empty controversies and idle fancies.

XLIV. Lastly, there are Idols which have immigrated into men's minds from the various dogmas of philosophies, and also from wrong laws of demonstration. These I call Idols of the Theatre; because in my judgment all the received systems are but so many stage-plays, representing worlds of their own creation after an unreal and scenic fashion. Nor is it only of the systems now in vogue, or only of the ancient sects and philosophies, that I speak; for many more plays of the same kind may yet be composed and in like artificial manner set forth; seeing that errors the most widely different have nevertheless causes for the most part alike. Neither again do I mean this only of entire systems, but also of many principles and axioms in science, which by tradition, credulity, and negligence have come to be received.

Isaac Newton

Isaac Newton (1642–1727) had formulated his theory of universal gravitation by the time he was twenty-four. But it was not until several years later, in 1687, that he published it, at the insistence of friends, under the title *The Mathematical Principles of Natural Philosophy*. This triumph of scientific genius, which has been called the greatest single monument of human learning, seems almost miraculous and its author somehow superhuman. Yet, without detracting from Newton's greatness, we must recognize that his theory of gravitation was the culmination of a scientific development that had been in progress for well over a hundred years and had included such names as Copernicus, Kepler, and Galileo. But Newton was the heir of other thinkers in an even broader sense. The selection from his *Optics* (1704) begins with a reaffirmation of the atomistic theory of matter, which was first developed by Democritus, an ancient Greek. However, instead of regarding the atoms as eternal, Newton, a Christian, argued that they were created by God.

The Newtonian picture of the universe gradually came to be accepted in the scientific world as the ultimate explanation of things and reigned supreme for over two hundred years, until it was superseded in the twentieth century by Einstein's theory of relativity. But Einstein did not negate Newton; rather his theory represented an improvement over that of Newton, being more general and thus able to explain phenomena the earlier theory could not.

During his long lifetime, spent mainly as a teacher at Cambridge University, Newton was widely honored, both in his own country and abroad. Yet toward the end of his life, he made this modest assessment of his career: "I know not what the world will think of my labors, but to myself it seems that I have been but as a child playing on the seashore; now finding some pebble rather more polished, and now some shell rather more agreeably variegated than another, while the immense ocean of truth extended itself unexplored before me."

---

1. Describe Newton's method. How does he arrive at his conclusions?

2. Would Newton be a good scientist according to Bacon? Why or why not?

Optics

All these things being considered, it seems probable to me, that God in the beginning formed matter in solid, massy, hard, impenetrable, moveable particles, of such sizes and figures, and with such other properties, and in such proportion to space, as most conduced to the end for which he formed them; and that these primitive particles, being solids, are incomparably harder than any porous bodies compounded of them; even so very hard, as never to wear or break in pieces; no ordinary power being able to divide what God himself made one in the first creation. While the particles continue entire, they may compose bodies of one and the same nature and texture in all ages: But should they wear away, or break in pieces, the nature of things depending on them would be changed. Water and earth, composed of old worn particles and fragments of particles, would not be of the same nature and texture now, with water and earth composed of entire particles in the beginning. And therefore, that nature may be lasting, the changes of corporeal things are to be placed only in the various separations and new associations and motions of these permanent particles; compound bodies being apt to break, not in the midst of solid particles, but where those particles are laid together, and only touch in a few points.

It seems to me farther, that those particles have not only a force of inertia accompanied with such passive laws of motion as naturally result from that force, but also that they are moved by certain active principles, such as is that of gravity, and that which causes fermentation, and the cohesion of bodies. These principles I consider, not as occult qualities, supposed to result from the specific forms of things, but as general laws of nature, by which the things themselves are formed; their truth appearing to us by phenomena, though their causes be not yet discovered. For these are manifest qualities, and their causes only are occult. And the Aristotelians gave the name of *occult qualities*, not to manifest qualities, but to such qualities only as they supposed to lie hid in bodies, and to be the unknown causes of manifest effects: Such as would be the causes of gravity, and of magnetic and electric attractions, and of fermentations, if we should suppose that these forces or actions arose from qualities unknown to us, and incapable of being discovered and made manifest. Such occult qualities put a stop to the improvement of natural philosophy, and therefore of late years have been rejected. To tell us that every species of things is endowed with an occult specific quality by which it acts and produces manifest effects, is to tell us nothing: But to derive two or three general principles of motion from

Isaac Newton, *Optics, or, a Treatise of the Reflections, Refractions, Inflections and Colours of Light*, 4th ed. (London, 1730). [Capitalization and spelling have been modernized.—*Ed.*]

phenomena, and afterwards to tell us how the properties and actions of all corporeal things follow from those manifest principles, would be a very great step in philosophy, though the causes of those principles were not yet discovered: And therefore I scruple not to propose the principles of motion above-mentioned, they being of very general extent, and leave their causes to be found out.

Now by the help of these principles, all material things seem to have been composed of the hard and solid particles above-mentioned, variously associated in the first creation by the counsel of an intelligent agent. For it became him who created them to set them in order. And if he did so, it's unphilosophical to seek for any other origin of the world, or to pretend that it might arise out of a chaos by the mere laws of nature; though being once formed, it may continue by those laws for many ages. For while comets move in very eccentric orbs in all manner of positions, blind fate could never make all the planets move one and the same way in orbs concentric, some inconsiderable irregularities excepted, which may have risen from the mutual actions of comets and planets upon one another, and which will be apt to increase, till this system wants a reformation. Such a wonderful uniformity in the planetary system must be allowed the effect of choice. And so much the uniformity in the bodies of animals, they having generally a right and a left side shaped alike, and on either side of their bodies two legs behind, and either two arms, or two legs, or two wings before their shoulders, a neck running down into a backbone, and a head upon it; and in the head two ears, two eyes, a nose, a mouth, and a tongue, alike situated. Also the first contrivance of those very artificial parts of animals, the eyes, ears, brain, muscles, heart, lungs, midriff, glands, larynx, hands, wings, swimming bladders, natural spectacles, and other organs of sense and motion; and the instinct of brutes and insects, can be the effect of nothing else than the wisdom and skill of a powerful ever-living agent, who being in all places, is more able by his will to move the bodies within his boundless uniform sensorium, and thereby to form and reform the parts of the universe, than we are by our will to move the parts of our bodies. And yet we are not to consider the world as the body of God, or the several parts thereof, as the parts of God. He is a uniform being, void of organs, members, or parts, and they are his creatures subordinate to him, and subservient to his will; and he is no more the soul of them, than the soul of man is the soul of the species of things carried through the organs of sense into the place of its sensation, where it perceives them by means of its immediate presence, without the intervention of any third thing. The organs of sense are not for enabling the soul to perceive the species of things in its sensorium, but only for conveying them thither; and God had no need of such organs, he being everywhere present to the things themselves. And since space is divisible *in infinitum*, and matter is not necessarily in all places, it may be also allowed that God is able to create particles of matter of several sizes and figures, and in several proportions to space, and perhaps of different densities and forces, and thereby to vary the laws of nature, and make worlds of several sorts in several parts of the universe. At least, I see nothing of contradiction in all this.

As in mathematics, so in natural philosophy, the investigation of difficult things by the method of analysis, ought ever to precede the method of composition. This analysis consists in making experiments and observations, and in drawing general conclusions from them by induction and admitting of no objections against the conclusions, but such as are taken from experiments, or other certain truths. For hypotheses are not to be regarded in experimental philosophy. And although the arguing from experiments and observations by induction be no demonstration of general conclusions; yet it is the best way of arguing which the nature of things admits of, and may be looked upon as so much the stronger, by how much the induction is more general. And if no exception occur from phenomena, the conclusion may be pronounced generally. But if at any time afterwards any exception shall occur from experiments, it may then begin to be pronounced with such exceptions as occur. By this way of analysis we may proceed from compounds to ingredients, and from motions to the forces producing them; and in general, from effects to their causes, and from particular causes to more general ones, till the argument ends in the most general. This is the method of analysis: And the synthesis consists in assuming the causes discovered, and established as principles, and by them explaining the phenomena proceeding from them, and proving the explanations.

The Mathematical Principles of Natural Philosophy

The Rules of Reasoning in Philosophy

Rule I.   We are to admit no more causes of natural things, than such as are both true and sufficient to explain their appearances.

To this purpose the philosophers say, that Nature does nothing in vain, and more is in vain, when less will serve; for Nature is pleased with simplicity, and affects not the pomp of superfluous causes.

Rule II.   Therefore to the same natural effects we must, as far as possible, assign the same causes.

As to respiration in a man, and in a beast; the descent of stones in Europe and in America; the light of our culinary fire and of the sun; the reflection of light in the earth, and in the planets.

Trans. A. Motte (London, 1729). [Capitalization and spelling have been modernized.—*Ed.*]

Rule III. The qualities of bodies, which admit neither intension nor remission of degrees, and which are found to belong to all bodies within reach of our experiments, are to be esteemed the universal qualities of all bodies whatsoever.

For since the qualities of bodies are only known to us by experiments, we are to hold for universal, all such as universally agree with experiments; and such as are not liable to diminution, can never be quite taken away. We are certainly not to relinquish the evidence of experiments for the sake of dreams and vain fictions of our own devising; nor are we to recede from the analogy of Nature, which is wont to be simple, and always consonant to itself. We no other way know the extension of bodies, than by our senses, nor do these reach it in all bodies; but because we perceive extension in all that are sensible, therefore we ascribe it universally to all others, also. That abundance of bodies are hard we learn by experience. And because the hardness of the whole arises from the hardness of the parts, we therefore justly infer the hardness of the undivided particles not only of the bodies we feel but of all others. That all bodies are impenetrable, we gather not from reason, but from sensation. The bodies which we handle we find impenetrable, and thence conclude impenetrability to be a universal property of all bodies whatsoever. That all bodies are moveable, and endowed with certain powers (which we call the forces of inertia) or persevering in their motion or in their rest, we only infer from the like properties observed in the bodies which we have seen. The extension, hardness, impenetrability, mobility, and force of inertia of the whole, result from the extension, hardness, impenetrability, mobility, and forces of inertia of the parts: and thence we conclude that the least particles of all bodies to be also all extended, and hard, and impenetrable, and moveable, and endowed with their proper forces of inertia. And this is the foundation of all philosophy. Moreover, that the divided but contiguous particles of bodies may be separated from one another, is a matter of observation; and, in the particles that remain undivided, our minds are able to distinguish yet lesser parts, as is mathematically demonstrated. But whether the parts so distinguished, and not yet divided, may, by the powers of nature, be actually divided and separated from one another, we cannot certainly determine. Yet had we the proof of but one experiment, that any undivided particle, in breaking a hard and solid body, suffered a division, we might by virtue of this rule, conclude, that the undivided as well as the divided particles, may be divided and actually separated into infinity.

Lastly, if it universally appears, by experiments and astronomical observations, that all bodies about the earth, gravitate toward the earth; and that in proportion to the quantity of matter which they severally contain; that the moon likewise, according to the quantity of its matter, gravitates toward the earth; that on the other hand our sea gravitates toward the moon; and all the planets mutually one toward another; and the comets in like manner towards the sun; we must, in consequence of this rule, universally allow, that all bodies whatsoever are endowed with a principle of mutual gravitation. For the argument from the appearances concludes with more force for the universal gravitation of all bodies, than for their impenetrability, of which among those in the celestial regions, we have no experiments, nor any manner of observation. Not that I affirm gravity to be essential to all bodies. By their inherent force I mean nothing but their force of inertia. This is immutable. Their gravity is diminished as they recede from the earth.

Rule IV. In experimental philosophy we are to look upon propositions collected by general induction from phenomena as accurately or very nearly true, notwithstanding any contrary hypotheses that may be imagined, till such time as other phenomena occur, by which they may either be made more accurate, or liable to exceptions.

This rule we must follow that the argument of induction may not be evaded by hypotheses.

THINKING ACROSS CULTURES

1. What role did religion play in European expansion?

2. Compare and contrast the Spanish expansion in the Americas with the Portuguese expansion in Asia.

3. For a European at that time, which event do you think would seem more significant: the Portuguese contact with Asia or the Spanish discovery of the Americas? Why?

4. The European maritime explorations, the Reformation, and the development of the New Science were roughly contemporary. By far the most significant event of the three for Europeans of that time was the Reformation. What does this tell us about sixteenth-century Europe?

5. From a twenty-first-century vantage point, which of the three events is most significant? Why? What does your answer tell us about contemporary society?

THE MODERN ERA

The question, When did the modern era begin? probably has no definitive answer. At the least, different historians answer it differently. Some point to the Renaissance, others to the rise of modern science, others even to the high Middle Ages in the thirteenth century. These divergences indicate that the concept of modernity itself is sufficiently amorphous to defy precise dating. Nevertheless, whether or not we select them as the progenitors of the modern era, two developments occurred in the eighteenth century that have gradually given shape to civilization throughout the world in the centuries that have followed. Both were revolutions, but of quite different kinds, the first being political and the second technological.

In Europe, monarchical rule reached its apex in the seventeenth century, expressing itself in the doctrine of the divine right of kings and in perhaps its most exaggerated form in the famous pronouncement of Louis XIV, "*L'etat c'est moi.*" But even before that century ended changes were under way. The two revolutions in England during the seventeenth century, although they did not bring the monarchy to an end, deprived the kings of much of their former power, placing it in the hands of Parliament. However, the seminal revolution did not occur in Europe but in the Western Hemisphere, when a group of English colonies successfully revolted against their colonial master, declaring their independence in 1776. The American Revolution proved an inspiration and was followed by other insurrections elsewhere. Of these, by far the most important occurred in France; the destruction of the *ancien regime* was to alter the course of history and politics in Europe and beyond far into the future. Also, revolutions soon began to erupt in the Latin-speaking areas of America. There, under leaders like Bolívar and San Martin, the various colonies rose up so that by the middle of the nineteenth century almost all of the Western Hemisphere, much of which had endured colonial status for three hundred years, was free. But the revolt against colonialism in the nineteenth century was far from worldwide. On the contrary, the century witnessed the apogee of imperialism, as the major powers of Europe—and, to a lesser extent, the United States—competed with each other in the acquisition of new colonies elsewhere.

The second, technological or Industrial Revolution cannot be dated; in fact, it is still in progress. It had its beginnings early in the eighteenth century, with England leading the way. The most important early technological achievement was the introduction of steam as a source of power. From the dawn of history almost the only source of power, other than that of wind and water, was muscle—that of humans and animals. But in 1712 Thomas

Newcomen devised the first steam engine, which was gradually made more efficient during the course of the century. Its greatest effects were in manufacturing and transportation. Steam power was particularly important in the textile industry; it made possible the weaving of cloth, especially from cotton imported from the American South, in factories centered in the city of Manchester, where large numbers of workers, mostly from the country, were brought together in a large urban setting. A little later steam was harnessed to carriages and the first railroads built. Thus the products of the new factories could be quickly and cheaply distributed throughout the country. The advent of steam-powered ships in the nineteenth century in turn fostered an expansion of trade around the world.

Both the political and technological revolutions of the eighteenth century were to have deep effects on society in the nineteenth. As the idea and practice of democratic government spread, a reaction developed. The established orders of Europe, including particularly members of the aristocracy and the landed gentry, fought a long but increasingly futile battle to preserve their ancient status and prerogatives. But the growth of industry and the economic system that helped make it possible produced a new class—the bourgeoisie or capitalists—who demanded and gained increasing political and social power. The rise of capitalism was given both a theoretical rationale and a justification by the writings of a new school of economists like Adam Smith, David Ricardo, and the French physiocrats, who advocated the doctrine of *laissez faire*.

The creation of a large class of factory workers, or proletarians, was a vital ingredient in the industrialization of Europe. For centuries these people had been farmers, or had worked in "cottage industries" located in rural areas. Now they became congregated in industrial cities, where they worked in large factories, as "appendages of machines." Because much of the work was simple and routine, children could be employed (and many were), beginning as early as the age of six. These employees proved particularly advantageous to the capitalists, because their wages could be held at the lowest possible subsistence level.

Conditions in the factories became so bad in the early nineteenth century that they attracted the attention of social reformers, who succeeded in enacting legislation to eliminate the worst abuses. They also attracted the attention of the greatest nineteenth-century economist and social theorist— Karl Marx. Starting from a basis provided by the German philosopher G. W. F. Hegel, Marx argued that the rise of capitalism, with the bourgeoisie as its leaders, represented simply a stage in a historical development that would lead inevitably to the triumph of the workers, or proletariat. When this occurred, social classes would disappear, to be followed by a "golden age"— the classless society. As the followers of Marx agitated for the proletarian revolution that would be the prelude to their vision of utopia, they were ruthlessly suppressed by the political regimes throughout Europe. Although

Marxist movements made scant progress in the major industrialized nations of the West, they proved much more successful in the early twentieth century in other parts of the world, particularly Russia and China.

The great political and technological advances of the eighteenth century gave rise to prosperity, as wealth spread among wider segments of society. Prosperity, in turn, resulted in optimism. Intellectuals, aware that the source of many of these advances lay in the scientific discoveries of the preceding century, which they attributed to the application of reason to nature, concluded that the future of civilization depended on the universal application of reason to human affairs, a belief eloquently expressed by the Marquis de Condorcet, even as he lay in hiding from the vengeance of his fellow revolutionaries. Led by people like Voltaire and the French *philosophes*, they proclaimed the Age of Reason. To mark their era off even more from the past, which they considered to be heavily tainted with the obscurantism of religious belief, they referred to it also as the Enlightenment.

The increasingly productive mills, particularly in England, required more and more raw cotton, which could be grown well in the southern United States. So the plantation system flourished. Since cotton farming was labor-intensive, large numbers of field workers were needed. To get a supply of cheap labor inhabitants of Africa were purchased or kidnapped, transported across the Atlantic, and put to work as slaves. This slave-trade, largely in the hands of British merchants and mariners, was an extension of an older, and much larger, trade in human beings between Africa and South and Central America.

Although trade with America, including the importation of raw materials and the exportation of finished products, proved lucrative for English industrialists, its loss as a colony was a serious blow. But there was recompense in the possession of India, which proved a profitable market for English goods. The English had penetrated this vast subcontinent as early as the seventeenth century, but it was not until the eighteenth century that they gained control over the country, under the leadership of the adventurer Robert Clive (1725–1774), who easily defeated the French who were also trying to colonize the land. British rule in India was for about a hundred years indirect, being exercised through a private enterprise, the English East India Company, but in 1858 Parliament, following a rebellion by Indian troops against the British, took over direct control of the country. On New Year's Day, 1877, Queen Victoria, in an elaborate and pompous ceremony in Delhi (which she did not attend), was formally proclaimed Empress of India. The British were to control the land for nearly another hundred years, until after the Second World War.

During the period of European industrialization, repeated attempts were made by the major maritime powers to develop trade relations with China, which was viewed as a potentially enormous market for manufactured goods and which had had some sporadic trade relations with the West for thousands of years. An ideal solution would have been the colonization of the country and certainly the British, and others, dreamed of such a magnificent conquest. But China was not to prove the easy prey that India had been. Under the Manchu dynasty, which ruled from 1644 to 1912, a policy of exclusion of foreigners was adopted and trading with the West limited to the ports of Macao and Canton on the southern coast. Although many attempts were made to expand these commercial contacts, the Chinese response was plain: The West had nothing to offer China that the Chinese needed or wanted. It was only in the middle of the nineteenth century that sufficient pressure could be brought to bear on a disintegrating dynasty to allow Western commercial and political influence to penetrate the country.

A history, similar at first but later quite different, describes Western contacts with Japan. Soon after coming to power the Tokugawa shogunate (1603–1868) began to close Japan's doors to foreigners. Only a small island off Nagasaki was reserved for Dutch traders. Other foreigners who tried to enter the country were either driven off or killed. The long period of Japanese isolation was brought to an end in 1858 when Commodore Matthew Perry, with an American naval fleet, entered Japanese waters and demanded the opening of the country. Because the Japanese had no power with which to resist they were forced to acquiesce and open their ports to American traders, as well as to those of other nations. Just over a decade later the last Tokugawa shogun resigned and the emperor assumed control of the government. Known as the Meiji Restoration, this shift in political power paved the way for the rapid modernization, as well as increasing Westernization, of Japan.

Although the tide of European imperialism in the Western Hemisphere had been reversed in the nineteenth century, it was replaced by a final wave of imperialistic expansion, mainly in Africa. Almost all the major European powers took part. In territory seized Britain and France assumed the lead, dividing about half of the continent between them. The remainder was parcelled out among various European powers, including Germany, Portugal, Italy, Belgium, and Spain. By the beginning of the twentieth century only two countries in Africa remained genuinely independent—Ethiopia, which had successfully repulsed Italian invaders in 1896, and Liberia, which had been established as a homeland for liberated American slaves in 1822. With Africa partitioned little remained for imperialists to seize. However, a few scattered islands, mainly in the Pacific Ocean and the Caribbean Sea, were still available. These were soon parcelled out, with the United States enthusiastically sharing in the division.

Revolutionary Declarations

If one conceives the genesis of modernity in political terms, the two documents that follow may well be considered to have originated the modern era. They set out, in dramatic language, both the philosophical assumptions that underlie the modern democratic state and the prerogatives that must be secured for its citizens if such a state is to be realized in practice. Thus, the United States and France initiated modern democracy, a form of society that has been adopted in large part first throughout the West and later in various other areas of the world. This is not to say, however, that other nations had no role in the development of democracy. England, in particular, made significant contributions to the theory and practice of democratic government even though she, herself, with her royal family and House of Lords, has not yet achieved full social democracy but still retains some of the trappings of her medieval feudal past.

To one studying the two documents that follow, a point that quickly becomes apparent is the similarities between them, particularly in their general statements about the nature and justification of government. These similarities can be explained in large part by the fact that the authors of both were drawing on a common heritage of European political and social thought, extending as far back as classical Greece. But the similarities also raise the question of the influence of the *Declaration of Independence* on the *Declaration of the Rights of Man and Citizen*. The first was written in 1776; the second was promulgated fifteen years later, in 1791. The French revolutionaries were well aware of events in America and sympathetic to the colonists' cause so it is hardly an undue speculation to reason that their thoughts and actions were stimulated by the American example.

One important difference distinguishes the two declarations. The Americans were in revolt against a power that had its seat far away, across the Atlantic Ocean, but the French were rebelling against a ruler who occupied their own land. In both cases the charges leveled against the oppressors are directed specifically to the persons of the respective kings, George III and Louis XVI, but it is questionable how much either monarch was responsible for the injustices described. Whatever the roles of the kings, the major onus for the acts that led to revolution probably lay with the senior ministers of state of the two regimes.

The third document seeks to expose some of the hypocrisy inherent in the first two. Women, especially educated, wealthy bourgeois women in France, often were supporters of the revolutionary ideals embodied in the first two declarations. Many were outraged that the *Declaration of the Rights of Man* applied only to males. Olympe de Gouges offered her *Declaration of the Rights of Woman* as a remedy for what she perceived as the fatal flaw in the masculine assumptions of the *Declaration of the Rights of Man*. Published in 1791, it was ignored by the leaders of the French Revolution. Indeed, under the Napoleonic Code of 1804, women were declared legally incompetent. Olympe de Gouges was guillotined in 1793 for her opposition to the execution of the French royal family.

---

1. In what ways does the Declaration of the Rights of Man show the influence of the Declaration of Independence? In what ways is it unlike the Declaration of Independence?

2. How does Olympe de Gouges use the assumptions and values embodied in the Declaration of Independence and Declaration of the Rights of Man to claim that women should be considered political actors possessing inherent rights?

The Declaration of Independence

In Congress, July 4, 1776
The Unanimous Declaration of the Thirteen
United States of America

When in the course of human events, it becomes necessary for one people to dissolve the political bands which have connected them with another, and to assume among the powers of the earth, the separate and equal station to which the Laws of Nature and of Nature's God entitle them, a decent respect to the opinions of mankind requires that they should declare the causes which impel them to the separation.

We hold these truths to be self-evident, that all men are created equal, that they are endowed by their Creator with certain unalienable rights, that among these are life, liberty and the pursuit of happiness. That to secure these rights, governments are instituted among men, deriving their just powers from the consent of the governed. That whenever any form of government becomes destructive of these ends, it is the right of the people to alter or to abolish it, and to institute new government, laying its foundation on such principles and organizing its powers in such form, as to them shall seem most likely to effect their safety and happiness. Prudence, indeed, will dictate that governments long established should not be changed for light and transient causes; and accordingly all experience hath shown, that mankind are more disposed to suffer, while evils are sufferable, than to right themselves by abolishing the forms to which they are accustomed. But when a long train of abuses and usurpations, pursuing invariably the same object evinces a design to reduce them under absolute despotism, it is their right, it is their duty, to throw off such government, and to provide new guards for their future security. Such has been the patient sufferance of these Colonies; and such is now the necessity which constrains them to alter their former systems of government. The history of the present King of Great Britain is a history of repeated injuries and usurpations, all having in direct object the establishment of an absolute tyranny over these States. To prove this, let facts be submitted to a candid world.

He has refused his assent to laws, the most wholesome and necessary for the public good.

He has forbidden his Governors to pass laws of immediate and pressing importance, unless suspended in their operation till his assent should be obtained; and when so suspended, he has utterly neglected to attend to them.

He has refused to pass other laws for the accommodation of large districts of people, unless those people would relinquish the right of representation in the Legislature, a right inestimable to them and formidable to tyrants only.

He has called together legislative bodies at places unusual, uncomfortable, and distant from the depository of their public records, for the sole purpose of fatiguing them into compliance with his measures.

He has dissolved representative houses repeatedly, for opposing with manly firmness his invasions on the rights of the people.

He has refused for a long time, after such dissolutions, to cause others to be elected; whereby the legislative powers, incapable of annihilation, have returned to the people at large for their exercise; the State remaining in the meantime exposed to all the dangers of invasion from without and convulsions within.

He has endeavoured to prevent the population of these states; for that purpose obstructing the laws of naturalization of foreigners; refusing to pass others to encourage their migration hither, and raising the conditions of new appropriations of lands.

He has obstructed the administration of justice, by refusing his assent to laws for establishing judiciary powers.

He has made judges dependent on his will alone, for the tenure of their offices, and the amount and payment of their salaries.

He has erected a multitude of new offices, and sent hither swarms of officers to harass our people, and eat out their substance.

He has kept among us, in times of peace, standing armies without the consent of our legislatures.

He has affected to render the military independent of and superior to the civil power.

He has combined with others to subject us to a jurisdiction foreign to our constitution, and unacknowledged by our laws; giving his assent to their acts of pretended legislation:

For quartering large bodies of armed troops among us:

For protecting them, by a mock trial, from punishment for any murders which they should commit on the inhabitants of these States:

For cutting off our trade with all parts of the world:

For imposing taxes on us without our consent:

For depriving us in many cases, of the benefits of trial by jury:

For transporting us beyond seas to be tried for pretended offences:

For abolishing the free system of English laws in a neighbouring Province, establishing therein an arbitrary government, and enlarging its boundaries so as to render it at once an example and fit instrument for introducing the same absolute rule into these Colonies:

For taking away our Charters, abolishing our most valuable laws, and altering fundamentally the forms of our governments:

For suspending our own Legislatures, and declaring themselves invested with power to legislate for us in all cases whatsoever.

He has abdicated government here, by declaring us out of his protection and waging war against us.

He has plundered our seas, ravaged our coasts, burnt our towns, and destroyed the lives of our people.

He is at this time transporting large armies of foreign mercenaries to complete the works of death, desolation and tyranny, already begun with circumstances of cruelty and perfidy scarcely paralleled in the most barbarous ages, and totally unworthy the head of a civilized nation.

He has constrained our fellow citizens taken captive on the high seas to bear arms against their country, to become the executioners of their friends and brethren, or to fall themselves by their hands.

He has excited domestic insurrections amongst us, and has endeavoured to bring on the inhabitants of our frontiers, the merciless Indian savages, whose known rule of warfare, is an undistinguished destruction of all ages, sexes, and conditions.

In every stage of these oppressions we have petitioned for redress in the most humble terms: our repeated petitions have been answered only by repeated injury. A prince whose character is thus marked by every act which may define a tyrant is unfit to be the ruler of a free people.

Nor have we been wanting in attention to our British brethren. We have warned them from time to time of attempts by their legislature to extend an unwarrantable jurisdiction over us. We have reminded them of the circumstances of our emigration and settlement here. We have appealed to their native justice and magnanimity, and we have conjured them by the ties of our common kindred to disavow these usurpations, which would inevitably interrupt our connections and correspondence. They too have been deaf to the voice of justice and of consanguinity. We must, therefore, acquiesce in the necessity, which denounces our separation, and hold them, as we hold the rest of mankind, enemies in war, in peace friends.

We, therefore, the Representatives of the United States of America, in General Congress assembled, appealing to the Supreme Judge of the world for the rectitude of our intentions, do, in the name, and by authority of the good people of these Colonies, solemnly publish and declare, That these United Colonies are, and of right ought to be Free and Independent States; that they are absolved from all allegiance to the British Crown, and that all political connection between them and the State of Great Britain, is and ought to be totally dissolved; and that as Free and Independent States, they have full power to levy war, conclude peace, contract alliances, establish commerce, and to do all other acts and things which Independent States may of right do. And for the support of this declaration, with a firm reliance on the protection of Divine Providence, we mutually pledge to each other our lives, our fortunes, and our sacred honor.

Declaration of the Rights of Man and Citizen

The representatives of the French people, organized in National Assembly, considering that ignorance, forgetfulness, or contempt of the rights of man are the sole causes of public misfortunes and of the corruption of governments, have resolved to set forth in a solemn declaration the natural, inalienable, and sacred rights of man, in order that such declaration, continually before all members of the social body, may be a perpetual reminder of their rights and duties; in order that the acts of the legislative power and those of the executive power may constantly be compared with the aim of every political institution and may accordingly be more respected; in order that the demands of the citizens, founded henceforth upon simple and incontestable principles, may always be directed towards the maintenance of the Constitution and the welfare of all.

Accordingly, the National Assembly recognizes and proclaims, in the presence and under the auspices of the Supreme Being, the following rights of man and citizen.

1. Men are born and remain free and equal in rights; social distinctions may be based only upon general usefulness.

2. The aim of every political association is the preservation of the natural and inalienable rights of man; these rights are liberty, property, security, and resistance to oppression.

3. The source of all sovereignty resides essentially in the nation; no group, no individual may exercise authority not emanating expressly therefrom.

4.   Liberty consists of the power to do whatever is not injurious to others; thus the enjoyment of the natural rights of every man has for its limits only those that assure other members of society the enjoyment of those same rights; such limits may be determined only by law.

5.   The law has the right to forbid only actions which are injurious to society. Whatever is not forbidden by law may not be prevented, and no one may be constrained to do what it does not prescribe.

6.   Law is the expression of the general will; all citizens have the right to concur personally, or through their representatives, in its formation; it must be the same for all, whether it protects or punishes. All citizens, being equal before it, are equally admissible to all public offices, positions, and employments, according to their capacity, and without other distinction than that of virtues and talents.

7.   No man may be accused, arrested, or detained except in the cases determined by law, and according to the forms prescribed thereby. Whoever solicit, expedite, or execute arbitrary orders, or have them executed, must be punished; but every citizen summoned or apprehended in pursuance of the law must obey immediately; he renders himself culpable by resistance.

8.   The law is to establish only penalties that are absolutely and obviously necessary; and no one may be punished except by virtue of a law established and promulgated prior to the offence and legally applied.

9.   Since every man is presumed innocent until declared guilty, if arrest be deemed indispensable, all unnecessary severity for securing the person of the accused must be severely repressed by law.

10.   No one is to be disquieted because of his opinions, even religious, provided their manifestation does not disturb the public order established by law.

11.   Free communication of ideas and opinions is one of the most precious of the rights of man. Consequently, every citizen may speak, write, and print freely, subject to responsibility for the abuse of such liberty in the cases determined by law.

12.   The guarantee of the rights of man and citizen necessitates a public force; such a force, therefore, is instituted for the advantage of all and not for the particular benefit of those to whom it is entrusted.

13.   For the maintenance of the public force and for the expenses of administration a common tax is indispensable; it must be assessed equally on all citizens in proportion to their means.

14.   Citizens have the right to ascertain, by themselves or through their representatives, the necessity of the public tax, to consent to it freely, to supervise its use, and to determine its quota, assessment, payment, and duration.

15.   Society has the right to require of every public agent an accounting of his administration.

16.   Every society in which the guarantee of rights is not assured or the separation of powers not determined has no constitution at all.

17.   Since property is a sacred and inviolate right, no one may be deprived thereof unless a legally established public necessity obviously requires it, and upon condition of a just and previous indemnity.

Declaration of the Rights of Woman and the Female Citizen

For the National Assembly to decree in its last sessions, or in those of the next legislature:

Preamble

Mothers, daughters, sisters [and] representatives of the nation demand to be constituted into a national assembly. Believing that ignorance, omission, or scorn for the rights of woman are the only causes of public misfortunes and of the corruption of governments, [the women] have resolved to set forth in a solemn declaration the natural, inalienable, and sacred rights of woman in order that this declaration, constantly exposed before all the members of the society, will ceaselessly remind them of their rights and duties; in order that the authoritative acts of women and the authoritative acts of men may be at any moment compared with and respectful of the purpose of all political institutions; and in order that citizens' demands, henceforth based on simple and incontestable principles, will always support the constitution, good morals, and the happiness of all.

Consequently, the sex that is as superior in beauty as it is in courage during the sufferings of maternity recognizes and declares in the presence and under the auspices of the Supreme Being, the following Rights of Woman and of Female Citizens.

Article I

Woman is born free and lives equal to man in her rights. Social distinctions can be based only on the common utility.

Article II

The purpose of any political association is the conservation of the natural and imprescriptible rights of woman and man; these rights are liberty, property, security, and especially resistance to oppression.

Article III

The principle of all sovereignty rests essentially with the nation, which is nothing but the union of woman and man; no body and no individual can exercise any authority which does not come expressly from it [the nation].

Article IV

Liberty and justice consist of restoring all that belongs to others; thus, the only limits on the exercise of the natural rights of woman are perpetual male tyranny; these limits are to be reformed by the laws of nature and reason.

Article V

Laws of nature and reason proscribe all acts harmful to society; everything which is not prohibited by these wise and divine laws cannot be prevented, and no one can be constrained to do what they do not command.

Article VI

The law must be the expression of the general will; all female and male citizens must contribute either personally or through their representatives to its formation; it must be the same for all: male and female citizens, being equal in the eyes of the law, must be equally admitted to all honors, positions, and public employment according to their capacity and without other distinctions besides those of their virtues and talents.

Article VII

No woman is an exception: she is accused, arrested, and detained in cases determined by law. Women, like men, obey this rigorous law.

Article VIII

The law must establish only those penalties that are strictly and obviously necessary, and no one can be punished except by virtue of a law established and promulgated prior to the crime and legally applicable to women.

Article IX

Once any woman is declared guilty, complete rigor is [to be] exercised by the law.

Article X

No one is to be disquieted for his very basic opinions; woman has the right to mount the scaffold; she must equally have the right to mount the rostrum, provided that her demonstrations do not disturb the legally established public order.

Article XI

The free communication of thoughts and opinions is one of the most precious rights of woman, since that liberty assures the recognition of children by their fathers. Any female citizen thus may say freely, I am the mother of a child which belongs to you, without being forced by a barbarous prejudice to hide the truth; [an exception may be made] to respond to the abuse of this liberty in cases determined by the law.

Article XII

For the support of the public force and the expenses of administration, the contributions of woman and man are equal: she shares all the duties [*corvées*] and all the painful tasks; therefore, she must have the same share in the distribution of positions, employment, offices, honors, and jobs [*industrie*].

Article XIII

Female and male citizens have the right to verify, either by themselves or through their representatives, the necessity of the public contribution. This can only apply to women if they are granted an equal share, not only of wealth, but also of public administration, and in the determination of the proportion, the base, the collection, and the duration of the tax.

Article XIV

The collectivity of women, joined for tax purposes to the aggregate of men, has the right to demand an accounting of his administration from any public agent.

Article XV

No society has a constitution without the guarantee of rights and the separation of powers; the constitution is null if the majority of individuals comprising the nation have not cooperated in drafting it.

Article XVI

Property belongs to both sexes whether united or separate; for each it is an inviolable and sacred right; no one can be deprived of it, since it is the true patrimony of nature, unless the legally determined public need obviously dictates it, and then only with a just and prior indemnity.

Postscript

Woman, wake up; the tocsin of reason is being heard throughout the whole universe; discover your rights. The powerful empire of nature is no longer surrounded by prejudice, fanaticism, superstition, and lies. The flame of truth has dispersed all the clouds of folly and usurpation. Enslaved man has multiplied his strength and needs recourse to yours to break his chains. Having become free, he has become unjust to his companion. Oh, women, women! When will you cease to be blind? What advantage have you received from the Revolution? A more pronounced scorn, a more marked disdain. In the centuries of corruption you ruled only over the weakness of men. The reclamation of your patrimony, based on the wise decrees of nature—what have you to dread from such a fine undertaking? The *bon mot* of the legislator of the marriage of Cana? Do you fear that our French legislators, correctors of that morality, long ensnared by political practices now out of date, will only say again to you women, what is there in common between you and us? Everything you will have to answer. If they persist in their weakness in putting this non sequitur in contradiction to their principles, courageously oppose the force of reason to the empty pretentions of superiority: unite yourselves beneath the standards of philosophy; deploy all the energy of your character, and you will soon see these haughty men, not groveling at your feet as servile adorers, but proud to share with you the treasures of the Supreme Being. Regardless of what barriers confront you, it is in your power to free yourselves; you have only to want to. Let us pass now to the shocking tableau of what you have been in society; and since national education is in question at this moment, let us see whether our wise legislators will think judiciously about the education of women.

Women have done more harm than good. Constraint and dissimulation have been their lot. What force had robbed them of, ruse returned to them: they had recourse to all the resources of their charms, and the most irreproachable person did not resist them. Poison and the sword were both subject to them; they commanded in crime as in fortune. The French government, especially, depended throughout the centuries on the nocturnal administration of women; the cabinet kept no secret from their indiscretion: ambassadorial post, command, ministry, presidency, pontificate, college of cardinals; finally, anything which characterizes the folly of men, profane and sacred, all have been subject to the cupidity and ambition of this sex, formerly contemptible and respected, and since the revolution, respectable and scorned.

In this sort of contradictory situation, what remarks could I not make! I have but a moment to make them, but this moment will fix the attention of the remotest posterity. Under the Old Regime, all was vicious, all was guilty; but could not the amelioration of conditions be perceived even in the substance of vices? A woman only had to be beautiful or amiable; when she possessed these two advantages, she saw a hundred fortunes at her feet. If she did not profit from them, she had a bizarre character or a rare philosophy which made her scorn wealth; then she was deemed to be like a crazy woman; the most indecent made herself respected with gold; commerce in women was a kind of industry in the first class [of society], which, henceforth, will have no more credit. If it still had it, the revolution would be lost, and under the new relationships we would always be corrupted; however, reason can always be deceived [into believing] that any other road to fortune is closed to the woman whom a man buys, like the slave on the African coasts. The difference is great; that is known. The slave is commanded by the master: but if the master gives her liberty without recompense, and at an age when the slave has lost all her charms, what will become of this unfortunate woman? The victim of scorn, even the doors of charity are closed to her; she is poor and old, they say; why did she not know how to make her fortune? Reason finds other examples that are even more touching. A young inexperienced woman, seduced by a man whom she loves, will abandon her parents to follow him; the ingrate will leave her after a few years, and the older she has become with him, the more inhuman is his inconstancy: if she has children, he will likewise abandon them. If he is rich, he will consider himself excused from sharing his fortune with his noble victims. If some involvement binds him to his duties, he will deny them, trusting that the laws will support him. If he is married, any other obligation loses its rights. Then what laws remain to extirpate vice all the way to its root? The law of dividing wealth and public administration between men and women. It can easily be seen that one who is born into a rich family gains very much from such equal sharing. But the one born into a poor family with merit and virtue—what is her lot? Poverty and opprobrium. If she does not precisely excel in music or painting, she cannot be admitted to any public function when she has all the capacity for it. I do not want to give only a sketch of things; I will go more deeply into this in the new edition of all my political writings, with notes, which I propose to give to the public in a few days.

I take up my text again on the subject of morals. Marriage is the tomb of trust and love. The married woman can with impunity give bastards to her husband, and also give them the wealth which does not belong to them. The woman who is unmarried has only one feeble right; ancient and inhuman laws refuse to her for her children the right to the name and the wealth of their father; no new laws have been made in this matter. If it is considered a paradox and an impossibility on my part to try to give my sex an honorable and just consistency. I leave it to men to attain glory for dealing with this matter; but while we wait, the way can be prepared through national education, the restoration of morals, and conjugal conventions.

Form for a Social Contract Between Man and Woman

We, _____ and _____ moved by our own will, unite ourselves for the duration of our lives, and for the duration of our mutual inclinations, under the following conditions: We intend and wish to make our wealth communal, meanwhile reserving to ourselves the right to divide it in favor of our children and of those toward whom we might have a particular inclination, mutually recognizing that our property belongs directly to our children, from whatever bed they come, and that all of them without distinction have the right to bear the name of the fathers and mothers who have acknowledged them, and we are charged to subscribe to the law which punishes the renunciation of one's own blood. We likewise obligate ourselves, in case of separation, to divide our wealth and to set aside in advance the portion the law indicates for our children, and in the event of a perfect union, the one who dies will divest himself of half his property in his children's favor, and if one dies childless, the survivor will inherit by right, unless the dying person has disposed of half the common property in favor of one whom he judged deserving.

Adam Smith

European economic practices before Adam Smith were guided by the theory of mercantilism. Often described as the doctrine that a nation's wealth consists in the amount of money, in the form of precious metals, it possesses, it follows from mercantile theory that the nation should adopt the policy of maximizing its exports (particularly in the form of valuable manufactured goods) and minimizing its imports, thus increasing its intake of bullion. But this is only a superficial account of a much more complex theory. To understand mercantilism one must view it in its historical context—that of the emerging nation-states of Europe. So understood, mercantilism, like warfare, can be seen as one of the methods employed by these burgeoning nations to increase their power, particularly in relation to that of their neighbors. Although one of the means to this end was to achieve a favorable balance of trade, others included the encouragement of manufacturing industries, the increase of an urban over a rural population, the acquisition of colonies (particularly in the Western Hemisphere), and others. But most important was the idea that economics was an organ of national power and that, therefore, the state should exercise tight control over every facet of its economy.

Although the mercantilist system was by no means a failure in serving the needs of the times, it began to come under attack during the eighteenth century. Perhaps the sharpest, and certainly the most influential, of its critics was the Scot, Adam Smith (1723–1790). By profession Smith was not an economist but a philosopher, being for several years a professor of moral philosophy at the University of Glasgow. His great work, whose full title is *An Inquiry into Nature and Causes of the Wealth of Nations*, was published in 1776.

Smith focused his attack on mercantilism on its central tenet—that the economic life of a nation should be under the strict control of the government. Rather than encouraging economic activity, he argued, such a policy increasingly stifles it. In his mind the best way to maximize the wealth of a nation is to allow each individual to pursue his own interests with a minimum of restraints. Thus he advocated the economics that has come to be known as the free enterprise system and his book *The Wealth of Nations* laid the theoretical foundations on which modern capitalism was to develop.

Smith believed that, if each individual pursued his own economic interests, the interests of all would be enhanced. But, as the later history of capitalism has made us realize, the pursuit of unbridled self-interest—particularly by large corporations—has often had a quite different effect. To critics of his economic theory Smith would undoubtedly have replied that, when he spoke of self-interest, he always meant *enlightened* self-interest, or the individual's recognition that his own best interests could be realized only with the realization of those of society as a whole. To what extent such a reply would constitute a repudiation of the capitalism his economic theory engendered is a question worthy of debate.

---

1.   Briefly restate, in your own words, Adam Smith's argument.

2.   Which classes of people in nineteenth-century Europe would be most likely to favor free enterprise? Which would be most likely to oppose it? Why?

An Inquiry into the Nature and Causes of the Wealth of Nations

Book IV, Chapter II

OF RESTRAINTS UPON THE IMPORTATION FROM FOREIGN COUNTRIES OF SUCH GOODS AS CAN BE PRODUCED AT HOME

By restraining, either by high duties, or by absolute prohibitions, the importation of such goods from foreign countries as can be produced at home, the monopoly of the home-market is more or less secured to the domestic industry employed in producing them. Thus the prohibition of importing either live cattle or salt provisions from foreign countries secures to the graziers of Great Britain the monopoly of the home market for butchers'-meat. The high duties upon the importation of corn, which in times of moderate plenty amount to a prohibition, give a like advantage to the growers of that commodity. The prohibition of the importation of foreign woollens is equally favourable to the woollen manufactures. The silk manufacture, though altogether employed upon foreign materials, has lately obtained the same advantage. The linen manufacture has not yet obtained it, but is making great strides towards it. Many other sorts of manufactures have, in the same manner, obtained in Great Britain, either altogether, or very nearly a monopoly against their countrymen. The variety of goods of which the importation into Great Britain is prohibited, either absolutely, or under certain circumstances, greatly exceeds what can easily be suspected by those who are not well acquainted with the laws of the customs.

Adam Smith, *An Inquiry into the Nature and Causes of the Wealth of Nations*, 8th ed.

That this monopoly of the home-market frequently gives great encouragement to that particular species of industry which enjoys it, and frequently turns toward that employment a greater share of both the labour and stock of the society than would otherwise have gone to it, cannot be doubted. But whether it tends either to increase the general industry of the society, or to give it the most advantageous direction, is not, perhaps, altogether so evident.

The general industry of the society never can exceed what the capital of the society can employ. As the number of workmen that can be kept in employment by any particular person must bear a certain proportion to his capital, so the number of those that can be continually employed by all the members of a great society, must bear a certain proportion to the whole capital of that society, and never can exceed that proportion. No regulation of commerce can increase the quantity of industry in any society beyond what its capital can maintain. It can only divert a part of it into a direction into which it might not otherwise have gone; and it is by no means certain that this artificial direction is likely to be more advantageous to the society than that into which it would have gone of its own accord.

Every individual is continually exerting himself to find out the most advantageous employment for whatever capital he can command. It is his own advantage, indeed, and not that of the society, which he has in view. But the study of his own advantage naturally, or rather necessarily leads him to prefer that employment which is most advantageous to the society.

First, every individual endeavours to employ his capital as near home as he can, and consequently as much as he can in the support of domestic industry; provided always that he can thereby obtain the ordinary, or not a great deal less than the ordinary profits of stock.

Thus, upon equal or nearly equal profits, every wholesale merchant naturally prefers the home-trade to the foreign trade of consumption, and the foreign trade of consumption to the carrying trade. In the home-trade his capital is never so long out of his sight as it frequently is in the foreign trade of consumption. He can know better the character and situation of the persons whom he trusts, and if he should happen to be deceived, he knows better the laws of the country from which he must seek redress. . . . Upon equal, or only nearly equal profits, therefore, every individual naturally inclines to employ his capital in the manner in which it is likely to afford the greater support to domestic industry, and to give revenue and employment to the greatest number of people of his own country.

Secondly, every individual who employs his capital in the support of domestic industry, necessarily endeavours so to direct that industry, that its produce may be of the greatest possible value.

The produce of industry is what it adds to the subject or materials upon which it is employed. In proportion as the value of this produce is great or small, so will likewise be the profits of the employer. But it is only for the sake of profit that any man employs a capital in the support of industry; and he will always, therefore, endeavour to employ it in the support of that industry of which the produce is likely to be of the greatest value, or to exchange for the greatest quantity either of money or of other goods.

But the annual revenue of every society is always precisely equal to the exchangeable value of the whole annual produce of its industry, or rather is precisely the same thing with that exchangeable value. As every individual, therefore, endeavours as much as he can both to employ his capital in the support of domestic industry, and so to direct that industry that its produce may be of the greatest value; every individual necessarily labours to render the annual revenue of the society as great as he can. He generally, indeed, neither intends to promote the public interest, nor knows how much he is promoting it. By preferring the support of domestic to that of foreign industry, he intends only his own security; and by directing that industry in such a manner as its produce may be of the greatest value, he intends only his own gain, and he is in this, as in many other cases, led by an invisible hand to promote an end which was no part of his intention. Nor is it always the worse for the society that it was no part of it. By pursuing his own interest he frequently promotes that of the society more effectually than when he really intends to promote it. I have never known much good done by those who affected to trade for the public good. It is an affectation, indeed, not very common among merchants, and very few words need be employed in dissuading them from it.

What is the species of domestic industry which his capital can employ, and of which the produce is likely to be of the greatest value, every individual, it is evident, can, in his local situation, judge much better than any statesman or lawgiver can do for him. The statesman, who should attempt to direct private people in what manner they ought to employ their capitals, would not only load himself with a most unnecessary attention, but assume an authority which could safely be trusted, not only to no single person, but to no council or senate whatever, and which would nowhere be so dangerous as in the hands of a man who had folly and presumption enough to fancy himself fit to exercise it.

To give the monopoly of the home-market to the produce of domestic industry, in any particular art or manufacture, is in some measure to direct private people in what manner they ought to employ their capitals, and must, in almost all cases, be either a useless or a hurtful regulation. If the produce of domestic can be brought there as cheap as that of foreign industry, the regulation is evidently useless. If it cannot, it must generally be hurtful. It is the maxim of every prudent master of a family, never to attempt to make at home what it will cost him more to make than to buy. The taylor does not attempt to make his own shoes, but buys them of the shoemaker. The shoemaker does not attempt to make his own clothes, but employs a taylor. The farmer attempts to make neither the one nor the other, but employs those different artificers. All of them find it for their interest to employ their whole industry in a way in which they have some advantage over their neighbours, and to purchase with a part of its produce, or what is the same thing, with the price of a part of it, whatever else they have occasion for.

What is prudence in the conduct of every family, can scarce be folly in that of a great kingdom. If a foreign country can supply us with a commodity cheaper than we ourselves can make it, better buy it of them with some part of the produce of our own industry, employed in a way in which we have some advantage. The general industry of the country, being always in proportion to the capital which employs it, will not thereby be diminished, no more than that of the above-mentioned artificers; but only left to find out the way in which it can be employed with the greatest advantage. It is certainly not employed to the greatest advantage, when it is thus directed towards an object which it can buy cheaper than it can make. The value of its annual produce is certainly more or less diminished, when it is thus turned away from producing commodities evidently of more value than the commodity which it is directed to produce. According to the supposition, that commodity could be purchased from foreign countries cheaper than it can be made at home. It could, therefore, have been purchased with a part only of the commodities, or, what is the same thing, with a part only of the price of the commodities, which the industry employed by an equal capital would have produced at home, had it been left to follow its natural course. The industry of the country, therefore, is thus turned away from a more to a less advantageous employment, and the exchangeable value of its annual produce, instead of being increased, according to the intention of the lawgiver, must necessarily be diminished by every such regulation.

By means of such regulations, indeed, a particular manufacture may sometimes be acquired sooner than it could have been otherwise, and after a certain time may be made at home as cheap or cheaper than in the foreign country. But though the industry of the society may be thus carried with advantage into a particular channel sooner than it could have been otherwise, it will by no means follow that the sum total, either of its industry, or of its revenue, can ever be augmented by any such regulation. The industry of the society can augment only in proportion as its capital augments, and its capital can augment only in proportion to what can be gradually saved out of its revenue. But the immediate effect of every such regulation is to diminish its revenue, and what diminishes its revenue is certainly not very likely to augment its capital faster than it would have augmented of its own accord, had both capital and industry been left to find out their natural employments.

Though for want of such regulations the society should never acquire the proposed manufacture, it would not, upon that account, necessarily be the poorer in any one period of its duration. In every period of its duration its whole capital and industry might still have been employed, though upon different objects, in the manner that was most advantageous at the time. In every period its revenue might have been the greatest which its capital could afford, and both capital and revenue might have been augmented with the greatest possible rapidity.

The natural advantages which one country has over another in producing particular commodities are sometimes so great, that it is acknowledged by all the world to be in vain to struggle with them. By means of glasses, hotbeds, and hotwalls, very good grapes can be raised in Scotland, and very good wine too can be made of them at about thirty times the expense for which at least equally good can be brought from foreign countries. Would it be a reasonable law to prohibit the importation of all foreign wines, merely to encourage the making of claret and burgundy in Scotland? But if there would be a manifest absurdity in turning towards any employment thirty times more of the capital and industry of the country, than would be necessary to purchase from foreign countries an equal quantity of the commodities wanted, there must be an absurdity, though not altogether so glaring, yet exactly of the same kind, in turning towards any such employment a thirtieth, or even a three hundredth part more of either. Whether the advantages which one country has over another be natural or acquired, is in this respect of no consequence. As long as the one country has those advantages, and the other wants them, it will always be more advantageous for the latter, rather to buy of the former than to make. It is an acquired advantage only, which one artificer has over his neighbour, who exercises another trade; and yet they both find it more advantageous to buy of one another, than to make what does not belong to their particular trades.

Merchants and manufacturers are the people who derive the greatest advantage from this monopoly of the home-market. The prohibition of the importation of foreign cattle, and of salt provisions, together with the high duties upon foreign corn, which in times of moderate plenty amount to a prohibition, are not near so advantageous to the graziers and farmers of Great Britain, as other regulations of the same kind are to its merchants and manufacturers. Manufactures, those of the finer kind especially, are more easily transported from one country to another than corn or cattle. It is in the fetching and carrying manufactures, accordingly, that foreign trade is chiefly employed. In manufactures, a very small advantage will enable foreigners to undersell our own workmen, even in the homemarket. It will require a very great one to enable them to do so in the rude produce of the soil. If the free importation of foreign manufactures were permitted, several of the home manufactures would probably suffer, and some of them, perhaps, go to ruin altogether, and a considerable part of the stock and industry at present employed in them would be forced to find out some other employment. But the freest importation of the rude produce of the soil could have no such effect upon the agriculture of the country.

• • •

Even the free importation of foreign corn could very little affect the interest of the farmers of Great Britain. Corn is a much more bulky commodity than butchers'-meat. A pound of wheat at a penny is as dear as a pound of butchers'-meat at fourpence. The small quantity of foreign corn imported even in times of the greatest scarcity, may satisfy our farmers that they can have nothing to fear from the freest importation. The average quantity imported one year with another, amounts only, according to the very well-informed author of the tracts upon the corn trade, to twenty-three thousand seven hundred and twenty-eight quarters of all sorts of grain, and does not exceed the five hundredth and seventy-one part of the annual consumption. But as the bounty upon corn occasions a greater exportation in years of plenty, so it must of consequence occasion a greater importation in years of scarcity, than in the actual state of tillage would otherwise take place. By means of it, the plenty of one year does not compensate the scarcity of another, and as the average quantity exported is necessarily augmented by it, so much likewise, in the actual state of tillage, the average quantity imported. If there were no bounty, as less corn would be exported, so it is probable that, one year with another, less would be imported than at present. The corn merchant, the fetchers and carriers of corn between Great Britain and foreign countries, would have much less employment, and might suffer considerably; but the country gentlemen and farmers could suffer very little. It is in the corn merchants accordingly, rather than in the country gentlemen and farmers, that I have observed the greatest anxiety for the renewal and continuation of the bounty.

Country gentlemen and farmers are, to their great honour, of all people, the least subject to the wretched spirit of monopoly. The undertaker of a great manufactory is sometimes alarmed if another work of the same kind is established within twenty miles of him. The Dutch undertaker of all the woollen manufacture at Abbeville stipulated, that no work of the same kind should be established within thirty leagues of that city. Farmers and country gentlemen, on the contrary, are generally disposed rather to promote than to obstruct the cultivation and improvement of their neighbours' farms and estates. They have no secrets, such as those of the greater part of manufacturers, but are generally rather fond of communicating to their neighbours, and of extending as far as possible any new practice which they have found to be advantageous. . . . Country gentlemen and farmers, dispersed in different parts of the country, cannot so easily combine as merchants and manufacturers, who being collected into towns, and accustomed to that exclusive corporation spirit which prevails in them, naturally endeavour to obtain against all their countrymen, the same exclusive privilege which they generally possess against the inhabitants of their respective towns. They accordingly seem to have been the original inventors of those restraints upon the importation of foreign goods, which secure to them the monopoly of the home-market. It was probably in imitation of them, and to put themselves upon a level with those who, they found, were disposed to oppress them, that the country gentlemen and farmers of Great Britain so far forgot the generosity which is natural to their station, as to demand the exclusive privilege of supplying their countrymen with corn and butchers'-meat. They did not perhaps take time to consider, how much less their interest could be affected by the freedom of trade than that of the people whose example they followed.

To prohibit by a perpetual law the importation of foreign corn and cattle, is in reality to enact, that the population and industry of the country shall at no time exceed what the rude produce of its own soil can maintain.

There seem, however, to be two cases in which it will generally be advantageous to lay some burden upon foreign, for the encouragement of domestic industry.

The first is, when some particular sort of industry is necessary for the defense of the country. The defense of Great Britain, for example, depends very much upon the number of its sailors and shipping. The act of navigation, therefore, very properly endeavours to give the sailors and shipping of Great Britain the monopoly of the trade of their own country, in some cases, by absolute prohibitions, and in others by heavy burdens upon the shipping of foreign countries. The following are the principal dispositions of this act.

First, all ships, of which the owners, masters, and three-fourths of the mariners are not British subjects, are prohibited, upon pain of forfeiting ship and cargo, from trading to the British settlements and plantations, or from being employed in the coasting trade of Great Britain.

Secondly, a great variety of the most bulky articles of importation can be brought into Great Britain only, either in such ships as are above described, or in ships of the country where those goods are produced, and of which the owners, masters, and three-fourths of the mariners, are of that particular country; and when imported even in ships of this latter kind, they are subject to double aliens duty. If imported in ships of any other country, the penalty is forfeiture of ship and goods. When this act was made, the Dutch were, what they still are, the great carriers of Europe, and by this regulation they were entirely excluded from being carriers to Great Britain, or from importing to us the goods of any other European country.

Thirdly, a great variety of the most bulky articles of importation are prohibited from being imported, even in British ships, from any country but that in which they are produced; under pain of forfeiting ship and cargo. This regulation too was probably intended against the Dutch. Holland was then, as now, the great emporium for all European goods, and by this regulation, British ships were hindered from loading in Holland the goods of any other European country.

Fourthly, salt fish of all kinds, whale fins, whale-bone, oil, and blubber, not caught by and cured on board British vessels, when imported into Great Britain, are subjected to double aliens duty. The Dutch, as they are still the principal, were then the only fishers in Europe that attempted to supply foreign nations with fish. By this regulation, a very heavy burden was laid upon their supplying Great Britain.

When the act of navigation was made, though England and Holland were not actually at war, the most violent animosity subsisted between the two nations. It had begun during the government of the long parliament, which first framed this act, and it broke out soon after in the Dutch wars during that of the Protector and of Charles the second. It is not impossible, therefore, that some of the regulations of this famous act may have proceeded from national animosity. They are as wise, however, as if they had all been dictated by the most deliberate wisdom. National animosity at that particular time aimed at the very same object which the most deliberate wisdom would have recommended, the diminution of the naval power of Holland, the only naval power which could endanger the security of England.

The act of navigation is not favourable to foreign commerce or to the growth of that opulence which can arise from it. The interest of a nation in its commercial relations to foreign nations is, like that of a merchant with regard to the different people with whom he deals, to buy as cheap and to sell as dear as possible. But it will be most likely to buy cheap, when by the most perfect freedom of trade it encourages all nations to bring to it the goods which it has occasion to purchase; and, for the same reason, it will be most likely to sell dear, when its markets are thus filled with the greatest number of buyers. The act of navigation, it is true, lays no burden upon foreign ships that come to export the produce of British industry. Even the ancient aliens duty, which used to be paid upon all goods exported as well as imported, has, by several subsequent acts, been taken off from the greater part of the articles of exportation. But if foreigners, either by prohibitions or high duties, are hindered from coming to sell, they cannot always afford to come to buy; because coming without a cargo, they must lose the freight from their own country to Great Britain. By diminishing the number of sellers, therefore, we necessarily diminish that of buyers, and are thus likely not only to buy foreign goods dearer, but to sell our own cheaper, than if there was a more perfect freedom of trade. As defense, however, is of much more importance than opulence, the act of navigation is, perhaps, the wisest of all the commercial regulations of England.

The second case, in which it will generally be advantageous to lay some burden upon foreign for the encouragement of domestic industry, is when some tax is imposed at home upon the produce of the latter. In this case, it seems reasonable that an equal tax should be imposed upon the like produce of the former. This would not give the monopoly of the home-market to domestic industry, not turn towards a particular employment a greater share of the stock and labour of the country, than what would naturally go to it. It would only hinder any part of what would naturally go to it from being turned away by the tax, into a less natural direction, and would leave the competition between foreign and domestic industry, after the tax, as nearly as possible upon the same footing as before it. In Great Britain, when any such tax is laid upon the produce of domestic industry, it is usual at the same time, in order to stop the clamorous complaints of our merchants and manufacturers, that they will be undersold at home, to lay a much heavier duty upon the importation of all foreign goods of the same kind.

This second limitation of the freedom of trade according to some people should, upon some occasions, be extended much farther than to the precise foreign commodities which could come into competition with those which had been taxed at home. When the necessaries of life have been taxed in any country, it becomes proper, they pretend, to tax not only the like necessaries of life imported from other countries, but all sorts of foreign goods which can come into competition with any thing that is the produce of domestic industry. Subsistence, they say, becomes necessarily dearer in consequence of such taxes; and the price of labour must always rise with the price of the labourers' subsistence. Every commodity, therefore, which is the produce of domestic industry, though not immediately taxed itself, becomes dearer in consequence of such taxes, because the labour which produces it becomes so. Such taxes, therefore, are really equivalent, they say, to a tax upon every particular commodity produced at home. In order to put domestic upon the same footing with foreign industry, therefore, it becomes necessary, they think, to lay some duty upon every foreign commodity, equal to this enhancement of the price of the home commodities with which it can come into competition.

Whether taxes upon the necessaries of life, such as those in Great Britain upon soap, salt, leather, candles, etc. necessarily raise the price of labour, and consequently that of all other commodities, I shall consider hereafter, when I come to treat of taxes. Supposing, however, in the mean time, that they have this effect, and they have it undoubtedly, this general enhancement of the price of all commodities, in consequence of that of labour, is a case which differs in the two following respects from that of a particular commodity, of which the price was enhanced by a particular tax immediately imposed upon it.

First, it might always be known with great exactness how far the price of such a commodity could be enhanced by such a tax: but how far the general enhancement of the price of labour might affect that of every different commodity about which labour was employed, could never be known with any tolerable exactness. It would be impossible, therefore, to proportion with any tolerable exactness the tax upon every foreign, to this enhancement of the price of every home commodity.

Secondly, taxes upon the necessaries of life have nearly the same effect upon the circumstances of the people as a poor soil and a bad climate. Provisions are thereby rendered dearer in the same manner as if it required extraordinary labour and expense to raise them. As in the natural scarcity arising from soil and climate, it would be absurd to direct the people in what manner they ought to employ their capitals and industry, so is it likewise in the artificial scarcity arising from such taxes. To be left to accommodate, as well as they could, their industry to their situation, and to find out those employments in which, notwithstanding their unfavourable circumstances, they might have some advantage either in the home or in the foreign market, is what in both cases would evidently be most for their advantage. To lay a new tax upon them, because they are already overburdened with taxes, and because they already pay too dear for the necessaries of life, to make them likewise pay too dear for the greater part of other commodities, is certainly a most absurd way of making amends.

Such taxes, when they have grown up to a certain height, are a curse equal to the barrenness of the earth and the inclemency of the heavens; and yet it is in the richest and most industrious countries that they have been most generally imposed. No other countries could support so great a disorder. As the strongest bodies only can live and enjoy health, under an unwholesome regimen; so the nations only, that in every sort of industry have the greatest natural and acquired advantages, can subsist and prosper under such taxes. Holland is the country in Europe in which they abound most, and which from peculiar circumstances continues to prosper, not by means of them, as has been most absurdly supposed, but in spite of them.

• • •

To expect, indeed, that the freedom of trade should ever be entirely restored in Great Britain, is as absurd as to expect that an Oceana or Utopia should ever be established in it. Not only the prejudices of the public, but what is much more unconquerable, the private interests of many individuals, irresistibly oppose it. Were the officers of the army to oppose with the same zeal and unanimity any reduction in the number of forces, with which master manufacturers set themselves against every law that is likely to increase the number of their rivals in the home-market; were the former to animate their soldiers, in the same manner as the latter inflame their workmen, to attack with violence and outrage the proposers of any such regulation; to attempt to reduce the army would be as dangerous as it has now become to attempt to diminish in any respect the monopoly which our manufacturers have obtained against us. This monopoly has so much increased the number of some particular tribes of them, that, like an overgrown standing army, they have become formidable to the government, and upon many occasions intimidate the legislature. The member of parliament who supports every proposal for strengthening this monopoly is sure to acquire not only the reputation of understanding trade, but great popularity and influence with the order of men whose numbers and wealth render them of great importance. If he opposes them, on the contrary, and still more if he has authority enough to be able to thwart them, neither the most acknowledged probity, nor the highest rank, nor the greatest public services, can protect him from the most infamous abuse and detraction, from personal insults, nor sometimes from real danger, arising from the insolent outrage of furious and disappointed monopolists.

Antoine-Nicolas de Condorcet

The eighteenth century in Europe presents an anomaly, long recognized by historians. Labeled the Age of Reason or the Enlightenment, it nevertheless came to an end with an act of national violence, the French Revolution, and the ascendancy of a "man on a white charger," Napoleon Bonaparte. The life of Marie-Jean-Antoine-Nicolas Caritat, Marquis de Condorcet (1743–1794), reflects in microcosm this anomaly. Born into a noble family, he broke away from the traditional constraints of his class at an early age to embrace the rationalistic intellectual and social ideas that were being championed most forcefully in France by Voltaire and the *philosophes* under the leadership of Denis Diderot, editor of the *Encyclopédie*. Imbued by these ideals, which were sweeping Europe, Condorcet joined in a campaign of agitation for social reforms that culminated in the French Revolution, in which he played an important role. However, as the level of violence rose, he drew back, only to be denounced by his more zealous revolutionary compatriots, tried in absentia, and sentenced to death. He went into hiding for nine months, then attempted to escape from Paris, was captured, and died in his cell under mysterious circumstances, a victim of the revolution he had helped to inspire.

The essay from which the following selection is taken exhibits many of the leading ideas of the Enlightenment, in particular the conviction that history reveals a record of human progress achieved through the application of reason to the natural and social problems facing humankind. After describing nine stages of this progress through history, Condorcet turns at the end of his essay to the future progress of the human mind. How accurate he was in the predictions appearing in the selection is a matter of historical record to us two hundred years later. The essay was never published by Condorcet; rather he left it at his death in the form of a sketch, written while he was hiding from the revolutionary authorities. Something of his state of mind at that time—both his faith in reason and his disillusionment with the course of the revolution—is revealed in the final paragraph.

---

1. What are Condorcet's assumptions about human nature?

2. What does Condorcet think are the goals of human history? To what extent has the modern West adopted those goals? To what extent have these goals been achieved?

The Progress of the Human Mind

Introduction

Man is born with the capacity to receive sensations. In those he receives, he is able to perceive and to distinguish the simple sensations of which they are composed. He can retain, recognize, and combine them. He can preserve or recall them to his memory; he can compare their different combinations; he can ascertain what they have in common and how they differ; lastly, he can attach signs to all these objects to recognize them more easily and to form new combinations from them.

This faculty is developed in him by the action of external objects, that is, by the action of certain complex sensations the constancy of which, even through change, is independent of himself. It is also exercised by communication with other individuals and by all the artificial means which, from the first development of this faculty, men have succeeded in inventing.

Sensations are accompanied by pleasure or pain and man has the further faculty of converting these momentary impressions into lasting feelings of a corresponding nature and of experiencing these feelings either at the sight or recollection of the pleasure or pain of beings like himself. From this faculty, united with that of forming and combining ideas, arise, between him and his fellow creatures, the ties of interest and duty, to which nature has attached the most precious part of our happiness and the most poignant of our sufferings.

If we were to confine our observations to an inquiry into the general facts and laws which the development of these faculties presents to us, in what is common to the different individuals of the human species, our inquiry would be called metaphysics.

But if we consider this development in relation to the individuals who live at the same time in any given place and follow it through from generation to generation, it then exhibits a picture of the progress of the human mind. This progress is subject to the same general laws, observable in the development of our individual faculties, and is the result of that development considered at once in a great number of individuals united in society. The result which every moment presents depends upon that of the preceding moments and has an influence on what the future will bring.

This picture, therefore, is historical; subject to constant change, it is the result of the successive observation of human societies during different stages through which they have passed. It will therefore record the order in which the changes have taken place, explain the influence of every past period upon that which follows it, and thus show, by the changes which the human species has experienced as it ceaselessly renews itself through the immensity of the ages, the course which it has pursued, and the steps which it has taken towards knowledge and happiness. From these observations on what man has been in the past and what he is now we shall be able to find the means of securing and of accelerating the further progress that human nature allows him to hope for.

Such is the aim of the work I have undertaken, the result of which will be to show, from reasoning and from facts, that no bounds have been set to the improvement of the human faculties; that the perfectibility of man is absolutely indefinite; that the progress of this perfectibility, now beyond the control of any power that would stop it, has no other limit than the duration of the globe on which nature has placed us. The course of this progress may no doubt be more or less rapid, but it can never be reversed, at least as long as the earth retains its place in the system of the universe and the laws of this system shall neither produce a general cataclysm on the globe nor cause such changes as will prevent the human race from preserving and exercising its present faculties and finding the same resources.

• • •

The Tenth Stage

THE FUTURE PROGRESS OF THE HUMAN MIND

If man can predict, almost with certainty, those phenomena of which he knows the laws; if, even when he does not know the laws, experience of the past enables him to foresee, with considerable probability, future phenomena, why should we suppose it an impossible undertaking to sketch, with some degree of truth, the future destiny of mankind based on the results of its history? The only foundation of the natural sciences is the principle that the general laws, known or unknown, which regulate the phenomena of the universe are regular and constant and why should this principle, applicable to the other operations of nature, be less true when applied to the development of the intellectual and moral faculties of man? Since beliefs based on experience of similar conditions are the only guide by which the wisest of men govern their conduct, why should the philosopher be prohibited from supporting his conjectures in a similar way as long as he does not give them a greater certainty than is warranted by the number, the consistency, and the accuracy of his actual observations?

Our hopes regarding the future condition of the human species may be stated in three points: the abolition of inequality between nations, the progress of equality within each nation, and the true perfection of man.

Will not every nation one day reach the state of civilization attained by those people who are most enlightened, most free, most exempt from prejudices, as the French, for instance, and the Anglo-Americans? . . . In a word, will not men be continually moving towards that state in which all will possess the knowledge needed to conduct themselves in the ordinary affairs of life by their own reason and to preserve that reason free of prejudice; to understand their rights and exercise them according to their beliefs and their conscience; to be able, by the development of their faculties, to secure the means of providing for their wants; lastly, to reach a state in which folly and wretchedness will be accidents, happening only now and then, and not the habitual lot of a considerable portion of society? . . .

In examining these three questions we shall find the strongest reasons to believe, from past experience, from observation of the progress which the sciences and civilization have hitherto made, and from the analysis of the progress of the human mind and the development of its faculties, that nature has set no limits to the realization of our hopes.

If we survey the existing state of the world, we shall find, in the first place, that in Europe the principles of the French constitution are those of every enlightened mind. We shall see that they are too widely disseminated and too openly professed for tyrants and priests to prevent them from penetrating by degrees into the miserable abodes of their slaves, where they will soon awaken those remnants of good sense and arouse that suppressed indignation which suffering and terror have failed to extinguish completely in the minds of the oppressed.

If we next look at the different nations, we shall observe in each what special obstacles oppose this revolution and what dispositions favor it. We shall find some in which it will be effected, perhaps slowly, by the wisdom of their governments and others in which the governments rendered violent by their resistance, will themselves become involved in its swift and terrible convulsions.

Can we doubt that either the wisdom or the senseless feuds of European nations adding to the slow but certain effects of the progress of their colonies will not soon bring about the independence of the entire new world and that then the European population of these colonies will fail to civilize or remove, even without conquest, those savage nations still occupying these immense tracts of country?

Run through the history of our projects and settlements in Africa or in Asia and you will see how our monopolies, our treachery, our bloody contempt for men of a different color or creed and the proselyting ardor or the intrigues of our priests have destroyed any feelings of respect and goodwill which the superiority of our knowledge and the advantages of our commerce had at first obtained from the inhabitants. But the time is doubtless approaching when, no longer appearing to these people simply as corruptors or tyrants, we shall become to them instruments for their benefit and the generous champions of their freedom from bondage.

• • •

Then the inhabitants of Europe, satisfied with an unrestricted commerce and too enlightened as to their own rights to deny those of others, will respect that independence which they have hitherto flagrantly violated. Then will their settlements—instead of being filled by power-hungry adventurers, who, using their place and privilege, hasten, by plunder and deceit, to amass wealth, in order to purchase honors and titles on their return home—be peopled with industrious men, seeking in those happy climates the ease and comfort lacking in their native country. They will remain there because of their love of liberty, ambition having lost its allurements and those settlements of robbers will then become colonies of citizens, who will plant in Africa and Asia the principles and examples of the freedom, reason, and illumination of Europe. Those monks too, who indoctrinate the natives of the countries in question in the most shameful superstitions and who arouse antagonism by menacing the people with a new tyranny, will be succeeded by men of integrity and benevolence, eager to spread among these people truths useful to their happiness and to inform them of their interests as well as their rights, for the love of truth is also a passion and when it shall have at home no gross prejudices to combat and no degrading errors to dissipate it will naturally extend itself to remote and foreign lands.

• • •

The progress of these people will be less slow and more sure than ours has been because they will borrow from us that illumination which we have had to discover and because for them to acquire the simple truths and infallible methods which we have obtained only after many errors they need only grasp our discoveries and developments as they appear in our writings. If the progress of the Greeks was lost to later nations, it was the result of a lack of communication between peoples; for this we have the tyrannical domination of the Romans to blame. But when mutual needs shall have drawn the ties of all mankind closer; when the most powerful nations shall have established the political principles of equality between societies as between individuals and respect for the independence of weaker states, as well as compassion for ignorance and misery; when the maxims which tend to crush human faculties shall be replaced by those which favor their action and energy will there still be reason to fear that the earth will contain lands devoid of knowledge or that the pride of despotism will be able to raise barriers to truth that cannot quickly be surmounted?

The moment will then arrive in which the sun will observe in its course free nations only, recognizing no other master than reason, in which tyrants and slaves, priests and their stupid or hypocritical instruments will exist only in works of history and on the stage; in which our only concern will be to pity their past victims and dupes, and by the memory of their horrid excesses to keep a vigilant watch so that we may be able instantly to recognize and effectually to stifle by the force of reason the seeds of superstition and tyranny, should they ever attempt to make their appearance upon the earth again.

In tracing the history of societies we have had occasion to remark that there frequently is a considerable difference between the rights which the law allows the citizens of a state and those which they really enjoy, between the equality established by political institutions and that which actually exists between individuals, and that this disproportion was a chief cause of the destruction of liberty in the ancient republics, of the storms which they had to encounter and the weakness that delivered them into the power of foreign tyrants.

These distinctions have three principal causes: inequality of wealth, inequality of condition between the individual whose means of subsistence are hereditary and one whose resources end with his life or rather that part of his life in which he is capable of labor, and lastly, inequality in education.

• • •

Let us compare the actual population with the extent of territory in the enlightened nations of Europe; let us observe the way in which labor and the means of subsistence are distributed in agriculture and industry and we shall see that it will be impossible to maintain these means to the same degree, and therefore to maintain the same level of population if a large number of individuals cease to have their labor, and the small capital necessary to set it at work or to make its profit sufficient to supply their own wants and those of their family. But this labor and the small capital we have mentioned can exist only as long as each head of a family is alive and healthy. Their small fortune is at best an annuity but in reality more precarious than an annuity; as a result there is an important difference between this class of society and the class of men whose income depends either on landed wealth or the interest on capital, which depend little on personal labor and are therefore not subject to similar risks.

Here then is a necessary cause of inequality, of dependence, and even of misery, which ceaselessly threatens the most numerous and active class in our society.

This inequality may, however, be greatly reduced by providing support for anyone who becomes aged taken from his savings, but augmented by the savings of other persons, who, having made a similar addition to a common stock, do not survive so long; in procuring, in the same way, an equal income for women who may lose their husbands or children who may lose their father; lastly, in providing for young men when they reach an age at which they can begin to work for themselves and to start a new family, sufficient capital to allow them to work, derived from those who die before they reach that age. It is to the application of mathematics to the probabilities of life and the investment of money that we owe the idea of these methods, which are already being employed with some success, though they have not been carried far enough or employed widely enough to make them truly beneficial, not merely to a few families, but to the entire society, which would as a result be able to avoid the periodic ruin observable in a number of families, causing recurrent misery and suffering.

•••

The equality in education we can hope to attain, and with which we ought to be satisfied, is that which excludes every kind of dependence, either forced or voluntary. An easy method by which this end may be attained can be found, given the actual state of human knowledge, even for those who can attend school for only a few years and in later life can devote only occasional hours of leisure to study. We might show that, by a careful choice of the subjects to be taught and of teaching methods, the entire population can be instructed in everything necessary for the management of their households, for the transaction of their business, for the free development of their labor and their faculties, for the knowledge, exercise and protection of their rights, for a recognition of their duties and the will to discharge them, for the capacity to judge both their own actions and those of others by their own understanding, for the acquisition of all the noble and delicate feelings that are an honor to humanity, for freeing themselves from a blind dependence on those to whom they may entrust the care of their interests and the security of their rights, for choosing and guarding themselves so as no longer to be the dupes of those popular errors that torment the life of man with superstitious fears and chimerical hopes, for defending themselves against prejudices by the strength of reason alone, and finally for escaping from the delusions of those who would spread snares for their fortune, their health, their freedom of thought and of conscience, under the pretext of enriching, healing, and saving them.

•••

The different causes of equality we have enumerated do not act in isolation; rather they unite, combine, and support each other, and their combined influence leads to stronger, surer, and more constant action. Greater equality of education will lead to greater equality of industry, and hence of wealth, and equality of wealth necessarily contributes to equality of education. Finally, the equality of nations, like that between individuals, has a similar effect.

To sum up, a proper kind of education corrects the natural inequality of men's abilities, instead of strengthening it, just as good laws remedy the natural inequality of the means of subsistence or just as, in societies whose institutions have achieved this equality, liberty, though subject to law, will be more extensive and complete than in the total independence of savage life. Then the social art will have accomplished its end—that of securing and extending to all the enjoyment of the common rights that nature has given to them.

•••

Men cannot become enlightened upon the nature and development of their moral feelings, upon the principles of morality, upon the reasons for conforming their conduct to those principles, and upon their interest, whether as individuals or as members of society, without at the same time improving their moral practice, an advance no less real than that of moral science itself. Is not a mistaken sense of interest the most frequent cause of actions contrary to the general welfare? Is not the violence of our passions the constant result either of habits we have developed through miscalculation or of ignorance about how to resist these passions or to divert, govern, and direct their action?

Is not the practice of reflecting on our conduct, of examining it through reason and conscience, of exercising those humane feelings that blend our happiness with that of others the necessary consequence of a well-conceived study of morality and of a greater equality in the provisions of the social compact? Will not the consciousness of his own dignity, in a man who is free, along with a system of education built on a more profound knowledge of our moral constitution, render common to almost every man those principles of strict and unsullied justice, those habits of an active and enlightened benevolence, of a delicate and generous sensibility, of which nature has planted the seeds in our hearts, whose flowering needs only the benign influence of knowledge and liberty? Just as the mathematical and physical sciences tend to improve the arts that we employ for our most simple wants, so is it not equally a part of the necessary order of nature that the moral and political sciences should have a similar influence on the motives that direct our feelings and actions?

What is the goal of the improvement of laws and public institutions, resulting from the progress of these sciences, but to reconcile, blend, and unite the interest of each individual with the common interest of all? What is the aim of the social art but to surmount the opposition between these two apparently conflicting interests? Will not the constitution and laws of a country be in closest accord with reason and nature whenever the practice of virtue becomes least difficult and the temptations to deviate from her path least numerous and least powerful?

What vicious habit, what practice contrary to good faith, what crime even, can we find that does not have its origin in the legislation, institutions, and prejudices of the country in which we observe this habit, this practice, or this crime to exist?

In short, will not the progress of the useful arts—a result of their being founded on sound theory as well as improved legislation derived from the truths of the political sciences—lead to a well-being and prosperity that will naturally dispose men to humanity, to benevolence, and to justice? Do not all the observations I have made and which I hope to develop further prove that the moral goodness of man, the necessary consequence of his constitution, is, like all his other faculties, capable of indefinite improvement and that nature has linked together in an unbreakable chain truth, happiness, and virtue?

Among the causes of human improvement that are of most importance to the general welfare there must be included the total elimination of the prejudices which have established an inequality of rights between sexes, fatal even to the sex that the inequality favors. We would search in vain to find reasons to justify this prejudice, whether we look to differences of physical organization, of intellect, or of moral sensibility. The inequality of the sexes had its origin solely in the abuse of strength and all attempts which have since been made to excuse it are nothing but vain sophisms.

Further, it can be shown that the elimination of the customs based on this prejudice and of the laws it has dictated would increase the happiness of family life by encouraging the practice of the domestic virtues, on which all the others depend. It would improve education by making it truly general, either because it would include both sexes with greater equality or because it cannot become general, even to men, without the support of the mothers of families. Would not this tribute, even though belated, to equity and good sense put an end to the too-fertile principles of injustice, cruelty, and crime, by overcoming the opposition between the natural inclination of self-interest, most strong and difficult to subdue though it may be, and the interests of mankind or one's duties to society? Would it not produce, what has until now been only a dream, national manners that are mild and pure and are formed, not by proud asceticism or hypocrisy or the fear of shame or religious terrors but by freely contracted habits that are inspired by nature and fortified by reason?

Once people become more enlightened and have recognized their right to dispose of their own life and wealth as they choose, they will gradually come to regard war as the most dreadful of all calamities, the most terrible of all crimes. The first wars that will disappear will be those into which the usurpers of power have in the past forced their subjects, in support of their pretended hereditary rights.

Nations will understand that they cannot become conquerors without losing their freedom, that permanent confederations are their only means of maintaining their independence, and that their goal should be security and not power. Gradually commercial prejudices will die away and a false sense of mercantile interest will lose the terrible power it has had of drenching the earth in blood and of ruining nations under the pretext of enriching them. As the people of different countries gradually are drawn together by the principles of politics and morality, as each, for its own welfare, permits foreigners to share the benefits it derives either from nature or its own industry, all the causes which produce, poison and perpetuate national animosities will disappear one by one, hence will no longer encourage or even arouse the insanity of war.

• • •

All the causes that contribute to the perfection of the human race, all the means we have listed that ensure its progress, must, from their very nature, exercise a continuing, active influence that constantly increases its scope. We have provided the proofs of this and their further development in the work itself will serve only to strengthen them. So we may conclude then that the perfectibility of man is indefinite. Meanwhile we have to this point considered him as possessing only the same natural faculties and the same organization as he has at present. How much greater would be the certainty, how much wider the scope of our hopes, if we could prove that these natural faculties themselves, this very organization, are themselves improvable? This is the last question we shall examine.

The organic perfectibility or deterioration of the classes of vegetables or the species of the animal kingdom can be regarded as one of the general laws of nature. This law applies to the human race as well. It cannot be doubted that the progress of medicine, the availability of more wholesome food and better housing, plus a mode of life that will develop our physical powers by exercise without at the same time impairing them by excess, in general, that the elimination of the two most active causes of deterioration—poverty and misery on the one hand and enormous wealth on the other—will necessarily result in prolonging the length of life and giving people better health and stronger bodies. It is obvious that the practice of medicine will improve and become more efficacious through the progress of reason and the social order and must finally eliminate infectious or contagious diseases, as well as those general illnesses resulting from climate, food, and conditions of labor. Nor would it be difficult to prove that we can have the same hope about almost every other malady, whose causes and cure we can reasonably expect to discover. Would it be absurd then to assume that this improvement of the human species is susceptible of indefinite progress, to suppose that a time must one day come when death will be the effect either of extraordinary accidents or of the slow and gradual decay of the vital powers and that the duration of life—of the time between the birth of man and this decay—will itself have no assignable limit? Certainly man will not become immortal but may not the time between the moment in which he draws his first breath and the common term when, in the natural course of nature, without disease or accident, he draws his last, be necessarily increased?

•••

But are not our physical faculties and the strength, dexterity, and acuteness of our senses included in the qualities whose perfection in the individual may be transmitted? Observation of the different breeds of domestic animals leads us to answer this question affirmatively, a conclusion that is confirmed by direct observation of the human species.

Finally, may we not say the same of the intellectual and moral faculties? May not our parents, who transmit to us the advantages or defects of their constitution and from whom we receive our features and shape, as well as our tendencies to certain physical affections, transmit to us also that part of their constitution on which intellect, intelligence, energy of soul, and moral sensibility depend as well? Is it not probable that education, by perfecting these qualities, will at the same time influence, modify, and perfect this organization itself? Analogy, investigation of the human faculties, and certain facts all appear to substantiate these conjectures and thus to enlarge the boundary of our hopes.

These are the questions with which we shall finish the final stage. How admirably does this view of the human race, emancipated from its chains, released from the dominion of chance, as well as from that of the enemies of progress, and advancing with a firm and sure step in the paths of truth, console the philosopher who laments the errors, the flagrant acts of injustice and the crimes with which the earth is still polluted. It is the contemplation of this prospect that rewards him for all his efforts to assist the progress of reason and the defense of liberty. He dares to regard these efforts as part of the eternal chain of human destiny and in this persuasion he finds the true delight of virtue and the pleasure of having performed a lasting service, which no stroke of fate calculated to restore the reign of prejudice and slavery can ever destroy. This contemplation is for him an asylum into which he retires, where the memory of his persecutors cannot follow him. He lives there in imagination, with man restored to his natural rights and dignity; he forgets human greed, fear or envy, which corrupt and torment. Here he truly lives with his peers in an elysium created by reason and embellished by the purest pleasures known to the lover of humanity.

China and Great Britain

From ancient times trade existed between China and the West, particularly over the long "silk road." Besides silk other Chinese products like tea, spices, and porcelain ("china") were greatly prized in Europe and later in America. But the overland route was long and difficult, so increasingly efforts were made to develop trade by sea. Two ports were opened on the south coast of China—Macao by the Portuguese in 1557 and nearby Canton by the British and others in the early eighteenth century. Because these allowed only a limited and restricted trade, European merchants and their governments began to apply pressure to have China opened more widely to them commercially. In their turn, the Chinese, suspicious and disdainful of the West, offered stiff and continuing resistance to any change.

An interesting episode in this long commercial struggle occurred in 1795. The British government decided to use the birthday celebration of the Manchu emperor of China, Ch'ien Lung (1711–1799), as an occasion to further their trading interests. So they dispatched their first ambassador, the Earl of Macartney, to the imperial court at Peking. The earl bore with him lavish birthday gifts but also a list of concessions for the advantage of England and of British merchants that he hoped to wrest from the aging emperor. The selection that follows contains the emperor's response to these English overtures. It is of importance not only because it describes in some detail the projects of the British (as well as of other Westerners) for the development of trade with China but also for the picture it gives of China's conception of its place in the world, that of other nations, and the relative status of the two. This is hardly a picture that Westerners were prepared to accept or even to comprehend and also one of which they lost no time in disabusing the Chinese. The British, rebuffed in their efforts to gain a privileged trading relationship with China, soon turned to illicit endeavors. They began the mass production of opium in India, which was then smuggled into China. This underground trade led eventually to the Opium War in 1839, in which the British were quickly victorious, so gaining the trading concessions that they had earlier sought without success from the Emperor Ch'ien Lung. Other nations soon demanded and got similar concessions, so China ended its virtual economic isolation and became open again to the world.

The second document, the Treaty of Nanking, stipulates the concessions that China made to the British following the Opium War.

1. How does the Emperor Chi'en Lung depict the relationship between China and the European countries?

2. Compare and contrast the relationship between China and Britain with the relationship between Japan and Portugal discussed in a previous section.

Mandate to King George III

You, O King, live beyond the confines of many seas, nevertheless, impelled by your humble desire to partake of the benefits of our civilisation, you have dispatched a mission respectfully bearing your memorial. Your Envoy has crossed the seas and paid his respects at my Court on the anniversary of my birthday. To show your devotion, you have also sent offerings of your country's produce.

I have perused your memorial: the earnest terms in which it is couched reveal a respectful humility on your part, which is highly praiseworthy. In consideration of the fact that your Ambassador and his deputy have come a long way with your memorial and tribute, I have shown them high favour and have allowed them to be introduced into my presence. To manifest my indulgence, I have entertained them at a banquet and made them numerous gifts. I have also caused presents to be forwarded to the Naval Commander and six hundred of his officers and men, although they did not come to Peking, so that they too may share in my all-embracing kindness.

As to your entreaty to send one of your nationals to be accredited to my Celestial Court and to be in control of your country's trade with China, this request is contrary to all usage of my dynasty and cannot possibly be entertained. It is true that Europeans, in the service of the dynasty, have been permitted to live at Peking, but they are compelled to adopt Chinese dress, they are strictly confined to their own precincts and are never permitted to return home. You are presumably familiar with our dynastic regulations. Your proposed Envoy to my Court could not be placed in a position similar to that of European officials in Peking who are forbidden to leave China, nor could he, on the other hand, be allowed liberty of movement and the privilege of corresponding with his own country; so that you would gain nothing by his residence in our midst.

Moreover, our Celestial dynasty possesses vast territories, and tribute missions from the dependencies are provided for by the Department for Tributary States, which ministers to their wants and exercises strict control over their movements. It would be quite impossible to leave them to their

From Backhouse, E., and J. O. P. Bland, *Annals & Memoirs of the Court of Peking.*

own devices. Supposing that your Envoy should come to our Court, his language and national dress differ from that of our people, and there would be no place in which to bestow him. It may be suggested that he might imitate the Europeans permanently resident in Peking and adopt the dress and customs of China, but, it has never been our dynasty's wish to force people to do things unseemly and inconvenient. Besides, supposing I sent an Ambassador to reside in your country, how could you possibly make for him the requisite arrangements? Europe consists of many other nations besides your own: if each and all demanded to be represented at our Court, how could we possibly consent? The thing is utterly impracticable. How can our dynasty alter its whole procedure and system of etiquette, established for more than a century, in order to meet your individual views? If it be said that your object is to exercise control over your country's trade, your nationals have had full liberty to trade at Canton for many a year, and have received the greatest consideration at our hands. Missions have been sent by Portugal and Italy, preferring similar requests. The Throne appreciated their sincerity and loaded them with favours, besides authorising measures to facilitate their trade with China. You are no doubt aware that, when my Canton merchant, Wu Chao-ping, was in debt to the foreign ships, I made the Viceroy advance the monies due, out of the provincial treasury, and ordered him to punish the culprit severely. Why then should foreign nations advance this utterly unreasonable request to be represented at my Court? Peking is nearly two thousand miles from Canton, and at such a distance what possible control could any British representative exercise?

If you assert that your reverence for Our Celestial dynasty fills you with a desire to acquire our civilisation, our ceremonies and code of laws differ so completely from your own that, even if your Envoy were able to acquire the rudiments of our civilisation, you could not possibly transplant our manners and customs to your alien soil. Therefore, however adept the Envoy might become, nothing would be gained thereby.

Surveying the wide world, I have but one aim in view, namely, to maintain a perfect governance and to fulfil the duties of the State: strange and costly objects do not interest me. If I have commanded that the tribute offerings sent by you, O King, are to be accepted, this was solely in consideration for the spirit which prompted you to dispatch them from afar. Our dynasty's majestic virtue has penetrated unto every country under Heaven, and Kings of all nations have offered their costly tribute by land and sea. As your Ambassador can see for himself, we possess all things. I set no value on objects strange or ingenious, and have no use for your country's manufactures. This then is my answer to your request to appoint a representative at my Court, a request contrary to our dynastic usage, which would only result in inconvenience to yourself. I have expounded my wishes in detail and have commanded your tribute Envoys to leave in peace on their homeward journey. It behoves you, O King, to respect my sentiments and to display even greater devotion and loyalty in future, so that, by perpetual submission to our Throne, you may secure peace and prosperity for your country hereafter. Besides making gifts (of which I enclose an inventory) to each member of your Mission, I confer upon you, O King, valuable presents in excess of the number usually bestowed on such occasions, including silks and curios—a list of which is likewise enclosed. Do you reverently receive them and take note of my tender goodwill towards you! A special mandate.

[A further mandate to King George III dealt in detail with the British Ambassador's proposals and the Emperor's reasons for declining them.]

You, O King, from afar have yearned after the blessings of our civilisation, and in your eagerness to come into touch with our converting influence have sent an Embassy across the sea bearing a memorial. I have already taken note of your respectful spirit of submission, have treated your mission with extreme favour and loaded it with gifts, besides issuing a mandate to you, O King, and honouring you with the bestowal of valuable presents. Thus has my indulgence been manifested.

Yesterday your Ambassador petitioned my Ministers to memorialise me regarding your trade with China, but his proposal is not consistent with our dynastic usage and cannot be entertained. Hitherto, all European nations, including your own country's barbarian merchants, have carried on their trade with our Celestial Empire at Canton. Such has been the procedure for many years, although our Celestial Empire possesses all things in prolific abundance and lacks no product within its own borders. There was therefore no need to import the manufactures of outside barbarians in exchange for our own produce. But as the tea, silk and porcelain which the Celestial Empire produces, are absolute necessities to European nations and to yourselves, we have permitted, as a signal mark of favour, that foreign *hongs* should be established at Canton, so that your wants might be supplied and your country thus participate in our beneficence. But your Ambassador has now put forward new requests which completely fail to recognise the Throne's principle to 'treat strangers from afar with indulgence,' and to exercise a pacifying control over barbarian tribes, the world over. Moreover, our dynasty, swaying the myriad races of the globe, extends the same benevolence towards all. Your England is not the only nation trading at Canton. If other nations, following your bad example, wrongfully importune my ear with further impossible requests, how will it be possible for me to treat them with easy indulgence? Nevertheless, I do not forget the lonely remoteness of your island, cut off from the world by intervening wastes of sea, nor do I overlook your excusable ignorance of the usages of our Celestial Empire. I have consequently commanded my Ministers to enlighten your Ambassador on the subject, and have ordered the departure of the mission. But I have doubts that, after your Envoy's return he may fail to acquaint you with my view in detail or that he may be lacking in lucidity, so that I shall now proceed to take your requests *seriatim* and to issue my mandate on each question separately. In this way you will, I trust, comprehend my meaning.

(1)   Your Ambassador requests facilities for ships of your nation to call at Ningpo, Chusan, Tientsin and other places for purposes of trade. Until now trade with European nations has always been conducted at Aomen, where the foreign *hongs* are established to store and sell foreign merchandise. Your nation has obediently complied with this regulation for years past without raising any objection. In none of the other ports named have *hongs* been established, so that even if your vessels were to proceed thither, they would have no means of disposing of their cargoes. Furthermore, no interpreters are available, so you would have no means of explaining your wants, and nothing but general inconvenience would result. For the future, as in the past, I decree that your request is refused and that the trade shall be limited to Aomen.

(2)   The request that your merchants may establish a repository in the capital of my Empire for the storing and sale of your produce, in accordance with the precedent granted to Russia, is even more impracticable than the last. My capital is the hub and centre about which all quarters of the globe revolve. Its ordinances are most august and its laws are strict in the extreme. The subjects of our dependencies have never been allowed to open places of business in Peking. Foreign trade has hitherto been conducted at Aomen, because it is conveniently near to the sea, and therefore an important gathering place for the ships of all nations sailing to and fro. If warehouses were established in Peking, the remoteness of your country, lying far to the north-west of my capital, would render transport extremely difficult Before Kiakhta was opened, the Russians were permitted to trade at Peking, but the accommodation furnished to them was only temporary. As soon as Kiakhta was available, they were compelled to withdraw from Peking, which has been closed to their trade these many years. Their frontier trade at Kiakhta is on all fours with your trade at Aomen. Possessing facilities at the latter place, you now ask for further privileges at Peking, although our dynasty observes the severest restrictions respecting the admission of foreigners within its boundaries, and has never permitted the subjects of dependencies to cross the Empire's barriers and settle at will amongst the Chinese people. This request is also refused.

(3)   Your request for a small island near Chusan, where your merchants may reside and goods be warehoused, arises from your desire to develop trade. As there are neither foreign *hongs* nor interpreters in or near Chusan, where none of your ships have ever called, such an island would be utterly useless for your purposes. Every inch of the territory of our Empire is marked on the map and the strictest vigilance is exercised over it all: even tiny islets and farlying sand-banks are clearly defined as part of the provinces to which they belong. Consider, moreover, that England is not the only barbarian land which wishes to establish relations with our civilisation and trade with our Empire: supposing that other nations were all to imitate your evil example and beseech me to present them each and all with a site

for trading purposes, how could I possibly comply? This also is a flagrant infringement of the usage of my Empire and cannot possibly be entertained.

(4)   The next request, for a small site in the vicinity of Canton city, where your barbarian merchants may lodge or, alternatively, that there be no longer any restrictions over their movements at Aomen, has arisen from the following causes. Hitherto, the barbarian merchants of Europe have had a definite locality assigned to them at Aomen for residence and trade, and have been forbidden to encroach an inch beyond the limits assigned to that locality. Barbarian merchants having business with the *hongs* have never been allowed to enter the city of Canton; by these measures, disputes between Chinese and barbarians are prevented, and a firm barrier is raised between my subjects and those of other nations. The present request is quite contrary to precedent; furthermore, European nations have been trading with Canton for a number of years and, as they make large profits, the number of traders is constantly increasing. How would it be possible to grant such a site to each country? The merchants of the foreign *hongs* are responsible to the local officials for the proceedings of barbarian merchants and they carry out periodical inspections. If these restrictions were withdrawn, friction would inevitably occur between the Chinese and your barbarian subjects, and the results would militate against the benevolent regard that I feel towards you. From every point of view, therefore, it is best that the regulations now in force should continue unchanged.

(5)   Regarding your request for remission or reduction of duties on merchandise discharged by your British barbarian merchants at Aomen and distributed throughout the interior, there is a regular tariff in force for barbarian merchants' goods, which applies equally to all European nations. It would be as wrong to increase the duty imposed on your nation's merchandise on the ground that the bulk of foreign trade is in your hands, as to make an exception in your case in the shape of specially reduced duties. In future, duties shall be levied equitably without discrimination between your nation and any other, and, in order to manifest my regard, your barbarian merchants shall continue to be shown every consideration at Aomen.

(6)   As to your request that your ships shall pay the duties leviable by tariff, there are regular rules in force at the Canton Custom house respecting the amounts payable, and since I have refused your request to be allowed to trade at other ports, this duty will naturally continue to be paid at Canton as heretofore.

(7)   Regarding your nation's worship of the Lord of Heaven, it is the same religion as that of other European nations. Ever since the beginning of history, sage Emperors and wise rulers have bestowed on China a moral system and inculcated a code, which from time immemorial has been religiously observed by the myriads of my subjects. There has been no hankering after heterodox doctrines. Even the European (missionary) officials in my capital are forbidden to hold intercourse with Chinese subjects; they are restricted within the limits of their appointed residences, and may not go about

propagating their religion. The distinction between Chinese and barbarian is most strict, and your Ambassador's request that barbarians shall be given full liberty to disseminate their religion is utterly unreasonable.

It may be, O King, that the above proposals have been wantonly made by your Ambassador on his own responsibility, or peradventure you yourself are ignorant of our dynastic regulations and had no intention of transgressing them when you expressed these wild ideas and hopes. I have ever shown the greatest condescension to the tribute missions of all States which sincerely yearn after the blessings of civilisation, so as to manifest my kindly indulgence. I have even gone out of my way to grant any requests which were in any way consistent with Chinese usage. Above all, upon you, who live in a remote and inaccessible region, far across the spaces of ocean, but who have shown your submissive loyalty by sending this tribute mission, I have heaped benefits far in excess of those accorded to other nations. But the demands presented by your Embassy are not only a contravention of dynastic tradition, but would be utterly unproductive of good result to yourself, besides being quite impracticable. I have accordingly stated the facts to you in detail, and it is your bounden duty reverently to appreciate my feelings and to obey these instructions henceforward for all time, so that you may enjoy the blessings of perpetual peace. If, after the receipt of this explicit decree, you lightly give ear to the representations of your subordinates and allow your barbarian merchants to proceed to Chêkiang and Tientsin, with the object of landing and trading there, the ordinances of my Celestial Empire are strict in the extreme, and the local officials, both civil and military, are bound reverently to obey the law of the land. Should your vessels touch the shore, your merchants will assuredly never be permitted to land or to reside there, but will be subject to instant expulsion. In that event your barbarian merchants will have had a long journey for nothing. Do not say that you were not warned in due time! Tremblingly obey and show no negligence! A special mandate!

The Treaty of Nanking: Treaty of Peace, Friendship, Commerce, Indemnity, etc., between Great Britain and China, August 29, 1842

Her Majesty the Queen of the United Kingdom of Great Britain and Ireland, and His Majesty the Emperor of China, being desirous of putting an end to the misunderstandings and consequent hostilities which have arisen between the two countries, have resolved to conclude a Treaty for that purpose, and have therefore named as their Plenipotentiaries, that is to say:—

Her Majesty the Queen of Great Britain and Ireland, Sir Henry Pottinger, Bart, a Major-General in the service of the East India Company, &c.;

And His Imperial Majesty the Emperor of China, the High Commissioners Keying, a Member of the Imperial House, a guardian of the Crown Prince, and General of the garrison of Canton; and Elepoo, of the Imperial Kindred, graciously permitted to wear the insignia of the first rank, and the distinction of a peacock's feather, lately Minister and Governor-General, &c., and now Lieutenant-General Commanding at Chapoo.

Who, after having communicated to each other their respective full powers, and found them to be in good and due form, have agreed upon and concluded the following Articles:—

Article I.

PEACE AND FRIENDSHIP. PROTECTION OF PERSONS AND PROPERTY.

There shall henceforward be peace and friendship between Her Majesty the Queen of the United Kingdom of Great Britain and Ireland and His Majesty the Emperor of China, and between their respective subjects, who shall enjoy full security and protection for their persons and property within the dominions of the other.

Article II.

CANTON, AMOY, FOOCHOW, NINGPO, AND SHANGHAI OPENED TO BRITISH SUBJECTS AND THEIR TRADE.

His Majesty the Emperor of China agrees, that British subjects, with their families and establishments, shall be allowed to reside, for the purpose of carrying on their mercantile pursuits, without molestation or restraint, at the cities and towns of Canton, Amoy, Foochowfoo, Ningpo, and Shanghai.

APPOINTMENT OF BRITISH SUPERINTENDENTS OR CONSULS AT THOSE PLACES; THEIR DUTIES.

And Her Majesty the Queen of Great Britain, &c., will appoint Superintendents or Consular Officers to reside at each of the above named cities or towns to be the medium of communication between the Chinese authorities and the said merchants, and to see that the just duties and other dues of the Chinese Government, as hereafter provided for, are duly discharged by Her Britannic Majesty's subjects.

Article III.

CESSION OF HONG KONG TO GREAT BRITAIN.

It being obviously necessary and desirable that British subjects should have some port at which they may careen and refit their ships, when required, and keep stores for that purpose, His Majesty the Emperor of China cedes to Her Majesty the Queen of Great Britain, &c., the Island of Hong Kong. to be possessed in perpetuity by Her Britannic Majesty, her heirs and successors, and to be governed by such laws and regulations as Her Majesty the Queen of Great Britain, &c., shall see fit to direct.

Article IV.

INDEMNITY. PAYMENT BY CHINA OF 6,000,000 DOLLARS FOR VALUE OF OPIUM DELIVERED UP AS A RANSOM FOR BRITISH SUBJECTS.

The Emperor of China agrees to pay the sum of 6,000,000 dollars, as the value of the Opium which was delivered up at Canton in the month of March, 1839, as a ransom for the lives of Her Britannic Majesty's Superintendent and subjects, who had been imprisoned and threatend with death by the Chinese High Officers.

Article V.

ABOLITION OF PRIVILEGES OF HONG MERCHANTS AT PORTS OF RESIDENCE OF BRITISH MERCHANTS. PAYMENT BY CHINA OF 3,000,000 DOLLARS FOR DEBTS DUE TO BRITISH SUBJECTS BY CERTAIN HONG MERCHANTS.

The Government of China having compelled the British merchants trading at Canton to deal exclusively with certain Chinese merchants, called Hong merchants (or Co-Hong), who had been licensed by the Chinese Government for that purpose, the Emperor of China agrees to abolish that practice in future at all ports where British merchants may reside, and to permit them to carry on their mercantile transactions with whatever persons they please: and His Imperial Majesty further agrees to pay to the British Government the sum of 3,000,000 dollars, on account of debts due to British subjects by some of the Hong merchants or Co-Hong, who have become insolvent, and who owe very large sums of money to subjects of Her Britannic Majesty.

Article VI.

INDEMNITY. PAYMENT BY CHINA OF 12,000,000 DOLLARS FOR EXPENSES OF BRITISH EXPEDITION TO DEMAND REDRESS. DEDUCTION OF RANSOM RECEIVED BY BRITISH FORCES FOR CHINESE TOWNS.

The Government of Her Britannic Majesty having been obliged to send out an expedition to demand and obtain redress for the violent and unjust proceedings of the Chinese High Authorities towards Her Britannic Majesty's Officers and subjects, the Emperor of China agrees to pay the sum of 12,000,000 dollars. on account of the expenses incurred; and Her Britannic Majesty's Plenipotentiary voluntarily agrees, on behalf of Her Majesty to deduct from the said amount of 12,000,000 dollars, any sums which may have been received by Her Majesty's combined forces, as ransom for cities and towns in China, subsequent to the 1st day of August. 1841.

Article VII.

PERIODS FOR PAYMENT TO BE MADE BY CHINA OF INDEMNITIES OF 21,000,000 DOLLARS.

It is agreed, that the total amount of 21,000,000 dollars, described in the 3 preceding Articles, shall be paid as follows:—
6,000,000 immediately.
6,000,000 in 1843; that is, 3,000,000 on or before the 30th of the month of June, and 3,000,000 on or before the 31st of December.
5,000,000 in 1844; that is, 2,500,000 on or before the 30th day of June, and 2,500,000 on or before the 31st of December.
4,000,000 in 1845; that is, 2,000,000 on or before the 30th of June, and 2,000,000 on or before the 31st of December.

INTEREST ON ARREARS.

And it is further stipulated, that interest, at the rate of 5 per cent, per annum, shall be paid by the Government of China on any portion of the above sums that are not punctually discharged at the periods fixed.

Article VIII.

ALL BRITISH SUBJECTS (EUROPEAN AND INDIAN) CONFINED IN CHINA TO BE RELEASED.

Article IX.

AMNESTY. RELEASE AND INDEMNITY TO CHINESE FORMERLY IN BRITISH EMPLOY.

Article X.

TARIFF TO BE ISSUED OF IMPORT, EXPORT, AND TRANSIT DUTIES.

His Majesty the Emperor of China agrees to establish at all the ports which are, by Article II of this Treaty, to be thrown open for the resort of British merchants, a fair and regular tariff of export and import customs and other dues, which tariff shall be publicly notified and promulgated for general information.

TRANSIT DUTIES ON BRITISH GOODS CONVEYED BY CHINESE INTO THE INTERIOR.

And the Emperor further engages, that when British merchandise shall have once paid at any of the said ports the regulated customs and dues, agreeable to the tariff to be herealter fixed, such merchandise may be conveyed by Chinese merchants to any province or city in the interior of the Empire of China on paying a further amount as transit duties, which shall not exceed   per cent, on the tariff value of such goods.

Article XI.

CORRESPONDENCE BETWEEN BRITISH AND CHINESE AUTHORITIES.

It is agreed that Her Britannic Majesty's Chief High Officer in China shall correspond with the Chinese High Officers, both at the capital and in the provinces, under the term "communication"; the subordinate British Officers and Chinese High Officers in the provinces, under the terms "statement" on the part of the former, and on the part of the latter, "declaration"; and the subordinates of both countries on a footing of perfect equality: merchants and others not holding official situations, and therefore not included in the above, on both sides, to use the term "representation" in all papers addressed to, or intended for the notice of, the respective Governments.

Article XII.

EVACUATION OF NANKING AND GRAND CANAL BY BRITISH FORCES.—KULANGSU AND CHUSAN TO BE HELD BY BRITISH FORCES UNTIL SETTLEMENT OF MONEY PAYMENTS.

On the assent of the Emperor of China to this Treaty being received, and the discharge of the first instalment of money, Her Britannic Majesty's forces will retire from Nanking and the Grand Canal, and will no longer molest or stop the trade of China. The military post at Chinhai will also be withdrawn: but the Islands of Kulangsu, and that of Chusan, will continue to be held by Her Majesty's forces until the money payments, and the arrangements for opening the ports to British merchants, be completed.

ARTICLE XIII.

RATIFICATIONS. PROVISIONS OF TREATY TO TAKE EFFECT IN THE MEANTIME.

The ratification of this Treaty by Her Majesty the Queen of Great Britain, &c., and His Majesty the Emperor of China, shall be exchanged as soon as the great distance which separates England from China will admit; but in the meantime, counterpart copies of it, signed and sealed by the Plenipotentiaries, on behalf of their respective Sovereigns, shall be mutually delivered, and all its provisions and arrangements shall take effect.

Done at Nanking, and signed and sealed by the Plenipotentiaries on board Her Britannic Majesty's ship "Cornwallis," this 29th day of August, 1842; corresponding with the Chinese date, 24th day of the 7th month, in the 22nd year of Taoukwang.

(L.S.) HENRY POTTINGER.
Her Majesty's Plenipotentiary.

Seal of the
Chinese High
Commissioner.

Signature of 3rd Chinese Plenipotentiary.	Signature of 2nd Chinese Plenipotentiary.	Signature of 1st Chinese Plenipotentiary.

Simón Bolívar

From the time of their occupation at the beginning of the sixteenth century, the lands of Latin America remained under the colonial domination of Spain and Portugal for three hundred years. In the wake of the American and French revolutions, however, winds of change began to blow throughout those lands. The chance for freedom came in 1810, following Napoleon's invasion of Spain, during which he deposed its king and put his own puppet on the Spanish throne. Latin America took this event as an opportunity to assert its independence from its European masters; thus began a long struggle that lasted until 1824 when, with the final defeat of the Spanish army in Peru, European domination of the continent came to an end.

The most important figure in the liberation of Latin America was Simón Bolívar (1783–1830). Born in Caracas, Venezuela, to a wealthy, aristocratic family of African-Spanish descent, Bolívar devoted his life to two tasks. The first was to drive the Spanish out of Latin America. (While in Rome during a tour of Europe in 1805 Bolívar had taken the following oath: "I swear before you, I swear by the God of my fathers, I swear by them, I swear upon my honor and by my homeland that I shall not let my arm rest, nor my soul repose until I have broken the chains laid upon us by our Spanish oppressors.") His second goal was to organize and structure the political regimes that would assume power once the Spanish had been driven out. Because of his great contributions to the liberation of Latin America Bolívar was given the title "The Liberator."

During the course of his long struggle against the Spanish, Bolívar was forced several times to flee from Venezuela. On one occasion in 1815 he took refuge on the Caribbean island of Jamaica. While there he received a letter from a local inhabitant, who asked him a number of questions about the current situation in Latin America as well as his expectations about the future. The selection that follows is Bolívar's response. In his letter Bolívar gives considerable information about the history and population of Latin America, the nature of Spanish rule, the course of the struggle for independence, and his own vision of the future development of the South American continent. A political realist, Bolívar concluded that the people of Latin America were not prepared for the kind of democracy that had been established in the United States. A visionary as well, he pictured a future in which the isthmus of Panama, complete with canal, would become the capital of the world.

1.   How does Bolívar describe Spanish imperialism?

2.   What political and cultural effects has Spanish imperialism had on Native Americans?

The Jamaica Letter

Kingston, Jamaica,
September 6, 1815.

My dear Sir:

I hasten to reply to the letter of the 29th ultimo which you had the honor of sending me and which I received with the greatest satisfaction.

Sensible though I am of the interest you desire to take in the fate of my country, and of your commiseration with her for the tortures she has suffered from the time of her discovery until the present at the hands of her destroyers, the Spaniards, I am no less sensible of the obligation which your solicitous inquiries about the principal objects of American policy place upon me. Thus, I find myself in conflict between the desire to reciprocate your confidence, which honors me, and the difficulty of rewarding it, for lack of documents and books and because of my own limited knowledge of a land so vast, so varied, and so little known as the New World.

In my opinion it is impossible to answer the questions that you have so kindly posed. Baron von Humboldt himself, with his encyclopedic theoretical and practical knowledge, could hardly do so properly, because, although some of the facts about America and her development are known, I dare say the better part are shrouded in mystery. Accordingly, only conjectures that are more or less approximate can be made, especially with regard to her future and the true plans of the Americans, inasmuch as our continent has within it potentialities for every facet of development revealed in the history of nations, by reason of its physical characteristics and because of the hazards of war and the uncertainties of politics.

As I feel obligated to give due consideration to your esteemed letter and to the philanthropic intentions prompting it, I am impelled to write you these words, wherein you will certainly not find the brilliant thoughts you seek but rather a candid statement of my ideas.

"Three centuries ago," you say, "began the atrocities committed by the Spaniards on this great hemisphere of Columbus." Our age has rejected these atrocities as mythical, because they appear to be beyond the human capacity for evil. Modern critics would never credit them were it not for the many and

Trans. L. Bertrand.

frequent documents testifying to these horrible truths. The humane Bishop of Chiapas, that apostle of America, Las Casas [1474–1564], has left to posterity a brief description of these horrors, extracted from the trial records in Sevilla relating to the cases brought against the *conquistadores*, and containing the testimony of every respectable person then in the New World, together with the charges [*procesos*], which the tyrants made against each other. All this is attested by the foremost historians of that time. Every impartial person has admitted the zeal, sincerity, and high character of that friend of humanity, who so fervently and so steadfastly denounced to his government and to his contemporaries the most horrible acts of sanguinary frenzy.

With what a feeling of gratitude I read that passage in your letter in which you say to me: "I hope that the success which then followed Spanish arms may now turn in favor of their adversaries, the badly oppressed people of South America." I take this hope as a prediction, if it is justice that determines man's contests. Success will crown our efforts, because the destiny of America has been irrevocably decided; the tie that bound her to Spain has been severed. Only a concept maintained that tie and kept the parts of that immense monarchy together. That which formerly bound them now divides them. The hatred that the Peninsula [Spain] has inspired in us is greater than the ocean between us. It would be easier to have the two continents meet than to reconcile the spirits of the two countries. The habit of obedience; a community of interest, of understanding, of religion; mutual goodwill; a tender regard for the birthplace and good name of our forefathers; in short, all that gave rise to our hopes, came to us from Spain. As a result there was born a principle of affinity that seemed eternal, notwithstanding the misbehavior of our rulers which weakened that sympathy, or, rather, that bond enforced by the domination of their rule. At present the contrary attitude persists: we are threatened with the fear of death, dishonor, and every harm; there is nothing we have not suffered at the hands of that unnatural stepmother—Spain. The veil has been torn asunder. We have already seen the light, and it is not our desire to be thrust back into darkness. The chains have been broken; we have been freed, and now our enemies seek to enslave us anew. For this reason America fights desperately, and seldom has desperation failed to achieve victory.

Because successes have been partial and spasmodic, we must not lose faith. In some regions the Independents triumph, while in others the tyrants have the advantage. What is the end result? Is not the entire New World in motion, armed for defense? We have but to look around us on this hemisphere to witness a simultaneous struggle at every point.

The war-like state of the La Plata River provinces [Argentina] has purged that territory and led their victorious armies to Upper Perú arousing Arequipa and worrying the royalists in Lima. Nearly one million inhabitants there now enjoy liberty.

The territory of Chile, populated by 800,000 souls, is fighting the enemy who is seeking her subjugation; but to no avail, because those who long ago put an end to the conquests of this enemy, the free and indomitable Araucanians, are their neighbors and compatriots. Their sublime example is proof to those fighting in Chile that a people who love independence will eventually achieve it.

The viceroyalty of Perú, whose population approaches a million and a half inhabitants, without doubt suffers the greatest subjection and is obliged to make the most sacrifices for the royal cause; and, although the thought of cooperating with that part of America may be vain, the fact remains that it is not tranquil, nor is it capable of restraining the torrent that threatens most of its provinces.

New Granada [Colombia], which is, so to speak, the heart of America, obeys a general government, save for the territory of Quito which is held only with the greatest difficulty by its enemies, as it is strongly devoted to the country's cause; and the provinces of Panamá and Santa Marta endure, not without suffering, the tyranny of their masters. Two and a half million people inhabit New Granada and are actually defending that territory against the Spanish army under General Morillo, who will probably suffer defeat at the impregnable fortress of Cartagena. But should he take that city, it will be at the price of heavy casualties, and he will then lack sufficient forces to subdue the unrestrained and brave inhabitants of the interior.

With respect to heroic and hapless Venezuela, events there have moved so rapidly and the devastation has been such that it is reduced to frightful desolation and almost absolute indigence, although it was once among the fairest regions that are the pride of America. Its tyrants govern a desert, and they oppress only those unfortunate survivors who, having escaped death, lead a precarious existence. A few women, children, and old men are all that remain. Most of the men have perished rather than be slaves; those who survive continue to fight furiously on the fields and in the inland towns, until they expire or hurl into the sea those who, insatiable in their thirst for blood and crimes, rival those first monsters who wiped out America's primitive race. Nearly a million persons formerly dwelt in Venezuela, and it is no exaggeration to say that one out of four has succumbed either to the land, sword, hunger, plague, flight, or privation, all consequences of the war, save the earthquake.

According to Baron von Humboldt, New Spain, including Guatemala, had 7,800,000 inhabitants in 1808. Since that time, the insurrection, which has shaken virtually all of her provinces, has appreciably reduced that apparently correct figure, for over a million men have perished, as you can see in the report of Mr. Walton, who describes faithfully the bloody crimes committed in that abundant kingdom. There the struggle continues by dint of human and every other type of sacrifice, for the Spaniards spare nothing that might enable them to subdue those who have had the misfortune of being born on this soil, which appears to be destined to flow with the blood of its offspring. In spite of everything, the Mexicans will be free. They have embraced the country's cause, resolved to avenge their forefathers or follow them to the grave. Already they saw with Raynal [French philosopher]: The time has come at last to repay the Spaniards torture for torture and to drown that race of annihilators in its own blood or in the sea.

The islands of Puerto Rico and Cuba, with a combined population of perhaps 700,000 to 800,000 souls, are the most tranquil possessions of the Spaniards, because they are not within range of contact with the Independents. But are not the people of those islands Americans? Are they not maltreated? Do they not desire a better life?

This picture represents, on a military map, an area of 2,000 longitudinal and 900 latitudinal leagues at its greatest point, wherein 16,000,000 Americans either defend their rights or suffer repression at the hands of Spain, which, although once the world's greatest empire, is now too weak, with what little is left her, to rule the new hemisphere or even to maintain herself in the old. And shall Europe, the civilized, the merchant, the lover of liberty allow an aged serpent, bent only on satisfying its venomous rage, devour the fairest part of our globe? What! Is Europe deaf to the clamor of her own interests? Has she no eyes to see justice? Has she grown so hardened as to become insensible? The more I ponder these questions, the more I am confused. I am led to think that America's disappearance is desired; but this is impossible because all Europe is not Spain. What madness for our enemy to hope to reconquer America when she has no navy, no funds, and almost no soldiers! Those troops which she has are scarcely adequate to keep her own people in a state of forced obedience and to defend herself from her neighbors. On the other hand, can that nation carry on the exclusive commerce of one-half the world when it lacks manufactures, agricultural products, crafts and sciences, and even a policy? Assume that this mad venture were successful, and further assume that pacification ensued, would not the sons of the Americans of today, together with the sons of the European *reconquistadores* twenty years hence, conceive the same patriotic designs that are now being fought for?

Europe could do Spain a service by dissuading her from her rash obstinacy, thereby at least sparing her the costs she is incurring and the blood she is expending. And if she will fix her attention on her own precincts she can build her prosperity and power upon more solid foundations than doubtful conquests, precarious commerce, and forceful exactions from remote and powerful peoples. Europe herself, as a matter of common sense policy, should have prepared and executed the project of American independence, not alone because the world balance of power so necessitated, but also because this is the legitimate and certain means through which Europe can acquire overseas commercial establishments. A Europe which is not moved by the violent passions of vengeance, ambition, and greed, as is Spain, would seem to be entitled, by all the rules of equity, to make clear to Spain where her best interests lie.

All of the writers who have treated this matter agree on this point. Consequently, we have had reason to hope that the civilized nations would hasten to our aid in order that we might achieve that which must prove to be advantageous to both hemispheres. How vain has been this hope! Not only the Europeans but even our brothers of the North [United States] have been apathetic bystanders in this struggle which, by its very essence, is the most just, and in its consequences the most noble and vital of any which have been raised in ancient or in modern times. Indeed, can the far-reaching effects of freedom for the hemisphere which Columbus discovered ever be calculated?

"The criminal action of Bonaparte," you say, "in seizing Charles IV and Ferdinand VII, the monarchs of that nation which three centuries ago treacherously imprisoned two rulers of South America, is a most evident sign of divine retribution, and, at the same time, positive proof that God espouses the just cause of the Americans and will grant them independence."

•••

"These several months," you add, "I have given much thought to the situation in America and to her hopes for the future. I have a great interest in her development, but I lack adequate information respecting her present state and the aspirations of her people. I greatly desire to know about the politics of each province, also its peoples, and whether they desire a republic or a monarchy; or whether they seek to form one unified republic or a single monarchy? If you could supply me with this information or suggest the sources I might consult, I should deem it a very special favor."

Generous souls always interest themselves in the fate of a people who strive to recover the rights to which the Creator and Nature have entitled them, and one must indeed be wedded to error and passion not to harbor this noble sentiment. You have given thought to my country and are concerned in its behalf, and for your kindness I am warmly grateful.

I have listed the population, which is based on more or less exact data, but which a thousand circumstances render deceiving. This inacuracy cannot easily be remedied, because most of the inhabitants live in rural areas and are often nomadic; they are farmers, herders, and migrants, lost amidst thick giant forests, solitary plains, and isolated by lakes and mighty streams. Who is capable of compiling complete statistics of a land like this? Moreover, the tribute paid by the Indians, the punishments of the slaves, the first fruits of the harvest [*primicias*], tithes [*diezmas*], and taxes levied on farmers, and other impositions have driven the poor Americans from their homes. This is not to mention the war of extermination that has already taken a toll of nearly an eighth part of the population and frightened another large part away. All in all, the difficulties are insuperable, and the tally is likely to show only half the true count.

It is even more difficult to foresee the future fate of the New World, to set down its political principles, or to prophesy what manner of government it will adopt. Every conjecture relative to America's future is, I feel, pure speculation. When mankind was in its infancy, steeped in uncertainty, ignorance, and error, was it possible to foresee what system it would adopt for its preservation? Who could venture to say that a certain nation would be a republic or a monarchy; this nation great, that nation small? To my way of thinking, such is our own situation. We are a young people. We inhabit a world apart, separated by broad seas. We are young in the ways of almost all the arts and sciences, although, in a certain manner, we are old in the ways of civilized society. I look upon the present state of America as similar to that of Rome after its fall. Each part of Rome adopted a political system conforming to its interest and situation or was led by the individual ambitions of certain chiefs, dynasties, or associations. But this important difference exists: those dispersed parts later reestablished their ancient nations, subject to the changes imposed by circumstances or events. But we scarcely retain a vestige of what once was; we are, moreover, neither Indian nor European, but a species midway between the legitimate proprietors of this country and the Spanish usurpers. In short, though Americans by birth we derive our rights from Europe, and we have to assert, these rights against the rights of the natives, and at the same time we must defend ourselves against the invaders. This places us in a most extraordinary and involved situation. Notwithstanding that it is a type of divination to predict the result of the political course which America is pursuing, I shall venture some conjectures which, of course, are colored by my enthusiasm and dictated by rational desires rather than by reasoned calculations.

The role of the inhabitants of the American hemisphere has for centuries been purely passive. Politically they were non-existent. We are still in a position lower than slavery, and therefore it is more difficult for us to rise to the enjoyment of freedom. Permit me these transgressions in order to establish the issue. States are slaves because of either the nature or the misuse of their constitutions; a people is therefore enslaved when the government, by its nature or its vices, infringes on and usurps the rights of the citizen or subject. Applying these principles, we find that America was denied not only its freedom but even an active and effective tyranny. Let me explain. Under absolutism there are no recognized limits to the exercise of governmental powers. The will of the great sultan, khan, bey, and other despotic rulers is the supreme law, carried out more or less arbitrarily by the lesser pashas, khans, and satraps of Turkey and Persia, who have an organized system of oppression in which inferiors participate according to the authority vested in them. To them is entrusted the administration of civil, military, political, religious, and tax matters. But, after all is said and done, the rulers of Ispahan are Persians; the viziers of the Grand Turk are Turks; and the sultans of Tartary are Tartars. China does not bring its military leaders and scholars from the land of Genghis Khan, her conqueror, notwithstanding that the Chinese of today are the lineal descendants of those who were reduced to subjection by the ancestors of the present-day Tartars.

How different is our situation! We have been harassed by a conduct which has not only deprived us of our rights but has kept us in a sort of permanent infancy with regard to public affairs. If we could at least have managed our domestic affairs and our internal administration, we could have acquainted ourselves with the processes and mechanics of public affairs. We should also have enjoyed a personal consideration, thereby commanding a certain unconscious respect from the people, which is so necessary to preserve amidst revolutions. That is why I say we have even been deprived of an active tyranny, since we have not been permitted to exercise its functions.

Americans today, and perhaps to a greater extent than ever before, who live within the Spanish system occupy a position in society no better than that of serfs destined for labor, or at best they have no more status than that of mere consumers. Yet even this status is surrounded with galling restrictions, such as being forbidden to grow European crops, or to store products which are royal monopolies, or to establish factories of a type the Peninsula itself does not possess. To this add the exclusive trading privileges, even in articles of prime necessity, and the barriers between American provinces, designed to prevent all exchange of trade, traffic, and understanding. In short, do you wish to know what our future held?—simply the cultivation of the fields of indigo, grain, coffee, sugar cane, cacao, and cotton; cattle raising on the broad plains; hunting wild game in the jungles; digging in the earth to mine its gold—but even these limitations could never satisfy the greed of Spain.

So negative was our existence that I can find nothing comparable in any other civilized society, examine as I may the entire history of time and the politics of all nations. Is it not an outrage and a violation of human rights to expect a land so splendidly endowed, so vast, rich, and populous, to remain merely passive?

As I have just explained, we were cut off and, as it were, removed from the world in relation to the science of government and administration of the state. We were never viceroys or governors, save in the rarest of instances; seldom archbishops and bishops; diplomats never; as military men, only subordinates; as nobles, without royal privileges. In brief, we were neither magistrates nor financiers and seldom merchants—all in flagrant contradiction to our institutions.

Emperor Charles V made a pact with the discoverers, conquerors, and settlers of America, and this, as Guerra puts it, is our social contract. The monarchs of Spain made a solemn agreement with them, to be carried out on their own account and at their own risk, expressly prohibiting them from drawing on the royal treasury. In return, they were made the lords of the land, entitled to organize the public administration and act as the court of last appeal, together with many other exemptions and privileges that are too numerous to mention. The King committed himself never to alienate the American provinces, inasmuch as he had no jurisdiction but that of sovereign domain. Thus, for themselves and their descendants, the *conquistadors* possessed what were tantamount to feudal holdings. Yet there are explicit laws respecting employment in civil, ecclesiastical, and tax-raising establishments. These laws favor, almost exclusively, the natives of the country who are of Spanish extraction. Thus, by an outright violation of the laws and the existing agreements, those born in America have been despoiled of their constitutional rights as embodied in the code.

• • •

The Americans have risen rapidly without previous knowledge of, and, what is more regrettable, without previous experience in public affairs, to enact upon the world stage the eminent roles of legislator, magistrate, minister of the treasury, diplomat, general, and every position of authority, supreme or subordinate, that comprises the hierarchy of a fully organized state.

When the French invasion, stopped only by the walls of Cádiz, routed the fragile governments of the Peninsula, we were left orphans. Prior to that invasion, we had been left to the mercy of a foreign usurper. Thereafter, the justice due us was dangled before our eyes, raising hopes that only came to nought. Finally, uncertain of our destiny, and facing anarchy for want of a legitimate, just, and liberal government, we threw ourselves headlong into the chaos of revolution. Attention was first given to obtaining domestic security against enemies within our midst, and then it was extended to the procuring of external security. Authorities were set up to replace those we had deposed, empowered to direct the course of our revolution and to take full advantage of the fortunate turn of events; thus we were able to found a constitutional government worthy of our century and adequate to our situation.

The first steps of all the new governments are marked by the establishment of *juntas* of the people. These *juntas* speedily draft rules for the calling of congresses, which produce great changes. Venezuela erected a democratic and federal government, after declaring for the rights of man. A system of checks and balances was established, and general laws were passed granting civil liberties, such as freedom of the press and others. In short, an independent government was created. New Granada uniformly followed the political institutions and reforms introduced by Venezuela, taking as the fundamental basis of her constitution the most elaborate federal system ever to be brought into existence. Recently the powers of the chief executive have been increased, and he has been given all the powers that are properly his. I understand that Buenos Aires and Chile have followed this same line of procedure, but, as the distance is so great and documents are so few and the news reports so unreliable, I shall not attempt even briefly to sketch their progress.

Events in Mexico have been too varied, confused, swift, and unhappy
to follow clearly the course of that revolution. We lack, moreover, the necessary documentary information to enable us to form a judgment. The
Independents of Mexico, according to our information, began their insurrection in September, 1810, and a year later they erected a central government
in Zitacuaro, where a national *junta* was installed under the auspices of
Ferdinand VII [of Spain], in whose name the government was carried on.
The events of the war caused this *junta* to move from place to place; and,
having undergone such modifications as events have determined, it may still
be in existence.

It is reported that a generalissimo or dictator [*sic*] has been appointed
and that he is the illustrious General Morelos, though others mention the
celebrated General Rayón. It is certain that one or both of these two great
men exercise the supreme authority in that country. And recently a constitution has been created as a framework of government. In March, 1812, the
government, then residing in Zultepec, submitted a plan for peace and war
to the Viceroy of Mexico that had been conceived with the utmost wisdom.
It acclaimed the law of nations and established principles that are true and
beyond question. The *junta* proposed that the war be fought as between
brothers and countrymen; that it need not be more cruel than a war between
foreign nations; that the rules of nations and of war, held inviolable even by
infidels and barbarians, must be more binding upon Christians, who are,
moreover, subject to one sovereign and to the same laws; that prisoners not
be treated as guilty of *lèse majesté*, nor those surrendering arms slain, but
rather held as hostages for exchange; and that peaceful towns not be put to
fire and sword. The *junta* concluded its proposal by warning that if this plan
were not accepted rigorous reprisal would be taken. This proposal was
received with scorn: no reply was made to the national *junta*. The original
communications were publicly burned in the plaza in Mexico City by the
executioner, and the Spaniards have continued the war of extermination
with their accustomed fury; meanwhile, the Mexicans and the other
American nations have refrained from instituting a war to the death respecting Spanish prisoners. Here it can be seen that as a matter of expediency an
appearance of allegiance to the King and even to the Constitution of the
monarchy has been maintained. The national *junta*, it appears, is absolute in
the exercise of the legislative, executive, and judicial powers, and its membership is very limited.

Events in Costa Firme have proved that institutions which are wholly
representative are not suited to our character, customs, and present knowledge. In Caracas party spirit arose in the societies, assemblies, and popular
elections; these parties led us back into slavery. Thus, while Venezuela has
been the American republic with the most advanced political institutions,
she has also been the clearest example of the inefficacy of the democratic and
federal system for our new-born states. In New Granada, the large number

of excess powers held by the provincial governments and the lack of centralization in the general government have reduced that fair country to her present state. For this reason her foes, though weak, have been able to hold out against all odds. As long as our countrymen do not acquire the abilities and political virtues that distinguish our brothers of the north, wholly popular systems, far from working to our advantage, will, I greatly fear, bring about our downfall. Unfortunately, these traits, to the degree in which they are required, do not appear to be within our reach. On the contrary, we are dominated by the vices that one learns under the rule of a nation like Spain, which has only distinguished itself in ferocity, ambition, vindictiveness, and greed.

It is harder, Montesquieu has written, to release a nation from servitude than to enslave a free nation. This truth is proven by the annals of all times, which reveal that most free nations have been put under the yoke, but very few enslaved nations have recovered their liberty. Despite the convictions of history, South Americans have made efforts to obtain liberal, even perfect, institutions, doubtless out of that instinct to aspire to the greatest possible happiness, which, common to all men, is bound to follow in civil societies founded on the principles of justice, liberty, and equality. But are we capable of maintaining in proper balance the difficult charge of a republic? Is it conceivable that a newly emancipated people can soar to the heights of liberty, and, unlike Icarus, neither have its wings melt nor fall into an abyss? Such a marvel is inconceivable and without precedent. There is no reasonable probability to bolster our hopes.

More than anyone, I desire to see America fashioned into the greatest nation in the world, greatest not so much by virtue of her area and wealth as by her freedom and glory. Although I seek perfection for the government of my country, I cannot persuade myself that the New World can, at the moment, be organized as a great republic. Since it is impossible, I dare not desire it; yet much less do I desire to have all America a monarchy because this plan is not only impracticable but also impossible. Wrongs now existing could not be righted, and our emancipation would be fruitless. The American states need the care of paternal governments to heal the sores and wounds of despotism and war. The parent country, for example, might be Mexico, the only country fitted for the position by her intrinsic strength, and without such power there can be no parent country. Let us assume it were to be the Isthmus of Panamá, the most central point of this vast continent. Would not all parts continue in their lethargy and even in their present disorder? For a single government to infuse life into the New World; to put into use all the resources for public prosperity; to improve, educate, and perfect the New World, that government would have to possess the authority of a god, much less the knowledge and virtues of mankind.

The party spirit that today keeps our states in constant agitation would assume still greater proportions were a central power established, for that power—the only force capable for checking this agitation—would be else-where. Furthermore, the chief figures of the capitals would not tolerate the preponderance of leaders at the metropolis, for they would regard these leaders as so many tyrants. Their resentments would attain such heights that they would compare the latter to the hated Spaniards. Any such monarchy would be a misshapen colossus that would collapse of its own weight at the slightest disturbance.

Mr. de Pradt [French writer] has wisely divided America into fifteen or seventeen mutually independent states, governed by as many monarchs. I am in agreement on the first suggestion, as America can well tolerate sev-enteen nations; as to the second, though it could easily be achieved, it would serve no purpose. Consequently, I do not favor American monarchies. My reasons are these: The well-understood interest of a republic is limited to the matter of its preservation, prosperity, and glory. Republicans, because they do not desire powers which represent a directly contrary viewpoint, have no reason for expanding the boundaries of their nation to the detriment of their own resources, solely for the purpose of having their neighbors share a lib-eral constitution. They would not acquire rights or secure any advantage by conquering their neighbors, unless they were to make them colonies, con-quered territory, or allies, after the example of Rome. But such thought and action are directly contrary to the principles of justice which characterize republican systems; and, what is more, they are in direct opposition to the interests of their citizens, because a state, too large of itself or together with its dependencies, ultimately falls into decay. Its free government becomes a tyranny. The principles that should preserve the government are disre-garded, and finally it degenerates into despotism. The distinctive feature of small republics is permanence: that of large republics varies, but always with a tendency toward empire. Almost all small republics have had long lives. Among the larger republics, only Rome lasted for several centuries, for its capital was a republic. The rest of her dominions were governed by divers laws and institutions.

The policy of a king is very different. His constant desire is to increase his possessions, wealth, and authority; and with justification, for his power grows with every acquisition, both with respect to his neighbors and his own vassals, who fear him because his power is as formidable as his empire, which he maintains by war and conquest. For these reasons I think that the Americans, being anxious for peace, science, art, commerce, and agricul-ture, would prefer republics to kingdoms. And, further, it seems to me that these desires conform with the aims of Europe.

We know little about the opinions prevailing in Buenos Aires, Chile, and Perú. Judging by what seeps through and by conjecture, Buenos Aires will have a central government in which the military, as a result of its inter-nal dissensions and external wars, will have the upper hand. Such a consti-tutional system will necessarily degenerate into an oligarchy or a monocracy, with a variety of restrictions the exact nature of which no one can now fore-see. It would be unfortunate if this situation were to follow because the people there deserve a more glorious destiny.

The Kingdom of Chile is destined, by the nature of its location, by the simple and virtuous character of its people, and by the example of its neigh-bors, the proud republicans of Arauco, to enjoy the blessings that flow from the just and gentle laws of a republic. If any American republic is to have a long life, I am inclined to believe it will be Chile. There the spirit of liberty has never been extinguished; the vices of Europe and Asia arrived too late or not at all to corrupt the customs of that distant corner of the world. Its area is limited; and, as it is remote from other peoples, it will always remain free from contamination. Chile will not alter her laws, ways, and practices. She will preserve her uniform political and religious views. In a word, it is possible for Chile to be free.

Perú on the contrary, contains two factors that clash with every just and liberal principle: gold and slaves. The former corrupts everything; the latter are themselves corrupt. The soul of a serf can seldom really appreciate true freedom. Either he loses his head in uprisings or his self-respect in chains. Although these remarks would be applicable to all America, I believe that they apply with greater justice to Lima, for the reasons I have given and because of the cooperation she has rendered her masters against her own brothers, those illustrious sons of Quito, Chile, and Buenos Aires. It is plain that he who aspires to obtain liberty will at least attempt to secure it. I imag-ine that in Lima the rich will not tolerate democracy, nor will the freed slaves and *pardos* accept aristocracy. The former will prefer the tyranny of a single man, to avoid the tumult of rebellion and to provide, at least, a peaceful sys-tem. If Perú intends to recover her independence, she has much to do.

From the foregoing, we can draw these conclusions: The American provinces are fighting for their freedom, and they will ultimately succeed. Some provinces as a matter of course will form federal and some central republics; the larger areas will inevitably establish monarchies, some of which will fare so badly that they will disintegrate in either present or future revolutions. To consolidate a great monarchy will be no easy task, but it will be utterly impossible to consolidate a great republic.

It is a grandiose idea to think of consolidating the New World into a single nation, united by pacts into a single bond. It is reasoned that, as these parts have a common origin, language, customs, and religion, they ought to have a single government to permit the newly formed states to unite in a confederation. But this is not possible. Actually, America is separated by cli-matic differences, geographic diversity, conflicting interests, and dissimilar characteristics. How beautiful it would be if the Isthmus of Panamá could be for us what the Isthmus of Corinth was for the Greeks! Would to God that some day we may have the good fortune to convene there an august assem-bly of representatives of republics, kingdoms, and empires to deliberate upon the high interests of peace and war with the nations of the other three-quarters of the globe. This type of organization may come to pass in some happier period of our regeneration. But any other plan, such as that of Abbé St. Pierre, who in laudable delirium conceived the idea of assembling a European congress to decide the fate and interests of those nations, would be meaningless.

Among the popular and representative systems, I do not favor the federal system. It is over-perfect, and it demands political virtues and talents far superior to our own. For the same reason I reject a monarchy that is part aristocracy and part democracy, although with such a government England has achieved much fortune and splendor. Since it is not possible for us to select the most perfect and complete form of government, let us avoid falling into demagogic anarchy or monocratic tyranny. These opposite extremes would only wreck us on similar reefs of misfortune and dishonor; hence, we must seek a mean between them. I say: Do not adopt the best system of government, but the one that is most likely to succeed.

By the nature of their geographic location, wealth, population, and character, I expect that the Mexicans, at the outset, intend to establish a representative republic in which the executive will have great powers. These will be concentrated in one person, who, if he discharges his duties with wisdom and justice, should almost certainly maintain his authority for life. If through incompetence or violence he should excite a popular revolt and it should be successful, this same executive power would then, perhaps, be distributed among the members of an assembly. If the dominant party is military or aristocratic, it will probably demand a monarchy that would be limited and constitutional at the outset, and would later inevitably degenerate into an absolute monarchy; for it must be admitted that there is nothing more difficult in the political world than the maintenance of a limited monarchy. Moreover, it must also be agreed that only a people as patriotic as the English are capable of controlling the authority of a king and of sustaining the spirit of liberty under the rule of sceptre and crown.

The states of the Isthmus of Panamá as far as Guatemala, will perhaps form a confederation. Because of their magnificent position between two mighty oceans, they may in time become the emporium of the world. Their canals will shorten distances throughout the world, strengthen commercial ties between Europe, America, and Asia, and bring to that happy area tribute from the four quarters of the globe. There some day, perhaps, the capital of the world may be located—reminiscent of the Emperor Constantine's claim that Byzantium was the capital of the ancient world.

New Granada will unite with Venezuela, if they can agree to the establishment of a central republic. Their capital may be Maracaibo or a new city to be named Las Casas (in honor of that humane hero) to be built on the borders of the two countries, in the excellent port area of Bahía-Honda. This location, though little known, is the most advantageous in all respects. It is readily accessible, and its situation is so strategic that it can be made impregnable. It has a fine, healthful climate, a soil as suitable for agriculture as for cattle raising, and a superabundance of good timber. The Indians living there can be civilized, and our territorial possessions could be increased with the acquisition of the Goajira Peninsula. This nation should be called Colombia as a just and grateful tribute to the discoverer of our hemisphere. Its government might follow the English pattern, except that in place of a king there will be an executive who will be elected, at most, for life, but his office will never be hereditary, if a republic is desired. There will be a hereditary legislative chamber or senate. This body can interpose itself between the violent demands of the people and the great powers of the government during periods of political unrest. The second representative body will be a legislature with restrictions no greater than those of the lower house in England. The Constitution will draw on all systems of government, but I do not want it to partake of all their vices. As Colombia is my country, I have an indisputable right to desire for her that form of government which, in my opinion, is best. It is very possible that New Granada may not care to recognize a central government, because she is greatly addicted to federalism; in such event, she will form a separate state which, if it endures, may prosper, because of its great and varied resources.

"Great and beneficial changes," you say, "can frequently be brought about through the efforts of individuals." The South Americans have a tradition to this effect: When Quetzalcoatl, the Hermes or Buddha of South America, gave up his ministry and left his people, he promised them he would return at an ordained time to reestablish his government and revive their prosperity. Does not this tradition foster a conviction that he may shortly reappear? Can you imagine the result if an individual were to appear among these people, bearing the features of Quetzalcoatl, their Buddha of the forest, or those of Mercury, of whom other nations have spoken? Do you suppose that this would affect all regions of America? Is it not unity alone that is needed to enable them to expel the Spaniards, their troops, and the supporters of corrupt Spain and to establish in these regions a powerful empire with a free government and benevolent laws?

Like you, I believe that the specific actions of individuals can produce general results, especially in revolutions. But is that hero, that great prophet or God of Anáhuac, Quetzalcoatl, capable of effecting the prodigious changes that you propose? This esteemed figure is not well known, if at all, by the Mexican people: such is the fate of the defeated, even if they be gods. Historians and writers, it is true, have undertaken a careful investigation of his origin, the truth or falsity of his doctrine, his prophesies, and the account of his departure from Mexico. Whether he was an apostle of Christ or a pagan is openly debated. Some would associate his name with St. Thomas; others, with the Feathered Serpent; while still others say he is the famous prophet of Yucatán, Chilan-Cambal. In a word, most Mexican authors, polemicists, and secular historians have discussed, at greater or lesser length, the question of the true character of Quetzalcoatl. The fact is, according to the historian, Father Acosta, that he established a religion which, in its rites, dogmas, and mysteries, bore a remarkable similarity to the religion of Jesus, the faith that it probably most resembles. Nevertheless, many Catholic writers have tried to dismiss the idea that he was a true prophet, and they refuse to associate him with St. Thomas, as other celebrated writers have done. The general opinion is that Quetzalcoatl was a divine lawgiver among the pagan peoples of Anáhuac; that their great Montezuma was his lieutenant, deriving his power from that divinity. Hence it may be inferred that our Mexicans would not follow the pagan Quetzalcoatl, however ingratiating the guise in which he might appear, for they profess the most intolerant and exclusive of all religions.

Happily, the leaders of the Mexican independence movement have made use of this fanaticism to excellent purpose by proclaiming the famous Virgin of Guadalupe the Queen of the Patriots, invoking her name in all difficult situations and placing her image on their banners. As a result, political enthusiasms have been commingled with religion, thus producing an intense devotion to the sacred cause of liberty. The veneration of this image in Mexico is greater than the exaltation that the most sagacious prophet could inspire.

Surely unity is what we need to complete our work of regeneration. The division among us, nevertheless, is nothing extraordinary, for it is characteristic of civil wars to form two parties, *conservatives* and *reformers*. The former are commonly the more numerous, because the weight of habit induces obedience to established powers; the latter are always fewer in number although more vocal and learned. Thus, the physical mass of the one is counterbalanced by the moral force of the other; the contest is prolonged, and the results are uncertain. Fortunately, in our case, the mass has followed the learned.

I shall tell you with what we must provide ourselves in order to expel the Spaniards and to found a free government. It is *union*, obviously; but such union will come about through sensible planning and well-directed actions rather than by divine magic. America stands together because it is abandoned by all other nations. It is isolated in the center of the world. It has no diplomatic relations, nor does it receive any military assistance; instead, America is attacked by Spain, which has more military supplies than any we can possibly acquire through furtive means.

When success is not assured, when the state is weak, and when results are distantly seen, all men hesitate; opinion is divided, passions rage, and the enemy fans these passions in order to win an easy victory because of them. As soon as we are strong and under the guidance of a liberal nation which will lend us her protection, we will achieve accord in cultivating the virtues and talents that lead to glory. Then will we march majestically toward that great prosperity for which South America is destined. Then will those sciences and arts which, born in the East, have enlightened Europe, wing their way to a free Colombia, which will cordially bid them welcome.

Such, Sir, are the thoughts and observations that I have the honor to submit to you, so that you may accept or reject them according to their merit. I beg you to understand that I have expounded them because I do not wish to appear discourteous and not because I consider myself competent to enlighten you concerning these matters.

Simón Bolívar

Child Labor

By the early nineteenth century, the Industrial Revolution had spread from England and was beginning to transform Europe from a rural to an urban society. In England, this transformation often depressed the living standards of workers beneath even those of the cottage manufacturing system of an earlier era. In doing so, however, it paved the way for its own reform, for it bared to the public eye in an aggravated form conditions that had long existed but had passed relatively unnoticed. Poverty and misery could be overlooked as long as the workers remained scattered about the countryside, but once they were congregated in the hideous slums of the Midlands industrial centers, their plight became too obvious to remain unheeded. Consequently, social reform became the order of the day.

Among the most prominent of the English reformers was the seventh Earl of Shaftesbury (1801–1885), who concentrated on working conditions in the factories. At Shaftesbury's instigation, another reformer, Michael Sadler, introduced a bill in Parliament in 1831 designed to regulate the working conditions of children in textile mills. The bill was referred to a committee, with Sadler as chairman. The selection that follows is an excerpt from the evidence presented before that committee. The committee's recommendations resulted in the Factory Act of 1833, which limited the working hours of children and set up a system of inspection to insure that its regulations would be carried out.

The Sadler Report requires no comment; it speaks for itself. The selection included here was picked almost at random from a bulky volume of testimony provided by hundreds of witnesses. Although these witnesses were presumably selected with some care, their accounts provide a generally accurate picture of the conditions of many factory workers, children in particular, in early-nineteenth-century England.

1. Summarize conditions in the factories.

2. What effect did factory work have on other aspects of the worker's lives?

The Sadler Report

Veneris, 18° Die Maii, 1832

MICHAEL THOMAS SADLER, ESQUIRE, IN THE CHAIR

MR. MATTHEW CRABTREE, *called in; and Examined.*

What age are you?_____Twenty-two.

What is your occupation?_____A blanket manufacturer.

Have you ever been employed in a factory?_____Yes.

At what age did you first go to work in one?_____Eight.

How long did you continue in that occupation?_____Four years.

Will you state the hours of labour at the period when you first went to the factory, in ordinary times?_____ From 6 in the morning to 8 at night.

Fourteen hours?_____Yes.

With what intervals for refreshment and rest?_____An hour at noon.

Then you had no resting time allowed in which to take your breakfast, or what is in Yorkshire called your "drinking"?_____No.

When trade was brisk what were your hours?_____From 5 in the morning to 9 in the evening.

Sixteen hours?_____Yes.

With what intervals at dinner?_____An hour.

How far did you live from the mill?_____About two miles.

Was there any time allowed for you to get your breakfast in the mill?_____No.

Did you take it before you left your home?_____Generally.

During those long hours of labour could you be punctual; how did you awake?_____I seldom did awake spontaneously; I was most generally awoke or lifted out of bed, sometimes asleep, by my parents.

Were you always in time?_____ No.

What was the consequence if you had been too late?_____I was most commonly beaten.

Severely?_____Very severely, I thought.

In whose factory was this? Messrs_____Hague & Cook's, of Dewsbury.

Will you state the effect that those long hours had upon the state of your health and feelings?_____I was, when working those long hours, commonly very much fatigued at night, when I left my work; so much so that I sometimes should have slept as I walked if I had not stumbled and started awake again; and so sick often that I could not eat, and what I did eat I vomited.

The Sadler Report: Report from the Committee on the Bill to Regulate the Labour of Children in the Mills and Factories of the United Kingdom (London: House of Commons, 1832).

Did this labour destroy your appetite?_____It did.

In what situation were you in that mill?_____I was a piecener.

Will you state to this Committee whether piecening is a very laborious employment for children, or not?_____It is a very laborious employment. Pieceners are continually running to and fro, and on their feet the whole day.

The duty of the piecener is to take the cardings from one part of the machinery, and to place them on another?_____Yes.

So that the labour is not only continual, but it is unabated to the last?_____It is unabated to the last.

Do you not think, from your own experience, that the speed of the machinery is so calculated as to demand the utmost exertions of a child supposing the hours were moderate?_____It is as much as they could do at the best; they are always upon the stretch, and it is commonly very difficult to keep up with their work.

State the condition of the children toward the latter part of the day, who have thus to keep up with the machinery._____It is as much as they do when they are not very much fatigued to keep up with their work, and toward the close of the day, when they come to be more fatigued, they cannot keep up with it very well, and the consequence is that they are beaten to spur them on.

Were you beaten under those circumstances?_____Yes.

Frequently?_____Very frequently.

And principally at the latter end of the day?_____Yes.

And is it your belief that if you had not been so beaten, you should not have got through the work?_____ I should not if I had not been kept up to it by some means.

Does beating then principally occur at the latter end of the day, when the children are exceedingly fatigued?_____It does at the latter end of the day, and in the morning sometimes, when they are very drowsy, and have not got rid of the fatigue of the day before.

What were you beaten with principally?_____A strap.

Anything else?_____Yes, a stick sometimes; and there is a kind of roller which runs on the top of the machine called a billy, perhaps two or three yards in length, and perhaps an inch and a half or more in diameter; the circumference would be four or five inches; I cannot speak exactly.

Were you beaten with that instrument?_____Yes.

Have you yourself been beaten, and have you seen other children struck severely with that roller?_____I have been struck very severely with it myself, so much so as to knock me down, and I have seen other children have their heads broken with it.

You think that it is a general practice to beat the children with the roller?_____It is.

You do not think then that you were worse treated than other children in the mill?_____No, I was not, perhaps not so bad as some were.

In those mills is chastisement towards the latter part of the day going on perpetually?_____Perpetually.

So that you can hardly be in a mill without hearing constant crying?_____Never an hour, I believe.

Do you think that if the overlooker were naturally a humane person it would be still found necessary for him to beat the children, in order to keep up their attention and vigilance at the termination of those extraordinary days of labour?_____Yes, the machine turns off a regular quantity of cardings, and of course they must keep as regularly to their work the whole of the day; they must keep with the machine, and therefore however humane the slubber may be, as he must keep up with the machine or be found fault with, he spurs the children to keep up also by various means but that which he commonly resorts to is to strap them when they become drowsy.

At the time when you were beaten for not keeping up with your work, were you anxious to have done it if you possibly could?_____Yes; the dread of being beaten if we could not keep up with our work was a sufficient impulse to keep us to it if we could.

When you got home at night after this labour, did you feel much fatigued?_____Very much so.

Had you any time to be with your parents, and to receive instruction from them?_____No.

What did you do?_____All that we did when we got home was to get the little bit of supper that was provided for us and go to bed immediately. If the supper had not been ready directly, we should have gone to sleep while it was preparing.

Did you not, as a child, feel it a very grievous hardship to be roused so soon in the morning?_____I did.

Were the rest of the children similarly circumstanced?_____Yes, all of them; but they were not all of them so far from their work as I was.

And if you had been too late you were under the apprehension of being cruelly beaten?_____I generally was beaten when I happened to be too late; and when I got up in the morning the apprehension of that was so great, that I used to run, and cry all the way as I went to the mill.

That was the way by which your punctual attendance was secured?_____Yes.

And you do not think it could have been secured by any other means?_____No.

Then it is your impression from what you have seen, and from your own experience, that those long hours of labour have the effect of rendering young persons who are subject to them exceedingly unhappy?_____Yes.

You have already said it had a considerable effect upon your health?_____Yes.

Do you conceive that it diminished your growth?_____I did not pay much attention to that; but I have been examined by some persons who said they thought I was rather stunted, and that I should have been taller if I had not worked at the mill.

What were your wages at that time?_____Three shillings [*per week—Ed*].

And how much a day had you for over-work when you were worked so exceedingly long?_____A half-penny a day.

Did you frequently forfeit that if you were not always there to a moment?_____Yes; I most frequently forfeited what was allowed for those long hours.

You took your food to the mill; was it in your mill, as is the case in cotton mills, much spoiled by being laid aside?_____It was very frequently covered by flues from the wool; and in that case they had to be blown off with the mouth, and picked off with the fingers before it could be eaten.

So that not giving you a little leisure for eating your food, but obliging you to take it at the mill, spoiled your food when you did get it?_____Yes, very commonly.

And that at the same time that this over-labour injured your appetite?_____Yes.

Could you eat when you got home?_____Not always.

What is the effect of this piecening upon the hands?_____It makes them bleed; the skin is completely rubbed off, and in that case they bleed in perhaps a dozen parts.

The prominent parts of the hand?_____Yes, all the prominent parts of the hand are rubbed down till they bleed; every day they are rubbed in that way.

All the time you continue at work?_____All the time we are working. The hands never can be hardened in that work, for the grease keeps them soft in the first instance, and long and continual rubbing is always wearing them down, so that if they were hard they would be sure to bleed.

Is it attended with much pain?_____Very much.

Do they allow you to make use of the back of the hand?_____No; the work cannot be so well done with the back of the hand, or I should have made use of that.

Is the work done as well when you are so many hours engaged in it, as it would be if you were at it a less time?_____I believe it is not done so well in those long hours; toward the latter end of the day the children become completely bewildered, and know not what they are doing, so that they spoil their work without knowing.

Then you do not think that the masters gain much by the continuance of the work to so great a length of time?_____I believe not.

Were there girls as well as boys employed in this manner?_____Yes.

Were they more tenderly treated by the overlookers, or were they worked and beaten in the same manner?_____There was no difference in their treatment.

Were they beaten by the overlookers, or by the slubber?_____By the slubber.

But the overlooker must have been perfectly aware of the treatment that the children endured at the mill?_____Yes; and sometimes the overlooker beat them himself; but the man that they wrought under had generally the management of them.

Did he pay them their wages?_____No; their wages were paid by the master.

But the overlooker of the mill was perfectly well aware that they could not have performed the duty exacted from them in the mill without being thus beaten?_____I believe he was.

You seem to say that this beating is absolutely necessary, in order to keep the children up to their work; is it universal throughout all factories?_____I have been in several other factories, and I have witnessed the same cruelty in them all.

Did you say that you were beaten for being too late?_____Yes.

Is it not the custom in many of the factories to impose fines upon children for being too late, instead of beating them?_____It was not in that factory.

What then were the fines by which you lost the money you gained by your long hours?_____The spinner could not get on so fast with his work when we happened to be too late; he could not begin his work so soon, and therefore it was taken by him.

Did the slubber pay you your wages?_____No, the master paid our wages.

And the slubber took your fines from you?_____Yes.

Then you were fined as well as beaten?_____There was nothing deducted from the ordinary scale of wages, but only from that received for over-hours, and I had only that taken when I was too late, so that the fine was not regular.

When you were not working over-hours, were you so often late as when you were working over-hours?_____Yes.

You were not very often late whilst you were not working over-hours?_____Yes, I was often late when I was not working over-hours; I had to go at six o'clock in the morning, and consequently had to get up at five to eat my breakfast and go to the mill, and if I failed to get up by five I was too late; and it was nine o'clock before we could get home, and then we went to bed; in the best times I could not be much above eight hours at home, reckoning dressing and eating my meals, and everything.

Was it a blanket-mill in which you worked?_____Yes.

Did you ever know that the beatings to which you allude inflicted a serious injury upon the children?_____I do not recollect any very serious injury, more than that they had their heads broken, if that may be called a serious injury; that has often happened; I, myself, had no more serious injury than that.

You say that the girls as well as the boys were employed as you have described, and you observed no difference in their treatment?_____ No difference.

The girls were beat in this unmerciful manner?_____They were.

They were subject, of course, to the same bad effects from this overworking?_____Yes.

Could you attend an evening-school during the time you were employed in the mill?_____No, that was completely impossible.

Did you attend the Sunday-school?_____Not very frequently when I work at the mill.

How then were you engaged during the Sunday?_____I very often slept till it was too late for school time or for divine worship, and the rest of the day I spent in walking out and taking a little fresh air.

Did your parents think that it was necessary for you to enjoy a little fresh air?_____I believe they did; they never said anything against it; before I went to the mill I used to go to the Sunday-school.

Did you frequently sleep nearly the whole of the day on Sunday?_____ Very often.

At what age did you leave that employment?_____I was about 12 years old.

Why did you leave that place?_____I went very late one morning, about seven o'clock, and I got severely beaten by the spinner, and he turned me out of the mill, and I went home, and never went any more.

Was your attendance as good as the other children?_____Being at rather a greater distance than some of them, I was generally one of the latest.

Where was your next work?_____I worked as bobbin-winder in another part of the works of the same firm.

How long were you a bobbin-winder?_____About two years, I believe.

What did you become after that?_____A weaver.

How long were you a weaver?_____I was a weaver till March in last year.

A weaver of what?_____A blanket-weaver.

With the same firm?_____With the same firm.

Did you leave them?_____No; I was dismissed from_____my work for a reason which I am willing and anxious to explain.

Have you had opportunities of observing the way in which the children are treated in factories up to a late period?_____Yes.

You conceive that their treatment still remains as you first found it, and that the system is in great want of regulation?_____It does.

Children you still observe to be very much fatigued and injured by the hours of labour?_____Yes.

From your own experience, what is your opinion as to the utmost labour that a child in piecening could safely undergo?_____If I were appealed to from my own feelings to fix a limit, I should fix it at ten hours, or less.

And you attribute to longer hours all the cruelties that you describe?_____A good deal of them.

Are the children sleepy in mills?_____Very.

Are they more liable to accidents in the latter part of the day than in the other part?_____I believe they are; I believe a greater number of accidents happen in the latter part of the day than in any other. I have known them so sleepy that in the short interval while the others have been going out, some of them have fallen asleep, and have been left there.

Is it an uncommon case for children to fall asleep in the mill, and remain there all night?_____Not to remain there all night; but I have known a case the other day, of a child whom the overlooker found when he went to lock the door, that had been left there.

So that you think there has been no change for the better in the treatment of those children; is it your opinion that there will be none, except Parliament interfere in their behalf?_____It is my decided conviction.

Have you recently seen any cruelties in mills?_____Yes; not long since I was in a mill and I saw a girl severely beaten; at a mill called Hicklane Mill, in Batley; I happened to be in at the other end of the room, talking; and I heard the blows, and I looked that way, and saw the spinner beating one of the girls severely with a large stick. Hearing the sound, led me to look round, and to ask what was the matter, and they said it was "Nothing but_____ paying [*beating—Ed.*] 'his ligger-on.'"

What age was the girl?_____About 12 years.

Was she very violently beaten?_____She was.

Was this when she was over-fatigued?_____It was in the afternoon.

Can you speak as to the effect of this labour in the mills and factories on the morals of the children, as far as you have observed?_____As far as I have observed with regard to morals in the mills, there is everything about them that is disgusting to every one conscious of correct morality.

Do you find that the children, the females especially, are very early demoralized in them?_____They are.

Is their language indecent?_____Very indecent; and both sexes take great familiarities with each other in the mills, without at all being ashamed of their conduct.

Do you connect their immorality of language and conduct with their excessive labour?_____It may be somewhat connected with it, for it is to be observed that most of that goes on toward night, when they begin to be drowsy; it is a kind of stimulus which they use to keep them awake; they say some pert thing or other to keep themselves from drowsiness, and it generally happens to be some obscene language.

Have not a considerable number of the females employed in mills illegitimate children very early in life?_____I believe there are; I have known some of them have illegitimate children when they were between 16 and 17 years of age.

How many grown-up females had you in the mill?_____I cannot speak to the exact number that were grown up; perhaps there might be thirty-four or so that worked in the mill at that time.

How many of those had illegitimate children?_____A great many of them; eighteen or nineteen of them, I think.

Did they generally marry the men by whom they had the children?_____No; it sometimes happens that young women have children by married men, and I have known an instance, a few weeks since, where one of the young women had a child by a married man.

Is it your opinion that those who have the charge of mills very often avail themselves of the opportunity they have to debauch the young women?_____No, not generally; most of the improper conduct takes place among the younger part of those that work in the mill.

Do you find that the children and young persons in those mills are moral in other respects, or does their want of education tend to encourage them in a breach of the law?_____I believe it does, for there are very few of them that can know anything about it; few of them can either read or write.

Are criminal offences then very frequent?_____Yes, theft is very common; it is practised a great deal in the mills, stealing their bits of dinner, or something of that sort. Some of them have not so much to eat as they ought to have, and if they can fall in with the dinner of some of their partners they steal it. The first day my brother and I went to the mill we had our dinner stolen, because we were not up to the tricks; we were more careful in future, but still we did not always escape.

Was there any correction going on at the mills for indecent language or improper conduct?_____No, I never knew of any.

From what you have seen and known of those mills, would you prefer that the hours of labour should be so long with larger wages, or that they should be shortened with a diminution of wages?_____If I were working at the mill now, I would rather have less labour and receive a trifle less, than so much labour and receive a trifle more.

Is that the general impression of individuals engaged in mills with whom you are acquainted?_____I believe it is.

What is the impression in the country from which you come with respect to the effect of this Bill upon wages?_____They do not anticipate that it will affect wages at all.

They think it will not lower wages?_____They do.

Do you mean that it will not lower wages by the hour, or that you will receive the same wages per day?_____They anticipate that it may perhaps lower their wages at a certain time of the year when they are working hard, but not at other times, so that they will have their wages more regular.

Does not their wish for this Bill mainly rest upon their anxiety to protect their children from the consequences of this excessive labour, and to have some opportunity of affording them a decent education?_____Yes; such are the wishes of every humane father that I have heard speak about the thing.

Have they not some feeling of having the labour equalized?_____ That is the feeling of some that I have heard speak of it.

Did your parents work in the same factories?_____No.

Were any of the slubbers' children working there?_____Yes.

Under what slubber did you work in that mill?_____Under a person of the name of Thomas Bennett, in the first place; and I was changed from him to another of the name of James Webster.

Did the treatment depend very much upon the slubber under whom you were?_____No, it did not depend directly upon him, for he was obliged to do a certain quantity of work, and therefore to make us keep up with that.

Were the children of the slubbers strapped in the same way?_____ Yes, except that it is very natural for a father to spare his own child.

Did it depend upon the feelings of a slubber toward his children?_____Very little.

Did the slubbers fine their own spinners?_____I believe not.

You said that the piecening was very hard labour; what labour is there besides moving about; have you anything heavy to carry or to lift?_____ We have nothing heavy to carry, but we are kept upon our feet in brisk times from 5 o'clock in the morning to 9 at night.

How soon does the hand get sore in piecening?_____How soon mine became sore I cannot speak to exactly; but they get a little hard on the Sunday, when we are not working, and they will get sore again very soon on the Monday.

Is it always the case in piecening that the hand bleeds, whether you work short or long hours?_____They bleed more when we work more.

Do they always bleed when you are working?_____Yes.

Do you think that the children would not be more competent to this task, and their hands far less hurt, if the hours were fewer every day, especially when their hands had become seasoned to the labour?_____I believe it would have an effect for the longer they are worked the more their hands are worn, and the longer it takes to heal them, and they do not get hard enough after a day's rest to be long without bleeding again; if they were not so much worn down, they might heal sooner, and not bleed so often or so soon.

After a short day's work, have you found your hands hard the next morning?_____They do not bleed much after we have ceased work; they then get hard; they will bleed soon in the morning when in regular work.

Do you think if the work of the children were confined to about ten hours a day, that they would not be able to perform this piecening without making their hands bleed?_____I believe they would.

So that it is your opinion, from your experience, that if the hours were mitigated, their hands would not be so much worn, and would not bleed by the business of piecening?_____Yes.

Do you mean to say that their hands would not bleed at all?_____ I cannot say exactly, for I always wrought long hours, and therefore my hands always did bleed.

Have you any experience of mills where they only work ten hours?_____I have never wrought at such mills, and in most of the mills I have seen their hands bleed.

At a slack time, when you were working only a few hours, did your hands bleed?_____No, they did not for three or four days, after we had been standing still for a week; the mill stood still sometimes for a week together, but when we did work we worked the common number of hours.

Were all the mills in the neighbourhood working the same number of hours in brisk times?_____Yes.

So that if any parent found it necessary to send his children to the mill for the sake of being able to maintain them, and wished to take them from any mill where they were excessively worked, he could not have found any other place where they would have been less worked?_____No, he could not; for myself, I had no desire to change, because I thought I was as well off as I could be at any other mill.

And if the parent, to save his child, had taken him from the mill, and had applied to the parish for relief, would the parish, knowing that he had withdrawn his child from its work, have relieved him?_____No.

So that the long labour which you have described, or actual starvation, was, practically, the only alternative that was presented to the parent under such circumstances?_____It was; they must either work at the mill they were at or some other, and there was no choice in the mills in that respect.

What, in your opinion, would be the effect of limiting the hours of labour upon the happiness, and the health, and the intelligence of the rising generation?_____If the hours are shortened, the children may, perhaps, have a chance of attending some evening-school, and learning to read and write; and those that I know who have been to school and learned to read and write; have much more comfort than those who have not. For myself, I went to a school when I was six years old, and I learned to read and write a little then.

At a free-school?_____Yes, at a free-school in Dewsbury; but I left school when I was six years old. The fact is, that my father was a small manufacturer, and in comfortable circumstances, and he got into debt with Mr. Cook for a wool bill, and as he had no other means of paying him, he came and agreed with my father, that my brother and I should go to work at his mill till that debt was paid; so that the whole of the time that we wrought at the mill we had no wages.

THOMAS BENNETT, *called in; and Examined.*

Where do you reside?_____At Dewsbury.

What is your business?_____A slubber.

What age are you?_____About 48.

Have you had much experience regarding the working of children in factories?_____Yes, about twenty-seven years.

Have you a family?_____Yes, eight children.

Have any of them gone to factories?_____All.

At what age?_____The first went at six years of age.

To whose mill?_____To Mr. Halliley's, to piece for myself.

What hours did you work at that mill?_____We have wrought from 4 to 9, from 4 to 10, and from 5 to 9, and from 5 to 10.

What sort of a mill was it?_____It was a blanket-mill; we sometimes altered the time, according as the days increased and decreased.

What were your regular hours?_____Our regular hours when we were not so throng, was from 6 to 7.

And when you were the throngest, what were your hours then?_____From 5 to 9, and from 5 to 10, and from 4 to 9.

Seventeen hours?_____Yes.

What intervals for meals had the children at that period?_____Two hours; an hour for breakfast, and an hour for dinner.

Did they always allow two hours for meals at Mr. Halliley's?_____ Yes, it was allowed, but the children did not get it, for they had business to do at that time, such as fettling and cleaning the machinery.

But they did not stop in at that time, did they?_____They all had their share of the cleaning and other work to do.

That is, they were cleaning the machinery?_____Cleaning the machinery at the time of dinner.

How long a time together have you known those excessive hours to continue?_____I have wrought so myself very nearly two years together.

Were your children working under you then?_____Yes, two of them.

State the effect upon your children._____Of a morning when they have been so fast asleep that I have had to go up stairs and lift them out of bed, and have heard them crying with the feelings of a parent; I have been much affected by it.

Were not they much fatigued at the termination of such a day's labour as that?_____Yes; many a time I have seen their hands moving while they have been nodding, almost asleep; they have been doing their business almost mechanically.

While they have been almost asleep, they have attempted to work?_____Yes; and they have missed the carding and spoiled the thread, when we have had to beat them for it.

Could they have done their work towards the termination of such a long day's labour, if they had not been chastised to it?_____No.

You do not think that they could have kept awake or up to their work till the seventeenth hour, without being chastised?_____No.

Will you state what effect it had upon your children at the end of their day's work?_____At the end of their day's work, when they have come home, instead of taking their victuals, they have dropped asleep with the victuals in their hands; and sometimes when we have sent them to bed with a little bread or something to eat in their hand, I have found it in their bed the next morning.

Had it affected their health?_____I cannot say much of that; they were very hearty children.

Do you live at a distance from the mill?_____Half a mile.

Did your children feel a difficulty in getting home?_____Yes, I have had to carry the lesser child on my back, and it has been asleep when I got home.

Did these hours of labour fatigue you?_____Yes, they fatigued me to that excess, that in divine worship I have not been able to stand according to order; I have sat to worship.

So that even during the Sunday you have felt fatigue from your labour in the week?_____Yes, we felt it, and always took as much rest as we could.

Were you compelled to beat your own children, in order to make them keep up with the machine?_____Yes, that was forced upon us, or we could not have done the work; I have struck them often, though I felt as a parent.

If the children had not been your own, you would have chastised them still more severely?_____Yes.

What did you beat them with?_____A strap sometimes; and when I have seen my work spoiled, with the roller.

Was the work always worse done at the end of the day?_____That was the greatest danger.

Do you conceive it possible that the children could do their work well at the end of such a day's labour as that?_____No.

Matthew Crabtree, the last Witness examined by this Committee, I think mentioned you as one of the slubbers under whom he worked?_____Yes.

He states that he was chastised and beaten at the mill?_____Yes, I have had to chastise him.

You can confirm then what he has stated as to the length of time he had to work as a child, and the cruel treatment that he received?_____Yes, I have had to chastise him in the evening, and often in the morning for being too late; when I had one out of the three wanting I could not keep up with the machine, and I was getting behindhand compared with what another man was doing; and therefore I should have been called to account on Saturday night if the work was not done.

Was he worse than others? _____ No.

Was it the constant practice to chastise the children? _____ Yes.

It was necessary in order to keep up your work? _____ Yes.

And you would have lost your place if you had not done so? _____ Yes; when I was working at Mr. Wood's mill, at Dewsbury, which at present is burnt down, but where I slubbed for him until it was, while we were taking our meals he used to come up and put the machine agoing; and I used to say, "You do not give us time to eat"; he used to reply, "Chew it at your work"; and I often replied to him, "I have not yet become debased like a brute, I do not chew my cud." Often has that man done that, and then gone below to see if a strap were off, which would have shown if the machinery was not working, and then he would come up again.

Was this at the drinking time? _____ Yes, at breakfast and at drinking.

Was this where the children were working? _____ Yes, my own children and others.

Were your own children obliged to employ most of their time at breakfast and at the drinking in cleansing the machine, and in fettling the spindles? _____ I have seen at that mill, and I have experienced and mentioned it with grief, that the English children were enslaved worse than the Africans. Once when Mr. Wood was saying to the carrier who brought his work in and out, "How long has that horse of mine been at work?" and the carrier told him the time, and he said "Loose him directly, he has been in too long," I made this reply to him, "You have more mercy and pity for your horse than you have for your men."

Did not this beating go on principally at the latter part of the day? _____ Yes.

Was it not also dangerous for the children to move about those mills when they became so drowsy and fatigued? _____ Yes, especially by lamplight.

Do the accidents principally occur at the latter end of those long days of labour? _____ Yes, I believe mostly so.

Do you know of any that have happened? _____ I know of one; it was at Mr. Wood's mill; part of the machinery caught a lass who had been drowsy and asleep, and the strap which ran close by her catched her at about her middle, and bore her to the ceiling, and down she came, and her neck appeared to be broken, and the slubber ran up to her and pulled her neck, and I carried her to the doctor myself.

Did she get well? _____ Yes, she came about again.

What time was that? _____ In the evening.

You say that you have eight children who have gone to the factories? _____ Yes.

There has been no opportunity for you to send them to a day-school? _____ No; one boy had about twelve months' schooling.

Have they gone to Sunday-schools? _____ Yes.

Can any of them write?_____Not one.

They do not teach writing at Sunday-schools?_____No; it is objected to, I believe.

So that none of your children can write?_____No.

What would be the effect of a proper limitation of the hours of labour upon the conduct of the rising generation?_____I believe it would have a very happy effect in regard to correcting their morals; for I believe there is a deal of evil that takes place in one or other in consequence of those long hours.

Is it your opinion that they would then have an opportunity of attending night-schools?_____Yes; I have often regretted, while working those long hours, that I could not get my children there.

Is it your belief that if they were better instructed, they would be happier and better members of society?_____Yes, I believe so.

Karl Marx and Friedrich Engels

According to Lenin, Marxism was derived from three sources: German philosophy, English political economy, and French socialism. The German philosophy was the absolute idealism of G. W. F. Hegel, which Karl Marx had imbibed while a student at the University of Berlin. Central to this philosophy was the notion of *dialectic*, the theory that history is a series of struggles between opposing forces, with each successive struggle occurring on a higher level than the one that preceded it. Hegel viewed the struggles as taking place between opposing ideas embodied in distinct national cultures. But Marx shifted the struggles from the ideational plane to the economic or material plane, and transformed the antagonists from nations to classes. In other words, he replaced Hegel's dialectical idealism with his own dialectical materialism; or, as he put it, he turned the dialectic, which Hegel had stood on its head, back on its feet again.

The English political economy that Lenin referred to consisted of the writings of the classical economists, Adam Smith and David Ricardo, whose labor theory of value provided Marx with the basic assumption underlying his greatest work, *Capital*. But Marx reversed the argument of the classical economists: Where they found in the labor theory of value a defense of capitalism, he found a weapon to attack it.

Finally, in his reference to French socialism Lenin had in mind the works of a group of writers, including Claude Saint-Simon, François Fourier, Pierre Proudhon, and Louis Blanc, whose views on the elimination of capitalism and the establishment of the ideal society greatly influenced Marx—even though later he scornfully brushed their theories aside as "utopian" socialism, while claiming that his own were "scientific."

Although Lenin and most other orthodox Marxists would undoubtedly deny it, Marxism owes a debt to a fourth source. This is a moral tradition, stretching back all the way to Socrates and the Old Testament prophets. Marx, the philosopher, historian, and economist, was above all else a moral reformer. Although he clothed his critique of capitalism in an elaborate intellectual framework, at heart it was a moral protest against the human misery and degradation resulting from early-nineteenth-century industrialism. And though he assiduously repeated that his socialism was scientific, the new era of human happiness that he envisioned in the classless society following the revolution was an ideal as utopian as that of Plato's *Republic*.

The *Communist Manifesto*, one of the greatest revolutionary documents in history, was the joint production of Marx (1818–1883) and his lifelong friend and collaborator Friedrich Engels (1820–1895). Composed in 1848 as a platform for the Communist League, a small organization of radical workmen, it contains in capsule form most of the major Marxist doctrines. The *Manifesto* is reproduced here complete except for Part III, in which the authors criticize other forms of socialism.

1. What do Marx and Engels mean by the terms "bourgeois" and "proleteriat"?

2. How do you think a nineteenth-century factory worker, as described in the last selection, would have responded to the Communist Manifesto? Why?

Manifesto of the Communist Party

A specter is haunting Europe—the specter of Communism. All the powers of Old Europe have entered into a holy alliance to exorcise this specter; Pope and Czar, Metternich and Guizot, French Radicals and German police-spies.

Where is the party in opposition that has not been decried as communistic by its opponents in power? Where is the opposition that has not hurled back the branding reproach of Communism, against the more advanced opposition parties, as well as against its reactionary adversaries?

Two things result from this fact.

I. Communism is already acknowledged by all European powers to be in itself a power.

II. It is high time that Communists should openly, in the face of the whole world, publish their views, their aims, their tendencies, and meet this nursery tale of the specter of Communism with a Manifesto of the party itself.

To this end Communists of various nationalities have assembled in London, and sketched the following Manifesto to be published in the English, French, German, Italian, Flemish, and Danish languages.

Bourgeois and Proletarians[1]

The history of all hitherto existing society is the history of class struggles.

Trans. S. Moore.

[1] By Bourgeoisie is meant the class of modern Capitalists, owners of the means of social production and employers of wage-labor. By proletariat the class of modern wage-laborers who, having no means of production of their own, are reduced to selling their labor-power in order to live.

Freeman and slave, patrician and plebeian, lord and serf, guild-master and journey-man, in a word, oppressor and oppressed, stood in constant opposition to one another, carried on an uninterrupted, now hidden, now open fight, that each time ended, either in a revolutionary reconstitution of society at large, or in the common ruin of the contending classes.

In the earlier epochs of history we find almost everywhere a complicated arrangement of society into various orders, a manifold gradation of social rank. In ancient Rome we have patricians, knights, plebeians, slaves; in the Middle Ages, feudal lords, vassals, guild-masters, journeymen, apprentices, serfs; in almost all of these classes, again, subordinate gradations.

The modern bourgeois society that has sprouted from the ruins of feudal society, has not done away with class antagonisms. It has but established new forms of struggle in place of the old ones.

Our epoch, the epoch of the bourgeoisie, possesses, however, this distinctive feature; it has simplified the class antagonisms. Society as a whole is more and more splitting up into two great hostile camps, into two great classes directly facing each other: Bourgeoisie and Proletariat.

From the serfs of the middle ages sprang the chartered burghers of the earliest towns. From these burgesses the first elements of the bourgeoisie were developed.

The discovery of America, the rounding of the Cape, opened up fresh ground for the rising bourgeoisie. The East-Indian and Chinese markets, the colonization of America, trade with the colonies, the increase in the means of exchange and in commodities generally, gave to commerce, to navigation, to industry, an impulse never before known, and thereby, to the revolutionary element in the tottering feudal society, a rapid development.

The feudal system of industry, under which industrial production was monopolized by closed guilds, now no longer sufficed for the growing wants of the new market. The manufacturing system took its place. The guild-masters were pushed on one side by the manufacturing middle class; division of labor between the different corporate guilds vanished in the face of division of labor in each single workshop.

Meantime the markets kept ever growing, the demand ever rising. Even manufacture no longer sufficed. Thereupon steam and machinery revolutionized industrial production. The place of manufacture was taken by the giant, Modern Industry, the place of the industrial middle class, by industrial millionaires, the leaders of whole industrial armies, the modern bourgeois.

Modern Industry has established the world's market, for which the discovery of America paved the way. This market has given an immense development to commerce, to navigation, to communication by land. This development has, in its turn, reacted on the extension of industry; and in proportion, as industry, commerce, navigation, railways extended, in the same proportion, the bourgeoisie developed, increased its capital, and pushed into the background every class handed down from the Middle Ages.

We see, therefore, how the modern bourgeoisie is itself the product of a long course of development, of a series of revolutions in the modes of production and of exchange.

Each step in the development of the bourgeoisie was accompanied by a corresponding political advance of that class. An oppressed class under the sway of the feudal nobility, an armed and self-governing association in the mediaeval commune, here independent urban republic (as in Italy and Germany), here taxable "third estate" of the monarchy (as in France), afterwards, in the period of manufacture proper, serving either the semi-feudal or the absolute monarchy as a counterpoise against the nobility, and, in fact, cornerstone of the great monarchies in general, the bourgeoisie has at last, since the establishment of Modern Industry and of the world's market, conquered for itself, in the modern representative State, exclusive political sway. The executive of the modern State is but a committee for managing the common affairs of the whole bourgeoisie.

The bourgeoisie, historically, has played a most revolutionary part.

The bourgeoisie, wherever it has got the upper hand, has put an end to all feudal, patriarchal, idyllic relations. It has pitilessly torn asunder the motley feudal ties that bound man to his "natural superiors," and has left remaining no other nexus between man and man than naked self-interest, than callous "cash payment." It has drowned the most heavenly ecstasies of religious fervor, of chivalrous enthusiasm, of Philistine sentimentalism, in the icy water of egotistical calculation. It has resolved personal worth into exchange value, and in place of the numberless indefeasible chartered freedoms, has set up that single, unconscionable freedom—Free Trade. In one word, for exploitation, veiled by religious and political illusions, it has substituted naked, shameless; direct, brutal exploitation.

The bourgeoisie has stripped of its halo every occupation hitherto honored and looked up to with reverent awe. It has converted the physician, the lawyer, the priest, the poet, the man of science, into its paid wage-laborers.

The bourgeoisie has torn away from the family its sentimental veil, and has reduced the family relation to a mere money relation.

The bourgeoisie has disclosed how it came to pass that the brutal display of vigor in the Middle Ages, which reactionists so much admire, found its fitting complement in the most slothful indolence. It has been the first to show what man's activity can bring about. It has accomplished wonders far surpassing Egyptian pyramids, Roman aqueducts, and Gothic cathedrals; it has conducted expeditions that put in the shade all former Exoduses of nations and crusades.

The bourgeoisie cannot exist without constantly revolutionizing the instruments of production, and thereby the relations of production, and with them the whole relations of society. Conservation of the old modes of production in unaltered form, was, on the contrary, the first condition of existence for all earlier industrial classes. Constant revolutionizing of production, uninterrupted disturbance of all social conditions, everlasting uncertainty and agitation, distinguish the bourgeois epoch from all earlier ones. All fixed, fast-frozen relations, with their train of ancient and venerable prejudices and opinions, are swept away; all new-formed ones become antiquated before they can ossify. All that is solid melts into air, all that is holy is profaned, and man is at last compelled to face with sober senses his real conditions of life, and his relations with his kind.

The need of a constantly expanding market for its products chases the bourgeoisie over the whole surface of the globe. It must nestle everywhere, settle everywhere, establish connections everywhere.

The bourgeoisie has through its exploitation of the world's market given a cosmopolitan character to production and consumption in every country. To the great chagrin of reactionists, it has drawn from under the feet of industry the national ground on which it stood. All old established national industries have been destroyed or are daily being destroyed. They are dislodged by new industries, whose introduction becomes a life and death question for all civilized nations, by industries that no longer work up indigenous raw material, but raw material drawn from the remotest zones, industries whose products are consumed, not only at home, but in every quarter of the globe. In place of the old wants, satisfied by the productions of the country, we find new wants, requiring for their satisfaction the products of distant lands and climes. In place of the old local and national seclusion and self-sufficiency we have had intercourse in every direction, universal interdependence of nations. And as in material, so also in intellectual production. The intellectual creations of individual nations become common property. National onesidedness and narrow-mindedness become more and more impossible, and from the numerous national and local literatures, there arises a world-literature.

The bourgeoisie, by the rapid improvement of all instruments of production, by the immensely facilitated means of communication, draws all, even the most barbarian, nations into civilization. The cheap prices of its commodities are the heavy artillery with which it batters down all Chinese walls, with which it forces the barbarians' intensely obstinate hatred of foreigners to capitulate. It compels all nations, on pain of extinction, to adopt the bourgeois mode of production; it compels them to introduce what it calls civilization into their midst, i.e., to become bourgeois themselves. In one word, it creates a world after its own image.

The bourgeoisie has subjected the country to the rule of the towns. It has created enormous cities, has greatly increased the urban population as compared with the rural, and has thus rescued a considerable part of the population from the idiocy of rural life. Just as it has made the country dependent on the towns, so it has made barbarian and semibarbarian countries dependent on the civilized ones, nations of peasants on nations of bourgeois, the East on the West.

The bourgeoisie keeps more and more doing away with the scattered state of the population, of the means of production, and of property. It has agglomerated population, centralized means of production, and has concentrated property in a few hands. The necessary consequence of this was political centralization. Independent, or but loosely connected provinces, with separate interests, laws, governments, and systems of taxation, became lumped together into one nation, with one government, one code of laws, one national class interest, one frontier, and one customs tariff.

The bourgeoisie, during its rule of scarce one hundred years, has created more massive and more colossal productive forces than have all preceding generations together. Subjection of Nature's forces to man, machinery, application of chemistry to industry and agriculture, steam-navigation, railways, electric telegraphs, clearing of whole continents for cultivation, canalization of rivers, whole populations conjured out of the ground—what earlier century had even a presentiment that such productive forces slumbered in the lap of social labor?

We see then: the means of production and of exchange on whose foundation the bourgeoisie built itself up, were generated in feudal society. At a certain stage in the development of these means of production and of exchange, the conditions under which feudal society produced and exchanged, the feudal organization of agriculture and manufacturing industry, in one word, the feudal relations of property, became no longer compatible with the already developed productive forces; they became so many fetters. They had to be burst asunder; they were burst asunder.

Into their places stepped free competition, accompanied by a social and political constitution adapted to it, and by the economical and political sway of the bourgeois class.

A similar movement is going on before our own eyes. Modern bourgeois society with its relations of production, of exchange, and of property, a society that has conjured up such gigantic means of production and of exchange, is like the sorcerer, who is no longer able to control the powers of the nether world whom he has called up by his spells. For many a decade past the history of industry and commerce is but the history of the revolt of modern productive forces against modern conditions of production, against the property relations that are the conditions for the existence of the bourgeoisie and of its rule. It is enough to mention the commercial crises that by their periodical return put on its trial, each time more threateningly, the existence of the bourgeois society. In these crises a great part not only of the existing products, but also of the previously created productive forces, is periodically destroyed. In these crises there breaks out an epidemic that, in all earlier epochs, would have seemed an absurdity—the epidemic of over-production. Society suddenly finds itself put back into a state of momentary barbarism; it appears as if a famine, a universal war of devastation, had cut off the supply of every means of subsistence; industry and commerce seem to be destroyed; and why? because there is too much civilization, too much means of subsistence, too much industry, too much commerce. The productive forces at the disposal of society no longer tend to further the development of the conditions of bourgeois property; on the contrary, they have become too powerful for these conditions, by which they are fettered, and as soon as they overcome these fetters, they bring disorder into the whole of bourgeois society, endanger the existence of bourgeois property. The conditions of bourgeois society are too narrow to comprise the wealth created by them. And how does the bourgeoisie get over these crises? On the one hand by enforced destruction of a mass of productive forces; on the other, by the conquest of new markets, and by the more thorough exploitation of the old ones. That is to say, by paving the way for more extensive and more destructive crises, and by diminishing the means whereby crises are prevented.

The weapons with which the bourgeoisie felled feudalism to the ground are now turned against the bourgeoisie itself.

But not only has the bourgeoisie forged the weapons that bring death to itself; it has also called into existence the men who are to wield those weapons—the modern working class—the proletarians.

In proportion as the bourgeoisie, *i.e.*, capital, is developed, in the same proportion is the proletariat, the modern working class, developed; a class of laborers, who live only so long as they find work, and who find work only so long as their labor increases capital. These laborers, who must sell themselves piece-meal, are a commodity, like every other article of commerce, and are consequently exposed to all the vicissitudes of competition, to all the fluctuations of the market.

Owing to the extensive use of machinery and to division of labor, the work of the proletarians has lost all individual character, and consequently, all charm for the workman. He becomes an appendage of the machine, and it is only the most simple, most monotonous, and most easily acquired knack, that is required of him. Hence, the cost of production of a workman is restricted almost entirely to the means of subsistence that he requires for his maintenance, and for the propagation of his race. But the price of a commodity, and therefore also of labor, is equal to its cost of production. In proportion, therefore, as the repulsiveness of the work increases, the wage decreases. Nay, more, in proportion as the use of machinery and division of labor increases, in the same proportion the burden of toil also increases, whether by prolongation of the working hours, by increase of the work enacted in a given time, or by increased speed of the machinery, etc.

Modern industry has converted the little workshop of patriarchal master into the great factory of the industrial capitalist. Masses of laborers, crowded into factories, are organized like soldiers. As privates of the industrialized army they are placed under the command of a perfect hierarchy of officers and sergeants. Not only are they the slaves of the bourgeois class, and of the bourgeois State, they are daily and hourly enslaved by the machine, by the over-looker, and, above all, by the individual bourgeois manufacturer himself. The more openly this despotism proclaims gain to be its end and aim, the more petty, the more hateful and the more embittering it is.

The less skill and exertion of strength implied in manual labor, in other words, the more modern industry becomes developed, the more is the labor of men superseded by that of women. Differences of age and sex have no longer any distinctive social validity for the working class. All are instruments of labor, more or less expensive to use, according to age and sex.

No sooner is the exploitation of the laborer by the manufacturer, so far at an end, that he receives his wages in cash, than he is set upon by the other portions of the bourgeoisie, the landlord, the shop-keeper, and pawnbroker, etc.

The lower strata of the middle class—the small tradespeople, shopkeepers, and retired tradesmen generally, the handicraftsmen and peasant—all these sink gradually into the proletariat, partly because their diminutive capital does not suffice for the scale on which modern industry is carried on, and is swamped in the competition with the large capitalists, partly because their specialized skill is rendered worthless by new methods of production. Thus the proletariat is recruited from all classes of the population.

The proletariat goes through various stages of development. With its birth begins its struggle with the bourgeoisie. At first the contest is carried on by individual laborers, then by the workpeople of a factory, then by the operatives of one trade, in one locality, against the individual bourgeois who directly exploits them. They direct their attacks not against the bourgeois conditions of production, but against the instruments of production themselves; they destroy imported wares that compete with their labor, they smash to pieces machinery, they set factories ablaze, they seek to restore by force the vanished status of the workman of the Middle Ages.

At this stage the laborers still form an incoherent mass scattered over the whole country, and broken up by their mutual competition. If anywhere they unite to form more compact bodies, this is not yet the consequence of their own active union, but of the union of the bourgeoisie, which class, in order to attain its own political ends, is compelled to set the whole proletariat in motion, and is moreover yet, for a time, able to do so. At this stage therefore, the proletarians do not fight their enemies, but the enemies of their enemies, the remnants of absolute monarchy, the landowners, the non-industrial bourgeois, the petty bourgeoisie. Thus the whole historical movement is concentrated in the hands of the bourgeoisie; every victory so obtained is a victory for the bourgeoisie.

But with the development of industry the proletariat not only increases in number; it becomes concentrated in greater masses, its strength grows and it feels that strength more. The various interests and conditions of life within the ranks of the proletariat are more and more equalized, in proportion as machinery obliterates all distinctions of labor, and nearly everywhere reduces wages to the same low level. The growing competition among the bourgeois, and the resulting commercial crises, make the wages of the workers even more fluctuating. The unceasing improvement of machinery, ever more rapidly developing, makes their livelihood more and more precarious; the collisions between individual workmen and individual bourgeois take more and more the character of collisions between two classes. Thereupon the workers begin to form combinations (Trades' Unions) against the bourgeois; they club together in order to keep up the rate of wages; they found permanent associations in order to make provision beforehand for these occasional revolts. Here and there the contest breaks out into riots.

Now and then the workers are victorious, but only for a time. The real fruit of their battles lies not in the immediate results but in the ever-improved means of communication that are created by modern industry, and that places the workers of different localities in contact with one another. It was just this contact that was needed to centralize the numerous local struggles, all of the same character, into one national struggle between classes. But every class struggle is a political struggle. And that union, to attain which the burghers of the Middle Ages, with their miserable highways, required centuries, the modern proletarians, thanks to railways, achieve in a few years.

This organization of the proletarians into a class, and consequently into a political party, is continually being upset again by the competition between the workers themselves. But it ever rises up again; stronger, firmer, mightier. It compels legislative recognition of particular interests of the workers, by taking advantage of the divisions among the bourgeoisie itself. Thus the ten-hours' bill in England was carried.

Altogether, collisions between the classes of the old society further, in many ways, the course of development of the proletariat. The bourgeoisie finds itself involved in a constant battle. At first with the aristocracy; later on, with those portions of the bourgeoisie itself, whose interests have become antagonistic to the progress of industry; at all times with the bourgeoisie of foreign countries. In all these countries it sees itself compelled to appeal to the proletariat, to ask for its help, and thus to drag it into the political arena. The bourgeoisie itself, therefore, supplies the proletariat with its own elements of political and general education, in other words, it furnishes the proletariat with weapons for fighting the bourgeoisie.

Further, as we have already seen, entire sections of the ruling classes are, by the advance of industry, precipitated into the proletariat, or are at least threatened in their conditions of existence. These also supply the proletariat with fresh elements of enlightenment and progress.

Finally, in times when the class struggle nears the decisive hour, the process of dissolution going on within the ruling class, in fact, within the whole range of an old society, assumes such a violent glaring character, that a small section of the ruling class cuts itself adrift, and joins the revolutionary class, the class that holds the future in its hands. Just as, therefore, at an earlier period, a section of the nobility went over to the bourgeoisie, so now a portion of the bourgeoisie goes over to the proletariat, and in particular, a portion of the bourgeoisie ideologists, who have raised themselves to the level of comprehending theoretically the historical movement as a whole.

Of all the classes that stand face to face with the bourgeoisie today the proletariat alone is a really revolutionary class. The other classes decay and finally disappear in the face of modern industry; the proletariat is its special and essential product.

The lower middle class, the small manufacturer, the shopkeeper, the artisan, the peasant, all these fight against the bourgeoisie to save from extinction their existence as fractions of the middle class. They are therefore not revolutionary, but conservative. Nay, more, they are reactionary, for they try to roll back the wheel of history. If by chance they are revolutionary, they are so only in view of their impending transfer into the proletariat; they thus defend not their present, but their future interests, they desert their own standpoint to place themselves at that of the proletariat.

The "dangerous class," the social scum, that passively rotting class thrown off by the lowest layers of old society, may, here and there, be swept into the movement by a proletarian revolution; its conditions of life, however, prepare it far more for the part of a bribed tool of reactionary intrigue.

In the conditions of the proletariat, those of the old society at large are already virtually swamped. The proletarian is without property; his relation to his wife and children has no longer anything in common with the bourgeois family relations; modern industrial labor, modern subjection to capital, the same in England as in France, in America as in Germany, has stripped him of every trace of national character. Law, morality, religion, are to him so many bourgeois prejudices, behind which lurk in ambush just as many bourgeois interests.

All the preceding classes that got the upper hand sought to fortify their already acquired status by subjecting society at large to their conditions of appropriation. The proletarians cannot become masters of the productive forces of society, except by abolishing their own previous mode of appropriation, and thereby also every other previous mode of appropriation. They have nothing of their own to secure and to fortify; their mission is to destroy all previous securities for, and insurances of, individual property.

All previous historical movements were movements of minorities, or in the interest of minorities. The proletarian movement is the self-conscious, independent movement of the immense majority, in the interest of the immense majority. The proletariat, the lowest stratum of our present society, cannot stir, cannot raise itself up, without the whole super-incumbent strata of official society being sprung into the air.

Though not in substance, yet in form, the struggle of the proletariat with the bourgeoisie is at first a national struggle. The proletariat of each country must, of course, first of all settle matters with its own bourgeoisie.

In depicting the most general phases of the development of the proletariat, we traced the more or less veiled civil war, raging within existing society, up to the point where the war breaks out into open revolution, and where the violent overthrow of the bourgeoisie lays the foundation for the sway of the proletariat.

Hitherto every form of society has been based, as we have already seen, on the antagonism of oppressing and oppressed classes. But in order to oppress a class certain conditions must be assured to it under which it can, at least, continue its slavish existence. The serf, in the period of serfdom, raised himself to membership in the commune, just as the petty bourgeois, under the yoke of feudal absolutism, managed to develop into a bourgeois. The modern laborer, on the contrary, instead of rising with the progress of industry, sinks deeper and deeper below the conditions of existence of his own class. He becomes a pauper and pauperism develops more rapidly than population and wealth. And here it becomes evident that the bourgeoisie is unfit any longer to be the ruling class in society and to impose its conditions of existence upon society as an overriding law. It is unfit to rule because it is incompetent to assure an existence to its slave within his slavery, because it cannot help letting him sink into such a state that it has to feed him instead of being fed by him. Society can no longer live under this bourgeoisie, in other words its existence is no longer compatible with society.

The essential condition for the existence and for the sway of the bourgeois class, is the formation and augmentation of capital; the condition for capital is wage-labor. Wage-labor rests exclusively on competition between the laborers. The advance of industry, whose involuntary promoter is the bourgeoisie, replaces the isolation of the laborers, due to competition, by their revolutionary combination, due to association. The development of modern industry, therefore, cuts from under its feet the very foundation on which the bourgeoisie produces and appropriates products. What the bourgeoisie therefore produces above all, are its own gravediggers. Its fall and the victory of the proletariat are equally inevitable.

II

PROLETARIANS AND COMMUNISTS

In what relation do the Communists stand to the proletarians as a whole?

The Communists do not form a separate party opposed to other working class parties.

They have no interests separate and apart from those of the proletariat as a whole.

They do not set up any sectarian principles of their own by which to shape and mould the proletarian movement.

The Communists are distinguished from the other working class parties by this only: 1. In the national struggles of the proletarians of the different countries, they point out and bring to the front the common interests of the entire proletariat, independently of all nationality. 2. In the various stages of development which the struggle of the working class against the bourgeoisie has to pass through, they always and everywhere represent the interests of the movement as a whole.

The Communists, therefore, are on the one hand, practically, the most advanced and resolute section of the working class parties of every country, that section which pushes forward all others; on the other hand, theoretically, they have over the great mass of the proletariat the advantage of clearly understanding the line of march, the conditions, and the ultimate general results of the proletarian movement.

The immediate aim of the Communists is the same as that of all the other proletarian parties: formation of the proletariat into a class, over-throw of the bourgeois supremacy, conquest of political power by the proletariat.

The theoretical conclusions of the Communists are in no way based on ideas or principles that have been invented, or discovered, by this or that would-be universal reformer.

They merely express, in general terms, actual relations springing from an existing class struggle, from a historical movement going on under our very eyes. The abolition of existing property relations is not at all a distinctive feature of Communism.

All property relations in the past have continually been subject to historical change, consequent upon the change in historical conditions.

The French Revolution, for example, abolished feudal property in favor of bourgeois property.

The distinguishing feature of Communism is not the abolition of property generally, but the abolition of bourgeois property. But modern bourgeois private property is the final and most complete expression of the system of producing and appropriating products, that is based on class antagonisms, on the exploitation of the many by the few.

In this sense the theory of the Communists may be summed up in the single sentence: Abolition of private property.

We Communists have been reproached with the desire of abolishing the right of personally acquiring property as the fruit of a man's own labor, which property is alleged to be the groundwork of all personal freedom, activity, and independence.

Hard-won, self-acquired, self-earned property! Do you mean the property of the petty artisan and of the small peasant, a form of property that preceded the bourgeois form? There is no need to abolish that; the development of industry has to a great extent already destroyed it, and is still destroying it daily.

Or do you mean modern bourgeois private property?

But does wage-labor create any property for the laborer? Not a bit. It creates capital, *i.e.*, that kind of property which exploits wage-labor, and which cannot increase except upon condition of begetting a new supply of wage-labor for fresh exploitation. Property, in its present form, is based on the antagonism of capital and wage-labor. Let us examine both sides of this antagonism.

To be a capitalist, is to have not only a purely personal, but a social *status* in production. Capital is a collective product, and only by the united action of many members, nay, in the last resort, only by the united action of all members of society, can it be set in motion.

Capital is therefore not a personal, it is a social power.

When, therefore, capital is converted into common property, into the property of all members of society, personal property is not thereby transformed into social property. It is only the social character of the property that is changed. It loses its class character.

Let us now take wage-labor.

The average price of wage-labor is the minimum wage, *i.e.*, that quantum of the means of subsistence, which is absolutely requisite to keep the laborer in bare existence as a laborer. What, therefore, the wage-laborer appropriates by means of his labor, merely suffices to prolong and reproduce a bare existence. We by no means intend to abolish this personal appropriation of the products of labor, an appropriation that is made for the maintenance and reproduction of human life, and that leaves no surplus wherewith to command the labor of others. All that we want to do away with, is the miserable character of this appropriation, under which the laborer lives merely to increase capital, and is allowed to live only in so far as the interest of the ruling class requires it.

In bourgeois society living labor is but a means to increase accumulated labor. In Communist society accumulated labor is but a means to widen, to enrich, to promote the existence of the laborer.

In bourgeois society, therefore, the past dominates the present; in Communist society, the present dominates the past. In bourgeois society capital is independent and has individuality, while the living person is dependent and has no individuality.

And the abolition of this state of things is called by the bourgeois: abolition of individuality and freedom! And rightly so. The abolition of bourgeois individuality, bourgeois independence, and bourgeois freedom is undoubtedly aimed at.

By freedom is meant, under the present bourgeois conditions of production, free trade, free selling, and buying.

But if selling and buying disappears, free selling and buying disappears also. This talk about free selling and buying, and all the other "brave words" of our bourgeoisie about freedom in general, have a meaning, if any, only in contrast with restricted selling and buying, with the fettered traders of the Middle Ages, but have no meaning when opposed to the Communistic abolition of buying and selling, of the bourgeois conditions of production, and of the bourgeoisie itself.

You are horrified at our intending to do away with private property. But in your existing society private property is already done away with for nine-tenths of the population; its existence for the few is solely due to its non-existence in the hands of those nine-tenths. You reproach us, therefore, with intending to do away with a form of property, the necessary condition for whose existence is, the nonexistence of any property for the immense majority of society.

In one word, you reproach us with intending to do away with your property. Precisely so: that is just what we intend.

From the moment when labor can no longer be converted into capital, money, or rent, into a social power capable of being monopolized, *i.e.*, from the moment when individual property can no longer be transformed into bourgeois property, into capital, from that moment, you say, individuality vanishes!

You must, therefore, confess that by "individual" you mean no other person than the bourgeois, than the middle-class owner of property. This person must, indeed, be swept out of the way, and made impossible.

Communism deprives no man of the power to appropriate the products of society: all that it does is to deprive him of the power to subjugate the labor of others by means of such appropriation.

It has been objected, that upon the abolition of private property all work will cease, and universal laziness will overtake us.

According to this, bourgeois society ought long ago to have gone to the dogs through sheer idleness; for those of its members who work, acquire nothing, and those who acquire anything, do not work. The whole of this objection is but another expression of the tautology: that there can no longer be any wage-labor when there is no longer any capital.

All objections against the communistic mode of producing and appropriating material products, have, in the same way, been urged against the communistic modes of producing and appropriating intellectual products. Just as, to the bourgeois, the disappearance of class property is the disappearance of production itself, so the disappearance of class structure is to him identical with the disappearance of all culture.

That culture, the loss of which he laments, is, for the enormous majority, a mere training to act as a machine.

But don't wrangle with us so long as you apply to our intended abolition of bourgeois property, the standard of your bourgeois notions of freedom, culture, law, etc. Your very ideas are but the outgrowth of the conditions of your bourgeois production and bourgeois property, just as your jurisprudence is but the will of your class made into a law for all, a will, whose essential character and direction are determined by the economical conditions of existence of your class.

The selfish misconception that induces you to transform into eternal laws of nature and of reason, the social forms springing from your present mode of production and form of property—historical relations that rise and disappear in the progress of production—this misconception you share with every ruling class that has preceded you. What you see clearly in the case of ancient property, what you admit in the case of feudal property, you are of course forbidden to admit in the case of your own bourgeois form of property.

Abolition of the family! Even the most radical flare up at this infamous proposal of the Communists.

On what foundation is the present family, the bourgeois family, based? On capital, on private gain. In its completely developed form this family exists only among the bourgeoisie. But this state of things finds its complement in the practical absence of the family among the proletarians and in public prostitution.

The bourgeois family will vanish as a matter of course when its complement vanishes, and both will vanish with the vanishing of capital.

Do you charge us with wanting to stop the exploitation of children by their parents? To this crime we plead guilty.

But, you will say, we destroy the most hallowed of relations, when we replace home education by social.

And your education! Is not that also social and determined by the social conditions under which you educate, by the intervention, direct or indirect, of society by means of schools, etc? The Communists have not invented the intervention of society in education; they do but seek to alter the character of that intervention, and to rescue education from the influence of the ruling class.

The bourgeois clap-trap about the family and education, about the hallowed co-relation of parent and child becomes all the more disgusting, as, by the action of modern industry, all family ties among the proletarians are torn asunder and their children transformed into simple articles of commerce and instruments of labor.

But you Communists would introduce community of women; screams the whole bourgeoisie in chorus.

The bourgeois sees in his wife a mere instrument of production. He heard that the instruments of production are to be exploited in common, and, naturally, can come to no other conclusion than that the lot of being common to all will likewise fall to the women.

He has not even a suspicion that the real point aimed at is to do away with the status of women as mere instruments of production.

For the rest nothing is more ridiculous than the virtuous indignation of our bourgeois at the community of women which, they pretend, is to be openly and officially established by the Communists. The Communists have no need to introduce community of women; it has existed almost from time immemorial.

Our bourgeois, not content with having the wives and daughters of their proletarians at their disposal, not to speak of common prostitutes, take the greatest pleasure in seducing each other's wives.

Bourgeois marriage is in reality a system of wives in common and thus, at the most, what the Communists might possibly be reproached with, is that they desire to introduce, in substitution for a hypocritically concealed, an openly legalized community of women. For the rest it is self-evident that the abolition of the present system of production must bring with it the abolition of the community of women springing from that system, *i.e.*, of prostitution both public and private.

The Communists are further reproached with desiring to abolish countries and nationality.

The workingmen have no country. We cannot take from them what they have not got. Since the proletariat must first of all acquire political supremacy, must rise to be the leading class of the nation, must constitute itself *the* nation, it is, so far, itself national though not in the bourgeois sense of the word.

National differences and antagonisms between peoples are daily more and more vanishing, owing to the development of the bourgeoisie, to freedom of commerce, to the world's market, to uniformity in the mode of production and in the conditions of life corresponding thereto.

The supremacy of the proletariat will cause them to vanish still faster. United action, of the leading civilized countries at least, is one of the first conditions for the emancipation of the proletariat.

In proportion as the exploitation of one individual by another is put an end to, the exploitation of one nation by another will also be put an end to. In proportion as the antagonism between classes within the nation vanishes, the hostility of one nation to another will come to an end.

The charges against Communism made from a religious, a philosophical, and, generally, from an ideological standpoint, are not deserving of serious examination.

Does it require deep intuition to comprehend that man's ideas, views, and conceptions, in one word, man's consciousness changes with every change in the conditions of his material existence, in his social relations and in his social life?

What else does the history of ideas prove than that intellectual production changes its character in proportion as material production is changed? The ruling ideas of each age have ever been the ideas of its ruling class.

When people speak of ideas that revolutionize society they do but express the fact that within the old society the elements of a new one have been created, and that the dissolution of the old ideas keeps even pace with the dissolution of the old conditions of existence.

When the ancient world was in its last throes, the ancient religions were overcome by Christianity. When Christian ideas succumbed in the eighteenth century to rationalist ideas, feudal society fought its death-battle with the then revolutionary bourgeoisie. The ideas of religious liberty and freedom of conscience merely gave expression to the sway of free competition within the domain of knowledge.

"Undoubtedly," it will be said, "religious, moral, philosophical," and juridical ideas have been modified in the course of historic development. But religion, morality, philosophy, political science, and law, constantly survived this change.

"There are besides, eternal truths, such as Freedom, Justice, etc., that are common to all states of society. But Communism abolishes eternal truths, it abolishes all religion and all morality, instead of constituting them on a new basis; it therefore acts as a contradiction to all past historical experience."

What does this accusation reduce itself to? The history of all past society has consisted in the development of class antagonisms, antagonisms that assumed different forms at different epochs.

But whatever form they may have taken, one fact is common to all past ages, *viz.*, the exploitation of one part of society by the other. No wonder, then, that the social consciousness of past ages, despite all the multiplicity and variety it displays, moves within certain common forms, or general ideas, which cannot completely vanish except with the total disappearance of class antagonisms.

The Communist revolution is the most radical rupture with traditional property relations; no wonder that its development involves the most radical rupture with traditional ideas.

But let us have done with the bourgeois objections to Communism.

We have seen above that the first step in the revolution by the working class is to raise the proletariat to the position of the ruling class, to win the battle of democracy.

The proletariat will use its political supremacy to wrest, by degrees, all capital from the bourgeoisie; to centralize all instruments of production in the hands of the State, *i.e.*, of the proletariat organized as the ruling class; and to increase the total of productive forces as rapidly as possible.

Of course, in the beginning this cannot be effected except by means of despotic inroads on the rights of property and on the conditions of bourgeois production; by means of measures, therefore, which appear economically insufficient and untenable, but which, in the course of the movement, outstrip themselves, necessitate further inroads upon the old social order and are unavoidable as a means of entirely revolutionizing the mode of production.

These measures will of course be different in different countries.

Nevertheless in the most advanced countries the following will be pretty generally applicable:

1. Abolition of property in land and application of all rents of land to public purposes.
2. A heavy progressive or graduated income tax.
3. Abolition of all rights of inheritance.
4. Confiscation of the property of all emigrants and rebels.
5. Centralization of credit in the hands of the State, by means of a national bank with State capital and an exclusive monopoly.
6. Centralization of the means of communication and transport in the hands of the State.
7. Extension of factories and instruments of production owned by the State; the bringing into cultivation of waste lands, and the improvement of the soil generally in accordance with a common plan.
8. Equal liability of all to labor. Establishment of industrial armies, especially for agriculture.
9. Combination of agriculture with manufacturing industries: gradual abolition of the distinction between town and country, by a more equable distribution of the population over the country.
10. Free education for all children in public schools. Abolition of children's factory labor in its present form. Combination of education with industrial production, etc.

When, in the course of development, class distinctions have disappeared and all production has been concentrated in the hands of a vast association of the whole nation, the public power will lose its political character. Political power, properly so called, is merely the organized power of one class for oppressing another. If the proletariat during its contest with the bourgeoisie is compelled, by the force of circumstances, to organize itself as a class, if, by means of a revolution, it makes itself the ruling class, and, as such, sweeps away by force the old conditions of production, then it will, along with these conditions, have swept away the conditions for the existence of class antagonism, and of classes generally, and will thereby have abolished its own supremacy as a class.

In place of the old bourgeois society with its classes and class antagonisms we shall have an association in which the free development of each is the condition for the free development of all.

...

IV

POSITION OF THE COMMUNISTS IN RELATION TO THE VARIOUS EXISTING OPPOSITION PARTIES

Section II has made clear the relations of the Communist to the existing working class parties, such as the Chartists in England and the Agrarian Reformers in America.

The Communists fight for the attainment of the immediate aims, for the enforcement of the momentary interests of the working class; but in the movement of the present they also represent and take care of the future of that movement. In France the Communists ally themselves with Social-Democrats, against the conservative and radical bourgeoisie, reserving, however, the right to take up a critical position in regard to phrases and illusions traditionally handed down from the great Revolution.

In Switzerland they support the Radicals, without losing sight of the fact that this party consists of antagonistic elements, partly of Democratic Socialists, in the French sense, partly of radical bourgeois.

In Poland they support the party that insists on an agrarian revolution, as the prime condition for national emancipation, that party which fomented the insurrection of Cracow in 1846.

In Germany they fight with the bourgeoisie whenever it acts in a revolutionary way against the absolute monarchy, the feudal squirearchy, and the petty bourgeoisie.

But they never cease, for a single instant, to instill into the working class the clearest possible recognition of the hostile antagonism between bourgeoisie and proletariat, in order that the German workers may straightway use, as so many weapons against the bourgeoisie the social and political conditions that the bourgeoisie must necessarily introduce along with its supremacy, and in order that, after the fall of the reactionary classes in Germany, the fight against the bourgeoisie itself may immediately begin.

The Communists turn their attention chiefly to Germany, because that country is on the eve of a bourgeois revolution that is bound to be carried out under more advanced conditions of European civilization, and with a much more developed proletariat, than that of England was in the seventeenth, and of France in the eighteenth century, and because the bourgeois revolution in Germany will be but the prelude to an immediately following proletarian revolution.

In short, the Communists everywhere support every revolutionary movement against the existing social and political order of things.

In all these movements they bring to the front, as the leading question in each, the property question, no matter what its degree of development at the time.

Finally, they labor everywhere for the union and agreement of the democratic parties of all countries.

The Communists disdain to conceal their views and aims. They openly declare that their ends can be attained only by the forcible overthrow of all existing social conditions. Let the ruling classes tremble at a communistic revolution. The proletarians have nothing to lose but their chains. They have a world to win.

Working men of all countries, unite!

Harriet Taylor Mill, On Marriage

The industrial and political revolutions that dominated the nineteenth century had a tremendously uneven impact on European society. Great wealth
was created and political systems more sensitive to the needs and desires
of the governed began to develop. But not all benefited from the changes.
We have seen that life for those who worked in the factories, which produced the wealth, was unimaginably harsh and desperate. If we look at
how the sweeping economic changes of the nineteenth century impacted
women, we are presented with a complex situation. Middle- and upper-
class women did benefit from the increase in wealth and freedom from
work outside the home and from harsh domestic chores. But the cost to
women for these benefits was high. In sharp contrast to the wider opportunities for men at the time, women's roles were sharply defined by the
domestic sphere. Since the development of factory production had
replaced the workshop, the domestic sphere itself had become much more
limited. Women were taught that their only function in life was to support
a husband and raise children. Many educated women, and some men, were
highly critical of these developments. One of them was Harriet Taylor Mill.

Harriet Taylor Mill (born Harriet Hardy in 1807) was eighteen when
she married a twenty-eight-year-old pharmaceuticals wholesaler named
John Taylor, with whom she had three children. Thus far, a very typical
life for a nineteenth-century middle-class Englishwoman. But Harriet
Taylor Mill would not live a typical life. Apparently frustrated by her husband's lack of intellectual curiosity, she began an intense, public, but pla-
tonic, relationship with the philosopher John Stuart Mill. Although the
relationship caused a great scandal, John Taylor was accommodating, even
setting up a separate residence for his wife. Two years after John Taylor
died of cancer in 1849, Harriet Taylor married John Stuart Mill. Scholars
disagree over the influence that the Mills had on each other's writings.
Both agreed, however, that the status of women in European culture was
the result of convention and tradition and should be changed. In the following selection Harriet Taylor Mill describes the status of married
women in nineteenth century Europe and how the marriage relationship
should be altered to benefit women.

---

1. What is the situation of women, according to Harriet Taylor Mill?

2. How can this situation be changed for the better?

If I could be providence to the world for a time, for the express purpose of raising the condition of women, I should come to you to know the
means—the *purpose* would be to remove all interference with affection, or
with any thing which is, or which even might be supposed to be, demonstrative of affection—In the present state of womens minds, perfectly uneducated, and with whatever of timidity and dependence is natural to them
increased a thousand fold by their habits of utter dependence, it would
probably be mischievous to remove at once all restraints, they would buy
themselves protectors at a dearer cost than even at present—but without
raising their natures at all, it seems to me, that once give women the desire
to raise their social condition, and they have a power which in the present
state of civilization and of mens characters, might be made of tremendous
effect. Whether nature made a difference in the nature of men and women
or not, it seems now that all men, with the exception of a few lofty minded,
are sensualists more or less—Women on the contrary are quite exempt
from this trait, however it may appear otherwise in the cases of some—It
seems strange that it should be so, unless it was meant to be a source of
power in demi-civilized states such as the present—or it may not be so—it
may be only that the habits of freedom and low indulgence in which boys
grow up and the contrary notion of what is called purity in girls may have
produced the appearance of different natures in the two sexes—As certain
it is that there is equality in nothing, now—all the pleasures such as there
are being mens, and all the disagreables and pains being womens, as that
every pleasure would be infinitely heightened both in kind and degree by
the perfect equality of the sexes. Women are educated for one single object,
to gain their living by marrying—(some poor souls get it without the
churchgoing in the same way—they do not seem to me a bit worse than
their honoured sisters)—To be married is the object of their existence and
that object being gained they do really cease to exist as to anything worth
calling life or any useful purpose. One observes very few marriages where
there is any real sympathy or enjoyment of companionship between
the parties—The woman knows what her power is, and gains by it what
she has been taught to consider "proper" to her state—The woman who
would gain power by such means is unfit for power, still they do use this
power for paltry advantages and I am astonished it has never occurred to
them to gain some large purpose: but their minds are degenerated by
habits of dependance—I should think that 500 years hence none of the
follies of their ancestors will so excite wonder and contempt as the fact of
legislative restraint as to matters of feeling—or rather in the expressions of
feeling. When once the law undertakes to say which demonstration of feeling shall be given to which, it seems quite inconsistent not to legislate for
all, and say how many shall be seen, how many heard, and what kind and
degree of feeling allows of shaking hands—The Turks is the only consistent mode—

I have no doubt that when the whole community is really educated, tho' the present laws of marriage were to continue they would be perfectly disregarded, because no one would marry—The widest and perhaps the quickest means to do away with its evils is to be found in promoting education—as it is the means of all good—but meanwhile it is hard that those who suffer most from its evils and who are always the best people, should be left without remedy. Would not the best plan be divorce which could be attained by *any, without any reason assigned*, and at small expence, but which could only be finally pronounced after a long period? not *less* time than two years should elapse between suing for divorce and permission to contract again— but what the decision will be *must* be certain at the moment of asking for it— *unless* during that time the suit should be withdrawn—

(I feel like a lawyer in talking of it only! O how absurd and little it all is!)

In the present system of habits and opinions, girls enter into what is called a contract perfectly ignorant of the conditions of it, and that they should be so is considered absolutely essential to their fitness for it!—But after all the one argument of the matter which I think might be said so as to strike both high and low natures is—Who would wish to have the person without the inclination? Whoever would take the benefit of a law of divorce must be those whose inclination is to separate and who on earth would wish another to remain with them against their inclination? I should think no one—people sophisticate about the matter now and will not believe that one "*really* would *wish to go*." Suppose instead of calling it a "law of divorce" it were to be called "Proof of affection"—They would like it better then—

At this present time, in this state of civilization, what evil would be caused by, first placing women on the most entire equality with men, as to all rights and privileges, civil and political, and then doing away with all laws whatever relating to marriage? Then if a woman had children she must take the charge of them, women would not then have children without considering how to maintain them. Women would have no more reason to barter person for bread, or for any thing else, than men have—public offices being open to them alike, all occupations would be divided between the sexes in their natural arrangement. Fathers would provide for their daughters in the same manner as for their sons—

All the difficulties about divorce seem to be in the consideration for the children—but on this plan it would be the women's *interest* not to have children—*now* it is thought to be the woman's interest to have children as so many *ties* to the man who feeds her.

Sex in its true and finest meaning, seems to be the way in which is manifested all that is highest best and beautiful in the nature of human beings—none but poets have approached to the perception of the beauty of the material world—still less of the spiritual—and there never yet existed a poet, except by the inspiration of that feeling which is the perception of beauty in all forms and by all the means which are given us, as well as by *sight*. Are we not born with the *five* senses, merely as a foundation for others which we may make by them—and who extends and refines those material senses to the highest—into infinity—best fulfils the end of creation—That is only saying—*Who enjoys most, is most virtuous*—It is for *you*—the most worthy to be the apostle of all loftiest virtue—to teach, such as may be taught, that the higher the *kind* of enjoyment, the *greater* the *degree*—perhaps there is but one class to whom this *can* be *taught*—the poetic nature struggling with superstition: *you* are fitted to be the saviour of such—

Charles Darwin

In 1831, having graduated from Cambridge University with a degree in theology, Charles Darwin (1809–1882) accepted the position of naturalist aboard the ship *Beagle*, which was setting sail on a surveying expedition to South America and the Pacific Ocean. During the voyage, which lasted five years, Darwin observed plant and animal life in widely scattered areas of the earth, gathering the evidence on which he was later to base his theory of biological evolution. To render the theory plausible, however, Darwin had to overcome two obstacles: First, he had to find evidence that the earth was old enough to provide time for the evolutionary process to have taken place, and second, he had to provide an explanation of this process.

His first problem was solved by the geologist Sir Charles Lyell, whose *Principles of Geology* (published in 1830) established that the earth had existed through vast periods of geological time. The clue to the solution of his second problem came from Malthus's *Essay on Population*, with its view that organic beings multiply faster than their food supply. Starting from Malthus's assumption, Darwin undertook in *The Origin of Species* to explain the process by which biological evolution is accomplished and to provide empirical evidence to support his explanation. Darwin's theory of evolution, in its claim that new species evolve from older ones, repudiated the doctrine of the immutability of species, which had stemmed from Aristotle and had been defended on theological grounds from the time of the Middle Ages. Thus, it marked a major revolution in the history of thought.

The selections that follow are taken from Darwin's two great works, *The Origin of Species* and *The Descent of Man*. The first book, published in 1859, contains his statement of the theory of biological evolution, along with the evidence on which it rests. In the second, published in 1871, Darwin completes his theory by including humans within the evolutionary process. It is, of course, Darwin's inclusion of human beings within his theory of evolution that has made his scientific views so controversial. The evolutionary explanation of the emergence of humankind has seemed to some to run counter to the account in Genesis of God's creation of Adam and Eve in his own image.

---

1. What methods and evidence does Darwin use to support his theory?

2. What does Darwin mean by "Natural Selection"?

The Origin of Species

•••

Nothing is easier than to admit in words the truth of the universal struggle for life, or more difficult—at least I have found it so—than constantly to bear this conclusion in mind. Yet, unless it be thoroughly engrained in the mind, the whole economy of nature, with every fact on distribution, rarity, abundance, extinction, and variation, will be dimly seen or quite misunderstood. We behold the face of nature bright with gladness, we often see superabundance of food; we do not see or we forget, that the birds which are idly singing round us mostly live on insects or seeds, and are thus constantly destroying life; or we forget how largely these songsters, or their eggs, or their nestlings, are destroyed by birds and beasts of prey; we do not always bear in mind, that, though food may be now super-abundant, it is not so at all seasons of each recurring year.

•••

A struggle for existence inevitably follows from the high rate at which all organic beings tend to increase. Every being, which during its natural life-time produces several eggs or seeds, must suffer destruction during some period of its life, and during some season or occasional year, otherwise, on the principle of geometrical increase, its numbers would quickly become so inordinately great that no country could support the product. Hence, as more individuals are produced than can possibly survive, there must in every case be a struggle for existence, either one individual with another of the same species, or with the individuals of distinct species, or with the physical conditions of life. It is the doctrine of Malthus applied with manifold force to the whole animal and vegetable kingdoms; for in this case there can be no artificial increase of food, and no prudential restraint from marriage. Although some species may be now increasing, more or less rapidly, in numbers, all cannot do so, for the world would not hold them.

There is no exception to the rule that every organic being naturally increases at so high a rate that, if not destroyed, the earth would soon be covered by the progeny of a single pair. Even slow-breeding man has doubled in twenty-five years, and at this rate, in less than a thousand years, there would literally not be standing-room for his progeny. Linnaeus[1] has calculated that if an annual plant produced only two seeds—and there is no plant so unproductive as this—and their seedlings next year produced two, and so on, then in twenty years there would be a million plants. The elephant is

---

[1]Swedish botanist (1707–1778)—*Ed.*
Charles Darwin, *The Origin of Species, by Means of Natural Selection or the Preservation of Favoured Races in the Struggle for Life,* 6th ed. (London, 1900).

reckoned the slowest breeder of all known animals, and I have taken some pains to estimate its probable minimum rate of natural increase; it will be safest to assume that it begins breeding when thirty years old, and goes on breeding till ninety years old, bringing forth six young in the interval, and surviving until one hundred years old; if this be so, after a period of from 740 to 750 years there would be nearly nineteen million elephants alive, descended from the first pair.

But we have better evidence on this subject than mere theoretical calculations, namely, the numerous recorded cases of the astonishingly rapid increase of various animals in a state of nature, when circumstances have been favourable to them during two or three following seasons. Still more striking is the evidence from our domestic animals of many kinds which have run wild in several parts of the world; if the statements of the rate of increase of slow-breeding cattle and horses in South America, and latterly in Australia, had not been well authenticated, they would have been incredible. So it is with plants; cases could be given of introduced plants which have become common throughout whole islands in a period of less than ten years. Several of the plants, such as the cardoon and a tall thistle, which are now the commonest over the wide plains of La Plata, clothing square leagues of surface almost to the exclusion of every other plant, have been introduced from Europe; and there are plants which now range in India, as I hear from Dr. Falconer, from Cape Comorin to the Himalaya, which have been imported from America since its discovery. In such cases, and endless others could be given, no one supposes, that the fertility of animals or plants has been suddenly and temporarily increased in any sensible degree. The obvious explanation is that the conditions of life have been highly favourable, and that there has consequently been less destruction of the old and young, and that nearly all the young have been enabled to breed. Their geometrical ratio of increase, the result of which never fails to be surprising, simply explains their extraordinarily rapid increase and wide diffusion in their new homes.

In a state of nature almost every full-grown plant annually produces seeds, and amongst animals there are very few which do not annually pair. Hence we may confidently assert, that all plants and animals are tending to increase at a geometrical ratio,—that all would rapidly stock every station in which they could anyhow exist,—and that this geometrical tendency to increase must be checked by destruction at some period of life. Our familiarity with the larger domestic animals tends, I think, to mislead us: we see no great destruction falling on them, but we do not keep in mind that thousands are annually slaughtered for food, and that in a state of nature an equal number would have somehow to be disposed of.

The only difference between organisms which annually produce eggs or seeds by the thousand, and those which produce extremely few, is, that the slow-breeders would require a few more years to people, under favourable conditions, a whole district, let it be ever so large. The condor lays a couple of eggs and the ostrich a score, and yet in the same country the condor may be the more numerous of the two; the Fulmar petrel lays but one egg, yet it is believed to be the most numerous bird in the world. One fly deposits hundreds of eggs, and another, like the hippobosca, a single one; but this difference does not determine how many individuals of the two species can be supported in a district. A large number of eggs is of some importance to those species which depend on a fluctuating amount of food, for it allows them rapidly to increase in number. But the real importance of a large number of eggs or seeds is to make up for much destruction at some period of life; and this period in the great majority of cases is an early one. If an animal can in any way protect its own eggs or young, a small number may be produced, and yet the average stock be fully kept up; but if many eggs or young are destroyed, many must be produced, or the species will become extinct. It would suffice to keep up the full number of a tree, which lived on an average for a thousand years, if a single seed were produced once in a thousand years, supposing that this seed were never destroyed, and could be ensured to germinate in a fitting place. So that, in all cases, the average number of any animal or plant depends only indirectly on the number of its eggs or seeds.

In looking at Nature, it is most necessary to keep the foregoing considerations always in mind—never to forget that every single organic being may be said to be striving to the utmost to increase in numbers; that each lives by a struggle at some period of its life; that heavy destruction inevitably falls either on the young or old, during each generation or at recurrent intervals. Lighten any check, mitigate the destruction ever so little, and the number of the species will almost instantaneously increase to any amount.

The causes which check the natural tendency of each species to increase are most obscure. Look at the most vigorous species; by as much as it swarms in numbers, by so much will it tend to increase still further. We know not exactly what the checks are even in a single instance. Nor will this surprise any one who reflects how ignorant we are on this head, even in regard to mankind, although so incomparably better known than any other animal. This subject of the checks to increase has been ably treated by several authors, and I hope in a future work to discuss it at considerable length, more especially in regard to the feral animals of South America. Here I will make only a few remarks, just to recall to the reader's mind some of the chief points. Eggs or very young animals seem generally to suffer most, but this is not invariably the case. With plants there is a vast destruction of seeds, but, from some observations which I have made it appears that the seedlings suffer most from germinating in ground already thickly stocked with other plants. Seedlings, also, are destroyed in vast numbers by various enemies; for instance, on a piece of ground three feet long and two wide, dug and cleared, and where there could be no choking from other plants, I marked all the seedlings of our native weeds as they came up, and out of 357 no less than 295 were destroyed, chiefly by slugs and insects. If turf which has long been mown, and the case would be the same with turf closely browsed by quadrupeds, be let to grow, the more vigorous plants gradually kill the less vigorous, though fully grown plants; thus out of twenty species growing on a little plot of mown turf (three feet by four) nine species perished, from the other species being allowed to grow up freely.

The amount of food for each species of course gives the extreme limit to which each can increase; but very frequently it is not the obtaining food, but the serving as prey to other animals, which determines the average number of a species. Thus, there seems to be little doubt that the stock of partridges, grouse, and hares on any large estate depends chiefly on the destruction of vermin. If not one head of game were shot during the next twenty years in England, and, at the same time, if no vermin were destroyed, there would, in all probability, be less game than at present, although hundreds of thousands of game animals are now annually shot. On the other hand, in some cases, as with the elephant, none are destroyed by beasts of prey; for even the tiger in India most rarely dares to attack a young elephant protected by its dam.

• • •

Many cases are on record showing how complex and unexpected are the checks and relations between organic beings, which have to struggle together in the same country.

• • •

[I give an] instance showing how plants and animals, remote in the scale of nature, are bound together by a web of complex relations. I shall hereafter have occasion to show that the exotic *Lobelia fulgens* is never visited in my garden by insects, and consequently, from its peculiar structure, never sets a seed. Nearly all our orchidaceous plants absolutely require the visits of insects to remove their pollen-masses and thus to fertilise them. I find from experiments that humble-bees are almost indispensable to the fertilisation of the heartsease (*Viola tricolor*), for other bees do not visit this flower. I have also found that the visits of bees are necessary for the fertilisation of some kinds of clover; for instance, 20 heads of Dutch clover (*Trifolium repens*) yielded 2,290 seeds, but 20 other heads protected from bees produced not one. Again, 100 heads of red clover (*T. pratense*) produced 2,700 seeds, but the same number of protected heads produced not a single seed. Humble-bees alone visit red clover, as other bees cannot reach the nectar. It has been suggested that moths may fertilise the clovers; but I doubt whether they could do so in the case of the red clover, from their weight not being sufficient to depress the wing petals. Hence we may infer as highly probable that, if the whole genus of humble-bees became extinct or very rare in England, the heartsease and red clover would become very rare, or wholly disappear. The number of humble-bees in any district depends in a great measure upon the number of field-mice, which destroy their combs and nests; and Col. Newman, who has long attended to the habits of humble-bees, believes that "more than two-thirds of them are thus destroyed all over England." Now the number of mice is largely dependent, as every one knows, on the number of cats; and Col. Newman says, "Near villages and small towns I have found the nests of humble-bees more numerous than elsewhere, which I attribute to the number of cats that destroy the mice." Hence it is quite credible that the presence of a feline animal in large numbers in a district might determine, through the intervention first of mice and then of bees, the frequency of certain flowers in that district!

• • •

If under changing conditions of life organic beings present individual differences in almost every part of their structure, and this cannot be disputed; if there be, owing to their geometrical rate of increase, a severe struggle for life at some age, season, or year, and this certainly cannot be disputed; then, considering the infinite complexity of the relations of all organic beings to each other and to their conditions of life, causing an infinite diversity in structure, constitution, and habits, to be advantageous to them, it would be a most extraordinary fact if no variations had ever occurred useful to each being's own welfare, in the same manner as so many variations have occurred useful to man. But if variations useful to any organic being ever do occur, assuredly individuals thus characterised will have the best chance of being preserved in the struggle for life; and from the strong principle of inheritance, these will tend to produce off-spring similarly characterised. This principle of preservation, or the survival of the fittest, I have called Natural Selection. It leads to the improvement of each creature in relation to its organic and inorganic conditions of life; and consequently, in most cases, to what must be regarded as an advance in organisation. Nevertheless, low and simple forms will long endure if well fitted for their simple conditions of life.

Natural selection, on the principle of qualities being inherited at corresponding ages, can modify the egg, seed, or young, as easily as the adult. Amongst many animals, sexual selection will have given its aid to ordinary selection, by assuring to the most vigorous and best adapted males the greatest number of offspring. Sexual selection will also give characters useful to the males alone, in their struggles or rivalry with other males; and these characters will be transmitted to one sex or to both sexes, according to the form of inheritance which prevails.

Whether natural selection has really thus acted in adapting the various forms of life to their several conditions and stations, must be judged by the general tenor and balance of evidence given in the following chapters. But we have already seen how it entails extinction; and how largely extinction has acted in the world's history, geology plainly declares. Natural selection, also, leads to divergence of character; for the more organic beings diverge in structure, habits, and constitution, by so much the more can a large number be supported on the area—of which we see proof by looking to the inhabitants of any small spot, and to the productions naturalised in foreign lands. Therefore, during the modification of the descendants of any one species, and during the incessant struggle of all species to increase in numbers, the more diversified the descendants become, the better will be their chance of success in the battle for life. Thus the small differences distinguishing varieties of the same species, steadily tend to increase, till they equal the greater differences between species of the same genus, or even of distinct genera.

We have seen that it is the common, the widely-diffused and widely-ranging species, belonging to the larger genera within each class, which vary most; and these tend to transmit to their modified offspring that superiority which now makes them dominant in their own countries. Natural selection, as has just been remarked, leads to divergence of character and to much extinction of the less improved and intermediate forms of life. On these principles, the nature of the affinities, and the generally well-defined distinctions between the innumerable organic beings in each class throughout the world, may be explained. It is a truly wonderful fact—the wonder of which we are apt to overlook from familiarity—that all animals and all plants throughout all time and space should be related to each other in groups, subordinate to groups, in the manner which we everywhere behold—namely, varieties of the same species most closely related, species of the same genus less closely and unequally related, forming section and subgenera, species of distinct genera related in different degrees, forming subfamilies, families, orders, subclasses and classes. The several subordinate groups in any class cannot be ranked in a single file, but seem clustered round points, and these round other points, and so on in almost endless cycles. If species had been independently created, no explanation would have been possible of this kind of classification; but it is explained through inheritance and the complex action of natural selection, entailing extinction and divergence of character, as we have seen illustrated in the diagram.

The affinities of all the beings of the same class have sometimes been represented by a great tree. I believe this simile largely speaks the truth. The green and building twigs may represent existing species; and those produced during former years may represent the long succession of extinct species. At each period of growth all the growing twigs have tried to branch out on all sides, and to overtop and kill the surrounding twigs and branches, in the same manner as species and groups of species have at all times overmastered other species in the great battle for life. The limbs divided into great branches, and these into lesser and lesser branches, were themselves once, when the tree was young, budding twigs; and this connection of the former and present buds by ramifying branches may well represent the classification of all extinct and living species in groups subordinate to groups. Of the many twigs which flourished when the tree was a mere bush, only two or three, now grown into great branches, yet survive and bear the other branches; so with the species which lived during long-past geological periods, very few have left living and modified descendants. From the first growth of the tree, many a limb and branch has decayed and dropped off; and these fallen branches of various sizes may represent those whole orders, families, and genera which have now no living representatives, and which are known to us only in a fossil state. As we here and there see a thin straggling branch springing from a fork low down in a tree, and which by some chance has been favoured and is still alive on its summit, so we occasionally see an animal like the Ornithorhynchus or Lepidosiren, which in some small degree connects by its affinities two large branches of life, and which has apparently been saved from fatal competition by having inhabited a protected station. As buds give rise by growth to fresh buds, and these, if vigorous, branch out and overtop on all sides many a feebler branch, so by generation I believe it has been with the Great Tree of Life, which fills with its dead and broken branches the crust of the earth, and covers the surface with its ever-branching and beautiful ramifications.

• • •

I have now recapitulated the facts and considerations which have thoroughly convinced me that species have been modified, during a long course of descent. This has been effected chiefly through the natural selection of numerous successive, slight, favourable variations; aided in an important manner by the inherited effects of the use and disuse of parts; and in an unimportant manner, that is in relation to adaptive structures, whether past or present, by the direct action of external conditions, and by variations which seem to us in our ignorance to rise spontaneously. It appears that I formerly underrated the frequency and value of these latter forms of variations, as leading to permanent modifications of structure independently of natural selection. But as my conclusions have lately been much misrepresented, and it has been stated that I attribute the modification of species exclusively to natural selection, I may be permitted to remark that in the first edition of this work, and subsequently, I placed in a most conspicuous position—namely, at the close of the Introduction—the following words: "I am convinced that the natural selection has been the main but not the exclusive means of modification." This has been of no avail. Great is the power of steady misrepresentation; but the history of science shows that fortunately this power does not long endure.

It can hardly be supposed that a false theory would explain, in so satisfactory a manner as does the theory of natural selection, the several large classes of facts above specified. It has recently been objected that this is an unsafe method of arguing; but it is a method used in judging of the common events of life, and has often been used by the greatest natural philosophers. The undulatory theory of light has thus been arrived at, and the belief in the revolution of the earth on its own axis was until lately supported by hardly any direct evidence. It is no valid objection that science as yet throws no light on the far higher problem of the essence or origin of life. Who can explain what is the essence of the attraction of gravity? No one now objects to following out the results consequent on this unknown element of attraction: not-with-standing that Leibnitz[2] formerly accused Newton of introducing "occult qualities and miracles into philosophy."

I see no good reason why the views given in this volume should shock the religious feelings of any one. It is satisfactory, as showing how transient such impressions are, to remember that the greatest discovery ever made by man, namely, the law of the attraction of gravity, was also attacked by Leibnitz, "as subversive of natural, and inferentially of revealed, religion." A celebrated author and divine has written to me that "he has gradually learnt to see that it is just as noble a conception of the Deity to believe that He created a few original forms capable of self-development into other and needful forms, as to believe that He required a fresh act of creation to supply the voids caused by the action of His laws."

Why, it may be asked, until recently did nearly all the most eminent living naturalists and geologists disbelieve in the mutability of species. It cannot be asserted that organic beings in a state of nature are subject to no variation; it cannot be proved that the amount of variation in the course of long ages is a limited quantity; no clear distinction has been, or can be, drawn between species and well-marked varieties. It cannot be maintained that species when intercrossed are invariably sterile, and varieties invariably fertile; or that sterility is a special endowment and sign of creation. The belief that species were immutable productions was almost unavoidable as long as the history of the world was thought to be of short duration; and now that we have acquired some idea of the lapse of time, we are too apt to assume, without proof, that the geological record is so perfect that it would have afforded us plain evidence of the mutation of species, if they had undergone mutation.

But the chief cause of our natural unwillingness to admit that one species has given birth to other and distinct species, is that we are always slow in admitting great changes of which we do not see the steps. The difficulty is the same as that felt by so many geologists, when Lyell first insisted that long lines of inland cliffs had been formed, and great valleys excavated, by the agencies which we see still at work. The mind cannot possibly grasp the full meaning of the term of even a million years; it cannot add up and perceive the full effects of many slight variations, accumulated during an almost infinite number of generations.

[2]German philosopher and mathematician (1646–1716)—*Ed.*

Although I am fully convinced of the truth of the views given in this volume under the form of an abstract, I by no means expect to convince experienced naturalists whose minds are stocked with a multitude of facts all viewed, during a long course of years, from a point of view directly opposite to mine. It is so easy to hide our ignorance under such expressions as the "plan of creation," "unity of design," etc., and to think that we give an explanation when we only restate a fact. Any one whose disposition leads him to attach more weight to unexplained difficulties than to the explanation of a certain number of facts will certainly reject the theory. A few naturalists, endowed with much flexibility of mind, and who have already begun to doubt the immutability of species, may be influenced by this volume; but I look with confidence to the future,—to young and rising naturalists, who will be able to view both sides of the question with impartiality. Whoever is led to believe that species are mutable will do good service by conscientiously expressing his conviction; for thus only can the load of prejudice by which this subject is overwhelmed be removed.

Several eminent naturalists have of late published their belief that a multitude of reputed species in each genus are not real species; but that other species are real, that is, have been independently created. This seems to me a strange conclusion to arrive at. They admit that a multitude of forms, which till lately they themselves thought were special creations, and which are still thus looked at by the majority of naturalists, and which consequently have all the external characteristic features of the species,—they admit that these have been produced by variation, but they refuse to extend the same view to other and slightly different forms. Nevertheless they do not pretend that they can define, or even conjecture, which are the created forms of life, and which are those produced by secondary laws. They admit variation as a *vera causa* in one case, they arbitrarily reject it in another, without assigning any distinction in the two cases. The day will come when this will be given as a curious illustration of the blindness of preconceived opinion. These authors seem no more startled at a miraculous act of creation than at an ordinary birth. But do they really believe that at innumerable periods in the earth's history certain elemental atoms have been commanded suddenly to flash into living tissues? Do they believe that at each supposed act of creation one individual or many were produced? Were all the infinitely numerous kinds of animals and plants created as eggs or seed, or as full grown? and in the case of mammals, were they created bearing the false marks of nourishment from the mother's womb? Undoubtedly some of these same questions cannot be answered by those who believe in the appearance or creation of only a few forms of life, or of some one form alone. It has been maintained by several authors that it is as easy to believe in the creation of a million beings as of one; but Maupertuis'[3] philosophical axiom "of least action" leads the mind more willingly to admit the smaller number; and certainly we

---

[3]French scientist and philosopher (1698–1759)—*Ed.*

ought not to believe that innumerable beings within each great class have been created with plain, but deceptive, marks of descent from a single parent.

As a record of a former state of things, I have retained in the foregoing paragraphs, and elsewhere, several sentences which imply that naturalists believe in the separate creation of each species; and I have been much censured for having thus expressed myself. But undoubtedly this was the general belief when the first edition of the present work appeared. I formerly spoke to very many naturalists on the subject of evolution, and never once met with any sympathetic agreement. It is probable that some did then believe in evolution, but they were either silent, or expressed themselves so ambiguously that it was not easy to understand their meaning. Now things are wholly changed, and almost every naturalist admits the great principle of evolution. There are, however, some who still think that species have suddenly given birth, through quite unexplained means, to new and totally different forms: but, as I have attempted to show, weighty evidence can be opposed to the admission of great and abrupt modifications. Under a scientific point of view, and as leading to further investigation, but little advantage is gained by believing that new forms are suddenly developed in an inexplicable manner from old and widely different forms, over the old belief in the creation of species from the dust of the earth.

It may be asked how far I extend the doctrine of the modification of species. The question is difficult to answer, because the more distinct the forms are which we consider, by so much the arguments in favour of community of descent become fewer in number and less in force. But some arguments of the greatest weight extend very far. All the members of whole classes are connected together by a chain of affinities, and all can be classed on the same principle, in groups subordinate to groups. Fossil remains sometimes tend to fill up very wide intervals between existing orders.

Organs in a rudimentary condition plainly show that an early progenitor had the organ in a fully developed condition; and this in some cases implies an enormous amount of modification in the descendants. Throughout whole classes various structures are formed on the same pattern and at a very early age the embryos closely resemble each other. Therefore I cannot doubt that the theory of descent with modification embraces all the members of the same great class or kingdom. I believe that animals are descended from at most only four or five progenitors, and plants from an equal or lesser number.

Analogy would lead me one step farther, namely, to the belief that all animals and plants are descended from some one prototype. But analogy may be a deceitful guide. Nevertheless all living things have much in common, in their chemical composition, their cellular structure, their laws of growth, and their liability to injurious influences. We see this even in so trifling a fact as that the same poison often similarly affects plants and animals; or that the poison secreted by the gall-fly produces monstrous growths on the wild rose or oak-tree. With all organic beings, excepting perhaps some of the very lowest, sexual reproduction seems to be essentially similar. With all, as far as is at present known, the germinal vesicle is the same; so that all organisms start from a common origin. If we look even to the two main divisions—namely, to the animal and vegetable kingdoms—certain low forms are so far intermediate in character that naturalists have disputed to which kingdom they should be referred. As Professor Asa Gray has remarked, "the spores and other reproductive bodies of many of the lower algae may claim to have first a characteristically animal, and then an unequivocally vegetable existence." Therefore, on the principle of natural selection with divergence of character, it does not seem incredible that, from such low and intermediate forms, both animals and plants may have been developed; and, if we admit this, we must likewise admit that all the organic beings which have ever lived on this earth may be descended from some one primordial form. But this inference is chiefly grounded on analogy, and it is immaterial whether or not it be accepted. No doubt it is possible, as Mr. G. H. Lewes has urged, that at the first commencement of life many different forms were evolved; but if so, we may conclude that only a very few have left modified descendants. For, as I have recently remarked in regard to the members of each great kingdom, such as the Vertebrata, Articulata, etc., we have distinct evidence in their embryological, homologous, and rudimentary structures, that within each kingdom all the members are descended from a single progenitor.

When the views advanced by me in this volume, and by Mr. Wallace, or when analogous views on the origin of species are generally admitted, we can dimly foresee that there will be a considerable revolution in natural history. Systematists will be able to pursue their labours as at present; but they will not be incessantly haunted by the shadowy doubt whether this or that form be a true species. This, I feel sure and I speak after experience, will be no slight relief. The endless disputes whether or not some fifty species of British brambles are good species will cease. Systematists will have only to decide (not that this will be easy) whether any form be sufficiently constant and disfinct from other forms, to be capable of definition; and if definable, whether the differences be sufficiently important to deserve a specific name. This latter point will become a far more essential consideration than it is at present; for differences, however slight, between any two forms, if not blended by intermediate gradations, are looked at by most naturalists as sufficient to raise both forms to the rank of species.

Hereafter we shall be compelled to acknowledge that the only distinction between species and well-marked varieties is, that the latter are known, or believed, to be connected at the present day by intermediate gradations whereas species were formerly thus connected. Hence, without rejecting the considerations of the present existence of intermediate gradations between any two forms, we shall be led to weigh more carefully and to value higher the actual amount of difference between them. It is quite possible that forms now generally acknowledged to be merely varieties may hereafter be thought worthy of specific names; and in this case scientific and common language will come into accordance. In short, we shall have to treat species in the same manner as those naturalists treat genera, who admit that genera are merely artificial combinations made for convenience. This may not be a cheering prospect; but we shall at least be freed from the vain search for the undiscovered and undiscoverable essence of the term species.

The other and more general departments of natural history will rise greatly in interest. The terms used by naturalists, of affinity, relationship, community of type, paternity, morphology, adaptive characters, rudimentary and aborted organs, etc., will cease to be metaphorical, and will have a plain signification. When we no longer look at an organic being as a savage looks at a ship, as something wholly beyond his comprehension; when we regard every production of nature as one which has had a long history; when we contemplate every complex structure and instinct as the summing up of many contrivances, each useful to the possessor, in the same way as any great mechanical invention is the summing up of the labour, the experience, the reason, and even the blunders of numerous workmen; when we thus view each organic being, how far more interesting—I speak from experience—does the study of natural history become!

A grand and almost untrodden field of inquiry will be opened, on the causes and laws of variation, on correlation, on the effects of use and disuse, on the direct action of external conditions, and so forth. The study of domestic productions will rise immensely in value. A new variety raised by man will be a more important and interesting subject for study than one more species added to the infinitude of already recorded species. Our classifications will come to be, as far as they can be so made, genealogies; and will then truly give what may be called the plan of creation. The rules for classifying will no doubt become simpler when we have a definite object in view. We possess no pedigrees or armorial bearings; and we have to discover and trace the many diverging lines of descent in our natural genealogies, by characters of any kind which have long been inherited. Rudimentary organs will speak infallibly with respect to the nature of long-lost structures. Species and groups of species which are called aberrant, and which may fancifully be called living fossils, will aid us in forming a picture of the ancient forms of life. Embryology will often reveal to us the structure, in some degree obscured, of the prototypes of each great class.

When we can feel assured that all the individuals of the same species, and all the closely allied species of most genera, have within a not very remote period descended from one parent, and have migrated from some one birth-place; and we better know the many means of migration, then, by the light which geology now throws, and will continue to throw, on former changes of climate and of the level of the land, we shall surely be enabled to trace in an admirable manner the former migrations of the inhabitants of the whole world. Even at present, by comparing the differences between the inhabitants of the sea on the opposite sides of a continent, and the nature of the various inhabitants on that continent in relation to their apparent means of immigration, some light can be thrown on ancient geography.

The noble science of Geology loses glory from the extreme imperfection of the record. The crust of the earth with its imbedded remains must not be looked at as a well-filled museum, but as a poor collection made at hazard and at rare intervals. The accumulation of each great fossiliferous formation will be recognised as having depended on an unusual concurrence of favourable circumstances, and the blank intervals between the successive stages as having been of vast duration. But we shall be able to gauge with some security the duration of these intervals by a comparison of the preceding and succeeding organic forms. We must be cautious in attempting to correlate as strictly contemporaneous two formations, which do not include many identical species, by the general succession of the forms of life. As species are produced and exterminated by slowly acting and still existing causes, and not by miraculous acts of creation; and as the most important of all causes of organic change is one which is almost independent of altered and perhaps suddenly altered physical conditions, namely the mutual relation of organism to organism,— the improvement of one organism entailing the improvement or the extermination of others; it follows, that the amount of organic change in the fossils of consecutive formations probably serves as a fair measure of the relative, though not actual lapse of time. A number of species, however, keeping in a body might remain for a long period unchanged, whilst within the same period several of these species by migrating into new countries and coming into competition with foreign associates, might become modified; so that we must not overrate the accuracy of organic change as a measure of time.

In the future I see open fields for far more important researches. Psychology will be securely based on the foundation already well laid by Mr. Herbert Spencer,[4] that of the necessary acquirements of each mental power and capacity by gradation. Much light will be thrown on the origin of man and his history.

Authors of the highest eminence seem to be fully satisfied with the view that each species has been independently created. To my mind it accords better with what we know of the laws impressed on matter by the Creator, that the production and extinction of the past and present inhabitants of the world should have been due to secondary causes, like those determining the birth and death of the individual. When I view all beings not as special creations, but as the lineal descendants of some few beings which lived long before the first bed of the Cambrian system was deposited, they seem to me to become ennobled. Judging from the past, we may safely infer that not one living species will transmit its unaltered likeness to a distant futurity. And of the species now living very few will transmit progeny of any kind to a far distant futurity; for the manner in which all organic beings are grouped, shows that the greater number of species in each genus, and all the species in many genera, have left no descendants, but have become utterly extinct. We

---

[4]English philosopher (1820-1903)—Ed.

can so far take a prophetic glance into futurity as to foretell that it will be the common and widely-spread species, belonging to the larger and dominant groups within each class, which will ultimately prevail and procreate new and dominant species. As all the living forms of life are the lineal descendants of those which lived long before the Cambrian epoch, we may feel certain that the ordinary succession by generation has never once been broken, and that no cataclysm has desolated the whole world. Hence we may look with some confidence to a secure future of great length. And as natural selection works solely by and for the good of each being, all corporeal and mental endowments will tend to progress towards perfection.

It is interesting to contemplate a tangled bank, clothed with many plants of many kinds, with birds singing on the bushes, with various insects flitting about, and with worms crawling through the damp earth, and to reflect that these elaborately constructed forms, so different from each other, and dependent upon each other in so complex a manner, have all been produced by laws acting around us. These laws, taken in the largest sense, being Growth with Reproduction; Inheritance which is almost implied by reproduction; Variability from the indirect and direct action of the conditions of life, and from use and disuse: a Ratio of Increase so high as to lead to a Struggle for Life, and as a consequence to Natural Selection, entailing Divergence of Character and the Extinction of less-improved forms. Thus, from the war of nature, from famine and death, the most exalted object which we are capable of conceiving, namely, the production of the higher animals, directly follows. There is grandeur in this view of life, with its several powers, having been originally breathed by the Creator into a few forms or into one; and that, whilst this planet has gone cycling on according to the fixed law of gravity, from so simple a beginning endless forms most beautiful and most wonderful have been and are being evolved.

The Descent of Man

Chapter XXI

General Summary and Conclusion

• • •

The main conclusion arrived at in this work, and now held by many naturalists who are well competent to form a sound judgment, is that man is descended from some less highly-organized form. The grounds upon which

Charles Darwin, *The Descent of Man, and Selection in Relation to Sex* (New York, 1872).

this conclusion rests will never be shaken, for the close similarity between man and the lower animals in embryonic development, as well as in innumerable points of structure and constitution, both of high, and of the most trifling importance—the rudiments which he retains, and the abnormal reversions to which he is occasionally liable—are facts which cannot be disputed. They have long been known, but until recently they told us nothing with respect to the origin of man. Now, when viewed by the light of our knowledge of the whole organic world, their meaning is unmistakable. The great principle of evolution stands up clear and firm, when these groups of facts are considered in connection with others, such as the mutual affinities of the members of the same group, their geographical distribution in past and present times, and their geological succession. It is incredible that all these facts should speak falsely. He who is not content to look, like a savage, at the phenomena of Nature as disconnected, cannot any longer believe that man is the work of a separate act of creation. He will be forced to admit that the close resemblance of the embryo of man to that, for instance, of a dog—the construction of his skull, limbs, and whole frame, independently of the uses to which the parts may be put, on the same plan with that of other mammals—the occasional reappearance of various structures, for instance, of several distinct muscles, which man does not normally possess, but which are common to the Quadrumana—and a crowd of analogous facts—all point in the plainest manner to the conclusion that man is the co-descendant with other mammals of a common progenitor.

[This] conclusion . . . that man is descended from some lowly-organized form, will, I regret to think, be highly distasteful to many persons. But there can hardly be a doubt that we are descended from barbarians. The astonishment which I felt on first seeing a party of Fuegians on a wild and broken shore will never be forgotten by me, for the reflection at once rushed into my mind—such were our ancestors. These men were absolutely naked and bedaubed with paint, their long hair was tangled, their mouths frothed with excitement, and their expression was wild, startled, and distrustful. They possessed hardly any arts, and, like wild animals, lived on what they could catch; they had no government, and were merciless to every one not of their own small tribe. He who has seen a savage in his native land will not feel much shame, if forced to acknowledge that the blood of some more humble creature flows in his veins. For my own part, I would as soon be descended from that heroic little monkey, who braved his dreaded enemy in order to save the life of his keeper; or from that old baboon, who, descending from the mountains, carried away in triumph his young comrade from a crowd of astonished dogs—as from a savage who delights to torture his enemies, offers up bloody sacrifices, practises infanticide without remorse, treats his wives like slaves, knows no decency, and is haunted by the grossest superstitions.

Man may be excused for feeling some pride at having risen, though not through his own exertions, to the very summit of the organic scale; and the fact of his having thus risen, instead of having been aboriginally placed there, may give him hopes for a still higher destiny in the distant future. But we are not here concerned with hopes or fears, only with the truth as far as our reason allows us to discover it. I have given the evidence to the best of my ability; and we must acknowledge, as it seems to me, that man with all his noble qualities, with sympathy which feels for the most debased, with benevolence which extends not only to other men but to the humblest living creature, with his godlike intellect which has penetrated into the movements and constitution of the solar system—with all these exalted powers—Man still bears in his bodily frame the indelible stamp of his lowly origin.

Rudyard Kipling

Imperialism has existed wherever more advanced civilizations have been able to exercise control over their weaker neighbors. Thus we have the ancient empires of the Assyrians, Babylonians, and even the Athenians, who prided themselves on respecting the liberties of their neighboring city-states while subjugating them to Athenian rule. So imperialism has flourished through the centuries. In modern times, following the discoveries of Columbus and others, all of the Western hemisphere was transformed into colonies of European powers. Spain and Portugal colonized South America, which did not become wholly free until the nineteenth century. England colonized North America; the United States drove the British out during the Revolutionary War, but even today Canada retains some colonial ties with the mother country.

Imperialism reached a climax in the nineteenth century, primarily because after that time few undeveloped lands remained to be annexed. These few consisted mainly of parts of Africa and scattered islands in the Caribbean sea and the Pacific Ocean. The United States occupied several of these islands while various European nations vied for colonies in Africa. The Kipling selection is concerned with both African and Indian colonization. Of special interest is the assumption that the colonizing powers did the natives a favor by bringing civilization to them. No mention is made of the fact that these same powers exploited their colonies economically and kept them in bondage.

---

1. In your own words, what is the "White Man's Burden"?

2. What would Símon Bolívar's reaction be to this poem?

The White Man's Burden (1899)

Take up the White Man's burden—
    Send forth the best ye breed—
Go bind your sons to exile
    To serve your captives' need;
To wait in heavy harness,

Rudyard Kipling, *Rudyard Kipling's Verse* (1885–1918) (Garden City, N.Y.: Doubleday, Page & Co. 1919).

On fluttered folk and wild—
Your new-caught, sullen peoples,
   Half-devil and half-child.

Take up the White Man's Burden—
   In patience to abide,
To veil the threat of terror
   And check the show of pride;
By open speech and simple,
   An hundred times made plain,
To seek another's profit,
   And work another's gain.

Take up the White Man's burden—
   The savage wars of peace—
Fill full the mouth of Famine
   And bid the sickness cease;
And when your goal is nearest
   The end for others sought,
Watch Sloth and heathen Folly
   Bring all your hope to nought.

Take up the White Man's burden—
   No tawdry rule of kings,
But toil of serf and sweeper—
   The tale of common things.
The ports ye shall not enter,
   The roads ye shall not tread,
Go make them with your living,
   And mark them with your dead.

Take up the White Man's burden—
   And reap his old reward:
The blame of those ye better,
   The hate of those ye guard—
The cry of hosts ye humour
   (Ah, slowly!) toward the light:—
"Why brought ye us from bondage,"
   "Our loved Egyptian night?"

Take up the White Man's burden—
   Ye dare not stoop to less—
Nor call too loud on Freedom
   To cloak your weariness;

By all ye cry or whisper,
   By all ye leave or do,
The silent, sullen peoples
   Shall weight your Gods and you.

Take up the White Man's burden—
   Have done with childish days—
The lightly proffered laurel,
   The easy, ungrudged praise.
Comes now, to search your manhood
   Through all the thankless years,
Cold, edged with dear-bought wisdom,
   The judgment of your peers!

THINKING ACROSS CULTURES

1. Based on these selections, what makes the modern era different from previous historical periods?

2. The nineteenth century has often been called the Age of Reason. Based on what you have read, do you think this is accurate? Why or why not?

3. The late eighteenth and nineteenth century produced many of the ideas and values that shape contemporary Western culture. Name some from these readings.

4. Who benefited from the political, economic, and technological advances of the nineteenth century? Who did not?

5. Compare and contrast the relation of European countries to the rest of the world in the Age of Encounters and the Modern Era.

THE RECENT PAST

Among historians with a penchant for labels, the twentieth century has come to be known as the Age of Anxiety. To decide whether this designation is apt one might ask whether people during this century have been particularly anxious, more so than in other historical eras. Because such a question is almost surely unanswerable, it might be better to ask: Has the history of this century been such that people have had good reason for heightened anxieties? Just what events have taken place that might have given rise to widespread concern?

The century began in a peaceful and apparently tranquil way. Indeed, peace had generally reigned for nearly a hundred years, since the end of the Napoleonic Wars early in the nineteenth century. Although there had been some conflicts, those on the international level had been relatively minor and those that had reached a larger scale, like the American Civil War, were internal. Nevertheless, the general tranquillity of the international scene, particularly in Europe, was a thin veneer for trouble was brewing beneath the surface. Deep-seated animosities, the legacy of old conflicts, as well as a contest for both political and economic primacy were a prelude to the struggle that was soon to come. The rise of nation-states in the modern era had engendered fierce feelings of nationalism that were ready to break into open conflict. This was particularly true of the most recently united countries, like Germany, which had grown into an economic giant and was chafing at its perceived lack of status among the great powers of Europe.

The explosion came in 1914 and for the next four years the major powers set about to destroy each other. The carnage was frightful; Germany, France, and England sacrificed most of a generation of their young men on the battlefields of the Western front. When the war ended, the victors were so vengeful that, instead of planning for the long-range future, they concentrated on the punishment of Germany. An exception was President Wilson, whose idea of a League of Nations displayed genuine statesmanship, but was repudiated by a myopic United States Senate. It is safe to say that most of the seeds of the Second World War, which was to erupt just twenty years later, were sown during the peace conference at Versailles in 1919.

The period after the first war witnessed three important developments in the world. First came the collapse of the Tsarist regime in Russia. The Communists, inspired by the writings of Karl Marx and led by the fiery revolutionary V. I. Lenin, seized power and established a new regime that, after the successful destruction of the bourgeoisie, was to usher in a classless society. Thus began a great social, economic, and political experiment whose reverberations were felt through most of the world for the remainder of the century. The second development was the Great Depression, which engulfed much of the world, including the United States, during the decade of the thirties, causing untold want and misery. In Germany the depression, as well as national resentment over the defeat suffered in the war, spawned the third interwar development—the rise of political extremism. Profiting by a national atmosphere of frustration and helplessness, a young, unscrupulous demagogue, Adolf Hitler, led his Nazi party into power, soon turning Germany into a totalitarian state and beginning preparations to overrun Europe. He was joined in this project by his Fascist partner, Benito Mussolini, who had come into power earlier in Italy under somewhat similar circumstances. So the stage was set for the Second World War.

Although the beginning of this war is usually dated from the German invasion of Poland in September 1939, it had actually been under way from 1931, when Japan invaded Manchuria. It continued until August, 1945, when it was brought to an end by the atomic bombs dropped by American planes on Hiroshima and Nagasaki. Unlike the first war, in which almost all the fighting occurred in small areas of Europe, this war was worldwide in scope. Although the heaviest fighting took place in Europe, particularly in Russia, and in Asia, no continent escaped. There was extensive combat in northern Africa and even some military activity along the coasts of both North and South America. Finally, a number of small islands in the Pacific Ocean were scenes of heavy battles. No one knows the number of casualties that resulted from the conflict but recent estimates of those killed range as high as fifty million. A large number of the fatalities were civilians, who were the victims of mass bombing raids. It is estimated that one American fire-bombing attack on Tokyo, for example, claimed the lives of over one hundred thousand people.

The Second World War was accompanied by the most heinous crime in history. Known as the Holocaust, it consisted in the wanton and systematic murder of approximately six million people, most but not all of whom were Jews. These victims were exterminated mainly by poison gas in specially constructed death camps, of which Auschwitz in Poland was the most notorious. The person who issued the order for these killings was the German dictator, Hitler, under the guise of the "racial purification" of Germany.

When peace finally came in 1945 it proved not to be peace. Instead, civilization was launched into the Cold War, which was to cast a chill on the world for the next forty years. The Cold War was caused by mutual suspicion, misunderstanding, and hostile intent, in approximately equal proportions. The Soviet Union, which had been with the democracies during the war, was nevertheless deeply suspicious of its wartime partners, with considerable reason. From the very beginning of the revolution in Russia in 1917 the Western powers had opposed the new order, doing whatever they could to undermine the Russian experiment because of their fear that communism would destroy the capitalistic system. Suspicion fostered misunderstanding; throughout the Cold War each side constantly repeated its desire for peace, but the other side interpreted any peaceful overtures made as merely camouflage covering a hostile intent. This, indeed, there was. Although both sides were undoubtedly sincere in their desire for peace, each was planning at the same time to secure whatever advantage it could over the other. Although the Cold War by no means marked the first occasion during which world powers confronted each other in a hostile stance, it contained an element that made it unique in history. Each side possessed nuclear weapons capable of destroying the other, as well as the ability to deliver these directly on the enemy. Although some analysts contend that the existence of such destructive weapons preserved the peace, arguing that the knowledge of their existence and the realization that any attack would produce an immediate and devastating counterattack was sufficient to deter the leaders of both sides from employing them, we have firm evidence that, during the Cuban missile crisis in 1962, both sides were on the very brink of ordering a nuclear attack on the other.

The Cold War came to an abrupt end with the astonishing collapse of communism in Russia during the decade of the 1980s, an event that, prior to its occurrence, almost every expert on international affairs affirmed to be an impossibility. Although the causes of this collapse are even now coming to light, it will probably be decades before scholars have a full understanding of what was wrong with Russian communism. Also, whether this collapse is a portent of the demise of communism in countries like China remains still to be seen.

Most readers of the past several pages will probably by now have concluded that the appellation Age of Anxiety is, if anything, an understatement when applied to the twentieth century, for its history sounds more like a litany of disaster. No one will, I think, point to this century in later years as a bright epoch in the history of the world. Yet there are to be found in it grounds for qualified optimism. The Fascist dictatorships were destroyed, even though it took the most costly war in history to accomplish the task. The Cold War, with the anxieties it caused for people throughout the world has at last come to an end. Also, the period since the Second World War has seen a major decline in political imperialism and the liberation of peoples from the yoke of colonialism.

Finally, nothing has yet been said of the constructive achievements of the century, which have been many. Science, particularly, has flourished, yielding new and exciting knowledge of the universe in all its aspects. Scientific discoveries, in turn, have led to an explosion of technology. Although some of the technological fruits of science, like nuclear weaponry, have been destructive, most have been beneficial to humanity. Great advances have been made in transportation and communications. In the mid-nineteenth century Pony Express riders on swift horses could carry the mail across America at about the same speed, twenty miles an hour, that Roman couriers did in Europe nearly two thousand years before; in the mid-twentieth century jet airplanes could carry it at speeds of six hundred miles an hour; by the end of the century computerized electronic mail could transmit messages in only seconds. The century has also witnessed the beginnings of the conquest of space with astronauts and cosmonauts circling the globe in rocket-powered ships. For the first time in history humans have left the earth to journey to the moon, heralding possible later voyages to other planets of the solar system.

In medicine great advances have been made. Smallpox, for centuries one of the greatest scourges of humanity, has been eliminated. And, although progress is slow, advances continue to be made toward the conquest of the dread disease of cancer. People on the whole are living healthier and longer lives than they did just a generation ago. The list of technological achievements of this century could be continued almost indefinitely. The computer revolution has contributed substantively to most of the other advances, and according to some historians of technology, might be ranked with that of the Industrial Revolution of two centuries ago for its impact on civilization.

In political affairs, the century has seen the birth of two international organizations designed to preserve world peace. That the League of Nations failed must be acknowledged, just as it must be recognized that the United Nations proved virtually impotent during the Cold War. But with that war now ended there are already indications that this international organization will develop into an effective organ for peace. Also a trend that began in the nineteenth century has continued—the liberation of much of the world from European imperialistic masters. India, under the influence of Mahatma Gandhi, gained its independence from England after the Second World War. Indonesia and other parts of East Asia have also become free as has most of Africa. Although independence has brought problems, both political and economic, there is new hope for all these lands.

Turning to a survey of the world as a whole, and its hopes for the future, it is fairly apparent now that the East–West struggle that has dominated the international scene for much of the century has ended. But it is also evident that it is being replaced by a North-South partition. This, rather than being political and military, is economic. Put in harsh but realistic terms, the nations of the Northern Hemisphere are almost uniformly rich while those of the Southern Hemisphere are poor. While this disparity might have been safely ignored in the past we now, because of advances in transportation and communication, all live in one world. The injustice of the situation can no longer be ignored. If world civilization is to have a viable future, something must be done to right the balance. This is an urgent task to which the present and future generations must direct their best will and energies.

Mohandas K. Gandhi

Mohandas K. Gandhi (1869–1948), known and revered throughout the world as Mahatma ("the Great Souled"), was one of the most influential figures in the political history of the twentieth century. Largely because of his tireless activities over a period of more than thirty years, India finally won its independence from British rule in 1947.

Gandhi's method for gaining his goal of *Swaraj*, or Home Rule, for India was extraordinary. Unlike most nationalists, who relied on arms to expel their oppressors, Gandhi repudiated the use of force in any form. His weapon was, in his language, *satyagraha*. This is a difficult term to translate into English. It is usually translated as "passive resistance" and Gandhi himself does so in the selection that follows. But he nevertheless insisted that this rendering fails to capture its essence. Literally the term means "insistence on truth" and Gandhi generally equated it with such phrases as "truth-force" or "soul-force." In political action this meant the practice of disobeying laws imposed by the government that Gandhi considered to be unjust and then accepting the consequences of his disobedience. As a result of his use of *satyagraha*, Gandhi was arrested on innumerable occasions, spending nearly seven years of his life behind bars. But with every incarceration his reputation and the body of his followers grew.

Gandhi was a deeply religious man, drawing his faith from a variety of sources. Central was his native Hindu religion, with its emphasis on nonviolence and its indifference to the comforts of material existence. But this was overlaid with ideas he had imbibed as a youthful law student in London, including the Christianity of the Sermon on the Mount and the pacifistic anarchism of the Russian, Peter Kropotkin (1842–1921). Finally, he was imbued with a deep moral sense, which led him to follow the guidance of his conscience, whatever the personal consequences might be.

Gandhi's life ended tragically. Following India's independence, its Hindu and Muslim populations found themselves in bitter internal conflict. Gandhi did his best to resolve the differences between them, but this led to antagonism against him by extremists from both camps. Early in 1948 he was assassinated by a young Hindu zealot while kneeling at his morning prayers. But there may be an even greater tragedy to relate. Gandhi was strongly opposed to what he considered to be the materialism of modern Western civilization and tried throughout his career to prevent the Westernization of India. In this he had some success, leading a movement to return Indian civilization to an earlier,

simpler mode of life. It is hard, therefore, to believe that Gandhi would
have looked on the subsequent history of his native land with anything
but despair.

---

1.   What does Gandhi mean by "love-force" or "soul-force"? Why does he
     think it will be effective?

2.   How does Gandhi define civilization?

Hind Swaraj or Indian Home Rule

• • •

READER: . . . Will you tell me something of what you have read and thought
of [modern] civilization?

EDITOR: Let us first consider what state of things is described by the word
"civilization." Its true test lies in the fact that people living in it make
bodily welfare the object of life. We will take some examples. The people
of Europe today live in better-built houses than they did a hundred
years ago. This is considered an emblem of civilization, and this is also
a matter to promote bodily happiness. Formerly, they wore skins, and
used spears as their weapons. Now, they wear long trousers, and, for
embellishing their bodies, they wear a variety of clothing, and, instead
of spears, they carry with them revolvers containing five or more chambers. If people of a certain country, who have hitherto not been in the
habit of wearing much clothing, boots, etc., adopt European clothing,
they are supposed to have become civilized out of savagery. Formerly,
in Europe, people ploughed their lands mainly by manual labour.
Now, one man can plough a vast tract by means of steam engines and
can thus amass great wealth. This is called a sign of civilization.
Formerly, only a few men wrote valuable books. Now, anybody writes
and prints anything he likes and poisons people's minds. Formerly, men
travelled in waggons. Now, they fly through the air in trains at the rate
of four hundred and more miles per day. This is considered the height
of civilization. It has been stated that, as men progress, they shall be able
to travel in airships and reach any part of the world in a few hours. Men
will not need the use of their hands and feet. They will press a button,
and they will have their clothing by their side. They will press another
button, and they will have their newspaper. A third, and a motor-car
will be in waiting for them. They will have a variety of delicately dished

Gandhi, Mohandas K., *Hind Swaraj or Indian Home Rule* (Ahmedabad: Navajivan Publishing
House, 1938). Courtesy of The Navajivan Trust.

up food. Everything will be done by machinery. Formerly, when people wanted to fight with one another, they measured between them their bodily strength; now it is possible to take away thousands of lives by one man working behind a gun from a hill. This is civilization. Formerly, men worked in the open air only as much as they liked. Now thousands of workmen meet together and for the sake of maintenance work in factories or mines. Their condition is worse than that of beasts. They are obliged to work, at the risk of their lives, at most dangerous occupations, for the sake of millionaires. Formerly, men were made slaves under physical compulsion. Now they are enslaved by temptation of money and of the luxuries that money can buy. There are now diseases of which people never dreamt before, and an army of doctors is engaged in finding out their cures, and so hospitals have increased. This is a test of civilization. Formerly, special messengers were required and much expense was incurred in order to send letters; today, anyone can abuse his fellow by means of a letter for one penny. True, at the same cost, one can send one's thanks also. Formerly, people had two or three meals consisting of home-made bread and vegetables; now, they require something to eat every two hours so that they have hardly leisure for anything else. What more need I say? All this you can ascertain from several authoritative books. These are all true tests of civilization. And if anyone speaks to the contrary, know that he is ignorant. This civilization takes note neither of morality nor of religion. Its votaries calmly state that their business is not to teach religion. Some even consider it to be a superstitious growth. Others put on the cloak of religion, and prate about morality. But, after twenty years' experience, I have come to the conclusion that immorality is often taught in the name of morality. Even a child can understand that in all I have described above there can be no inducement to morality. Civilization seeks to increase bodily comforts, and it fails miserably even in doing so.

● ● ●

READER: . . . What, then, is [true] civilization?

EDITOR: The answer to that question is not difficult. I believe that the civilization India has evolved is not to be beaten in the world. Nothing can equal the seeds sown by our ancestors. Rome went, Greece shared the same fate; the might of the Pharaohs was broken; Japan has become westernized; of China nothing can be said; but India is still, somehow or other, sound at the foundation. The people of Europe learn their lessons from the writings of the men of Greece or Rome, which exist no longer in their former glory. In trying to learn from them, the Europeans imagine that they will avoid the mistakes of Greece and Rome. Such is their pitiable condition. In the midst of all this India remains immoveable and that is her glory. It is a charge against India that her people are so uncivilized, ignorant and stolid, that it is not possible to induce them to adopt any changes. It is a charge really against our merit. What we have tested and found true on the anvil of experience, we dare not change. Many thrust their advice upon India, and she remains steady. This is her beauty; it is the sheet-anchor of our hope.

Civilization is that mode of conduct which points out to man the path of duty. Performance of duty and observance of morality are convertible terms. To observe morality is to attain mastery over our mind and our passions. So doing, we know ourselves. The Gujarati equivalent for civilization means "good conduct."

If this definition be correct, then India, as so many writers have shown, has nothing to learn from anybody else, and this is as it should be. We notice that the mind is a restless bird; the more it gets the more it wants, and still remains unsatisfied. The more we indulge our passions the more unbridled they become. Our ancestors, therefore, set a limit to our indulgences. They saw that happiness was largely a mental condition. A man is not necessarily happy because he is rich, or unhappy because he is poor. The rich are often seen to be unhappy, the poor to be happy. Millions will always remain poor. Observing all this, our ancestors dissuaded us from luxuries and pleasures. We have managed with the same kind of plough as existed thousands of years ago. We have retained the same kind of cottages that we had in former times and our indigenous education remains the same as before. We have had no system of life-corroding competition. Each followed his own occupation or trade and charged a regulation wage. It was not that we did not know how to invent machinery, but our forefathers knew that, if we set our hearts after such things, we would become slaves and lose our moral fibre. They, therefore, after due deliberation decided that we should only do what we could with our hands and feet. They saw that our real happiness and health consisted in a proper use of our hands and feet. They further reasoned that large cities were a snare and a useless encumbrance and that people would not be happy in them, that there would be gangs of thieves and robbers, prostitution and vice flourishing in them and that poor men would be robbed by rich men. They were, therefore, satisfied with small villages. They saw that kings and their swords were inferior to the sword of ethics, and they, therefore, held the sovereigns of the earth to be inferior to the Rishis and the Fakirs. A nation with a constitution like this is fitter to teach others than to learn from others. This nation had courts, lawyers and doctors, but they were all within bounds. Everybody knew that these professions were not particularly superior; morever, these vakils and vaids did not rob people; they were considered people's dependants, not their masters. Justice was tolerably fair. The ordinary rule was to avoid courts. There were no touts to lure people into them. This evil, too, was noticeable only in and around capitals. The common people lived independently and followed their agricultural occupation. They enjoyed true Home Rule.

And where this cursed modern civilization has not reached, India remains as it was before. The inhabitants of that part of India will very properly laugh at your newfangled notions. The English do not rule over them, nor will you ever rule over them. Those in whose name we speak we do not know, nor do they know us. I would certainly advise you and those like you who love the motherland to go into the interior that has yet been not polluted by the railways and to live there for six months; you might then be patriotic and speak of Home Rule.

Now you see what I consider to be real civilization. Those who want to change conditions such as I have described are enemies of the country and are sinners.

READER: It would be all right if India were exactly as you have described it, but it is also India where there are hundreds of child widows, where two-year-old babies are married, where twelve-year-old girls are mothers and house wives, where women practice polyandry, where the practice of Niyoga obtains, where, in the name of religion, girls dedicate themselves to prostitution, and in the name of religion sheep and goats are killed. Do you consider these also symbols of the civilization that you have described?

EDITOR: You make a mistake. The defects that you have shown are defects. Nobody mistakes them for ancient civilization. They remain in spite of it. Attempts have always been made and will be made to remove them. We may utilize the new spirit that is born in us for purging ourselves of these evils. But what I have described to you as emblems of modern civilization are accepted as such by its votaries. The Indian civilization, as described by me, has been so described by its votaries. In no part of the world, and under no civilization, have all men attained perfection. The tendency of the Indian civilization is to elevate the moral being, that of the Western civilization is to propagate immorality. The latter is godless, the former is based on a belief in God. So understanding and so believing, it behoves every lover of India to cling to the old Indian civilization even as a child clings to the mother's breast.

READER: I appreciate your views about civilization. I will have to think over them. I cannot take them in all at once. What, then, holding the views you do, would you suggest for freeing India?

EDITOR: I do not expect my views to be accepted all of a sudden. My duty is to place them before readers like yourself. Time can be trusted to do the rest. We have already examined the conditions for freeing India, but we have done so indirectly; we will now do so directly. It is a world-known maxim that the removal of the cause of a disease results in the removal of the disease itself. Similarly if the cause of India's slavery be removed, India can become free.

READER: If Indian civilization is, as you say, the best of all, how do you account for India's slavery?

EDITOR: This civilization is unquestionably the best, but it is to be observed that all civilizations have been on their trial. That civilization which is permanent outlives it. Because the sons of India were found wanting, its civilization has been placed in jeopardy. But its strength is to be seen in its ability to survive the shock. Moreover, the whole of India is not touched. Those alone who have been affected by Western civilization have become enslaved. We measure the universe by our own miserable footrule. When we are slaves, we think that the whole universe is enslaved. Because we are in an abject condition, we think that the whole of India is in that condition. As a matter of fact, it is not so, yet it is as well to impute our slavery to the whole of India. But if we bear in mind the above fact, we can see that if we become free, India is free. And in this thought you have a definition of *Swaraj*. It is *Swaraj* when we learn to rule ourselves. It is, therefore, in the palm of our hands. Do not consider this *Swaraj* to be like a dream. There is no idea of sitting still. The *Swaraj* that I wish to picture is such that, after we have once realized it, we shall endeavour to the end of our life-time to persuade others to do likewise. But such *Swaraj* has to be experienced, by each one for himself. One drowning man will never save another. Slaves ourselves, it would be a mere pretension to think of freeing others. Now you will have seen that it is not necessary for us to have as our goal the expulsion of the English. If the English become Indianized, we can accommodate them. If they wish to remain in India along with their civilization, there is no room for them. It lies with us to bring about such a state of things.

• • •

READER: . . . You know that what the English obtained in their own country they obtained by using brute force. I know you have argued that what they have obtained is useless, but that does not affect my argument. They wanted useless things and they got them. My point is that their desire was fulfilled. What does it matter what means they adopted? Why should we not obtain our goal, which is good, by any means whatsoever, even by using violence?

EDITOR: . . . Two kinds of force can back petitions. "We shall hurt you if you do not give this," is one kind of force; it is the force of arms, whose evil results we have already examined. The second kind of force can thus be stated: "If you do not concede our demand, we shall be no longer your petitioners. You can govern us only so long as we remain the governed; we shall no longer have any dealings with you." The force implied in this may be described as love-force, soul-force, or more popularly, but less accurately, passive resistance. This force is indestructible. He who uses it perfectly understands his position. We have an ancient proverb which literally means: "One negative cures thirty-six diseases." The force of arms is powerless when matched against the force of love or the soul.

•••

READER: Is there any historical evidence as to the success of what you have called soul-force or truth-force? No instance seems to have happened of any nation having risen through soul-force. I still think that the evil-doers will not cease doing evil without physical punishment.

EDITOR: The poet Tulsidas has said: "Of religion, pity, or love, is the root, as egotism of the body. Therefore, we should not abandon pity so long as we are alive." This appears to me to be a scientific truth. I believe in it as much as I believe in two and two being four. The force of love is the same as the force of the soul or truth. We have evidence of its working at every step. The universe would disappear without the existence of that force. But you ask for historical evidence. It is, therefore, necessary to know what history means. The Gujarati equivalent means: "It so happened." If that is the meaning of history, it is possible to give copious evidence. But, if it means the doings of kings and emperors, there can be no evidence of soul-force or passive resistance in such history. You cannot expect silver ore in a tin mine. History, as we know it, is a record of the wars of the world; and so there is a proverb among Englishmen that a nation which has no history, that is, no wars, is a happy nation. How kings played, how they became enemies of one another, how they murdered one another, is found accurately recorded in history, and if this were all that had happened in the world, it would have been ended long ago. If the story of the universe had commenced with wars, not a man would have been found alive today. Those people who have been warred against have disappeared as, for instance, the natives of Australia of whom hardly a man was left alive by the intruders. Mark, please, that these natives did not use soul-force in self-defence, and it does not require much foresight to know that the Australians will share the same fate as their victims. "Those that take the sword shall perish by the sword." With us the proverb is that professional swimmers will find a watery grave.

The fact that there are so many men still alive in the world shows that it is based not on the force of arms but on the force of truth or love. Therefore, the greatest and most unimpeachable evidence of the success of the force is to be found in the fact that, in spite of the wars of the world, it still lives on.

Thousands, indeed tens of thousands, depend for their existence on a very active working of this force. Little quarrels of millions of families in their daily lives disappear before the exercise of this force. Hundreds of nations live in peace. History does not and cannot take note of this fact. History is really a record of every interruption of the even working of the force of love or of the soul. Two brothers quarrel; one of them repents and re-awakens the love that was lying dormant in him; the two again begin to live in peace; nobody takes note of this. But if the two brothers, through the intervention of solicitors or some other reason take up arms or go to law—which is another form of the exhibition of brute force,—their doings would be immediately noticed in the press, they would be the talk of their neighbours and would probably go down to history. And what is true of families and communities is true of nations. There is no reason to believe that there is one law for families and another for nations. History, then, is a record of an interruption of the course of nature. Soul-force, being natural, is not noted in history.

READER: According to what you say, it is plain that instances of this kind of passive resistance are not to be found in history. It is necessary to understand this passive resistance more fully. It will be better, therefore, if you enlarge upon it.

EDITOR: Passive resistance is a method of securing rights by personal suffering; it is the reverse of resistance by arms. When I refuse to do a thing that is repugnant to my conscience, I use soul-force. For instance, the Government of the day has passed a law which is applicable to me. I do not like it. If by using violence I force the Government to repeal the law, I am employing what may be termed body-force. If I do not obey the law and accept the penalty for its breach, I use soul-force. It involves sacrifice of self.

Everybody admits that sacrifice of self is infinitely superior to sacrifice of others. Moreover, if this kind of force is used in a cause that is unjust, only the person using it suffers. He does not make others suffer for his mistakes. Men have before now done many things which were subsequently found to have been wrong. No man can claim that he is absolutely in the right or that a particular thing is wrong because he thinks so, but it is wrong for him so long as that is his deliberate judgment. It is therefore meet that he should not do that which he knows to be wrong, and suffer the consequence whatever it may be. This is the key to the use of soul-force.

READER: You would then disregard laws—this is rank disloyalty. We have always been considered a law-abiding nation. You seem to be going even beyond the extremists. They say that we must obey the laws that have been passed, but if the laws be bad, we must drive out the law-givers even by force.

EDITOR: Whether I go beyond them or whether I do not is a matter of no consequence to either of us. We simply want to find out what is right and to act accordingly. The real meaning of the statement that we are a law-abiding nation is that we are passive resisters. When we do not like certain laws, we do not break the heads of law-givers but we suffer and do not submit to the laws. That we should obey laws whether good or bad is a new-fangled notion. There was no such thing in former days. The people disregarded those laws they did not like and suffered the penalties for their breach. It is contrary to our manhood if we obey laws repugnant to our conscience. Such teaching is opposed to religion and means slavery. If the Government were to ask us to go about without any clothing, should we do so? If I were a passive resister, I would say to them that I would have nothing to do with their law. But we have so forgotten ourselves and become so compliant that we do not mind any degrading law.

A man who has realized his manhood, who fears only God, will fear no one else. Man-made laws are not necessarily binding on him. Even the Government does not expect any such thing from us. They do not say "You must do such and such a thing," but they say; "If you do not do it, we will punish you." We are sunk so low that we fancy that it is our duty and our religion to do what the law lays down. If man will only realize that it is unmanly to obey laws that are unjust, no man's tyranny will enslave him. This is the key to self-rule or Home Rule.

It is a superstition and ungodly thing to believe that an act of a majority binds a minority. Many examples can be given in which acts of majorities will be found to have been wrong and those of minorities to have been right. All reforms owe their origin to the initiation of minorities in opposition to majorities. If among a band of robbers a knowledge of robbing is obligatory, is a pious man to accept the obligation? So long as the superstition that men should obey unjust laws exists, so long will their slavery exist. And a passive resister alone can remove such a superstitition.

To use brute-force, to use gunpowder, is contrary to passive resistance, for it means that we want our opponent to do by force that which we desire but he does not. And if such a use of force is justifiable, surely he is entitled to do likewise by us. And so we should never come to an agreement. We may simply fancy, like the blind horse moving in a circle round a mill, that we are making progress. Those who believe that they are not bound to obey laws which are repugnant to their conscience have only the remedy of passive resistance open to them. Any other must lead to disaster.

READER: From what you say I deduce that passive resistance is a splendid weapon of the weak, but that when they are strong they may take up arms.

EDITOR: This is gross ignorance. Passive resistance, that is, soul-force, is matchless. It is superior to the force of arms. How, then, can it be considered only a weapon of the weak? Physical-force men are strangers to the courage that is requisite in a passive resister. Do you believe that a coward can ever disobey a law that he dislikes? Extremists are considered to be advocates of brute force. Why do they, then, talk about obeying laws? I do not blame them. They can say nothing else. When they succeed in driving out the English and they themselves have become governors, they will want you and me to obey their laws. And that is a fitting thing for their constitution. But a passive resister will say he will not obey a law that is against his conscience, even though he may be blown to pieces at the mouth of a cannon.

What do you think? Wherein is courage required—in blowing others to pieces from behind a cannon, or with a smiling face to approach a cannon and be blown to pieces? Who is the true warrior— he who keeps death always as a bosom-friend, or he who controls the death of others? Believe me that a man devoid of courage and manhood can never be a passive resister.

This, however, I will admit; that even a man weak in body is capable of offering this resistance. One man can offer it just as well as millions. Both men and women can indulge in it. It does not require the training of an army; it needs no jiu-jitsu. Control over the mind is alone necessary, and when that is attained, man is free like the king of the forest and his very glance withers the enemy.

Passive resistance is an all-sided sword, it can be used anyhow; it blesses him who uses it and him against whom it is used. Without drawing a drop of blood it produces far-reaching results. It never rusts and cannot be stolen. Competition between passive resisters does not exhaust. The sword of passive resistance does not require a scabbard. It is strange indeed that you should consider such a weapon to be a weapon merely of the weak.

READER: You have said that passive resistance is a speciality of India. Have cannons never been used in India?

EDITOR: Evidently, in your opinion, India means its few princes. To me it means its teeming millions on whom depends the existence of its princes and our own.

Kings will always use their kingly weapons. To use force is bred in them. They want to command, but those who have to obey commands do not want guns; and these are in a majority throughout the world. They have to learn either body-force or soul-force. Where they learn the former, both the rulers and the ruled become like so many madmen; but where they learn soul-force, the commands of the rulers do not go beyond the point of their swords, for true men disregard unjust commands. Peasants have never been subdued by the sword, and never will be. They do not know the use of the sword, and they are not frightened by the use of it by others. That nation is great which rests its head upon death as its pillow. Those who defy death are free from all fear. For those who are labouring under the delusive charms of brute-force, this picture is not overdrawn. The fact is that, in India, the nation at large has generally used passive resistance in all departments of life. We cease to co-operate with our rulers when they displease us. This is passive resistance.

•••

In order to restore India to its pristine condition, we have to return to it. In our own civilization there will naturally be progress, retrogression, reforms, and reactions; but one effort is required, and that is to drive out Western civilization. All else will follow.

READER: When you speak of driving out Western civilization, I suppose you will also say that we want no machinery?

EDITOR: ...Machinery has begun to desolate Europe. Ruination is now knocking at the English gates. Machinery is the chief symbol of modern civilization; it represents a great sin.

The workers in the mills of Bombay have become slaves. The condition of the women working in the mills is shocking. When there were no mills, these women were not starving. If the machinery craze grows in our country, it will become an unhappy land. It may be considered a heresy, but I am bound to say that it were better for us to send money to Manchester [England] and to use flimsy Manchester cloth than to multiply mills in India. By using Manchester cloth we only waste our money; but by reproducing Manchester in India, we shall keep our money at the price of our blood, because our very moral being will be sapped, and I call in support of my statement the very mill-hands as witnesses. And those who have amassed wealth out of factories are not likely to be better than other rich men. It would be folly to assume that an Indian Rockefeller would be better than the American Rockefeller. Impoverished India can become free, but it will be hard for any India made rich through immorality to regain its freedom. I fear we shall have to admit that moneyed men support British rule; their interest is bound up with its stability. Money renders a man helpless. The other thing which is equally harmful is sexual vice. Both are poison. A snake-bite is a lesser poison than these two, because the former merely destroys the body but the latter destroy body, mind, and soul. We need not, therefore, be pleased with the prospect of the growth of the millindustry.

READER: Are the mills, then, to be closed down?

EDITOR: That is difficult. It is no easy task to do away with a thing that is established. We, therefore, say that the non-beginning of a thing is supreme wisdom. We cannot condemn the mill-owners; we can but pity them. It would be too much to expect them to give up their mills, but we may implore them not to increase them. If they would be good they would gradually contract their business. They can establish in thousands of households the ancient and sacred handlooms and they can but out the cloth that may be thus woven. Whether the mill-owners do this or not, people can cease to use machine-made goods.

READER: You have so far spoken about machine-made cloth, but there are innumerable machine-made things. We have either to import them or to introduce machinery into our country.

EDITOR: Indeed, our goods even are made in Germany. What need, then, to speak of matches, pins, and glassware? My answer can be only one. What did India do before these articles were introduced? Precisely the same should be done today. As long as we cannot make pins without machinery so long will we do without them.

• • •

READER: What, then, would you say to the English?

EDITOR: To them I would respectfully say: "I admit you are my rulers. It is not necessary to debate the question whether you hold India by the sword or by my consent. I have no objection to your remaining in my country, but although you are the rulers, you will have to remain as servants of the people. It is not we who have to do as you wish, but it is you who have to do as we wish. You may keep the riches that you have drained away from this land, but you may not drain riches henceforth. Your function will be, if you so wish, to police India; you must abandon the idea of deriving any commercial benefit from us. We hold the civilization that you support to be the reverse of civilization. We consider our civilization to be far superior to yours. If you realize this truth, it will be to your advantage and, if you do not, according to your own proverb, you should only live in our country in the same manner as we do. You must not do anything that is contrary to our religions. It is your duty as rulers that for the sake of the Hindus you should eschew beef, and for the sake of Mahomedans you should avoid bacon and ham. We have hitherto said nothing because we have been cowed down, but you need not consider that you have not hurt our feelings by your conduct. We are not expressing our sentiments either through base selfishness or fear, but because it is our duty now to speak out boldly. We consider your schools and law courts to be useless. We want our own ancient schools and courts to be restored. The common language of India is not English but Hindi. You should, therefore, learn it. We can hold communication with you only in our national language.

We cannot tolerate the idea of your spending money on railways and the military. We see no occasion for either. You may fear Russia; we do not. When she comes we shall look after her. If you are with us, we may then receive her jointly. We do not need any European cloth. We shall manage with articles produced and manufactured at home. You may not keep one eye on Manchester and the other on India. We can work together only if our interests are identical.

This has not been said to you in arrogance. You have great military resources. Your naval power is matchless. If we wanted to fight with you on your own ground, we should be unable to do so, but if the above submissions be not acceptable to you, we cease to play the part of the ruled. You may, if you like, cut us to pieces. You may shatter us at the cannon's mouth. If you act contrary to our will, we shall not help you; and without our help, we know that you cannot move one step forward.

It is likely that you will laugh at all this in the intoxication of your power. We may not be able to disillusion you at once; but if there be any manliness in us, you will see shortly that your intoxication is suicidal and that your laugh at our expense is an aberration of intellect. We believe that at heart you belong to a religious nation. We are living in a land which is the source of religions. How we came together need not be considered, but we can make mutual good use of our relations. "You, English, who have come to India are not good specimens of the English nation, nor can we, almost half-Anglicized Indians, be considered good specimens of the real Indian nation. If the English nation were to know all you have done, it would oppose many of your actions. The mass of the Indians have had few dealings with you. If you will abandon your so-called civilization and search into your own scriptures, you will find that our demands are just. Only on condition of our demands being fully satisfied may you remain in India; and if you remain under those conditions, we shall learn several things from you and you will learn many from us. So doing we shall benefit each other and the world. But that will happen only when the root of our relationship is sunk in a religious soil."

READER: What will you say to the nation?

EDITOR: Who is the nation?

READER: For our purposes it is the nation that you and I have been thinking of, that is those of us who are affected by European civilization, and who are eager to have Home Rule.

EDITOR: To these I would say, "It is only those Indians who are imbued with real love who will be able to speak to the English in the above strain without being frightened, and only those can be said to be so imbued who conscientiously believe that Indian civilization is the best and that the European is a nine days' wonder. Such ephemeral civilizations have often come and gone and will continue to do so. Those only can be considered to be so imbued who, having experienced the force of the soul within themselves, will not cower before brute-force, and will not, on any account, desire to use brute-force. Those only can be considered to have been so imbued who are intensely dissatisfied with the present pitiable condition, having already drunk the cup of poison.

"If there be only one such Indian, he will speak as above to the English and the English will have to listen to him."

• • •

In my opinion, we have used the term "*Swaraj*" without understanding its real significance. I have endeavored to explain it as I understand it, and my conscience testifies that my life henceforth is dedicated to its attainment.

International Organizations

Each of the two great wars of the twentieth century gave birth to an international organization designed to preserve peace—the First World War to the League of Nations and the Second World War to the United Nations. The driving force behind the League, which began operations in 1920 with its headquarters in Geneva, Switzerland, was President Woodrow Wilson, who insisted that the Covenant of the League be included as an integral part of the peace treaties signed at the conclusion of the war. In his mind the heart of the Covenant lay in Article 10, which stipulated that the members "undertake to respect and preserve as against external aggression the territorial integrity and existing political independence of all Members of the League."

The League functioned sporadically throughout the interwar period, until it was eclipsed by the outbreak of the Second World War. Although weakened from the outset by the refusal of the United States to become a member—the U.S. Senate thus repudiating Wilson—it achieved some significant results. It sponsored and supported treaties on the reduction of armaments, settled border disputes between nations, and averted a possible war between Greece and Bulgaria. But on the main issues of the times it was to prove powerless. Its failure was made apparent by its inability to prevent two acts of aggression by major powers—the Japanese occupation of Manchuria in 1931 and the Italian seizure of Ethiopia in 1935.

Planning for a new international organization to replace the League and to be known as the United Nations began well before the end of the Second World War. As the war was drawing to a close, representatives of most of the nations of the world came together in San Francisco in April of 1945 and drafted the Charter of the United Nations. The organization began operations soon afterward, with its headquarters in New York City. Although the United Nations and its subsidiary agencies have accomplished much in the years since its founding, its primary goal of preserving world peace was frustrated for over forty years by the Cold War. Organized with a Security Council including the United States, Great Britain, France, the Soviet Union, and China, each of which had a veto power over any proposed action, it soon became apparent that the organization would be unable to intervene effectively in any dispute arising out of the conflict between the great powers. However, with the dissolution of the Soviet Union and the consequent relaxation of international tensions, the role of the United Nations in world affairs has been enhanced.

Whether its authority and its ability to maintain peace and security in the future will prove effective remains to be seen.

The following selection includes the complete covenant of the League of Nations, the first fifty-one articles of the Charter of the United Nations, and the United Nations' Universal Declaration of Human Rights.

1. Compare and contrast the purposes of the two organizations.

2. To what extent does the Universal Declaration of Human Rights reflect the ideas behind the Declaration of Independence and the Declaration of the Rights of Man and the Citizen?

The Covenant of the League of Nations

The high contracting parties, in order to promote international cooperation and to achieve international peace and security by the acceptance of obligations not to resort to war, by the prescription of open, just and honourable relations between nations, by the first establishment of the understandings of international law as the actual law of conduct among Governments, and by the maintenance of justice and a scrupulous respect for all treaty obligations in the dealings of organized peoples with one another, agree to this Covenant of the League of Nations.

Article 1

1. The original Members of the League of Nations shall be those of the Signatories which are named in the Annex to this Covenant and also such of those other States named in the Annex as shall accede without reservation to this Covenant. Such accession shall be effected by a Declaration deposited with the Secretariat within two months of the coming into force of the Covenant. Notice thereof shall be sent to all other Members of the League.

2. Any fully self-governing State, Dominion or Colony not named in the Annex may become a Member of the League if its admission is agreed to by two-thirds of the Assembly, provided that it shall give effective guarantees of its sincere intention to observe its international obligations, and shall accept such regulations as may be prescribed by the League in regard to its military, naval and air forces and armaments.

3. Any Member of the League may, after two years' notice of its intention so to do, withdraw from the League, provided that all its international obligations and all its obligations under this Covenant shall have been fulfilled at the time of its withdrawal.

Article 2

The action of the League under this Covenant shall be effected through the instrumentality of an Assembly and of a Council, with a permanent Secretariat.

Article 3

1. The Assembly shall consist of Representatives of the Members of the League.

2. The Assembly shall meet at stated intervals and from time to time as occasion may require, at the Seat of the League or at such other place as may be decided upon.

3. The Assembly may deal at its meetings with any matter within the sphere of action of the League or affecting the peace of the world.

4. At meetings of the Assembly, each Member of the League shall have one vote, and may have not more than three Representatives.

Article 4

1. The Council shall consist of Representatives of the Principal Allied and Associated Powers, together with Representatives of four other Members of the League. These four Members of the League shall be selected by the Assembly from time to time in its discretion. Until the appointment of the Representatives of the four Members of the league first selected by the Assembly, Representatives of Belgium, Brazil, Spain, and Greece shall be members of the Council.

2. With the approval of the majority of the Assembly, the Council may name additional Members of the League whose Representatives shall always be members of the Council; the Council with like approval may increase the number of Members of the League to be selected by the Assembly for representation on the Council. The Assembly shall fix by a two-thirds majority the rules dealing with the election of the non-permanent Members of the Council, and particularly such regulations as relate to their term of office and the conditions of re-eligibility.

3. The Council shall meet from time to time as occasion may require, and at least once a year, at the Seat of the League, or at such other place as may be decided upon.

4. The Council may deal at its meetings with any matter within the sphere of action of the League or affecting the peace of the world.

5. Any Member of the League not represented on the Council shall be invited to send a Representative to sit as a member at any meeting of the Council during the consideration of matters specially affecting the interest of that Member of the League.

6.   At meetings of the Council each member of the League represented on the Council shall have one vote, and may have not more than one Representative.

Article 5

1.   Except where otherwise expressly provided in this Covenant or by the terms of the present Treaty, decisions at any meeting of the Assembly or of the Council shall require the agreement of all the Members of the League represented at the meeting.

2.   All matters of procedure at meetings of the Assembly or of the Council, including the appointment of Committees to investigate particular matters, shall be regulated by the Assembly or by the Council, and may be decided by a majority of the Members of the League represented at the meeting.

3.   The first meeting of the Assembly and the first meeting of the Council shall be summoned by the President of the United States of America.

Article 6

1.   The permanent Secretariat shall be established at the Seat of the League. The Secretariat shall comprise a Secretary-General and such secretaries and staff as may be required.

2.   The first Secretary-General shall be the person named in the Annex; thereafter the Secretary-General shall be appointed by the Council with the approval of the majority of the Assembly.

3.   The secretaries and staff of the Secretariat shall be appointed by the Secretary-General with the approval of the Council.

4.   The Secretary-General shall act in that capacity at all meetings of the Assembly and of the Council.

5.   The expenses of the League shall be borne by the Members of the League in the proportion decided by the Assembly.

Article 7

1.   The Seat of the League is established at Geneva.

2.   The Council may at any time decide that the Seat of the League shall be established elsewhere.

3.   All positions under or in connection with the League, including the Secretariat, shall be open equally to men and women.

4.   Representatives of the Members of the League and officials of the League when engaged on the business of the League shall enjoy diplomatic privileges and immunities.

5.   The buildings and other property occupied by the League or its officials or by Representatives attending its meetings shall be inviolable.

Article 8

1.   The Members of the League recognize that the maintenance of peace requires the reduction of national armaments to the lowest point consistent with national safety and the enforcement by common action of international obligations.

2.   The Council, taking account of the geographical situation and circumstances of each state, shall formulate plans for such reduction for the consideration and action of the several Governments.

3.   Such plans shall be subject to reconsideration and revision at least every ten years.

4.   After these plans shall have been adopted by the several Governments, the limits of armaments therein fixed shall not be exceeded without the concurrence of the Council.

5.   The Members of the League agree that the manufacture by private enterprise of munitions and implements of war is open to grave objections. The Council shall advise how the evil effects attendant upon such manufacture can be prevented, due regard being had to the necessities of those Members of the League which are not able to manufacture the munitions and implements of war necessary for their safety.

6.   The Members of the League undertake to interchange full and frank information as to the scale of their armaments, their military, naval and air programmes and the condition of such of their industries as are adaptable to war-like purposes.

Article 9

A permanent Commission shall be constituted to advise the Council on the execution of the provisions of Articles 1 and 8 and on military, naval and air questions generally.

Article 10

The Members of the League undertake to respect and preserve as against external aggression the territorial integrity and existing political independence of all Members of the League. In case of any such aggression or in case of any threat or danger of such aggression the Council shall advise upon the means by which this obligation shall be fulfilled.

Article 11

1.   Any war or threat of war, whether immediately affecting any of the members of the League or not, is hereby declared a matter of concern to the whole League, and the League shall take any action that may be deemed wise and effectual to safeguard the peace of nations. In case any such emergency should arise the Secretary-General shall on the request of any Member of the League forthwith summon a meeting of the Council.

2.   It is also declared to be the friendly right of each Member of the League to bring to the attention of the Assembly or of the Council any circumstances whatever affecting international relations which threatens to disturb international peace or the good understanding between nations upon which peace depends.

Article 12

1.   The Members of the League agree that if there should arise between them any dispute likely to lead to a rupture, they will submit the matter either to arbitration or judicial settlement or to inquiry by the Council, and they agree in no case to resort to war until three months after the award by the arbitrators or the judicial decision or the report by the Council.

2.   In any case under this Article the award of the arbitrators or the judicial decision shall be made within a reasonable time, and the report of the Council shall be made within six months after the submission of the dispute.

Article 13

1.   The Members of the League agree that whenever any dispute shall arise between them which they recognize to be suitable for submission to arbitration or judicial settlement and which cannot be satisfactorily settled by diplomacy, they will submit the whole subject-matter to arbitration or judicial settlement.

2.   Disputes as to the interpretation of a treaty, as to any question of international law, as to the existence of any fact which if established would constitute a breach of any international obligation, or as to the extent and nature of the reparation to be made for any such breach, are declared to be

among those which are generally suitable for submission to arbitration or judicial settlement.

3. For the consideration of any such dispute, the court to which the case is referred shall be the Permanent Court of International Justice, established in accordance with Article 14, or any tribunal agreed on by the parties to the dispute or stipulated in any convention existing between them.

4. The Members of the League agree that they will carry out in full good faith any award or decision that may be rendered and that they will not resort to war against a Member of the League which complies therewith. In the event of any failure to carry out such an award or decision, the Council shall propose what steps should be taken to give effect thereto.

Article 14

The Council shall formulate and submit to the Members of the League for adoption plans for the establishment of a Permanent Court of International Justice. The Court shall be competent to hear and determine any dispute of an international character which the parties thereto submit to it. The Court may also give an advisory opinion upon any dispute or question referred to it by the Council or by the Assembly.

Article 15

1. If there should arise between Members of the League any dispute likely to lead to a rupture, which is not submitted to arbitration or judicial settlement in accordance with Article 13, the Members of the League agree that they will submit the matter to the Council. Any party to the dispute may effect such submission by giving notice of the existence of the dispute to the Secretary-General, who will make all necessary arrangements for a full investigation and consideration thereof.

2. For this purpose the parties to the dispute will communicate to the Secretary-General, as promptly as possible, statements of their case with all the relevant facts and papers, and the Council may forthwith direct the publication thereof.

3. The Council shall endeavour to effect a settlement of the dispute, and if such efforts are successful, a statement shall be made public giving such facts and explanations regarding the dispute and the terms of settlement thereof as the Council may deem appropriate.

4. If the dispute is not thus settled, the Council, either unanimously or by a majority vote, shall make and publish a report containing a statement of the facts of the dispute and the recommendations which are deemed just and proper in regard thereto.

5.   Any Member of the League represented on the Council may make public a statement of the facts of the dispute and of its conclusions regarding the same.

6.   If a report by the Council is unanimously agreed to by the members thereof other than the Representatives of one or more of the parties to the dispute, the Members of the League agree that they will not go to war with any party to the dispute which complies with the recommendations of the report.

7.   If the Council fails to reach a report which is unanimously agreed to by the members thereof, other than the Representatives of one or more of the parties to the dispute, the Members of the League reserve to themselves the right to take such action as they shall consider necessary for the maintenance of right and justice.

8.   If the dispute between the parties is claimed by one of them, and is found by the Council to arise out of a matter which by international law is solely within the domestic jurisdiction of that party, the Council shall so report, and shall make no recommendation as to its settlement.

9.   The Council may in any case under this Article refer the dispute to the Assembly. The dispute shall be so referred at the request of either party to the dispute, provided that such a request be made within fourteen days after the submission of the dispute to the Council.

10.   In any case referred to the Assembly, all the provisions of this Article and Article 12 relating to the action and powers of the Council shall apply to the action and powers of the Assembly, provided that a report made by the Assembly, if concurred in by the Representatives of those Members of the League represented on the Council and of a majority of the other Members of the League, exclusive in each case of the Representatives of the parties to the dispute, shall have the same force as a report by the Council concurred in by all the members thereof other than the Representatives of one or more of the parties to the dispute.

Article 16

1.   Should any Member of the League resort to war in disregard of its covenants under Articles 12, 13 or 15, it shall *ipso facto* be deemed to have committed an act of war against all other Members of the League, which hereby undertake immediately to subject it to the severance of all trade or financial relations, the prohibition of all intercourse between their nationals and the nationals of the covenant-breaking State, and the prevention of all financial, commercial or personal intercourse between the nationals of the covenant-breaking State and the nationals of any other State, whether a Member of the League or not.

2.   It shall be the duty of the Council in such case to recommend to the several Governments concerned what effective military, naval or air force

the Members of the League shall severally contribute to the armed forces to be used to protect the covenants of the League.

3. The Members of the League agree further, that they will mutually support one another in the financial and economic measures which are taken under this article, in order to minimize the loss and inconvenience resulting from the above measures, and that they will mutually support one another in resisting any special measures aimed at one of their number by the covenant-breaking State, and that they will take the necessary steps to afford passage through their territory to the forces of any of the Members of the League which are co-operating to protect the covenants of the League.

4. Any Member of the League which has violated any covenant of the League may be declared to be no longer a Member of the League by a vote of the Council concurred in by the Representatives of all the other Members of the League represented thereon.

Article 17

1. In the event of a dispute between a Member of the League and a State which is not a Member of the League, or between States not Members of the League, the State or States not Members of the League shall be invited to accept the obligations of membership in the League for the purposes of such dispute, upon such conditions as the Council may deem just. If such invitation is accepted, the provisions of Articles 12 to 16 inclusive shall be applied with such modifications as may be deemed necessary by the Council.

2. Upon such invitation being given the council shall immediately institute an inquiry into the circumstances of the dispute and recommend such action as may seem best and most effectual in the circumstances.

3. If a State so invited shall refuse to accept the obligations of membership in the League for the purposes of such dispute, and shall resort to war against a Member of the League, the provisions of Article 16 shall be applicable as against the State taking such action.

4. If both parties to the dispute when so invited refuse to accept the obligations of membership in the League for the purpose of such dispute, the Council may take such measures and make such recommendations as will prevent hostilities and will result in the settlement of the dispute.

Article 18

Every treaty or international engagement entered into hereafter by any Member of the League shall be forthwith registered with the Secretariat and shall as soon as possible be published by it. No such treaty or international engagement shall be binding until so registered.

Article 19

The Assembly may from time to time advise the reconsideration by Members of the League of treaties which have become inapplicable and the consideration of international conditions whose continuance might endanger the peace of the world.

Article 20

1.   The Members of the League severally agree that this Covenant is accepted as abrogating all obligations or understandings *inter se* which are inconsistent with the terms thereof, and solemnly undertake that they will not hereafter enter into any engagements inconsistent with the terms thereof.

2.   In case any Member of the League shall, before becoming a Member of the League, have undertaken any obligations inconsistent with the terms of this covenant, it shall be the duty of such Member to take immediate steps to procure its release from such obligations.

Article 21

Nothing in this Covenant shall be deemed to affect the validity of international engagements, such as treaties of arbitration or regional understandings like the Monroe Doctrine, for securing the maintenance of peace.

Article 22

1.   To those colonies and territories which as a consequence of the late war have ceased to be under the sovereignty of the States which formerly governed them and which are inhabited by the peoples not yet able to stand by themselves under the strenuous conditions of the modern world, there should be applied the principle that the well-being and development of such peoples form a sacred trust of civilization and that securities for the performance of this trust should be embodied in this Covenant.

2.   The best method of giving practical effect to this principle is that the tutelage of such peoples should be entrusted to advanced nations who by reason of their resources, their experience or their geographical position can best undertake this responsibility, and who are willing to accept it, and

that this tutelage should be exercised by them as Mandatories on behalf of the League.

3.   The character of the mandate must differ according to the stage of the development of the people, the geographical situation of the territory, its economic conditions and other similar circumstances.

4.   Certain communities formerly belonging to the Turkish Empire have reached a stage of development where their existence as independent nations can be provisionally recognized subject to the rendering of administrative advice and assistance by a Mandatory until such time as they are able to stand alone. The wishes of these communities must be a principal consideration in the selection of the Mandatory.

5.   Other peoples, especially those of Central Africa, are at such a stage that the Mandatory must be responsible for the administration of the territory under conditions which will guarantee freedom of conscience and religion, subject only to the maintenance of public order and morals, the prohibition of abuses such as the slave trade, the arms traffic and the liquor traffic, and the prevention of the establishment of fortifications or military and naval bases and of military training of the natives for other than police purposes and the defence of territory, and will also secure equal opportunities for the trade and commerce of other Members of the League.

6.   There are territories, such as South-West Africa and certain of the South Pacific Islands, which, owing to the sparseness of their population, or their small size, or their remoteness from the centres of civilization, or their geographical contiguity to the territory of the Mandatory, and other circumstances, can be best administered under the laws of the Mandatory as integral portions of its territory, subject to the safeguards above mentioned in the interests of the indigenous population.

7.   In every case of mandate, the Mandatory shall render to the Council an annual report in reference to the territory committed to its charge.

8.   The degree of authority, control, or administration to be exercised by the Mandatory shall, if not previously agreed upon by the Members of the League, be explicitly defined in each case by the Council.

9.   A permanent Commission shall be constituted to receive and examine the annual reports of the Mandatories and to advise the Council on all matters relating to the observance of the mandates.

Article 23

Subject to and in accordance with the provisions of international conventions existing or hereafter to be agreed upon, the Members of the League:

(a) will endeavour to secure and maintain fair and humane conditions and labour for men, women, and children, both in their own countries and in all countries to which their commercial and industrial relations extend, and for that purpose will establish and maintain the necessary international organizations;

(b) undertake to secure just treatment of the native inhabitants of territories under their control;

(c) will entrust the League with the general supervision over the execution of agreements with regard to the traffic in women and children, and the traffic in opium and other dangerous drugs;

(d) will entrust the League with the general supervision of the trade in arms and ammunition with the countries in which the control of this traffic is necessary in the common interest;

(e) will make provision to secure and maintain freedom of communications and of transit and equitable treatment for the commerce of all Members of the League. In this connexion, the special necessities of the regions devastated during the war of 1914–1918 shall be borne in mind;

(f) will endeavour to take steps in matters of international concern for the prevention and control of disease.

Article 24

1. There shall be placed under the direction of the League all international bureaux already established by general treaties if the parties to such treaties consent. All such international bureaux and all commissions for the regulation of matters of international interest hereafter constituted shall be placed under the direction of the League.

2. In all matters of international interest which are regulated by general conventions but which are not placed under the control of international bureaux or commissions, the Secretariat of the League shall, subject to the consent of the Council and if desired by the parties, collect and distribute all relevant information and shall render any other assistance which may be necessary or desirable.

3. The Council may include as part of the expenses of the Secretariat the expenses of any bureau or commission which is placed under the direction of the League.

Article 25

The Members of the League agree to encourage and promote the establishment and co-operation of duly authorized voluntary national Red Cross organizations having as purposes the improvement of health, the prevention of disease and the mitigation of suffering throughout the world.

Article 26

1. Amendments to this Covenant will take effect when ratified by the Members of the League whose Representatives compose the Council and by a majority of the Members of the League whose Representatives compose the Assembly.

2. No such amendments shall bind any Member of the League which signifies its dissent therefrom, but in that case it shall cease to be a Member of the League.

Charter of the United Nations[1]

We the Peoples of the United Nations Determined

to save succeeding generations from the scourge of war, which twice in our lifetime has brought untold sorrow to mankind, and

to reaffirm faith in fundamental human rights, in the dignity and worth of the human person, in the equal rights of men and women and of nations large and small, and

to establish conditions under which justice and respect for the obligations arising from treaties and other sources of international law can be maintained, and

to promote social progress and better standards of life in larger freedom,

And for These Ends

to practice tolerance and live together in peace with one another as good neighbours, and

to unite our strength to maintain international peace and security, and

to ensure by the acceptance of principles and the institution of methods, that armed force shall not be used, save in the common interest, and

to employ international machinery for the promotion of the economic and social advancement of all peoples,

---

[1]Amendments to Articles 23 and 27 of the Charter of the United Nations, adopted by the General Assembly on 17 December 1963, came into force on 31 August 1965.

The Amendment to Article 23 enlarged the Security Council from 11 to 15 members.

The amended Article 27 provided that decisions of the Security Council on procedural matters shall be made by an affirmative vote of nine members (formerly seven) and on all other matters by an affirmative vote of nine members (formerly seven), including the concurring votes of the five permanent members of the Security Council.

Have Resolved to Combine Our Efforts to Accomplish These Aims

Accordingly, our respective Governments, through representatives assembled in the city of San Francisco, who have exhibited their full powers found to be in good and due form, have agreed to the present Charter of the United Nations and do hereby establish an international organization to be known as the United Nations.

Chapter I

PURPOSES AND PRINCIPLES

Article 1. The Purposes of the United Nations are:

1. To maintain international peace and security, and to that end: to take effective collective measures for the prevention and removal of threats to the peace, and for the suppression of acts of aggression or other breaches of the peace, and to bring about by peaceful means, and in conformity with the principles of justice and international law, adjustment or settlement of international disputes or situations which might lead to a breach of the peace;

2. To develop friendly relations among nations based on respect for the principle of equal rights and self-determination of peoples, and to take other appropriate measures to strengthen universal peace;

3. To achieve international cooperation in solving international problems of an economic, social, cultural or humanitarian character, and in promoting and encouraging respect for human rights and for fundamental freedoms for all without distinction as to race, sex, language, or religion; and

4. To be a centre for harmonizing the actions of nations in the attainment of these common ends.

Article 2. The Organization and its Members, in pursuit of the Purposes stated in Article 1, shall act in accordance with the following Principles.

1. The Organization is based on the principle of the sovereign equality of all its Members.

2. All Members, in order to ensure to all of them the rights and benefits resulting from membership, shall fulfil in good faith the obligations assumed by them in accordance with the present Charter.

3. All Members shall settle their international disputes by peaceful means in such a manner that international peace and security, and justice, are not endangered.

4. All Members shall refrain in their international relations from the threat or use of force against the territorial integrity or political independence of any state, or in any other manner inconsistent with the Purposes of the United Nations.

5. All Members shall give the United Nations every assistance in any action it takes in accordance with the present Charter, and shall refrain from giving assistance to any state against which the United Nations is taking preventive or enforcement action.

6. The Organization shall ensure that states which are not Members of the United Nations act in accordance with these Principles so far as may be necessary for the maintenance of international peace and security.

7. Nothing contained in the present Charter shall authorize the United Nations to intervene in matters which are essentially within the domestic jurisdiction of any state or shall require the Members to submit such matters to settlement under the present Charter; but this principle shall not prejudice the application of enforcement measures under Chapter VII.

Chapter II

MEMBERSHIP

Article 3. The original Members of the United Nations shall be the states which, having participated in the United Nations Conference on International Organization at San Francisco, or having previously signed the Declaration by United Nations of 1 January 1942, sign the present Charter and ratify it in accordance with Article 110.

Article 4.

1. Membership to the United Nations is open to all other peace-loving states which accept the obligations contained in the present Charter and, in the judgment of the Organization, are able and willing to carry out these obligations.

2. The admission of any such state to membership in the United Nations will be effected by a decision of the General Assembly upon the recommendation of the Security Council.

Article 5. A member of the United Nations against which preventive or enforcement action has been taken by the Security Council may be suspended from the exercise of the rights and privileges of membership by the General

Assembly upon the recommendation of the Security Council. The exercise of these rights and privileges may be restored by the Security Council.

Article 6. A member of the United Nations which has persistently violated the Principles contained in the present Charter may be expelled from the Organization by the General Assembly upon the recommendation of the Security Council.

Chapter III

ORGANS

Article 7.

1.   There are established as the principal organs of the United Nations: a General Assembly, a Security Council, an Economic and Social Council, a Trusteeship Council, an International Court of Justice, and a Secretariat.

2.   Such subsidiary organs as may be found necessary may be established in accordance with the present Charter.

Article 8. The United Nations shall place no restrictions on the eligibility of men and women to participate in any capacity and under conditions of equality in its principal and subsidiary organs.

Chapter IV

THE GENERAL ASSEMBLY

Composition

Article 9.

1.   The General Assembly shall consist of all the members of the United Nations.

2.   Each Member shall have not more than five representatives in the General Assembly.

Functions and Powers

Article 10. The General Assembly may discuss any questions or any matters within the scope of the present Charter or relating to the powers and functions of any organs provided for in the present Charter, and except as provided in Article 12, may make recommendations to the Members of the United Nations or to the Security Council or to both on any such questions or matters.

Article 11.

1. The General Assembly may consider the general principles of cooperation in the maintenance of international peace and security, including the principles governing disarmament and the regulation of armaments, and may make recommendations with regard to such principles to the Members or to the Security Council or to both.

2. The General Assembly may discuss any questions relating to the maintenance of international peace and security brought before it by any Member of the United Nations, or by the Security Council, or by a state which is not a Member of the United Nations in accordance with Article 35, paragraph 2, and, except as provided in Article 12, may make recommendations with regard to any such question to the state or states concerned or to the Security Council or to both. Any such question on which action is necessary shall be referred to the Security Council by the General Assembly either before or after discussion.

3. The General Assembly may call the attention of the Security Council to situations which are likely to endanger international peace and security.

4. The powers of the General Assembly set forth in this Article shall not limit the general scope of Article 10.

Article 12.

1. While the Security Council is exercising in respect of any dispute or situation the functions assigned to it in the present Charter, the General Assembly shall not make any recommendation with regard to that dispute or situation unless the Security Council so requests.

2. The Secretary-General, with the Security Council, shall notify the General Assembly at each session of any matters relative to the maintenance of international peace and security which are being dealt with by the Security Council and shall similarly notify the General Assembly or the Members of the United Nations if the General Assembly is not in session, immediately the Security Council ceases to deal with such matters.

Article 13.

1. The General Assembly shall initiate studies and make recommendations for the purpose of:

a. promoting international cooperation in the political field and encouraging the progressive developments of international law and its codification;

b. promoting international cooperation in the economic, social, cultural, educational, and health fields, and assisting in the realization of human rights and fundamental freedoms for all without distinction as to race, sex, language, or religion.

2. The further responsibilities, functions and powers of the General Assembly with respect to matters mentioned in paragraph 1b above are set forth in Chapters IX and X.

Article 14. Subject to the provisions of Article 12, the General Assembly may recommend measures for the peaceful adjustment of any situation, regardless of origin, which it deems likely to impair the general welfare or friendly relations among nations, including situations resulting from a violation of the provisions of the present Charter setting forth the Purposes and Principles of the United Nations.

Article 15.

1. The General Assembly shall receive and consider annual and special reports from the Security Council; these reports shall include an account of the measures that the Security Council has decided upon or taken to maintain international peace and security.

2. The General Assembly shall receive and consider reports from the other organs of the United Nations.

Article 16. The General Assembly shall perform such functions with respect to the international trusteeship system as are assigned to it under Chapters XII and XIII, including the approval of the trusteeship agreements for areas not designed as strategic.

Article 17.

1. The General Assembly shall consider and approve the budget of the Organization.

2. The expenses of the Organization shall be borne by the Members as apportioned by the General Assembly.

3. The General Assembly shall consider and approve any financial and budgetary arrangements with specialized agencies referred to in Article 57 and shall examine the administrative budgets of such

specialized agencies with a view to making recommendations to the agencies concerned.

Voting

Article 18.

    1.   Each member of the General Assembly shall have one vote.

    2.   Decisions of the General Assembly on important questions shall be made by a two-thirds majority of the members present and voting. These questions shall include: recommendations with respect to the maintenance of international peace and security, the election of the non-permanent members of the Security Council, the election of the members of the Economic and Social Council, the election of members of the Trusteeship Council in accordance with paragraph 1c of Article 86, the admission of new members to the United Nations, the suspension of the rights and privileges of membership, the expulsion of Members, questions relating to the operation of the trusteeship system, and budgetary questions.

    3.   Decisions on other questions including the determination of additional categories of questions to be decided by a two-thirds majority, shall be made by a majority of the members present and voting.

Article 19. A member of the United Nations which is in arrears in the payment of its financial contributions to the Organization shall have no vote in the General Assembly if the amount of its arrears equals or exceeds the amount of the contributions due from it for the preceding two full years. The General Assembly may, nevertheless, permit such a Member to vote if it is satisfied that the failure to pay is due to conditions beyond the control of the Member.

Procedure

Article 20. The General Assembly shall meet in regular annual sessions and in such special sessions as occasion may require. Special sessions shall be convoked by the Secretary-General at the request of the Security Council or of a majority of the Members of the United Nations.

Article 21. The General Assembly shall adopt its own rules of procedure. It shall elect its President for each session.

Article 22. The General Assembly may establish such subsidiary organs as it deems necessary for the performance of its functions.

Chapter V

THE SECURITY COUNCIL

Composition

Article 23.

    1. The Security Council shall consist of fifteen members of the United Nations. The Republic of China, France, the Union of Soviet Socialist Republics, the United Kingdom of Great Britain and Northern Ireland, and the United States of America shall be permanent members of the Security Council. The General Assembly shall elect ten other Members of the United Nations to be nonpermanent members of the Security Council, due regard being specially paid, in the first instance to the contribution of Members of the United Nations to the maintenance of international peace and security and to the other purposes of the Organization, and also to equitable geographical distribution.

    2. The nonpermanent members of the Security Council shall be elected for a term of two years. In the first election of the nonpermanent members after the increase of the membership of the Security Council from eleven to fifteen, two of the four additional members shall be chosen for a term of one year. A retiring member shall not be eligible for immediate re-election.

    3. Each member of the Security Council shall have one representative.

Functions and Powers

Article 24.

    1. In order to ensure prompt and effective action by the United Nations, its Members confer on the Security Council primary responsibility for the maintenance of international peace and security, and agree that in carrying out its duties under this responsibility the Security Council acts on their behalf.

    2. In discharging these duties the Security Council shall act in accordance with the Purposes and Principles of the United Nations. The specific powers granted to the Security Council for the discharge of these duties are laid down in Chapters VI, VII, VIII, and XII.

    3. The Security Council shall submit annual and, when necessary, special reports to the General Assembly for its consideration.

Article 25. The Members of the United Nations agree to accept and carry out the decisions of the Security Council in accordance with the present Charter.

Article 26. In order to promote the establishment and maintenance of international peace and security with the least diversion for armaments of the world's human economic resources, the Security Council shall be responsible for formulating, with the assistance of the Military Staff Committee referred to in Article 47, plans to be submitted to the Members of the United Nations for the establishment of a system for the regulation of armaments.

Voting

Article 27.

1. Each member of the Security Council shall have one vote.
2. Decisions of the Security Council on procedural matters shall be made by an affirmative vote of nine members.
3. Decisions of the Security Council on all other matters shall be made by an affirmative vote of nine members including the concurring votes of the permanent members; provided that, in decisions under Chapter VI, and under paragraph 3 of Article 52, a party to a dispute shall abstain from voting.

Procedure

Article 28.

1. The Security Council shall be so organized as to be able to function continuously. Each member of the Security Council shall for this purpose be represented at all times at the seat of the Organization.
2. The Security Council shall hold periodic meetings at which each of its members may, if it so desires, be represented by a member of the government or by some other specially designated representative.
3. The Security Council may hold meetings at such places other than the seat of the Organization as in its judgment will best facilitate its work.

Article 29. The Security Council may establish such subsidiary organs as it deems necessary for the performance of its functions.

Article 30. The Security Council shall adopt its own rules of procedure, including the method of selecting its President.

Article 31. Any Member of the United Nations which is not a member of the Security Council may participate, without vote, in the discussion of any question brought before the Security Council whenever the latter considers that the interests of that Member are specially affected.

Article 32.   Any Member of the United Nations which is not a member of the Security Council or any state which is not a Member of the United Nations, if it is a party to a dispute under consideration by the Security Council, shall be invited to participate, without vote, in the discussion relating to the dispute. The Security Council shall lay down such conditions as it deems just for the participation of such a state which is not a Member of the United Nations.

Chapter VI

PACIFIC SETTLEMENT OF DISPUTES

Article 33.

1.   The parties to any dispute, the continuance of which is likely to endanger the maintenance of international peace and security, shall, first of all, seek a solution by negotiation, enquiry, mediation, conciliation, arbitration, judicial settlement, resort to regional agencies or arrangements, or other peaceful means of their own choice.

2.   The Security Council shall, when it deems necessary, call upon the parties to settle their dispute by such means.

Article 34. The Security Council may investigate any dispute, or any situation which might lead to international friction or give rise to a dispute, in order to determine whether the continuance of the dispute or situation is likely to endanger the maintenance of international peace and security.

Article 35.

1.   Any Member of the United Nations may bring any dispute, or any situation of the nature referred to in Article 34, to the attention of the Security Council or of the General Assembly.

2.   A state which is not a Member of the United Nations may bring to the attention of the Security Council or of the General Assembly any dispute to which it is a party if it accepts in advance, for the purposes of the dispute, the obligations of pacific settlement provided in the present Charter.

3.   The proceedings of the General Assembly in respect of matters brought to its attention under this Article will be subject to the provisions of Articles 11 and 12.

Article 36.

    1. The Security Council may, at any stage of a dispute of the nature referred to in Article 33 or of a situation of like nature, recommend appropriate procedures or methods of adjustment.

    2. The Security Council should take into consideration any procedures for the settlement of the dispute which have already been adopted by the parties.

    3. In making recommendations under this Article the Security Council should also take into consideration that legal disputes should as a general rule be referred by the parties to the International Court of Justice in accordance with the provisions of the Statute of the Court.

Article 37.

    1. Should the parties to a dispute of the nature referred to in Article 33 fail to settle it by the means indicated in that Article, they shall refer it to the Security Council.

    2. If the Security Council deems that the continuance of the dispute is in fact likely to endanger the maintenance of international peace and security, it shall decide whether to take action under Article 36 or to recommend such terms of settlement as it may consider appropriate.

Article 38. Without prejudice to the provisions of Article 33 to 37, the Security Council may, if all the parties to any dispute so request, make recommendations to the parties with a view to a pacific settlement of the dispute.

Chapter VII

ACTION WITH RESPECT TO THREATS TO THE PEACE, BREACHES OF THE PEACE, AND ACTS OF AGGRESSION

Article 39. The Security Council shall determine the existence of any threat to the peace, breach of the peace, or act of aggression and shall make recommendations, or decide what measures shall be taken in accordance with Articles 41 and 42, to maintain or restore international peace and security.

Article 40. In order to prevent an aggravation of the situation, the Security Council may, before making the recommendations or deciding upon the measures provided for in Article 39, call upon the parties concerned to comply with such provisional measures as it deems necessary or desirable. Such provisional measures shall be without prejudice to the rights, claims, or position of the parties concerned. The Security Council shall duly take account of failure to comply with such provisional measures.

Article 41. The Security Council may decide what measures not involving the use of armed forces are to be employed to give effect to its decisions, and it may call upon the Members of the United Nations to apply such measures. These may include complete or partial interruption of economic relations and of rail, sea, air, postal, telegraphic, radio, and other means of communication, and the severance of diplomatic relations.

Article 42. Should the Security Council consider that measures provided for in Article 41 would be inadequate or have proved to be inadequate, it may take such action by air, sea, or land forces as may be necessary to maintain or restore international peace and security. Such action may include demonstrations, blockade, and other operations by air, sea, or land forces of Members of the United Nations.

Article 43.

1. All Members of the United Nations, in order to contribute to the maintenance of international peace and security, undertake to make available to the Security Council, on its call and in accordance with a special agreement or agreements, armed forces, assistance, and facilities, including rights of passage, necessary for the purpose of maintaining international peace and security.

2. Such agreement or agreements shall govern the numbers and types of forces, the degree of readiness and general location, and the nature of the facilities and assistance to be provided.

3. The agreement or agreements shall be negotiated as soon as possible on the initiative of the Security Council. They shall be concluded between the Security Council and Members or between the Security Council and groups of Members and shall be subject to ratification by the signatory states in accordance with their respective constitutional processes.

Article 44. When the Security Council has decided to use force it shall, before calling upon a Member not represented on it to provide armed forces in fulfillment of the obligations assumed under Article 43, invite that Member, if the Member so desires, to participate in the decisions of the Security Council concerning the employment of contingents of that Member's armed forces.

Article 45. In order to enable the United Nations to take urgent military measures, Members shall hold immediately available national air-force contingents for combined international enforcement action. The strength and degree of readiness of these contingents and plans for their combined action shall be determined, within the limits laid down in the special agreement or agreements referred to in Article 43, by the Security Council with the assistance of the Military Staff Committee.

Article 46. Plans for the application of armed force shall be made by the Security Council with the assistance of the Military Staff Committee.

Article 47.

1. There shall be established a Military Staff Committee to advise and assist the Security Council on all questions relating to the Security Council's military requirements for the maintenance of international peace and security, the employment and command of forces placed at its disposal, the regulation of armaments, and possible disarmament.

2. The Military Staff Committee shall consist of the Chiefs of Staff, of the permanent members of the Security Council or their representatives. Any Member of the United Nations not permanently represented on the Committee shall be invited by the Committee to be associated with it when the efficient discharge of the Committee's responsibilities requires the participation of that Member in its work.

3. The Military Staff Committee shall be responsible under the Security Council for the strategic direction of any armed forces placed at the disposal of the Security Council. Questions relating to the command of such forces shall be worked out subsequently.

4. The Military Staff Committee, with the authorization of the Security Council and after consultation with appropriate regional agencies, may establish regional subcommittees.

Article 48.

1. The action required to carry out the decisions of the Security Council for the maintenance of international peace and security shall be taken by all the Members of the United Nations or by some of them, as the Security Council may determine.

2. Such decisions shall be carried out by the Members of the United Nations directly and through their action in the appropriate international agencies of which they are members.

Article 49. The Members of the United Nations shall join in affording mutual assistance in carrying out the measures decided upon by the Security Council.

Article 50. If preventive or enforcement measures against any state are taken by the Security Council, any other state, whether a Member of the United Nations or not, which finds itself confronted with special economic problems arising from the carrying out of those measures shall have the right to consult the Security Council with regard to a solution of those problems.

Article 51. Nothing in the present Charter shall impair the inherent right of individual or collective self-defence if an armed attack occurs against a Member of the United Nations until the Security Council has taken measures necessary to maintain international peace and security. Measures taken by Members in the exercise of this right of self-defence shall be immediately reported to the Security Council and shall not in any way affect the authority and responsibility of the Security Council under the present Charter to take at any time such action as it deems necessary in order to maintain or restore international peace and security.

Universal Declaration of Human Rights

Preamble

Whereas recognition of the inherent dignity and of the equal and inalienable rights of all members of the human family is the foundation of freedom, justice and peace in the world,

Whereas disregard and contempt for human rights have resulted in barbarous acts which have outraged the conscience of mankind, and the advent of a world in which human beings shall enjoy freedom of speech and belief and freedom from fear and want has been proclaimed as the highest aspiration of the common people,

Whereas it is essential, if man is not to be compelled to have recourse, as a last resort, to rebellion against tyranny and oppression, that human rights should be protected by the rule of law,

Whereas it is essential to promote the development of friendly relations between nations,

Whereas the peoples of the United Nations have in the Charter reaffirmed their faith in fundamental human rights, in the dignity and worth of the human person and in the equal rights of men and women and have determined to promote social progress and better standards of life in larger freedom,

Whereas Member States have pledged themselves to achieve, in cooperation with the United Nations, the promotion of universal respect for and observance of human rights and fundamental freedoms,

Whereas a common understanding of these rights and freedoms is of the greatest importance for the full realization of this pledge,

Now, therefore,
The General Assembly

Proclaims this Universal Declaration of Human Rights as a common standard of achievement for all peoples and all nations, to the end that every individual and every organ of society, keeping this Declaration constantly in mind, shall strive by teaching and education to promote respect for these rights and freedoms and by progressive measures, national and international, to secure their universal and effective recognition and observance, both among the peoples of Member States themselves and among the peoples of territories under their jurisdiction.

Article 1

All human beings are born free and equal in dignity and rights. They are endowed with reason and conscience and should act towards one another in a spirit of brotherhood.

Article 2

Everyone is entitled to all the rights and freedoms set forth in this Declaration, without distinction of any kind, such as race, colour, sex, language, religion, political or other opinion, national or social origin, property, birth, or other status.

Furthermore, no distinction shall be made on the basis of the political, jurisdictional or international status of the country or territory to which a person belongs, whether it be independent, trust, non-self-governing, or under any other limitation of sovereignty.

Article 3

Everyone has the right to life, liberty, and the security of person.

Article 4

No one shall be held in slavery or servitude; slavery and the slave trade shall be prohibited in all their forms.

Article 5

No one shall be subjected to torture or to cruel, inhuman, or degrading treatment or punishment.

Article 6

Everyone has the right to recognition everywhere as a person before the law.

Article 7

All are equal before the law and are entitled without any discrimination to equal protection of the law. All are entitled to equal protection against any discrimination in violation of this Declaration and against any incitement to such discrimination.

Article 8

Everyone has the right to an effective remedy by the competent national tribunals for acts violating the fundamental rights granted him by the constitution or by law.

Article 9

No one shall be subjected to arbitrary arrest, detention, or exile.

Article 10

Everyone is entitled in full equality to a fair, and public hearing by an independent and impartial tribunal, in the determination of his rights and obligations and of any criminal charge against him.

Article 11

1. Everyone charged with a penal offence has the right to be presumed innocent until proved guilty according to law in a public trial at which he has had all the guarantees necessary for his defence.

2. No one shall be held guilty of any penal offence on account of any act or omission which did not constitute a penal offence, under national or international law, at the time when it was committed. Nor shall a heavier penalty be imposed than the one that was applicable at the time the penal offence was committed.

Article 12

No one shall be subjected to arbitrary interference with his privacy, family, home, or correspondence, nor to attacks upon his honour and reputation. Everyone has the right to the protection of the law against such interference or attacks.

Article 13

1.   Everyone has the right to freedom of movement and residence within the borders of each State.

2.   Everyone has the right to leave any country, including his own, and to return to his country.

Article 14

1.   Everyone has the right to seek and to enjoy in other countries asylum from persecution.

2.   This right may not be invoked in the case of prosecutions genuinely arising from non-political crimes or from acts contrary to the purposes and principles of the United Nations.

Article 15

1.   Everyone has the right to a nationality.

2.   No one shall be arbitrarily deprived of his nationality nor denied the right to change his nationality.

Article 16

1.   Men and women of full age, without any limitation due to race, nationality, or religion, have the right to marry and to found a family. They are entitled to equal rights as to marriage, during marriage, and at its dissolution.

2.   Marriage shall be entered into only with the free and full consent of the intending spouses.

3.   The family is the natural and fundamental group unit of society and is entitled to protection by society and the State.

Article 17

1.   Everyone has the right to own property alone as well as in association with others.
2.   No one shall be arbitrarily deprived of his property.

Article 18

Everyone has the right to freedom of thought, conscience and religion; this right includes freedom to change his religion or belief, and freedom, either alone or in community with others and in public or private, to manifest his religion or belief in teaching, practice, worship, and observance.

Article 19

Everyone has the right to freedom of opinion and expression; this right includes freedom to hold opinions without interference and to seek, receive and impart information and ideas through any media and regardless of frontiers.

Article 20

1.   Everyone has the right to freedom of peaceful assembly and association.
2.   No one may be compelled to belong to an association.

Article 21

1.   Everyone has the right to take part in the government of his country, directly or through freely chosen representatives.
2.   Everyone has the right of equal access to public service in his country.
3.   The will of the people shall be the basis of the authority of government; this will shall be expressed in periodic and genuine elections which shall be by universal and equal suffrage and shall be held by secret vote or by equivalent free voting procedures.

Article 22

Everyone, as a member of society, has the right to social security and is entitled to realization, through national effort and international co-operation and in accordance with the organization and resources of each State, of the economic, social and cultural rights indispensable for his dignity and the free development of his personality.

Article 23

1.   Everyone has the right to work, to free choice of employment, to just and favourable conditions of work and to protection against unemployment.

2.   Everyone, without any discrimination, has the right to equal pay for equal work.

3.   Everyone who works has the right to just and favourable remuneration ensuring for himself and his family an existence worthy of human dignity, and supplemented, if necessary, by other means of social protection.

4.   Everyone has the right to form and to join trade unions for the protection of his interests.

Article 24

Everyone has the right to rest and leisure, including reasonable limitation of working hours and periodic holidays with pay.

Article 25

1.   Everyone has the right to a standard of living adequate for the health and well-being of himself and of his family, including food, clothing, housing, and medical care and necessary social services, and the right to security in the event of unemployment, sickness, disability, widowhood, old age, or other lack of livelihood in circumstances beyond his control.

2.   Motherhood and childhood are entitled to special care and assistance. All children, whether born in or out of wedlock, shall enjoy the same social protection.

Article 26

1.   Everyone has the right to education. Education shall be free, at least in the elementary and fundamental stages. Elementary education shall be compulsory. Technical and professional education shall be made generally available and higher education shall be equally accessible to all on the basis of merit.

2.   Education shall be directed to the full development of the human personality and to the strengthening of respect for human

rights and fundamental freedoms. It shall promote understanding, tolerance, and friendship among all nations, racial, or religious groups, and shall further the activities of the United Nations for the maintenance of peace.

3.   Parents have a prior right to choose the kind of education that shall be given to their children.

Article 27

1.   Everyone has the right freely to participate in the cultural life of the community, to enjoy the arts and to share in scientific advancement and its benefits.

2.   Everyone has the right to the protection of the moral and material interests resulting from any scientific, literary or artistic production of which he is the author.

Article 28

Everyone is entitled to a social and international order in which the rights and freedoms set forth in this Declaration can be fully realized.

Article 29

1.   Everyone has duties to the community in which alone the free and full development of his personality is possible.

2.   In the exercise of his rights and freedoms, everyone shall be subject only to such limitations as are determined by law solely for the purpose of securing due recognition and respect for the rights and freedoms of others and of meeting the just requirements of morality, public order, and the general welfare in a democratic society.

3.   These rights and freedoms may in no case be exercised contrary to the purposes and principles of the United Nations.

Article 30

Nothing in this Declaration may be interpreted as implying for any State, group, or person any right to engage in any activity or to perform any act aimed at the destruction of any of the rights and freedoms set forth herein.

Mao Tse-Tung

If Karl Marx would have been surprised to see communism taking root in Russia he would have been astonished to see it conquer China; for China, even more than Russia, was a land of peasant farmers, with only a minuscule population of industrial proletarians. Clearly, it was no place for a Communist revolution, according to orthodox Marxist theory.

As in Russia, the success of communism in China was in large part the result of the activities of a single individual—in this case Mao Tse-tung (1893–1976). Mao was instrumental in accomplishing two goals. First, he revised Marxist theory and practice to fit the actual conditions in his country. Lacking a nucleus of industrial workers, but with hundreds of millions of agricultural laborers at hand, most living under conditions of dire poverty, he turned to these peasants for his revolutionary force. (He did suggest that China had undergone an earlier bourgeois revolution in 1911, when Dr. Sun Yat-sen had overthrown the Manchu dynasty and set up a republic.)

Mao's second task was a different, more formidable one that took him over twenty years to accomplish. This was to mount the revolution and to guarantee that it would lead to the establishment of a Communist regime in China. Two obstacles stood in his way; both were military. Scarcely had he begun organizing the peasants and getting the revolution under way than Japan invaded and occupied Manchuria (in 1931) and later much of the rest of China. The Japanese occupation frustrated Mao's revolutionary movement for over a decade until the end of the Second World War in 1945. The other military opposition was internal. During the long struggle against the Japanese a substantial portion of the Chinese army belonged to the *Kuomintang*, under the leadership of Chiang Kai-shek. Chiang, who had originally been a compatriot of Mao, had, over the years, become increasingly reactionary. So, after the expulsion of the Japanese, these two leaders became bitter antagonists, in a struggle for control of China. Mao won, forcing Chiang and his followers to flee to Formosa (Taiwan) in 1949. Finally, he was able to realize his goal of establishing a Communist state in China.

The selection that follows is Mao's account of the beginning phases of the peasant revolt that was to lead to a Communist victory over twenty years later. In 1926 peasants in the interior of China had begun to rise against their landlords, but many of Mao's co-workers belittled their efforts. Mao decided to go to the area himself to see what actually was happening. In the selection he reports on what he found.

1. According to Mao, who were the revolutionary classes? Who were the counterrevolutionary classes?

2. In what ways has Mao changed the Communist ideas of Marx?

Report of an Investigation into the Peasant Movement in Hunan

The Importance of the Peasant Problem

During my recent visit to Hunan I conducted an investigation on the spot into the conditions in the five counties of Siangtan, Siangsiang, Hengshan, Liling and Changsha. In the thirty-two days from January 4 to February 5, in villages and in county towns, I called together for fact-finding conferences experienced peasants and comrades working for the peasant movement, listened attentively to their reports and collected a lot of material. Many of the hows and whys of the peasant movement were quite the reverse of what I had heard from the gentry in Hankow and Changsha. And many strange things there were that I had never seen or heard of before. I think these conditions exist in many other places.

All kinds of arguments against the peasant movement must be speedily set right. The erroneous measures taken by the revolutionary authorities concerning the peasant movement must be speedily changed. Only thus can any good be done for the future of the revolution. For the rise of the present peasant movement is a colossal event. In a very short time, in China's central, southern and northern provinces, several hundred million peasants will rise like a tornado or tempest, a force so extraordinarily swift and violent that no power, however great, will be able to suppress it. They will break all trammels that now bind them and rush forward along the road to liberation. They will send all imperialists, warlords, corrupt officials, local bullies and bad gentry to their graves. All revolutionary parties and all revolutionary comrades will stand before them to be tested, and to be accepted or rejected as they decide.

To march at their head and lead them? Or to follow at their rear, gesticulating at them and criticising them? Or to face them as opponents?

Every Chinese is free to choose among the three alternatives, but circumstances demand that a quick choice be made.

Mao Tse-tung, *Selected Readings from the Works of Mao Tse-tung* (Peking: Foreign Languages Press, 1971). Courtesy of Foreign Languages Press.

Get Organised!

The peasant movement in Hunan, so far as it concerns the counties in the central and southern sections of the province, where the movement is already developed, can be roughly divided into two periods.

The first period was the period of organisation, extending from January to September of last year. In this period, there was the stage from January to June—a stage of underground activities, and the stage from July to September when the revolutionary army expelled Chao Hengti[1]—a stage of open activities. In this period, the membership of the peasant association totalled only 300,000–400,000, and the masses it could directly lead numbered but little more than a million; as there was hardly any struggle in the rural areas, very little criticism of the association was heard. Since its members served as guides, scouts and carriers, the officers in the Northern Expedition Army even had a good word or two for the peasant association.

The second period was the period of revolutionary action, extending from last October to this January. The membership of the peasant association jumped to two million and the masses over whom it could exercise direct leadership increased to ten million people. As the peasants mostly entered only one name for each family when joining the association, a membership of two million therefore means a mass following of about ten million. Of all the peasants in Hunan, almost half are organised. In counties like Siangtan, Siangsiang, Liuyang, Changsha, Liling, Ningsiang, Pingkiang, Siangyin, Hengshan, Hengyang, Leiyang, Chen and Anhwa, nearly all the peasants have rallied organisationally in the association and followed its leadership. The peasants, with their extensive organisation, went right into action and within four months brought about a great and unprecedented revolution in the countryside.

Down with the Local Bullies and Bad Gentry! All Power to the Peasant Association!

The peasants attack as their main targets the local bullies and bad gentry and the lawless landlords, hitting in passing against patriarchal ideologies and institutions, corrupt officials in the cities and evil customs in the rural areas. In force and momentum, the attack is like a tempest or hurricane; those who submit to it survive and those who resist it perish. As a result, the privileges which the feudal landlords have enjoyed for thousands of years are being shattered to pieces. The dignity and prestige of the landlords are dashed to the ground. With the fall of the authority of the landlords, the peasant association becomes the sole organ of authority, and what people call "All power to the peasant

[1]The ruler of Hunan—*Ed.*

association" has come to pass. Even such a trifle as a quarrel between man and wife has to be settled at the peasant association. Nothing can be settled in the absence of people from the association. The association is actually dictating in all matters in the countryside, and it is literally true that "what ever it says, goes." The public can only praise the association and must not condemn it. The local bullies and bad gentry and the lawless landlords have been totally deprived of the right to have their say, and no one dares mutter the word "No." To be safe from the power and pressure of the peasant association, the first-rank local bullies and bad gentry fled to Shanghai; the second-rank ones to Hankow; the third-rank ones to Changsha; and the fourth-rank ones to the county towns; the fifth-rank ones and even lesser fry can only remain in the countryside and surrender to the peasant association.

"I'll donate ten dollars, please admit me to the peasant association," one of the smaller gentry would say.

"Pshaw! Who wants your filthy money!" the peasants would reply.

Many middle and small landlords, rich peasants and middle peasants, formerly opposed to the peasant association, now seek admission in vain. Visiting various places, I often came across such people, who solicited my help. "I beg," they would say, "the committeeman from the provincial capital to be my guarantor."

The census book compiled by the local authorities under the Manchu régime consisted of a regular register and a special register; in the former honest people were entered, and in the latter burglars, bandits and other undesirables. The peasants in some places now use the same method to threaten people formerly opposed to the association: "Enter them in the special register!"

Such people, afraid of being entered in the special register, try various means to seek admission to the association and do not feel at ease until, as they eagerly desire, their names are entered in its register. But they are as a rule sternly turned down, and so spend their days in a constant state of suspense; barred from the doors of the association, they are like homeless people. In short, what was generally sneered at four months ago as the "peasants' gang" has now become something most honourable. Those who prostrated themselves before the power of the gentry now prostrate themselves before the power of the peasants. Everyone admits that the world has changed since last October.

"An Awful Mess!" and "Very Good Indeed!"

The revolt of the peasants in the countryside disturbed the sweet dreams of the gentry. When news about the countryside reached the cities, the gentry there immediately burst into an uproar. When I first arrived in Changsha, I met people from various circles and picked up a good deal of street gossip. From the middle strata upwards to the rightwingers of the Kuomintang, there was not a single person who did not summarise the whole thing in one phrase: "An awful mess!" Even quite revolutionary people, carried away by the opinion of the "awful mess" school which prevailed like a storm over the whole city, became downhearted at the very thought of the conditions in the countryside, and could not deny the word "mess." Even very progressive people could only remark, "Indeed a mess, but inevitable in the course of the revolution." In a word, nobody could categorically deny the word "mess."

But the fact is, as stated above, that the broad peasant masses have risen to fulfil their historic mission, that the democratic forces in the rural areas have risen to overthrow the rural feudal power. The patriarchal-feudal class of local bullies, bad gentry and lawless landlords has formed the basis of autocratic government for thousands of years, the cornerstone of imperialism, warlordism and corrupt officialdom. To overthrow this feudal power is the real objective of the national revolution. What Dr. Sun Yat-sen wanted to do in the forty years he devoted to the national revolution but failed to accomplish, the peasants have accomplished in a few months. This is a marvellous feat which has never been achieved in the last forty or even thousands of years. It is very good indeed. It is not "a mess" at all. It is anything but "an awful mess."

"An awful mess"—that is obviously a theory which, in line with the interests of the landlords, aims at combating the rise of the peasants, a theory of the landlord class for preserving the old order of feudalism and obstructing the establishment of a new order of democracy, and a counter-revolutionary theory. No revolutionary comrade should blindly repeat it. If you have firmly established your revolutionary viewpoint and have furthermore gone the round of the villages for a look, you will feel overjoyed as never before. There, great throngs of tens of thousands of slaves, *i.e.*, the peasants, are overthrowing their cannibal enemies. Their actions are absolutely correct; their actions are very good indeed! "Very good indeed!" is the theory of the peasants and of all other revolutionaries. Every revolutionary comrade should know that the national revolution requires a profound change in the countryside. The Revolution of 1911[2] did not bring about this change, hence its failure. Now the change is taking place, which is an important factor necessary for completing the revolution. Every revolutionary comrade must support this change, or he will be taking the counter-revolutionary stand.

[2]The revolution that ended the autocratic rule of the Manchu dynasty. On October 10, 1911, under the influence of the bourgeois and petty-bourgeois revolutionary groups, a section of the imperial "New Army" staged an uprising in Wuchang, provincial capital of Hupeh. Similar uprisings in other provinces followed in rapid succession and the Manchu regime soon crumbled. On New Year's Day, 1912, the Provisional Government of the Republic of China was inaugurated in Nanking with Sun Yat-sen as President.—*Ed.*

The Question of "Going too Far"

There is another section of people who say, "although the peasant association ought to be formed, it has gone rather too far in its present actions." This is the opinion of the middle-of-the-roaders. But how do matters stand in reality? True, the peasants do in some ways "act unreasonably" in the countryside. The peasant association, supreme in authority, does not allow the landlords to have their say and makes a clean sweep of all their prestige. This is tantamount to trampling the landlords underfoot after knocking them down. The peasants threaten: "Put you in the special register"; they impose fines on the local bullies and bad gentry and demand contributions; they smash their sedan-chairs. Crowds of people swarm into the homes of the local bullies and bad gentry who oppose the peasant association, slaughtering their pigs and consuming their grain. They may even loll for a minute or two on the ivory beds of the young mesdames and mademoiselles in the families of the bullies and gentry. At the slightest provocation they make arrests, crown the arrested with tall paperhats, and parade them through the villages: "You bad gentry, now you know who we are!" Doing whatever they like and turning everything upside down, they have even created a kind of terror in the countryside. This is what some people call "going too far," or "going beyond the proper limit to right a wrong," or "really too outrageous."

The opinion of this group, reasonable on the surface, is erroneous at bottom.

First, the things described above have all been the inevitable results of the doings of the local bullies and bad gentry and lawless landlords themselves. For ages these people, with power in their hands, tyrannised over the peasants and trampled them underfoot; that is why the peasants have now risen in such a great revolt. The most formidable revolts and the most serious troubles invariably occur at places where the local bullies and bad gentry and the lawless landlords were the most ruthless in their evil deeds. The peasants' eyes are perfectly discerning. As to who is bad and who is not, who is the most ruthless and who is less so, and who is to be severely punished and who is to be dealt with lightly, the peasants keep perfectly clear accounts and very seldom has there been any discrepancy between the punishment and the crime.

Secondly, a revolution is not the same as inviting people to dinner, or writing an essay, or painting a picture, or doing fancy needlework; it cannot be anything so refined, so calm and gentle, or so mild, kind, courteous, restrained and magnanimous. A revolution is an uprising, an act of violence whereby one class overthrows another. A rural revolution is a revolution by which the peasantry overthrows the authority of the feudal landlord class. If the peasants do not use the maximum of their strength, they can never overthrow the authority of the landlords which has been deeply rooted for thousands of years. In the rural areas, there must be a great, fervent revolutionary upsurge, which alone can arouse hundreds and thousands of the people of form a great force. All the action mentioned above, labelled as "going too far," are caused by the power of the peasants, generated by a great, fervent, revolutionary upsurge in the countryside. Such actions were quite necessary in the second period of the peasant movement (the period of revolutionary action). In this period, it was necessary to establish the absolute authority of the peasants. It was necessary to stop malicious criticisms against the peasant association. It was necessary to overthrow all the authority of the gentry, to knock them down and even trample them underfoot. All actions labelled as "going too far" had a revolutionary significance in the second period. To put it bluntly, it was necessary to bring about a brief reign of terror in every rural area; otherwise one could never suppress the activities of the counter-revolutionaries in the countryside or overthrow the authority of the gentry. To right a wrong it is necessary to exceed the proper limits, and the wrong cannot be righted without the proper limits being exceeded.

The opinion of this school that the peasants are "going too far" is on the surface different from the opinion of the other school mentioned earlier that the peasant movement is "an awful mess," but in essence it adheres to the same viewpoint, and is likewise a theory of the landlords which supports the interests of the privileged classes. Since this theory hinders the rise of the peasant movement and consequently disrupts the revolution, we must oppose it resolutely.

The So-Called "Movement of the Riffraff"

The right wing of the Kuomintang says, "The peasant movement is a movement of the riffraff, a movement of the lazy peasants." This opinion has gained much currency in Changsha. I went to the countryside and heard the gentry say, "It is all right to set up the peasant association, but the people now running it are incompetent; better put others on the job." This opinion and the dictum of the right wing come to the same thing; both admit that the peasant movement may be carried on (as the peasant movement has already risen, no one dares say that it shouldn't); but both regard the people leading the movement as incompetent and hate particularly those in charge of the associations at the lower levels, labelling them "riffraff." In short, all those who were formerly despised or kicked into the gutter by the gentry, who had no social standing, and who were denied the right to have a say, have now, to everyone's surprise, raised their heads. They have not only raised their heads, but have also taken power into their hands. They are now running the township peasant associations (peasant associations at the lowest level), which have been turned into a formidable force in their hands. They raise their rough, blackened hands and lay them on the gentry. They bind the bad gentry with ropes, put tall paper-hats on them and lead them in a parade through the villages. (This is called "parading through the township" in Siangtan and Siangsiang, and "parading through the fields" in Liling.) Every day the coarse, harsh sound of their denunciation assails the ears of the gentry. They are giving orders and directions in all matters. They rank above everybody else, they who used to rank below everybody else—that is what people mean by "upside down."

Vanguard of the Revolution

When there are two opposite approaches to a thing or a kind of people, there will be two opposite opinions. "An awful mess" and "very good indeed," "riffraff" and "vanguard of the revolution," are both suitable examples.

We have seen the peasants' accomplishment of a revolutionary task for many years left unaccomplished, and their important contributions to the national revolution. But have all the peasants taken part in accomplishing such a great revolutionary task and in making important contributions? No. The peasantry consist of three sections—the rich peasants, the middle peasants and the poor peasants. The circumstances of the three sections differ, and so do their reactions to the revolution. In the first period, what reached the ears of the rich peasants was that the Northern Expedition Army had met with a crushing defeat in Kiangsi, that Chiang Kai-shek had been wounded in the leg and had flown back to Kwangtung, and that Wu P'ei-fu had recaptured Yochow. So they thought that the peasant association certainly could not last long and that the Three People's Principles[3] could never succeed, because such things were never heard of before. The officials of a township peasant association (generally of the so-called "riffraff" type), bringing the membership register and entering the house of a rich peasant, would say to him, "Please join the peasant association." How would the rich peasant answer? "Peasant association? For years I have lived here and tilled the fields; I have not seen anything like the peasant association but I get along all the same. You had better give it up!"—this from a moderate rich peasant. "What peasant association? Association for having one's head chopped off—don't get people into trouble!"—this from a violent rich peasant.

Strangely enough, the peasant association has now been established for several months, and has even dared to oppose the gentry. The gentry in the

[3]The Three People's Principles—Nationalism, Democracy, and the People's Welfare—were proposed by Sun Yat-sen as guiding principles for China's bourgeois-democratic revolution. In the *Manifesto of the First National Congress of the Kuomintang,* issued in 1924, he reinterpreted these principles, defining his Nationalism as the fight against imperialism and pledging active support for the workers' and peasants' movements. The *old* Three People's Principles thus gave way to the *new,* which embody the three cardinal policies of alliance with Russia, cooperation with the Communists, and assistance to the peasants and workers. The new Three People's Principles of the three cardinal policies served as the political basis of Kuomintang-Communist cooperation during the First Revolutionary Civil War period.—*Ed.*

neighbourhood have been arrested by the association and paraded through the villages because they refused to surrender their opium-smoking kits. In the county towns, moreover, prominent members of the gentry have been put to death, such as Yen Yung-ch'iu of Siangtan and Yang Chih-tse of Ningsiang. At the meeting celebrating the anniversary of the October Revolution, the anti-British rally and the grand celebration of the victory of the Northern Expedition, at least ten thousand peasants in every county, carrying big and small banners, with poles and hoes thrown in, marched in demonstrations in great columns like rolling waves. When all this happened, the rich peasants began to feel perplexed. In the grand celebration of the victory of the Northern Expedition, they learnt that Kiu-kiang had been taken, that Chiang Kai-shek had not been wounded in the leg and that Wu P'ei-fu had been finally defeated. Furthermore, "Long live the Three People's Principles!" "Long live the peasant association!" and "Long live the peasants!" were clearly written on the "decrees on red and green paper" [posters]. "Long live the peasants! Are these people to be regarded as emperors?" The rich peasants were greatly puzzled.

So the peasant association put on grand airs. People from the association said to the rich peasants, "We'll enter you in the special register," or, "In another month, the admission fee will be ten dollars!" It was only in these circumstances that the rich peasants tardily joined the peasant association, some paying fifty cents or a dollar (the regular fee being only one hundred cash), others securing admission only after people had put in a good word for them at their request. There are also quite a number of die-hards who, even up to the present, have not joined the association. When the rich peasants join the association they generally enter the name of some old man of sixty or seventy of their family, for they are always afraid of "the drafting of the adult males." After joining the association they never work for it enthusiastically. They remain inactive throughout.

How about the middle peasants? Their attitude is vacillating. They think that the revolution will not do them much good. They have rice in their pots and are not afraid of bailiffs knocking at their doors at midnight. They too, judging a thing by whether it ever existed before, knit their brows and think hard: "Can the peasant association really stand on its own feet?" "Can the Three People's Principles succeed?" Their conclusion is, "Afraid not." They think that all these things depend entirely on the will of Heaven; "To run a peasant association? Who knows if Heaven wills it or not?" In the first period, people from the peasant association, registers in hand, would enter the house of a middle peasant and say to him, "Please join the peasant association!" "No hurry!" replied the middle peasant. It was not until the second period, when the peasant association enjoyed great power, that the middle peasants joined up. In the association they behave better than the rich peasants, but are as yet not very active, and still want to wait and see. It is certainly necessary for the peasant association to explain a good deal more to the middle peasants in order to get them to join.

The main force in the countryside which has always put up the bitterest fight is the poor peasants. Throughout both the period of underground organisation and that of open organisation, the poor peasants have fought militantly all along. They accept most willingly the leadership of the Communist Party. They are the deadliest enemies of the local bullies and bad gentry and attack their strongholds without the slightest hesitation. They say to the rich peasants: "We joined the peasant association long ago, why do you still hesitate?" The rich peasants answer in a mocking tone, "You people have neither a tile over your head nor a pinpoint of land beneath your feet, what should have kept you from joining!" Indeed, the poor peasants are not afraid of losing anything. Many of them really have "neither a tile over their head nor a pinpoint of land beneath their feet"—what should have kept them from joining the association?

According to a survey of Changsha county, the poor peasants comprise 70 per cent of the rural population; the middle peasants, 20 per cent; and the rich peasants and landlords, 10 per cent. The poor peasants who comprise 70 per cent can be subdivided into two groups, the utterly impoverished and the less impoverished. The completely dispossessed, *i.e.*, those who have neither land nor money, and who, without any means of livelihood, are forced to leave home and become mercenary soldiers, or hired labourers, or tramp about as beggars—all belong to the "utterly impoverished" and comprise 20 per cent. The partly dispossessed, *i.e.*, those who have a little land or a little money, but consume more than they receive and live in the midst of toil and worry all the year round, *e.g.*, the handicraftsmen, tenant-peasants (except the rich tenant-peasants) and semi-tenant peasants—all belong to the "less impoverished" and comprise 50 per cent. The enormous mass of poor peasants, altogether comprising 70 per cent of the rural population, are the backbone of the peasant association, the vanguard in overthrowing the feudal forces, and the foremost heroes who have accomplished the great revolutionary undertaking left unaccomplished for many years. Without the poor peasants (the "riffraff" as the gentry call them) it would never have been possible to bring about in the countryside the present state of revolution, to overthrow the local bullies and bad gentry, or to complete the democratic revolution. Being the most revolutionary, the poor peasants have won the leadership in the peasant association. Almost all the posts of chairmen and committee members in the peasant associations at the lowest level were held by poor peasants in both the first and second periods (of the officials in the township associations in Hangshan the utterly impoverished comprise 50 per cent, the less impoverished comprise 40 per cent, and the impoverished intellectuals comprise 10 per cent). This leadership of the poor peasants is absolutely necessary. Without the poor peasants there can be no revolution. To reject them is to reject the revolution. To attack them is to attack the revolution. Their general direction of the revolution has never been wrong.

They have hurt the dignity of the local bullies and bad gentry. They have beaten the big and small local bullies and bad gentry to the ground and trampled them underfoot. Many of their deeds in the period of revolutionary action, described as "going too far," were in fact the very needs of the revolution. Some of the county governments, county headquarters of the party and county peasant associations in Hunan have committed a number of mistakes; there are even some which at the request of the landlords sent soldiers to arrest the lower officials of the peasant associations. Many chairmen and committeemen of the township associations are imprisoned in the jails in Hengshan and Siangsiang. This is a serious mistake, which greatly encourages the arrogance of the reactionaries. To judge whether or not it is a mistake, one need only see how, as soon as the chairmen and committeemen of the peasant associations are arrested, the local lawless landlords are elated and reactionary sentiments grow. We must oppose such counter-revolutionary calumnies as "riffraff movement" and "movement of the lazy peasants" and must be especially careful not to commit the mistake of helping the local bullies and bad gentry to attack the poor peasants.

As a matter of fact, although some of the poor peasant leaders certainly had shortcomings in the past, most of them have reformed themselves by now. They are themselves energetically prohibiting gambling and exterminating banditry. Where the peasant association is powerful, gambling and banditry have vanished. In some places it is literally true that people do not pocket articles dropped on the road and that doors are not bolted at night. According to a survey of Hengshan, 85 per cent of the poor peasant leaders have now turned out to be quite reformed, capable and energetic. Only 15 per cent of them retain some bad habits. They can only be regarded as "the few undesirables," and we must not echo the local bullies and bad gentry in condemning indiscriminately everybody as "riffraff." To tackle this problem of "the few undesirables," we can only, on the basis of the association's slogan of strengthening discipline, carry on propaganda among the masses and educate the undesirables themselves, so that the discipline of the association may be strengthened; but we must not wantonly send soldiers to make arrests, lest we should undermine the prestige of the poor peasantry and encourage the arrogance of the local bullies and bad gentry. This is a point we must particularly attend to.

Adolf Hitler

Anyone who has doubts about the progress of civilization can find ample support for his pessimism in the career of Adolf Hitler (1889–1945), for this twentieth-century political leader was the greatest mass murderer in human history. Although the exact number will never be known, best estimates place the total of those killed on his orders in the region of six million people. These people, it should be emphasized, did not die in war or even incidentally in Hitler's prosecution of other projects but simply because he decided to exterminate them. Although most of his victims were Jews, others were murdered as well, including gypsies, Poles, Russians, and other "undesirables." Known to history as the Holocaust, these deaths were the result of the deliberate, systematic murder of innocent victims from all over Europe.

Hitler wrote the book *Mein Kampf* ("My Struggle") nearly twenty years before the Holocaust, while he was serving a term in a Bavarian prison following his unsuccessful Munich "Beer Hall Putsch" against the government in 1923. The book, in two volumes, covers a number of topics, including an autobiography of the author up to the time of its writing, discussions of various political topics, Hitler's own theories of government, his plans for the development of his National Socialist (Nazi) party, and his eventual conquest of Europe following his release from jail. It has been remarked by an astute political observer that the nations of the world could have spared themselves much bloodshed, grief, and destruction had their leaders of the time read *Mein Kampf* carefully, taken its message seriously, and responded appropriately.

In the chapter "Nation and Race," from which the following selection is taken, Hitler cloaks his racism, including his slander of the Jewish people, in the garments of pseudoscience. Of special interest are his evaluation of the contributions of the Aryans (an undefined term) to culture and his understanding of the concept of idealism.

Hitler did not survive the Second World War. He committed suicide in his bunker far below the streets of Berlin as the Russian army was moving into the city, just after his partner in crime, the Italian dictator, Benito Mussolini, was captured by partisans and executed as he was trying to escape from Italy to Switzerland.

1. How does Hitler justify his racist views?

2. What attributes do "Aryans" possess, according to Hitler?

Mein Kampf

XI. NATION AND RACE

There are some truths which are so obvious that for this very reason they are not seen or at least not recognized by ordinary people. They sometimes pass by such truisms as though blind and are most astonished when someone suddenly discovers what everyone really ought to know. Columbus's eggs lie around by the hundreds of thousands, but Columbuses are met with less frequently.

Thus men without exception wander about in the garden of Nature; they imagine that they know practically everything and yet with few exceptions pass blindly by one of the more patent principles of Nature's rule: the inner segregation of the species of all living beings on this earth.

Even the most superficial observation shows that Nature's restricted form of propagation and increase is an almost rigid basic law of all the innumerable forms of expression of her vital urge. Every animal mates only with a member of the same species. The titmouse seeks the titmouse, the finch the finch, the stork the stork, the field mouse the field mouse, the dormouse the dormouse, the wolf the she-wolf, etc.

Only unusual circumstances can change this, primarily the compulsion of captivity or any other cause that makes it impossible to mate within the same species. But then Nature begins to resist this with all possible means, and her most visible protest consists either in refusing further capacity for propagation to bastards or in limiting the fertility of later offspring; in most cases, however, she takes away the power of resistance to disease or hostile attacks.

This is only too natural.

Any crossing of two beings not at exactly the same level produces a medium between the level of the two parents. This means: the offspring will probably stand higher than the racially lower parent, but not as high as the higher one. Consequently, it will later succumb in the struggle against the higher level. Such mating is contrary to the will of Nature for a higher breeding of all life. The precondition for this does not lie in associating superior and inferior, but in the total victory of the former. The stronger must dominate and not blend with the weaker, thus sacrificing his own greatness. Only the born weakling can view this as cruel, but he after all is only a weak and limited man; for if this law did not prevail, any conceivable higher development of organic living beings would be unthinkable.

The consequence of this racial purity, universally valid in Nature, is not only the sharp outward delimitation of the various races, but their uniform character in themselves. The fox is always a fox, the goose a goose, the tiger a tiger, etc., and the difference can lie at most in the varying measure of force, strength, intelligence, dexterity, endurance, etc., of the individual specimens. But you will never find a fox who in his inner attitude might, for example, show humanitarian tendencies toward geese, as similarly there is no cat with a friendly inclination toward mice.

Therefore, here, too, the struggle among themselves arises less from inner aversion than from hunger and love. In both cases, Nature looks on calmly, with satisfaction, in fact. In the struggle for daily bread all those who are weak and sickly or less determined succumb, while the struggle of the males for the female grants the right or opportunity to propagate only to the healthiest. And struggle is always a means for improving a species' health and power of resistance and, therefore, a cause of its higher development.

If the process were different, all further and higher development would cease and the opposite would occur. For, since the inferior always predominates numerically over the best, if both had the same possibility of preserving life and propagating, the inferior would multiply so much more rapidly that in the end the best would inevitably be driven into the background, unless a correction of this state of affairs were undertaken. Nature does just this by subjecting the weaker part to such severe living conditions that by them alone the number is limited, and by not permitting the remainder to increase promiscuously, but making a new and ruthless choice according to strength and health.

No more than Nature desires the mating of weaker with stronger individuals, even less does she desire the blending of a higher with a lower race, since, if she did, her whole work of higher breeding, over perhaps hundreds of thousands of years, might be ruined with one blow.

Historical experience offers countless proofs of this. It shows with terrifying clarity that in every mingling of Aryan blood with that of lower peoples the result was the end of the cultured people. North America, whose population consists in by far the largest part of Germanic elements who mixed but little with the lower colored peoples, shows a different humanity and culture from Central and South America, where the predominantly Latin immigrants often mixed with the aborigines on a large scale. By this one example, we can clearly and distinctly recognize the effect of racial mixture. The Germanic inhabitant of the American continent, who has remained racially pure and unmixed, rose to be master of the continent; he will remain the master as long as he does not fall a victim to defilement of the blood.

The result of all racial crossing is therefore in brief always the following:

(a) Lowering of the level of the higher race;
(b) Physical and intellectual regression and hence the beginning of a slowly but surely progressing sickness.

To bring about such a development is, then, nothing else but to sin against the will of the eternal creator. . . .

Everything we admire on this earth today—science and art, technology and inventions—is only the creative product of a few peoples and originally perhaps of one race. On them depends the existence of this whole culture. If they perish, the beauty of this earth will sink into the grave with them.

However much the soil, for example, can influence men, the result of the influence will always be different depending on the races in question. The low fertility of a living space may spur the one race to the highest achievements; in others it will only be the cause of bitterest poverty and final undernourishment with all its consequences. The inner nature of peoples is always determining for the manner in which outward influences will be effective. What leads the one to starvation trains the other to hard work.

All great cultures of the past perished only because the originally creative race died out from blood poisoning.

The ultimate cause of such a decline was their forgetting that all culture depends on men and not conversely; hence that to preserve a certain culture the man who creates it must be preserved. This preservation is bound up with the rigid law of necessity and the right to victory of the best and stronger in this world.

Those who want to live, let them fight, and those who do not want to fight in this world of eternal struggle do not deserve to live.

Even if this were hard—that is how it is! Assuredly, however, by far the harder fate is that which strikes the man who thinks he can overcome Nature, but in the last analysis only mocks her. Distress, misfortune, and diseases are her answer.

The man who misjudges and disregards the racial laws actually forfeits the happiness that seems destined to be his. He thwarts the triumphal march of the best race and hence also the precondition for all human progress, and remains, in consequence, burdened with all the sensibility of man, in the animal realm of helpless misery.

It is idle to argue which race or races were the original representative of human culture and hence the real founders of all that we sum up under the word "humanity." It is simpler to raise this question with regard to the present, and here an easy, clear answer results. All the human culture, all the results of art, science, and technology that we see before us today, are almost exclusively the creative product of the Aryan. This very fact admits of the not unfounded inference that he alone was the founder of all higher humanity, therefore representing the prototype of all that we understand by the word "man." He is the Prometheus of mankind from whose bright forehead the divine spark of genius has sprung at all times, forever kindling anew that fire of knowledge which illumined the night of silent mysteries and thus caused man to climb the path to mastery over the other beings of this earth. Exclude him—and perhaps after a thousand years darkness will again descend on the earth, human culture will pass, and the world turn to a desert.

If we were to divide mankind into three groups, the founders of culture, the bearers of culture, the destroyers of culture, only the Aryan could be considered as the representative of the first group. From him originate the foundations and walls of all human creation, and only the outward form and color are determined by the changing traits of character of the various peoples. He provides the mightiest building stones and plans for all human progress and only the execution corresponds to the nature of the varying men and races. . . .

The question of the inner causes of the Aryan's importance can be answered to the effect that they are to be sought less in a natural instinct of self-preservation than in the special type of its expression. The will to live, subjectively viewed, is everywhere equal and different only in the form of its actual expression. In the most primitive living creatures the instinct of self-preservation does not go beyond concern for their own ego. Egoism, as we designate this urge, goes so far that it even embraces time; the moment itself claims everything, granting nothing to the coming hours. In this condition the animal lives only for himself, seeks food only for his present hunger, and fights only for his own life. As long as the instinct of self-preservation expresses itself in this way, every basis is lacking for the formation of a group, even the most primitive form of family. Even a community between male and female, beyond pure mating, demands an extension of the instinct of self-preservation, since concern and struggle for the ego are now directed toward the second party; the male sometimes seeks food for the female, too, but for the most part both seek nourishment for the young. Nearly always one comes to the defense of the other, and thus the first, though infinitely simple, forms of a sense of sacrifice result. As soon as this sense extends beyond the narrow limits of the family, the basis for the formation of larger organisms and finally formal states is created.

In the lowest peoples of the earth this quality is present only to a very slight extent, so that often they do not go beyond the formation of the family. The greater the readiness to subordinate purely personal interests, the higher rises the ability to establish comprehensive communities.

This self-sacrificing will to give one's personal labor and if necessary one's own life for others is most strongly developed in the Aryan. The Aryan is not greatest in his mental qualities as such, but in the extent of his willingness to put all his abilities in the service of the community. In him the instinct of self-preservation has reached the noblest form, since he willingly subordinates his own ego to the life of the community and, if the hour demands, even sacrifices it.

Not in his intellectual gift lies the source of the Aryan's capacity for creating and building culture. If he had just this alone, he could only act destructively, in no case could he organize; for the innermost essence of all organization requires that the individual renounce putting forward his personal opinion and interests and sacrifice both in favor of a larger group. Only by way of this general community does he again recover his share. Now, for example, he no longer works directly for himself, but with his activity articulates himself with the community, not only for his own advantage, but for the advantage of all. The most wonderful elucidation of this attitude is provided by his word "work," by which he does not mean an activity for maintaining life in itself, but exclusively a creative effort that does not conflict with the interests of the community. Otherwise he designates human activity, in so far as it serves the instinct of self-preservation without consideration for his fellow men, as theft, usury, robbery, burglary, etc.

This state of mind, which subordinates the interests in the ego to the conservation of the community, is really the first premise for every truly human culture. From it alone can arise all the great works of mankind, which bring the founder little reward, but the richest blessings to posterity. Yes, from it alone can we understand how so many are able to bear up faithfully under a scanty life which imposes on them nothing but poverty and frugality, but gives the community the foundation of its existence. Every worker, every peasant, every inventor, official, etc., who works without ever being able to achieve any happiness or prosperity for himself, is a representative of his lofty idea, even if the deeper meaning of his activity remains hidden in him.

What applies to work as the foundation of human sustenance and all human progress is true to an even greater degree for the defense of man and his culture. In giving one's own life for the existence of the community lies the crown of all sense of sacrifice. It is this alone that prevents what human hands have built from being overthrown by human hands or destroyed by Nature.

Our own German language possesses a word which magnificently designates this kind of activity: *Pflichterfüllung* [fulfillment of duty]; it means not to be self-sufficient but to serve the community.

The basic attitude from which such activity arises, we call—to distinguish it from egoism and selfishness—idealism. By this we understand only the individual's capacity to make sacrifices for the community, for his fellow men.

How necessary it is to keep realizing that idealism does not represent a superfluous expression of emotion, but that in truth it has been, is, and will be, the premise for what we designate as human culture, yes, that it alone created the concept of "man." It is to this inner attitude that the Aryan owes his position in this world, and to it the world owes man; for it alone formed from pure spirit the creative force which, by a unique pairing of the brutal fist and the intellectual genius, created the monuments of human culture.

Without his idealistic attitude all, even the most dazzling faculties of the intellect, would remain mere intellect as such—outward appearance without inner value, and never creative force.

But, since true idealism is nothing but the subordination of the interests and life of the individual to the community, and this in turn is the precondition for the creation of organizational forms of all kinds, it corresponds in its innermost depths to the ultimate will of Nature. It alone leads men to voluntary recognition of the privilege of force and strength, and thus makes them into a dust particle of that order which shapes and forms the whole universe.

The purest idealism is unconsciously equivalent to the deepest knowledge.

How correct this is, and how little true idealism has to do with playful flights of the imagination, can be seen at once if we let the unspoiled child, a healthy boy, for example, judge. The same boy who feels like throwing up when he hears the tirades of a pacifist "idealist" is ready to give his young life for the ideal of his nationality.

Here the instinct of knowledge unconsciously obeys the deeper necessity of the preservation of the species, if necessary at the cost of the individual, and protests against the visions of the pacifist windbag who in reality is nothing but a cowardly, though camouflaged, egoist, transgressing the laws of development; for development requires willingness on the part of the individual to sacrifice himself for the community, and not the sickly imaginings of cowardly know-it-alls and critics of Nature.

Especially, therefore, at times when the ideal attitude threatens to disappear, we can at once recognize a diminution of that force which forms the community and thus creates the premises of culture. As soon as egoism becomes the ruler of a people, the bands of order are loosened and in the chase after their own happiness men fall from heaven into a real hell.

Yes, even posterity forgets the men who have only served their own advantage and praises the heroes who have renounced their own happiness.

The mightiest counterpart to the Aryan is represented by the Jew. In hardly any people in the world is the instinct of self-preservation developed more strongly than in the so-called "chosen." Of this, the mere fact of the survival of this race may be considered the best proof. Where is the people which in the last two thousand years has been exposed to so slight changes of inner disposition, character, etc., as the Jewish people? What people, finally, has gone through greater upheavals than this one—and nevertheless issued from the mightiest catastrophes of mankind unchanged? What an infinitely tough will to live and preserve the species speaks from these facts!

The mental qualities of the Jew have been schooled in the course of many centuries. Today he passes as "smart," and this in a certain sense he has been at all times. But his intelligence is not the result of his own development, but of visual instruction through foreigners. For the human mind cannot climb to the top without steps; for every step upward he needs the foundation of the past, and this in the comprehensive sense in which it can be revealed only in general culture. All thinking is based only in small part on man's own knowledge, and mostly on the experience of the time that has preceded. The general cultural level provides the individual man, without his noticing it as a rule, with such a profusion of preliminary knowledge that, thus armed, he can more easily take further steps of his own. The boy of today, for example, grows up among a truly vast number of technical acquisitions of the last centuries, so that he takes for granted and no longer pays attention to much that a hundred years ago was a riddle to even the greatest minds, although for following and understanding our progress in the field in question it is of decisive importance to him. If a very genius from the twenties of the past century should suddenly leave his grave today, it would be harder for him even intellectually to find his way in the present era than for an average boy of fifteen today. For he would lack all the infinite preliminary education which our present contemporary unconsciously, so to speak, assimilates while growing up amidst the manifestation of our present general civilization.

Since the Jew—for reasons which will at once become apparent—was never in possession of a culture of his own, the foundations of his intellectual work were always provided by others. His intellect at all times developed through the cultural world surrounding him.

The reverse process never took place.

For if the Jewish people's instinct of self-preservation is not smaller but larger than that of other peoples, if his intellectual faculties can easily arouse the impression that they are equal to the intellectual gifts of other races, he lacks completely the most essential requirement for a cultured people, the idealistic attitude.

In the Jewish people the will to self-sacrifice does not go beyond the individual's naked instinct of self-preservation. Their apparently great sense of solidarity is based on the very primitive herd instinct that is seen in many other living creatures in this world. It is a noteworthy fact that the herd instinct leads to mutual support only as long as a common danger makes this seem useful or inevitable. The same pack of wolves which has just fallen on its prey together disintegrates when hunger abates into its individual beasts. The same is true of horses which try to defend themselves against an assailant in a body, but scatter again as soon as the danger is past.

It is similar with the Jew. His sense of sacrifice is only apparent. It exists only as long as the existence of the individual makes it absolutely necessary. However, as soon as the common enemy is conquered, the danger threatening all averted and the booty hidden, the apparent harmony of the Jews among themselves ceases, again making way for their old causal tendencies. The Jew is only united when a common danger forces him to be or a common booty entices him; if these two grounds are lacking, the qualities of the crassest egoism come into their own, and in the twinkling of an eye the united people turns into a horde of rats, fighting bloodily among themselves.

If the Jews were alone in this world, they would stifle in filth and offal; they would try to get ahead of one another in hate-filled struggle and exterminate one another, in so far as the absolute absence of all sense of self-sacrifice, expressing itself in their cowardice, did not turn battle into comedy here too.

So it is absolutely wrong to infer any ideal sense of sacrifice in the Jews from the fact that they stand together in struggle, or, better expressed, in the plundering of their fellow men.

Here again the Jew is led by nothing but the naked egoism of the individual.

That is why the Jewish state—which should be the living organism for preserving and increasing a race—is completely unlimited as to territory. For a state formation to have a definite spatial setting always presupposes an idealistic attitude on the part of the state-race, and especially a correct interpretation of the concept of work. In the exact measure in which this attitude is lacking any attempt at forming, even of preserving, a spatially delimited state fails. And thus the basis on which alone culture can arise is lacking.

Hence the Jewish people, despite all apparent intellectual qualities, is without any true culture, and especially without any true culture of its own. For what sham culture the Jew today possesses is the property of other peoples, and for the most part it is ruined in his hands.

In judging the Jewish people's attitude on the question of human culture, the most essential characteristic we must always bear in mind is that there has never been a Jewish art and accordingly there is none today either; that above all the two queens of all the arts, architecture and music, owe nothing original to the Jews. What they do accomplish in the field of art is either patchwork or intellectual theft. Thus, the Jews lack those qualities which distinguish the races that are creative and hence culturally blessed.

To what an extent the Jew takes over foreign culture, imitating or rather ruining it, can be seen from the fact that he is mostly found in the art which seems to require the least original invention, the art of acting. But even here, in reality, he is only a "juggler," or rather an ape; for even here he lacks the last touch that is required for real greatness; even here he is not the creative genius, but a superficial imitator, and all the twists and tricks that he uses are powerless to conceal the inner lifelessness of his creative gift. Here the Jewish press most lovingly helps him along by raising such a roar of hosannahs about even the most mediocre bungler, just so long as he is a Jew, that the rest of the world actually ends up by thinking that they have an artist before them, while in truth it is only a pitiful comedian.

No, the Jew possesses no culture-creating force of any sort, since the idealism, without which there is no true higher development of man, is not present in him and never was present. Hence his intellect will never have a constructive effect, but will be destructive, and in very rare cases perhaps will at most be stimulating, but then as the prototype of the "force which always wants evil and nevertheless creates good."[1] Not through him does any progress of mankind occur, but in spite of him.

[1]Goethe's Faust, lines 1336–37: Mephistopheles to Faust.

Japanese Imperialism

In the waning years of the nineteenth century, as European imperialism was beginning to ebb, a new imperial power was rising in the Far East—Japan. The Japanese embarked on their imperialistic expansion soon after beginning their own internal modernization following the Meiji Restoration in 1868. With the hope of becoming a world power, comparable to those in the West, they realized that they needed vast material resources, which their small islands could not provide, to attain their goal. So they turned their eyes to the mainland of Asia. After a preliminary move against the island of Formosa (Taiwan) in 1874, they put military and diplomatic pressure on Korea, gaining important economic concessions there. This effort was followed in 1894 by direct invasion, precipitating a war with China. The Japanese were easily victorious, taking over control of Korea (which was formally annexed in 1910) and forcing the Chinese to cede the island of Formosa and the strategically important Liaotung peninsula of Manchuria to them. Under pressure from the European powers, however, they were forced to return the Liaotung peninsula to China. After a successful war against Russia in 1904 Japan won important economic concessions (which the Russians had held) in Manchuria, as well as the southern half of Sakhalin Island, north of Hokkaido.

During the First World War, as the ally of England, Japan was able with little effort to take control of German colonies in Asia, both on the mainland and among the islands of the western Pacific. Also she saw the war as an opportunity for domination of China itself. In 1915 she presented the Chinese with a set of "Twenty-one Demands," which, had they been granted, would virtually have converted China into a colony of Japan. Although the new republican government of China was able to resist the most sweeping of these demands, Japan did gain some important economic concessions from it. Finally, in 1931, Japan launched her main drive for the conquest of East Asia, beginning with the invasion of Manchuria, which she quickly conquered and annexed. This led to further warfare in China, which was pursued relentlessly for a decade against stubborn Chinese resistance. By 1941 the Japanese had concluded that they needed to eliminate any possibility of American intervention in the war. This they (mistakenly) believed they could do by the destruction of the United States Pacific fleet; hence the surprise attack on Pearl Harbor, which precipitated the American war against Japan.

Outside of Japan little was known directly of the extent of her imperial ambitions. Only at the end of the war were documents uncovered revealing her long-range goals. One of the most important of these was a secret plan, prepared at the beginning of 1942 for the Japanese government by the Total War Research Institute. The product of this plan was to be called "The Greater East Asia Co-Prosperity Sphere."

1. What is the Greater East Asia Co-Prosperity Sphere?

2. Were Japanese imperialist goals different from the goals of nineteenth-century European imperialism? If so, how were they different?

Draft of Basic Plan for Establishment of Greater East Asia Co-Prosperity Sphere

Part I. Outline of Construction

. . . .**The Plan.** The Japanese empire is a manifestation of morality and its special characteristic is the propagation of the Imperial Way. It strives but for the achievement of *Hakkō Ichiu*, the spirit of its founding. . . . It is necessary to foster the increased power of the empire, to cause East Asia to return to its original form of independence and co-prosperity by shaking off the yoke of Europe and America, and to let its countries and peoples develop their respective abilities in peaceful cooperation and secure livelihood.

THE FORM OF EAST ASIATIC INDEPENDENCE AND CO-PROSPERITY

The states, their citizens, and resources, comprised in those areas pertaining to the Pacific, Central Asia, and the Indian Oceans formed into one general union are to be established as an autonomous zone of peaceful living and common prosperity on behalf of the peoples of the nations of East Asia. The area including Japan, Manchuria, North China, lower Yangtze River, and the Russian Maritime Province, forms the nucleus of the East Asiatic Union. The Japanese empire possesses a duty as the leader of the East Asiatic Union.

The above purpose presupposes the inevitable emancipation or independence of Eastern Siberia, China, Indo-China, the South Seas, Australia, and India.

Sources of Japanese Tradition, ed. W.T. de Bary, 1958, © Columbia University Press, New York. Reprinted by permission of the publishers.

REGIONAL DIVISION IN THE EAST ASIATIC UNION AND THE NATIONAL DEFENSE SPHERE FOR THE JAPANESE EMPIRE

In the Union of East Asia, the Japanese empire is at once the stabilizing power and the leading influence. To enable the empire actually to become the central influence in East Asia, the first necessity is the consolidation of the inner belt of East Asia; and the East Asiatic Sphere shall be divided as follows for this purpose:

The Inner Sphere—the vital sphere for the empire—includes Japan, Manchuria, North China, the lower Yangtze Area and the Russian Maritime area.

The Smaller Co-Prosperity Sphere—the smaller self-supplying sphere of East Asia—includes the inner sphere plus Eastern Siberia, China, Indo-China and the South Seas.

The Greater Co-Prosperity Sphere—the larger self-supplying sphere of East Asia—includes the smaller co-prosperity sphere, plus Australia, India, and island groups in the Pacific. . . .

For the present, the smaller co-prosperity sphere shall be the zone in which the construction of East Asia and the stabilization of national defense are to be aimed at. After their completion there shall be a gradual expansion toward the construction of the Greater Co-Prosperity Sphere.

OUTLINE OF EAST ASIATIC ADMINISTRATION

It is intended that the unification of Japan, Manchoukuo, and China in neighborly friendship be realized by the settlement of the Sino-Japanese problems through the crushing of hostile influences in the Chinese interior, and through the construction of a new China in tune with the rapid construction of the Inner Sphere. Aggressive American and British influences in East Asia shall be driven out of the area of Indo-China and the South Seas, and this area shall be brought into our defense sphere. The war with Britain and America shall be prosecuted for that purpose.

The Russian aggressive influence in East Asia will be driven out. Eastern Siberia shall be cut off from the Soviet regime and included in our defense sphere. For this purpose, a war with the Soviets is expected. It is considered possible that this Northern problem may break out before the general settlement of the present Sino-Japanese and the Southern problems if the situation renders this unavoidable. Next the independence of Australia, India, etc. shall gradually be brought about. For this purpose, a recurrence of war with Britain and her allies is expected. The construction of a Greater Mongolian State is expected during the above phase. The construction of the Smaller Co-Prosperity Sphere is expected to require at least twenty years from the present time.

THE BUILDING OF THE NATIONAL STRENGTH

Since the Japanese empire is the center and pioneer of Oriental moral and cultural reconstruction, the officials and people of this country must return to the spirit of the Orient and acquire a thorough understanding of the spirit of the national moral character.

In the economic construction of the country, Japanese and Manchurian national power shall first be consolidated, then the unification of Japan, Manchoukuo and China, shall be effected. . . . Thus a central industry will be constructed in East Asia, and the necessary relations established with the Southern Seas.

The standard for the construction of the national power and its military force, so as to meet the various situations that might affect the stages of East Asiatic administration and the national defense sphere, shall be so set as to be capable of driving off any British, American, Soviet or Chinese counter influences in the future. . . .

Chapter 3. Political Construction

BASIC PLAN

The realization of the great ideal of constructing Greater East Asia Co-Prosperity requires not only the complete prosecution of the current Greater East Asia War but also presupposes another great war in the future. Therefore, the following two points must be made the primary starting points for the political construction of East Asia during the course of the next twenty years: 1) Preparation for war with the other spheres of the world; and 2) Unification and construction of the East Asia Smaller Co-Prosperity Sphere.

The following are the basic principles for the political construction of East Asia, when the above two points are taken into consideration:

a.   The politically dominant influence of European and American countries in the Smaller Co-Prosperity Sphere shall be gradually driven out and the area shall enjoy its liberation from the shackles hitherto forced upon it.

b.   The desires of the peoples in the sphere for their independence shall be respected and endeavors shall be made for their fulfillment, but proper and suitable forms of government shall be decided for them in consideration of military and economic requirements and of the historical, political and cultural elements peculiar to each area

It must also be noted that the independence of various peoples of East Asia should be based upon the idea of constructing East Asia as "independent countries existing within the New Order of East Asia" and that this conception differs from an independence based on the idea of liberalism and national self-determination.

c.   During the course of construction, military unification is deemed particularly important, and the military zones and key points necessary for defense shall be directly or indirectly under the control of our country.

d.   The peoples of the sphere shall obtain their proper positions, the unity of the people's minds shall be effected and the unification of the sphere shall be realized with the empire as its center. . . .

Chapter 4. Thought and Cultural Construction

GENERAL AIM IN THOUGHT

The ultimate aim in thought construction in East Asia is to make East Asiatic peoples revere the imperial influence by propagating the Imperial Way based on the spirit of construction, and to establish the belief that uniting solely under this influence is the one and only way to the eternal growth and development of East Asia.

And during the next twenty years (the period during which the above ideal is to be reached) it is necessary to make the nations and peoples of East Asia realize the historical significance of the establishment of the New Order in East Asia, and in the common consciousness of East Asiatic unity, to liberate East Asia from the shackles of Europe and America and to establish the common conviction of constructing a New Order based on East Asiatic morality.

Occidental individualism and materialism shall be rejected and a moral world view, the basic principle of whose morality shall be the Imperial Way, shall be established. The ultimate object to be achieved is not exploitation but co-prosperity and mutual help, not competitive conflict but mutual assistance and mild peace, not a formal view of equality but a view of order based on righteous classification, not an idea of rights but an idea of service, and not several world views but one unified world view.

GENERAL AIM IN CULTURE

The essence of the traditional culture of the Orient shall be developed and manifested. And, casting off the negative and conservative cultural characteristics of the continents (India and China) on the one hand, and taking in the good points of Western culture on the other, an Oriental culture and morality, on a grand scale and subtly refined, shall be created.

Hiroshima and Nagasaki

Although heavy fighting had been waged on the mainland of Asia since the Japanese invasion of Manchuria in 1931, the beginning of the Second World War is usually dated from September 1, 1939, when Nazi Germany launched its surprise attack on Poland. Unlike the First World War, in which hostilities were generally confined to relatively small areas of Europe, the Second World War was virtually global in extent. Land, sea, and aerial combat spread throughout most of Europe, large areas of Asia and Africa, along the coastlines of both North and South America, and on innumerable islands scattered across the Pacific Ocean. The United States entered the war following the Japanese surprise attack on the Pacific Fleet at Pearl Harbor, Hawaii, on December 7, 1941. The war finally came to an end, first with the German collapse in May 1945, and then the Japanese surrender three months later, following the American atomic bomb attacks on Hiroshima and Nagasaki. One of the unanswerable questions of history is that of how long the war would have continued and how many lives would have been lost had the United States not dropped the two atomic bombs.

The bomb had been developed over several years by American scientists and engineers working in great secrecy under the code name "Manhattan Project." It had been tested only once—in the desert of New Mexico—before being released over Hiroshima. The decision to drop the bomb in Japan, probably the most awesome decision ever to face a human being, was made by President Harry S. Truman.

It is difficult to describe in words the effects of the atomic explosions over the two Japanese cities. Nevertheless, the following selection, although written largely in factual, unemotional terms, succeeds in capturing something of the essence not only of the material destruction wreaked but also of the human suffering, both physical and psychological, of the victims of the attacks. It is taken from a report prepared shortly after the war by a team of American investigators who visited both cities, examined the effects of the bombing, and questioned many survivors of the attacks.

---

1.   What is the purpose of this report?

2.   What unexpected effects of the bombings did the investigators find?

The Effects of Atomic Bombs on Hiroshima and Nagasaki

I. Introduction

The available facts about the power of the atomic bomb as a military weapon lie in the story of what it did at Hiroshima and Nagasaki. Many of these facts have been published, in official and unofficial form, but mingled with distortions or errors. The United States Strategic Bombing Survey, therefore, in partial fulfillment of the mission for which it was established, has put together in these pages a fairly full account of just what the atomic bombs did at Hiroshima and Nagasaki. Together with an explanation of how the bomb achieved these effects, this report states the extent and nature of the damage, the casualties, and the political repercussions from the two attacks. The basis is the observation, measurement, and analysis of the Survey's investigators. The conjecture that is necessary for understanding of the complex phenomena and for applying the findings to the problems of defense of the United States is clearly labelled.

When the atomic bombs fell, the United States Strategic Bombing Survey was completing a study of the effects of strategic bombing on Germany's ability and will to resist. A similar study of the effects of strategic bombing on Japan was being planned. The news of the dropping of the atomic bomb gave a new urgency to this project, for a study of the air war against Japan clearly involved new weapons and new possibilities of concentration of attack that might qualify or even change the conclusions and recommendations of the Survey as to the effectiveness of air power. The directors of the Survey, therefore, decided to examine exhaustively the effects of the atomic bombs, in order that the full impact on Japan and the implications of their results could be confidently analyzed. Teams of experts were selected to study the scenes of the bombings from the special points of emphasis of physical damage, civilian defense, morale, casualties, community life, utilities and transportation, various industries, and the general economic and political repercussions. In all, more than 110 men— engineers, architects, fire experts, economists, doctors, photographers, draftsmen—participated in the field study at each city, over a period of 10 weeks from October to December, 1945. Their detailed studies are now being published.

• • •

The Effects of Atomic Bombs on Hiroshima and Nagasaki (Washington, D.C.: U.S. Government Printing Office, 1946).

II. The Effects of the Atomic Bombings

A. THE ATTACKS AND DAMAGE

1. The attacks. A single atomic bomb, the first weapon of its type ever used against a target, exploded over the city of Hiroshima at 0815 on the morning of 6 August 1945. Most of the industrial workers had already reported to work, but many workers were enroute and nearly all the school children and some industrial employees were at work in the open on the program of building removal to provide firebreaks and disperse valuables to the country. The attack came 45 minutes after the "all clear" had been sounded from a previous alert. Because of the lack of warning and the populace's indifference to small groups of planes, the explosion came as an almost complete surprise, and the people had not taken shelter. Many were caught in the open, and most of the rest in flimsily constructed homes or commercial establishments.

The bomb exploded slightly northwest of the center of the city. Because of this accuracy and the flat terrain and circular shape of the city, Hiroshima was uniformly and extensively devastated. Practically the entire densely or moderately built-up portion of the city was leveled by blast and swept by fire. A "fire-storm," a phenomenon which has occurred infrequently in other conflagrations, developed in Hiroshima: fires springing up almost simultaneously over the wide flat area around the center of the city drew in air from all directions. The inrush of air easily overcame the natural ground wind, which had a velocity of only about 5 miles per hour. The "fire-wind" attained a maximum velocity of 30 to 40 miles per hour 2 to 3 hours after the explosion. The "fire-wind" and the symmetry of the built-up center of the city gave a roughly circular shape to the 4.4 square miles which were almost completely burned out.

The surprise, the collapse of many buildings, and the conflagration contributed to an unprecedented casualty rate. Seventy to eighty thousand people were killed, or missing and presumed dead, and an equal number were injured. . . .

At Nagasaki, 3 days later, the city was scarcely more prepared, though vague references to the Hiroshima disaster had appeared in the newspaper of 8 August. From the Nagasaki Prefectural Report on the bombing, something of the shock of the explosion can be inferred:

> The day was clear with not very much wind—an ordinary midsummer's day. The strain of continuous air attack on the city's population and the severity of the summer had vitiated enthusiastic air raid precautions. Previously, a general alert had been sounded at 0748, with a raid alert at 0750; this was canceled at 0830, and the alertness of the people was dissipated by a great feeling of relief.
>
> The city remained on the warning alert, but when two B-29s were again sighted coming in the raid signal was not given immediately; the bomb was

dropped at 1102 and the raid signal was given a few minutes later, at 1109. Thus only about 400 people were in the city's tunnel shelters, which were adequate for about 30 percent of the population.

When the atomic bomb exploded, an intense flash was observed first, as though a large amount of magnesium had been ignited, and the scene grew hazy with white smoke. At the same time at the center of the explosion, and a short while later in other areas, a tremendous roaring sound was heard and a crushing blast wave and intense heat were felt. The people of Nagasaki, even those who lived on the outer edge of the blast, all felt as though they had sustained a direct hit, and the whole city suffered damage such as would have resulted from direct hits everywhere by ordinary bombs.

The zero area, where the damage was most severe, was almost completely wiped out and for a short while after the explosion no reports came out of that area. People who were in comparatively damaged areas reported their condition under the impression that they had received a direct hit. If such a great amount of damage could be wreaked by a near miss, then the power of the atomic bomb is unbelievably great.

In Nagasaki, no fire-storm arose, and the uneven terrain of the city confined the maximum intensity of damage to the valley over which the bomb exploded. The area of nearly complete devastation was thus much smaller; only about 1.8 square miles. Casualties were lower also; between 35,000 and 40,000 were killed, and about the same number injured. People in the tunnel shelters escaped injury, unless exposed in the entrance shaft.

• • •

Hiroshima before the war was the seventh largest city in Japan, with a population of over 340,000, and was the principal administrative and commercial center of the southwestern part of the country. As the headquarters of the Second Army and of the Chugoku Regional Army, it was one of the most important military command stations in Japan, the site of one of the largest military supply depots, and the foremost military shipping point for both troops and supplies. Its shipping activities had virtually ceased by the time of the attack, however, because of sinkings and the mining of the Inland Sea. It had been relatively unimportant industrially before the war, ranking only twelfth, but during the war new plants were built that increased its significance. These factories were not concentrated, but spread over the outskirts of the city; this location, we shall see, accounts for the slight industrial damage.

The impact of the atomic bomb shattered the normal fabric of community life and disrupted the organizations for handling the disaster. In the 30 percent of the population killed and the additional 30 percent seriously injured were included corresponding proportions of the civic authorities and rescue groups. A mass flight from the city took place, as persons sought safety from the conflagration and a place for shelter and food. Within

24 hours, however, people were streaming back by the thousands in search of relatives and friends and to determine the extent of their property loss. Road blocks had to be set up along all routes leading into the city, to keep curious and unauthorized people out. The bulk of the dehoused population found refuge in the surrounding countryside; within the city the food supply was short and shelter virtually nonexistent.

On 7 August, the commander of the Second Army assumed general command of the counter-measures, and all military units and facilities in the area were mobilized for relief purposes. Army buildings on the periphery of the city provided shelter and emergency hospital space, and dispersed Army supplies supplemented the slight amounts of food and clothing that had escaped destruction. The need far exceeded what could be made available. Surviving civilians assisted; although casualties in both groups had been heavy, 190 policemen and over 2,000 members of the Civilian Defense Corps reported for duty on 7 August.

The status of medical facilities and personnel dramatically illustrates the difficulties facing authorities. Of more than 200 doctors in Hiroshima before the attack, over 90 percent were casualties and only about 30 physicians were able to perform their normal duties a month after the raid. Out of 1,780 nurses, 1,654 were killed or injured. Though some stocks of supplies had been dispersed, many were destroyed. Only three out of 45 civilian hospitals could be used, and two large Army hospitals were rendered unusable. Those within 3,000 feet of ground zero were totally destroyed, and the mortality rate of the occupants was practically 100 percent. Two large hospitals of reinforced concrete construction were located 4,900 feet from ground zero. The basic structures remained erect but there was such severe interior damage that neither was able to resume operation as a hospital for some time and the casualty rate was approximately 90 percent, due primarily to falling plaster, flying glass, and fire. Hospitals and clinics beyond 7,000 feet, though often remaining standing, were badly damaged and contained many casualties from flying glass or other missiles.

With such elimination of facilities and personnel, the lack of care and rescue activities at the time of the disaster is understandable; still, the eyewitness account of Father Siemes[1] shows how this lack of first-aid contributed to the seriousness of casualties. At the improvised first-aid stations, he reports:

> . . . Iodine is applied to the wounds but they are left uncleansed. Neither ointment nor other therapeutic agents are available. Those that have been brought in are laid on the floor and no one can give them any further care. What could one do when all means are lacking? Among the passersby, there are many who are uninjured. In a purposeless, insensate manner, distraught by the magnitude of the disaster, most of them rush by and none conceives

---

[1]German-born Jesuit professor at Jochi University, Tokyo; in the Hiroshima area when the bomb fell.—Ed.

the thought of organizing help on his own initiative. They are concerned only with the welfare of their own families—in the official aid stations and hospitals, a good third or half of those that had been brought in died. They lay about there almost without care, and a very high percentage succumbed. Everything was lacking, doctors, assistants, dressings, drugs, etc. . . .

Effective medical help had to be sent in from the outside, and arrived only after a considerable delay.

Fire-fighting and rescue units were equally stripped of men and equipment. Father Siemes reports that 30 hours elapsed before any organized rescue parties were observed. In Hiroshima, only 16 pieces of fire-fighting equipment were available for fighting the conflagration, three of them borrowed. However, it is unlikely that any public fire department in the world, even without damage to equipment or casualties to personnel, could have prevented development of a conflagration in Hiroshima, or combatted it with success at more than a few locations along its perimeter. The total fire damage would not have been much different.

When the atomic bomb fell, Nagasaki was comparatively intact. Because the most intense destruction was confined to the Urukami Valley, the impact of the bomb on the city as a whole was less shattering than at Hiroshima. In addition, no fire-storm occurred; indeed, a shift in wind direction helped control the fires. Medical personnel and facilities were hard-hit, however. Over 80 percent of the city's hospital beds and the Medical College were located within 3,000 feet of the center of the explosion, and were completely gutted by fire; buildings of wooden construction were destroyed by fire and blast. The mortality rate in this group of buildings was between 75 and 80 percent. Exact casualty figures for medical personnel are unknown, but the city seems to have fared better than Hiroshima: 120 doctors were at work on 1 November, about one-half of the preraid roster. Casualties were undoubtedly high: 600 out of 850 medical students at the Nagasaki Medical College were killed and most of the others injured; and of the 20 faculty members, 12 were killed and 4 others injured.

• • •

The city's repair facilities were completely disorganized by the atomic bomb, so that with the single exception of shutting off water to the affected areas no repairs were made to roads, bridges, water mains, or transportation installations by city forces. The prefecture took full responsibility for such restoration as was accomplished, delegating to the scattered city help the task of assisting in relief of victims. There were only 3 survivors of 115 employees of the street car company, and as late as the middle of November 1945 no cars were running. A week after the explosion, the water works officials made an effort to supply water to persons attempting to live in the bombed-out areas, but the leakage was so great that the effort was abandoned. It fell to the prefecture, therefore, to institute recovery measures even in those streets normally the responsibility of the city. Of the entire public works construction group covering the Nagasaki city area, only three members appeared for work and a week was required to locate and notify other survivors. On the morning of 10 August, police rescue units and workers from the Kawaminami shipbuilding works began the imperative task of clearing the Omura-Nagasaki pike, which was impassable for 8,000 feet. A path 6-1/2 feet wide was cleared despite the intense heat from smouldering fires, and by 15 August had been widened to permit two-way traffic. No trucks, only rakes and shovels, were available for clearing the streets, which were filled with tile, bricks, stone, corrugated iron, machinery, plaster, and stucco. Street areas affected by blast and not by fire were littered with wood. Throughout the devastated area, all wounded had to be carried by stretcher, since no motor vehicles were able to proceed through the cluttered streets for several days. The plan for debris removal required clearance of a few streets leading to the main highway; but there were frequent delays caused by the heat of smouldering fires and by calls for relief work. The debris was simply raked and shoveled off the streets. By 20 August the job was considered complete. The streets were not materially damaged by the bomb nor were the surface or the abutments of the concrete bridges, but many of the wooden bridges were totally or partially destroyed by fire.

Under the circumstances—fire, flight of entire families, destruction of official records, mass cremation—identification of dead and the accurate count of casualties was impossible. As at Hiroshima, the season of the year made rapid disposal of bodies imperative, and mass cremation and mass burial were resorted to in the days immediately after the attack. Despite the absence of sanitary measures, no epidemics broke out here. The dysentery rate rose from 25 per 100,000 to 125 per 100,000. A census taken on 1 November 1945 found a population of 142,700 in the city.

At Nagasaki, the scale of destruction was greater than at Hiroshima, though the actual area destroyed was smaller because of the terrain and the point of fall of the bomb. The Nagasaki Prefectural Report described vividly the impress of the bomb on the city and its inhabitants:

Within a radius of 1 kilometer from ground zero, men and animals died almost instantaneously from the tremendous blast pressure and heat; houses and other structures were smashed, crushed and scattered; and fires broke out. The strong complex steel members of the structures of the Mitsubishi Steel Works were bent and twisted like jelly and the roofs of the reinforced concrete National Schools were crumpled and collapsed, indicating a force beyond imagination. Trees of all sizes lost their branches or were uprooted or broken off at the trunk.

Outside a radius of 1 kilometer and within a radius of 2 kilometers from ground zero, some men and animals died instantly from the great blast and heat, but the great majority were seriously or superficially injured. Houses and other structures were completely destroyed while fires broke out everywhere. Trees were uprooted and withered by the heat.

Outside a radius of 2 kilometers and within a radius of 4 kilometers from ground zero, men and animals suffered various degrees of injury from window glass and other fragments scattered about by the blast and many were burned by the intense heat. Dwelling and other structures were half damaged by blast.

Outside a radius of 4 kilometers and within a radius of 8 kilometers from ground zero, living creatures were injured by materials blown about by the blast; the majority were only superficially wounded. Houses were half or only partially damaged.

While the conflagration with its uniformly burnt-out area caught the attention at Hiroshima, the blast effects, with their resemblance to the aftermath of a hurricane, were most striking at Nagasaki. Concrete buildings had their sides facing the blast stove in like boxes. Long lines of steel-framed factory sheds, over a mile from ground zero, leaned their skeletons away from the explosion. Blast resistant objects such as telephone poles leaned away from the center of the explosion; on the surrounding hills trees were blown down within considerable areas. Although there was no general conflagration, fires contributed to the total damage in nearly all concrete structures. Evidence of primary fire is more frequent than at Hiroshima.

• • •

B. GENERAL EFFECTS

1. Casualties. The most striking result of the atomic bombs was the great number of casualties. The exact number of dead and injured will never be known because of the confusion after the explosions. Persons unaccounted for might have been burned beyond recognition in the falling buildings, disposed of in one of the mass cremations of the first week of recovery, or driven out of the city to die or recover without any record remaining. No sure count of even the preraid population existed. Because of the decline in activity in the two port cities, the constant threat of incendiary raids, and the formal evacuation programs of the Government, an unknown number of the inhabitants had either drifted away from the cities or been removed according to plan. In this uncertain situation, estimates of casualties have generally ranged between 100,000 and 180,000 for Hiroshima, and between 50,000 and 100,000 for Nagasaki. The Survey believes the dead at Hiroshima to have been between 70,000 and 80,000 with an equal number injured; at Nagasaki over 35,000 dead and somewhat more than that injured seems the most plausible estimate.

Most of the immediate casualties did not differ from those caused by incendiary or high-explosive raids. The outstanding difference was the presence of radiation effects, which became unmistakable about a week after the bombing. At the time of impact, however, the causes of death and injury were flash burns, secondary effects of blast and falling debris, and burns from blazing buildings. No records are available that give the relative importance of the various types of injury, especially for those who died immediately after the explosion. Indeed, many of these people undoubtedly died several times over, theoretically, since each was subjected to several injuries, any one of which would have been fatal.

Radiation disease. The radiation effects upon survivors resulted from the gamma rays liberated by the fission process rather than from induced radio-activity or the lingering radio-activity of deposits of primary fission products. Both at Nagasaki and at Hiroshima, pockets of radio-activity have been detected where fission products were directly deposited, but the degree of activity in these areas was insufficient to produce casualties. Similarly, induced radio-activity from the interaction of neutrons with matter caused no authenticated fatalities. But the effects of gamma rays—here used in a general sense to include all penetrating high-frequency radiations and neutrons that caused injury—are well established, even though the Allies had no observers in the affected areas for several weeks after the explosions.

Our understanding of radiation casualties is not complete. In part the deficiency is in our basic knowledge of how radiation effects animal tissue.

According to the Japanese, those individuals very near the center of the explosion but not affected by flash burns or secondary injuries became ill within 2 or 3 days. Bloody diarrhea followed, and the victims expired, some within 2 to 3 days after the onset and the majority within a week. Autopsies showed remarkable changes in the blood picture—almost complete absence of white blood cells, and deterioration of bone marrow. Mucous membranes of the throat, lungs, stomach, and the intestines showed acute inflammation.

The majority of the radiation cases, who were at greater distances, did not show severe symptoms until 1 to 4 weeks after the explosion, though many felt weak and listless on the following day. After a day or two of mild nausea and vomiting, the appetite improved and the person felt quite well until symptoms reappeared at a later date. In the opinion of some Japanese physicians, those who rested or subjected themselves to less physical exertion showed a longer delay before the onset of subsequent symptoms. The first signs of recurrence were loss of appetite, lassitude, and general discomfort. Inflammation of the gums, mouth, and pharynx appeared next. Within 12 to 48 hours, fever became evident. In many instances it reached only 100° Fahrenheit and remained for only a few days. In other cases, the temperature went as high as 104° or 106° Fahrenheit. The degree of fever apparently had a direct relation to the degree of exposure to radiation. Once developed, the fever was usually well sustained, and in those cases terminating fatally it continued high until the end. If the fever subsided, the patient usually showed a rapid disappearance of other symptoms and soon regained his feeling of good health. The other symptoms commonly seen were shortage of white corpuscles, loss of hair, inflammation and gangrene of the gums, inflammation of the mouth and pharynx, ulceration of the lower gastro-intestinal tract, small livid spots (petechiae) resulting from escape of blood into the tissues of the skin or mucous membrane, and larger hemorrhages of gums, nose and skin.

Loss of hair usually began about 2 weeks after the bomb explosion, though in a few instances it is reported to have begun as early a 4 to 5 days afterward. The areas were involved in the following order of frequency with variations depending on the degree of exposure: scalp, armpits, beard, pubic region, and eyebrows. Complete baldness was rare. Microscopic study of the body areas involved has shown atrophy of the hair follicles. In those patients who survived after 2 months, however, the hair has commenced to regrow. An interesting but unconfirmed report has it that loss of the hair was less marked in persons with grey hair than in those with dark hair. . . .

The effects of the bomb on pregnant women are marked, however. Of women in various stages of pregnancy who were within 3,000 feet of ground zero, all known cases have had miscarriages. Even up to 6,500 feet they have had miscarriages or premature infants who died shortly after birth. In the group between 6,500 and 10,000 feet, about one-third have given birth to apparently normal children. Two months after the explosion, the city's total incidence of miscarriages, abortions, and premature births was 27 percent as compared with a normal rate of 6 percent. Since other factors than radiation contributed to this increased rate, a period of years will be required to learn the ultimate effects of mass radiation upon reproduction.

Treatment of victims by the Japanese was limited by the lack of medical supplies and facilities. Their therapy consisted of small amounts of vitamins, liver extract, and an occasional blood transfusion. Allied doctors used penicillin and plasma with beneficial effects. Liver extract seemed to benefit the few patients on whom it was used: It was given in small frequent doses when available. A large percentage of the cases died of secondary disease, such as septic bronchopneumonia or tuberculosis, as a result of lowered resistance. Deaths from radiation began about a week after exposure and reached a peak in 3 to 4 weeks. They had practically ceased to occur after 7 to 8 weeks.

Unfortunately, no exact definition of the killing power of radiation can yet be given, nor a satisfactory account of the sort and thickness of concrete or earth that will shield people. From the definitive report of the Joint Commission will come more nearly accurate statements on these matters. In the meanwhile the awesome lethal effects of the atomic bomb and the insidious additional peril of the gamma rays speak for themselves.

2. Morale. As might be expected, the primary reaction to the bomb was fear—uncontrolled terror, strengthened by the sheer horror of the destruction and suffering witnessed and experienced by the survivors. Between one-half and two-thirds of those interviewed in the Hiroshima and Nagasaki areas confessed having such reactions, not just for the moment but for some time. As two survivors put it:

Whenever a plane was seen after that, people would rush into their shelters; they went in and out so much that they did not have time to eat. They were so nervous they could not work.

After the atomic bomb fell, I just couldn't stay home. I would cook, but while cooking I would always be watching out and worrying whether an atomic bomb would fall near me.

The behavior of the living immediately after the bombings, as described earlier, clearly shows the state of shock that hindered rescue efforts. A Nagasaki survivor illustrates succinctly the mood of survivors:

All I saw was the flash and I felt my body get warm and then I saw everything flying around. My grandmother was hit on the head by a flying piece of roof and she was bleeding. . . . I became hysterical seeing my grandmother bleeding and we just ran around without knowing what to do.

I was working at the office. I was talking to a friend at the window. I saw the whole city in a red flame, then I ducked. The pieces of the glass hit my back and face. My dress was torn off by the glass. Then I got up and ran to the mountain where the good shelter was.

The two typical impulses were these: Aimless, even hysterical activity or flight from the city to shelter and food.

Martin Luther King, Jr.

The letter that follows was written by Dr. King while he was serving a jail sentence in Birmingham, Alabama, in 1963. The offense for which he was jailed consisted of his participation in civil rights demonstrations throughout Alabama. He joined a growing number of demonstrators in this activity and several others also were jailed by the authorities. The civil rights movement had its origins in the Second World War in which many black soldiers participated with distinction and valor. Their experiences taught them that there was a better life possible than what they had endured as second-class citizens in the south. Many of these men became active in attempts to improve conditions for black people in their home areas. Dr. King is a notable example of such a person. He bases his case on the idea of justice and the American commitment, expressed so well by Thomas Jefferson in the Declaration of Independence, to the idea that all people are equal. As Dr. King makes clear, segregation is the opposite of this idea so it is un-American as well as unjust. His efforts on behalf of social justice for black people have been fruitful, with many beneficial results, particularly in the southern states, but also elsewhere in the country. So he did not languish in the Birmingham jail in vain.

1. Why is King protesting? How does he justify breaking the law?

2. Compare King's notion of nonviolent resistance with Gandhi's notion of love-force.

Letter from Birmingham City Jail

My dear Fellow Clergymen,

While confined here in the Birmingham city jail, I came across your recent statement calling our present activities "unwise and untimely." Seldom, if ever, do I pause to answer criticism of my work and ideas. If I sought to answer all of the criticisms that cross my desk, my secretaries would be engaged in little else in the course of the day, and I would have no time for constructive work. But since I feel that you are men of genuine good

Martin Luther King's "Letter from Birmingham Jail" from *A Testament of Hope*, ed. J. M. Washington, pp. 289–302. (San Francisco: Harper & Row, 1986).

will and your criticisms are sincerely set forth, I would like to answer your statement in what I hope will be patient and reasonable terms.

I think I should give the reason for my being in Birmingham, since you have been influenced by the argument of "outsiders coming in." I have the honor of serving as president of the Southern Christian Leadership Conference, an organization operating in every southern state, with headquarters in Atlanta, Georgia. We have some eighty-five affiliate organizations all across the South—one being the Alabama Christian Movement for Human Rights. Whenever necessary and possible we share staff, educational and financial resources with our affiliates. Several months ago our local affiliate here in Birmingham invited us to be on call to engage in a nonviolent direct-action program if such were deemed necessary. We readily consented and when the hour came we lived up to our promises. So I am here, along with several members of my staff, because we were invited here. I am here because I have basic organizational ties here.

Beyond this, I am in Birmingham because injustice is here. Just as the eighth century prophets left their little villages and carried their "thus saith the Lord" far beyond the boundaries of their hometowns; and just as the Apostle Paul left his little village of Tarsus and carried the gospel of Jesus Christ to practically every hamlet and city of the Graeco-Roman world, I too am compelled to carry the gospel of freedom beyond my particular hometown. Like Paul, I must constantly respond to the Macedonian call for aid.

Moreover, I am cognizant of the interrelatedness of all communities and states. I cannot sit idly by in Atlanta and not be concerned about what happens in Birmingham. Injustice anywhere is a threat to justice everywhere. We are caught in an inescapable network of mutuality, tied in a single garment of destiny. Whatever affects one directly affects all indirectly. Never again can we afford to live with the narrow, provincial "outside agitator" idea. Anyone who lives in the United States can never be considered an outsider anywhere in this country.

You deplore the demonstrations that are presently taking place in Birmingham. But I am sorry that your statement did not express a similar concern for the conditions that brought the demonstrations into being. I am sure that each of you would want to go beyond the superficial social analyst who looks merely at effects, and does not grapple with underlying causes. I would not hesitate to say that it is unfortunate that so-called demonstrations are taking place in Birmingham at this time, but I would say in more emphatic terms that it is even more unfortunate that the white power structure of this city left the Negro community with no other alternative.

In any nonviolent campaign there are four basic steps: (1) collection of the facts to determine whether injustices are alive, (2) negotiation, (3) self-purification, and (4) direct action. We have gone through all of these steps in Birmingham. There can be no gainsaying of the fact that racial injustice engulfs this community.

Birmingham is probably the most thoroughly segregated city in the United States. Its ugly record of police brutality is known in every section of this country. Its injust treatment of Negroes in the courts is a notorious reality. There have been more unsolved bombings of Negro homes and churches in Birmingham than any city in this nation. These are the hard, brutal and unbelievable facts. On the basis of these conditions Negro leaders sought to negotiate with the city fathers. But the political leaders consistently refused to engage in good faith negotiation.

Then came the opportunity last September to talk with some of the leaders of the economic community. In these negotiating sessions certain promises were made by the merchants—such as the promise to remove the humiliating racial signs from the stores. On the basis of these promises Rev. Shuttlesworth and the leaders of the Alabama Christian Movement for Human Rights agreed to call a moratorium on any type of demonstrations. As the weeks and months unfolded we realized that we were the victims of a broken promise. The signs remained. Like so many experiences of the past we were confronted with blasted hopes, and the dark shadow of a deep disappointment settled upon us. So we had no alternative except that of preparing for direct action, whereby we would present our very bodies as a means of laying our case before the conscience of the local and national community. We were not unmindful of the difficulties involved. So we decided to go through a process of self-purification. We started having workshops on nonviolence and repeatedly asked ourselves the questions, "Are you able to accept blows without retaliating?" "Are you able to endure the ordeals of jail?" We decided to set our direct-action program around the Easter season, realizing that with the exception of Christmas, this was the largest shopping period of the year. Knowing that a strong economic withdrawal program would be the byproduct of direct action, we felt that this was the best time to bring pressure on the merchants for the needed changes. Then it occurred to us that the March election was ahead and so we speedily decided to postpone action until after election day. When we discovered that Mr. Connor was in the run-off, we decided again to postpone action so that the demonstrations could not be used to cloud the issues. At this time we agreed to begin our nonviolent witness the day after the run-off.

This reveals that we did not move irresponsibly into direct action. We too wanted to see Mr. Connor defeated; so we went through postponement after postponement to aid in this community need. After this we felt that direct action could be delayed no longer.

You may well ask, "Why direct action? Why sit-ins, marches, etc.? Isn't negotiation a better path?" You are exactly right in your call for negotiation. Indeed, this is the purpose of direct action. Nonviolent direct action seeks to create such a crisis and establish such creative tension that a community that has constantly refused to negotiate is forced to confront the issue. It seeks so to dramatize the issue that it can no longer be ignored. I just referred to the creation of tension as a part of the work of the nonviolent resister. This may sound rather shocking. But I must confess that I am not afraid of the word tension. I have earnestly worked and preached against violent tension, but there is a type of constructive nonviolent tension that is necessary for growth. Just as Socrates felt that it was necessary to create a tension in the mind so that individuals could rise from the bondage of myths and half-truths to the unfettered realm of creative analysis and objective appraisal, we must see the need of having nonviolent gadflies to create the kind of tension in society that will help men to rise from the dark depths of prejudice and racism to the majestic heights of understanding and brotherhood. So the purpose of the direct action is to create a situation so crisis-packed that it will inevitably open the door to negotiation. We, therefore, concur with you in your call for negotiation. Too long has our beloved Southland been bogged down in the tragic attempt to live in monologue rather than dialogue.

One of the basic points in your statement is that our acts are untimely. Some have asked, "Why didn't you give the new administration time to act?" The only answer that I can give to this inquiry is that the new administration must be prodded about as much as the outgoing one before it acts. We will be sadly mistaken if we feel that the election of Mr. Boutwell will bring the millennium to Birmingham. While Mr. Boutwell is much more articulate and gentle than Mr. Connor, they are both segregationists, dedicated to the task of maintaining the status quo. The hope I see in Mr. Boutwell is that he will be reasonable enough to see the futility of massive resistance to desegregation. But he will not see this without pressure from the devotees of civil rights. My friends, I must say to you that we have not made a single gain in civil rights without determined legal and nonviolent pressure. History is the long and tragic story of the fact that privileged groups seldom give up their privileges voluntarily. Individuals may see the moral light and voluntarily give up their unjust posture; but as Reinhold Niebuhr has reminded us, groups are more immoral than individuals.

We know through painful experience that freedom is never voluntarily given by the oppressor; it must be demanded by the oppressed. Frankly, I have never yet engaged in a direct action movement that was "well-timed," according to the timetable of those who have not suffered unduly from the disease of segregation. For years now I have heard the words "Wait!" It rings in the ear of every Negro with a piercing familiarity. This "Wait" has almost always meant "Never." It has been a tranquilizing thalidomide, relieving the emotional stress for a moment, only to give birth to an ill-formed infant of frustration. We must come to see with the distinguished jurist of yesterday that "justice too long delayed is justice denied." We have waited for more than 340 years for our constitutional and God-given rights. The nations of Asia and Africa are moving with jetlike speed toward the goal of political independence, and we still creep at horse and buggy pace toward the gaining of a cup of coffee at a lunch counter. I guess it is easy for those who have never felt the stinging darts of segregation to say, "Wait." But when you have seen vicious mobs lynch your mothers and fathers at will and drown your sisters and brothers at whim; when you have seen hate-filled policemen curse, kick, brutalize and even kill your black brothers and sisters with impunity; when you see the vast majority of your twenty million Negro brothers smothering in an airtight cage of poverty in the midst of an affluent society; when you suddenly find your tongue twisted and your speech stammering as you seek to explain to your six-year-old daughter why she can't go to the public amusement park that has just been advertised on television, and see tears welling up in her little eyes when she is told that Funtown is closed to colored children, and see the depressing clouds of inferiority begin to form in her little mental sky, and see her begin to distort her little personality by unconsciously developing a bitterness toward white people; when you have to concoct an answer for a five-year-old son asking in agonizing pathos: "Daddy, why do white people treat colored people so mean?"; when you take a cross-country drive and find it necessary to sleep night after night in the uncomfortable corners of your automobile because no motel will accept you; when you are humiliated day in and day out by nagging signs reading "white" and "colored"; when your first name becomes "nigger" and your middle name becomes "boy" (however old you are) and your last name becomes "John," and when your wife and mother are never given the respected title "Mrs."; when you are harried by day and haunted by night by the fact that you are a Negro, living constantly at tiptoe stance never quite knowing what to expect next, and plagued with inner fears and outer resentments; when you are forever fighting a degenerating sense of "nobodiness"; then you will understand why we find it difficult to wait. There comes a time when the cup of endurance runs over, and men are no longer willing to be plunged into an abyss of injustice where they experience the blackness of corroding despair. I hope, sirs, you can understand our legitimate and unavoidable impatience.

You express a great deal of anxiety over our willingness to break laws. This is certainly a legitimate concern. Since we so diligently urge people to obey the Supreme Court's decision of 1954 outlawing segregation in the public schools, it is rather strange and paradoxical to find us consciously breaking laws. One may well ask, "How can you advocate breaking some laws and obeying others?" The answer is found in the fact that there are two types of laws: there are *just* and there are *unjust* laws. I would agree with Saint Augustine that "An unjust law is no law at all."

Now what is the difference between the two? How does one determine when a law is just or unjust? A just law is a man-made code that squares with the moral law or the law of God. An unjust law is a code that is out of harmony with the moral law. To put it in the terms of Saint Thomas Aquinas, an unjust law is a human law that is not rooted in eternal and natural law. Any law that uplifts human personality is just. Any law that degrades human personality is unjust. All segregation statutes are unjust because segregation distorts the soul and damages the personality. It gives the segregator a false sense of superiority, and the segregated a false sense of inferiority. To use the words of Martin Buber, the great Jewish philosopher, segregation substitutes an "I-it" relationship for the "I-thou" relationship, and ends up relegating persons to the status of things. So segregation is not only politically, economically and sociologically unsound, but it is morally wrong and sinful. Paul Tillich has said that sin is separation. Isn't segregation an existential expression of man's tragic separation, an expression of his awful estrangement, his terrible sinfulness? So I can urge men to disobey segregation ordinances because they are morally wrong.

Let us turn to a more concrete example of just and unjust laws. An unjust law is a code that a majority inflicts on a minority that is not binding on itself. This is difference made legal. On the other hand a just law is a code that a majority compels a minority to follow that it is willing to follow itself. This is sameness made legal.

Let me give another explanation. An unjust law is a code inflicted upon a minority which that minority had no part in enacting or creating because they did not have the unhampered right to vote. Who can say that the legislature of Alabama which set up the segregation laws was democratically elected? Throughout the state of Alabama all types of conniving methods are used to prevent Negroes from becoming registered voters and there are some counties without a single Negro registered to vote despite the fact that the Negro constitutes a majority of the population. Can any law set up in such a state be considered democratically structured?

These are just a few examples of unjust and just laws. There are some instances when a law is just on its face and unjust in its application. For instance, I was arrested Friday on a charge of parading without a permit. Now there is nothing wrong with an ordinance which requires a permit for a parade, but when the ordinance is used to preserve segregation and to deny citizens the First Amendment privilege of peaceful assembly and peaceful protest, then it becomes unjust.

I hope you can see the distinction I am trying to point out. In no sense do I advocate evading or defying the law as the rabid segregationist would do. This would lead to anarchy. One who breaks an unjust law must do it *openly, lovingly* (not hatefully as the white mothers did in New Orleans when they were seen on television screaming, "nigger, nigger, nigger"), and with a willingness to accept the penalty. I submit that an individual who breaks a law that conscience tells him is unjust, and willingly accepts the penalty by staying in jail to arouse the conscience of the community over its injustice, is in reality expressing the very highest respect for law.

Of course, there is nothing new about this kind of civil disobedience. It was seen sublimely in the refusal of Shadrach, Meshach, and Abednego to obey the laws of Nebuchadnezzar because a higher moral law was involved.

It was practiced superbly by the early Christians who were willing to face hungry lions and the excruciating pain of chopping blocks, before submitting to certain unjust laws of the Roman Empire. To a degree academic freedom is a reality today because Socrates practiced civil disobedience.

We can never forget that everything Hitler did in Germany was "legal" and everything the Hungarian freedom fighters did in Hungary was "illegal." It was "illegal" to aid and comfort a Jew in Hitler's Germany. But I am sure that if I had lived in Germany during that time I would have aided and comforted my Jewish brothers even though it was illegal. If I lived in a Communist country today where certain principles dear to the Christian faith are suppressed, I believe I would openly advocate disobeying these anti-religious laws. I must make two honest confessions to you, my Christian and Jewish brothers. First, I must confess that over the last few years I have been gravely disappointed with the white moderate. I have almost reached the regrettable conclusion that the Negro's great stumbling block in the stride toward freedom is not the White Citizen's Counciler or the Ku Klux Klanner, but the white moderate who is more devoted to "order" than to justice; who prefers a negative peace which is the absence of tension to a positive peace which is the presence of justice; who constantly says, "I agree with you in the goal you seek, but I can't agree with your methods of direct action"; who paternalistically feels that he can set the timetable for another man's freedom; who lives by the myth of time and who constantly advises the Negro to wait until a "more convenient season." Shallow understanding from people of good will is more frustrating than absolute misunderstanding from people of ill will. Lukewarm acceptance is much more bewildering than outright rejection.

I had hoped that the white moderate would understand that law and order exist for the purpose of establishing justice, and that when they fail to do this they become dangerously structured dams that block the flow of social progress. I had hoped that the white moderate would understand that the present tension of the South is merely a necessary phase of the transition from an obnoxious negative peace, where the Negro passively accepted his unjust plight, to a substance-filled positive peace, where all men will respect the dignity and worth of human personality. Actually, we who engage in nonviolent direct action are not the creators of tension. We merely bring to the surface the hidden tension that is already alive. We bring it out in the open where it can be seen and dealt with. Like a boil that can never be cured as long as it is covered up but must be opened with all its pus-flowing ugliness to the natural medicines of air and light, injustice must likewise be exposed, with all of the tension its exposing creates, to the light of human conscience and the air of national opinion before it can be cured.

In your statement you asserted that our actions, even though peaceful, must be condemned because they precipitate violence. But can this assertion be logically made? Isn't this like condemning the robbed man because his possession of money precipitated the evil act of robbery? Isn't this like condemning Socrates because his unswerving commitment to truth and his philosophical delvings precipitated the misguided popular mind to make him drink the hemlock? Isn't this like condemning Jesus because His unique God-consciousness and never-ceasing devotion to his will precipitated the evil act of crucifixion? We must come to see, as federal courts have consistently affirmed, that it is immoral to urge an individual to withdraw his efforts to gain his basic constitutional rights because the quest precipitates violence. Society must protect the robbed and punish the robber.

I had also hoped that the white moderate would reject the myth of time. I received a letter this morning from a white brother in Texas which said: "All Christians know that the colored people will receive equal rights eventually, but it is possible that you are in too great of a religious hurry. It has taken Christianity almost two thousand years to accomplish what it has. The teachings of Christ take time to come to earth." All that is said here grows out of a tragic misconception of time. It is the strangely irrational notion that there is something in the very flow of time that will inevitably cure all ills. Actually time is neutral. It can be used either destructively or constructively. I am coming to feel that the people of ill will have used time much more effectively than the people of good will. We will have to repent in this generation not merely for the vitriolic words and actions of the bad people, but for the appalling silence of the good people. We must come to see that human progress never rolls in on wheels of inevitability. It comes through the tireless efforts and persistent work of men willing to be co-workers with God, and without this hard work time itself becomes an ally of the forces of social stagnation. We must use time creatively, and forever realize that the time is always ripe to do right. Now is the time to make real the promise of democracy, and transform our pending national elegy into a creative psalm of brotherhood. Now is the time to lift our national policy from the quicksand of racial injustice to the solid rock of human dignity.

You spoke of our activity in Birmingham as extreme. At first I was rather disappointed that fellow clergymen would see my nonviolent efforts as those of the extremist. I started thinking about the fact that I stand in the middle of two opposing forces in the Negro community. One is a force of complacency made up of Negroes who, as a result of long years of oppression, have been so completely drained of self-respect and a sense of "somebodiness" that they have adjusted to segregation, and, of a few Negroes in the middle class who, because of a degree of academic and economic security, and because at points they profit by segregation, have unconsciously become insensitive to the problems of the masses. The other force is one of bitterness and hatred, and comes perilously close to advocating violence. It is expressed in the various black nationalist groups that are springing up over the nation, the largest and best known being Elijah Muhammad's Muslim movement. This movement is nourished by the contemporary frustration over the continued existence of racial discrimination. It is made up of people who have lost faith in America, who have absolutely repudiated Christianity, and who have concluded that the white man is an incurable "devil." I have tried to stand between these two forces, saying that we need not follow the "do-nothingism" of the complacent or the hatred and despair of the black nationalist. There is the more excellent way of love and nonviolent protest. I'm grateful to God that, through the Negro church, the dimension of nonviolence entered our struggle. If this philosophy had not emerged, I am convinced that by now many streets of the South would be flowing with floods of blood. And I am further convinced that if our white brothers dismiss us as "rabble-rousers" and "outside agitators" those of us who are working through the channels of nonviolent direct action and refuse to support our nonviolent efforts, millions of Negroes, out of frustration and despair, will seek solace and security in black nationalist ideologies, a development that will lead inevitably to a frightening racial nightmare.

Oppressed people cannot remain oppressed forever. The urge for freedom will eventually come. This is what happened to the American Negro. Something within has reminded him of his birthright of freedom; something without has reminded him that he can gain it. Consciously and unconsciously, he has been swept in by what the Germans call the *Zeitgeist*, and with his black brothers of Africa, and his brown and yellow brothers of Asia, South America and the Caribbean, he is moving with a sense of cosmic urgency toward the promised land of racial justice. Recognizing this vital urge that has engulfed the Negro community, one should readily understand public demonstrations. The Negro has many pent-up resentments and latent frustrations. He has to get them out. So let him march sometime; let him have his prayer pilgrimages to the city hall; understand why he must have sit-ins and freedom rides. If his repressed emotions do not come out in these nonviolent ways, they will come out in ominous expressions of violence. This is not a threat; it is a fact of history. So I have not said to my people "get rid of your discontent." But I have tried to say that this normal and healthy discontent can be channelized through the creative outlet of nonviolent direct action. Now this approach is being dismissed as extremist. I must admit that I was initially disappointed in being so categorized.

But as I continued to think about the matter I gradually gained a bit of satisfaction from being considered an extremist. Was not Jesus an extremist in love—"Love your enemies, bless them that curse you, pray for them that despitefully use you." Was not Amos an extremist for justice—"Let justice roll down like waters and righteousness like a mighty stream." Was not Paul an extremist for the gospel of Jesus Christ—"I bear in my body the marks of the Lord Jesus." Was not Martin Luther an extremist—"Here I stand; I can do none other so help me God." Was not John Bunyan an extremist—"I will stay in jail to the end of my days before I make a butchery of my conscience." Was not Abraham Lincoln an extremist—"This nation cannot survive half slave and half free." Was not Thomas Jefferson an extremist—"We hold these truths to be self-evident, that all men are created equal." So the question is not whether we will be extremist but what kind of extremist will we be. Will we be extremists for hate or will we be extremists for love? Will we be extremists for the preservation of injustice—or will we be extremists for the cause of justice? In that dramatic scene on Calvary's hill, three men were crucified. We must not forget that all three were crucified for the same crime—the crime of extremism. Two were extremists for immorality, and thusly fell below their environment. The other, Jesus Christ, was an extremist for love, truth and goodness, and thereby rose above his environment. So, after all, maybe the South, the nation and the world are in dire need of creative extremists.

I had hoped that the white moderate would see this. Maybe I was too optimistic. Maybe I expected too much. I guess I should have realized that few members of a race that has oppressed another race can understand or appreciate the deep groans and passionate yearnings of those that have been oppressed and still fewer have the vision to see that injustice must be rooted out by strong, persistent and determined action. I am thankful, however, that some of our white brothers have grasped the meaning of this social revolution and committed themselves to it. They are still all too small in quantity, but they are big in quality. Some like Ralph McGill, Lillian Smith, Harry Golden, and James Dabbs have written about our struggle in eloquent, prophetic and understanding terms. Others have marched with us down nameless streets of the South. They have languished in filthy roach-infested jails, suffering the abuse and brutality of angry policemen who see them as "dirty nigger-lovers." They, unlike so many of their moderate brothers and sisters, have recognized the urgency of the moment and sensed the need for powerful "action" antidotes to combat the disease of segregation.

Let me rush on to mention my other disappointment. I have been so greatly disappointed with the white church and its leadership. Of course, there are some notable exceptions. I am not unmindful of the fact that each of you has taken some significant stands on this issue. I commend you, Rev. Stallings, for your Christian stance on this past Sunday, in welcoming Negroes to your worship service on a non-segregated basis. I commend the Catholic leaders of this state for integrating Springhill College several years ago.

But despite these notable exceptions I must honestly reiterate that I have been disappointed with the church. I do not say that as one of the negative critics who can always find something wrong with the church. I say it as a minister of the gospel, who loves the church; who was nurtured in its bosom; who has been sustained by its spiritual blessings and who will remain true to it as long as the cord of life shall lengthen.

I had the strange feeling when I was suddenly catapulted into the leadership of the bus protest in Montgomery several years ago that we would have the support of the white church. I felt that the white ministers, priests and rabbis of the South would be some of our strongest allies. Instead, some have been outright opponents, refusing to understand the freedom movement and misrepresenting its leaders; all too many others have been more cautious than courageous and have remained silent behind the anesthetizing security of the stained-glass windows.

In spite of my shattered dreams of the past, I came to Birmingham with the hope that the white religious leadership of this community would see the justice of our cause, and with deep moral concern, serve as the channel through which our just grievances would get to the power structure. I had hoped that each of you would understand. But again I have been disappointed. I have heard numerous religious leaders of the South call upon their worshippers to comply with a desegregation decision because it is the *law*, but I have longed to hear white ministers say, "Follow this decree because integration is morally *right* and the Negro is your brother." In the midst of blatant injustices inflicted upon the Negro, I have watched white churches stand on the sideline and merely mouth pious irrelevancies and sanctimonious trivialities. In the midst of a mighty struggle to rid our nation of racial and economic injustice, I have heard so many ministers say, "Those are social issues with which the gospel has no real concern," and I have watched so many churches commit themselves to a completely otherworldly religion which made a strange distinction between body and soul, the sacred and the secular.

So here we are moving toward the exit of the twentieth century with a religious community largely adjusted to the status quo, standing as a taillight behind other community agencies rather than a headlight leading men to higher levels of justice.

I have traveled the length and breadth of Alabama, Mississippi, and all the other southern states. On sweltering summer days and crisp autumn mornings I have looked at her beautiful churches with their lofty spires pointing heavenward. I have beheld the impressive outlay of her massive religious education buildings. Over and over again I have found myself asking: "What kind of people worship here? Who is their God? Where were their voices when the lips of Governor Barnett dripped with words of interposition and nullification? Where were they when Governor Wallace gave the clarion call for defiance and hatred? Where were their voices of support when tired, bruised, and weary Negro men and women decided to rise from the dark dungeons of complacency to the bright hills of creative protest?"

Yes, these questions are still in my mind. In deep disappointment, I have wept over the laxity of the church. But be assured that my tears have been tears of love. There can be no deep disappointment where there is not deep love. Yes, I love the church; I love her sacred walls. How could I do otherwise? I am in the rather unique position of being the son, the grandson, and the great-grandson of preachers. Yes, I see the church as the body of Christ. But, oh! How we have blemished and scarred that body through social neglect and fear of being nonconformists.

There was a time when the church was very powerful. It was during that period when the early Christians rejoiced when they were deemed worthy to suffer for what they believed. In those days the church was not merely a thermometer that recorded the ideas and principles of popular opinion; it was a thermostat that transformed the mores of society. Wherever the early Christians entered a town the power structure got disturbed and immediately sought to convict them for being "disturbers of the peace" and "outside agitators." But they went on with the conviction that they were "a colony of heaven," and had to obey God rather than man. They were small in number but big in commitment. They were too God-intoxicated to be "astronomically intimidated." They brought an end to such ancient evils as infanticide and gladiatorial contest.

Things are different now. The contemporary church is often a weak, ineffectual voice with an uncertain sound. It is so often the arch-supporter of the status quo. Far from being disturbed by the presence of the church, the power structure of the average community is consoled by the church's silent and often vocal sanction of things as they are.

But the judgment of God is upon the church as never before. If the church of today does not recapture the sacrificial spirit of the early church, it will lose its authentic ring, forfeit the loyalty of millions, and be dismissed as an irrelevant social club with no meaning for the twentieth century. I am meeting young people every day whose disappointment with the church has risen to outright disgust.

Maybe again, I have been too optimistic. Is organized religion too inextricably bound to the status quo to save our nation and the world? Maybe I must turn my faith to the inner spiritual church, the church within the church, as the true *ecclesia* and the hope of the world. But again I am thankful to God that some noble souls from the ranks of organized religion have broken loose from the paralyzing chains of conformity and joined us as active partners in the struggle for freedom. They have left their secure congregations and walked the streets of Albany, Georgia, with us. They have gone through the highways of the South on tortuous rides for freedom. Yes, they have gone to jail with us. Some have been kicked out of their churches, and lost support of their bishops and fellow ministers. But they have gone with the faith that right defeated is stronger than evil triumphant. These men have been the leaven in the lump of the race. Their witness has been the spiritual salt that has preserved the true meaning of the gospel in these troubled times. They have carved a tunnel of hope through the dark mountain of disappointment.

I hope the church as a whole will meet the challenge of this decisive hour. But even if the church does not come to the aid of justice, I have no despair about the future. I have no fear about the outcome of our struggle in Birmingham, even if our motives are presently misunderstood. We will reach the goal of freedom in Birmingham and all over the nation, because the goal of America is freedom. Abused and scorned though we may be, our destiny is tied up with the destiny of America. Before the Pilgrims landed at Plymouth we were here. Before the pen of Jefferson etched across the pages of history the majestic words of the Declaration of Independence, we were here. For more than two centuries our foreparents labored in this country without wages; they made cotton king; and they built the homes of their masters in the midst of brutal injustice and shameful humiliation—and yet out of a bottomless vitality they continued to thrive and develop. If the inexpressible cruelties of slavery could not stop us, the opposition we now face will surely fail. We will win our freedom because the sacred heritage of our nation and the eternal will of God are embodied in our echoing demands.

I must close now. But before closing I am impelled to mention one other point in your statement that troubled me profoundly. You warmly commended the Birmingham police force for keeping "order" and "preventing violence." I don't believe you would have so warmly commended the police force if you had seen its angry violent dogs literally biting six unarmed, nonviolent Negroes. I don't believe you would so quickly commend the policemen if you would observe their ugly and inhuman treatment of Negroes here in the city jail; if you would watch them push and curse old Negro women and young Negro girls; if you would see them slap and kick old Negro men and young boys; if you will observe them, as they did on two occasions, refuse to give us food because we wanted to sing our grace together. I'm sorry that I can't join you in your praise for the police department.

It is true that they have been rather disciplined in their public handling of the demonstrators. In this sense they have been rather publicly "nonviolent." But for what purpose? To preserve the evil system of segregation. Over the last few years I have consistently preached that non-violence demands that the means we use must be as pure as the ends we seek. So I have tried to make it clear that it is wrong to use immoral means to attain moral ends. But now I must affirm that it is just as wrong, or even more so, to use moral means to preserve immoral ends. Maybe Mr. Connor and his policemen have been rather publicly nonviolent, as Chief Pritchett was in Albany, Georgia, but they have used the moral means of nonviolence to maintain the immoral end of flagrant racial injustice. T. S. Eliot has said that there is no greater treason than to do the right deed for the wrong reason.

I wish you had commended the Negro sit-inners and demonstrators of Birmingham for their sublime courage, their willingness to suffer and their amazing discipline in the midst of the most inhuman provocation. One day the South will recognize its real heroes. They will be the James Merediths, courageously and with a majestic sense of purpose facing jeering and hostile mobs and the agonizing loneliness that characterizes the life of the pioneer. They will be old, oppressed, battered Negro women, symbolized in a seventy-two-year-old woman of Montgomery, Alabama, who rose up with a sense of dignity and with her people decided not to ride the segregated buses, and responded to one who inquired about her tiredness with ungrammatical profundity: "My feet is tired, but my soul is rested." They will be the young high school and college students, young ministers of the gospel and a host of their elders courageously and nonviolently sitting-in at lunch counters and willingly going to jail for conscience's sake. One day the South will know that when these disinherited children of God sat down at lunch counters they were in reality standing up for the best in the American dream and the most sacred values in our Judeo-Christian heritage, and thusly, carrying our whole nation back to those great wells of democracy which were dug deep by the Founding Fathers in the formulation of the Constitution and the Declaration of Independence.

Never before have I written a letter this long (or should I say a book?). I'm afraid that it is much too long to take your precious time. I can assure you that it would have been much shorter if I had been writing from a comfortable desk, but what else is there to do when you are alone for days in the dull monotony of a narrow jail cell other than write long letters, think strange thoughts, and pray long prayers?

If I have said anything in this letter that is an overstatement of the truth and is indicative of an unreasonable impatience, I beg you to forgive me. If I have said anything in this letter that is an understatement of the truth and is indicative of my having a patience that makes me patient with anything less than brotherhood, I beg God to forgive me.

I hope this letter finds you strong in the faith. I also hope that circumstances will soon make it possible for me to meet each of you, not as an integrationist or a civil rights leader, but as a fellow clergyman and a Christian brother. Let us all hope that the dark clouds of racial prejudice will soon pass away and the deep fog of misunderstanding will be lifted from our fear-drenched communities and in some not too distant tomorrow the radiant stars of love and brotherhood will shine over our great nation with all of their scintillating beauty. Yours for the cause of Peace and Brotherhood,

Martin Luther King, Jr.

The United States and the World after the Cold War

The Cold War dominated world history after the Second World War. But 1991 saw two events that radically changed the international situation: the disintegration of the Soviet Union and the display of military power by the U.S.-led coalition of Western nations in the Persian Gulf War. While the end of the Cold War relieved the world of the imminent possibility of a worldwide conventional and nuclear conflict between rival superpowers, it did not bring about an era of peace. Ethnic and historic tensions, suppressed by the Cold War rivals, led to bloody conflicts in southern Europe, central Africa, and many parts of Asia. The victors of the Cold War, the United States and its NATO allies, cast about for new purpose. Militarily and economically superior to any other nation or group of nations in the world, there was much discussion about how that power should be employed. The NATO intervention in the Balkans in 1997 to protect Albanian Kosovars from Serbian nationalists and the destruction of the World Trade Center by Muslim radicals on September 11, 2001, refocused the question on the appropriate and effective use of *American* military power in the world. In 1997 the U.S. military demonstrated that it had far surpassed even its Western allies in military ability. But the terrorist attacks in 2001 proved that an open, democratic society, no matter how powerful, was vulnerable. The American response to the attacks also highlighted a new rift among Western nations. European countries, having experienced the tragedy of two world wars, favored a system of international relations governed by multilateral decision making in accordance with international law. The United States, wary of submitting to international law and fully capable of taking action on its own, proved willing to act unilaterally. The following selections focus on this issue of U.S. foreign policy. In the first, journalist Michael Barone describes how the United States went from a marginal nation to the sole superpower during the twentieth century. The next three selections follow a debate in print between two American foreign affairs experts over the proper role of the United States in world affairs. William Pfaff, a Paris-based journalist and author, cautions the United States against imperialism. Robert Kagan, a Washington-based scholar influential in the George W. Bush administration, argues that the United States has an obligation to use its power for the good of the rest of the world.

1. What flaws and dangers does William Pfaff point to in U.S. foreign policy?

2. How does Robert Kagan defend U.S. foreign policy?

The American Century

Michael Barone, U.S. News and World Report, December 27, 1999

On Dec. 8, 1941, the day after the attack on Pearl Harbor, Franklin D. Roosevelt stood before Congress and called for a declaration of war. "The American people in their righteous might," the president proclaimed, "will win through to absolute victory."

Absolute victory: No compromise, no deals with the enemy. *Righteous might*: Not just a strong America—a virtuous one. *The American people*: A people united, not just the military, or a few elected leaders.

With those 13 words, FDR sketched a history of the 20th century that, if exceedingly short, was also disarmingly accurate. In February 1941, Henry Luce, in his famous "American Century" editorial in *Life*, called on Americans to "accept whole-heartedly our duty and our opportunity as the most powerful and vital nation in the world . . . to exert upon the world the full import of our interests."

And so we have. The most riveting story of the 20th century is the rise of totalitarianism and its defeat at the hands of America. But there are other stories, other chapters. Luce could have no way of knowing it when he penned his editorial, but Americans literally took him at his word, thrusting upon the world the full import of their interests and energies over the course of these hundred years. At the dawn of a new millennium now, one may look back at the old and find it impossible not to recognize an indelible American imprint in virtually every area of human endeavor—in science and medicine, business and industry, arts and letters—it has been Uncle Sam's century. Over the years, America has been criticized by friend and foe for a dominance both real and perceived. But there is no gainsaying the fact that, if nations were people, Uncle Sam would be the man of the century.

The American legacy is impressive—but it is one no one could have predicted at the dawn of the now departing century. A hundred years ago, America was the largest of the great powers. Its economy had surged ahead of those in Europe. For all of America's sweep and swagger, however, Britain was the dominant world power, with the largest empire and Navy, rivaled only by Germany, with its huge Army and strength in science.

America, for many reasons, was unwilling and unready to inherit the mantle of leadership. The United States was united in name only, the wounds of the Civil War still far from healed. Though wages in the North were twice those in the South, few Southerners deigned to cross the Mason-Dixon line. On both sides of the divide, racial segregation was the order of the day. On the borders, meanwhile, immigrants were pouring in—17 million between 1890 and 1914. The new arrivals gave cold comfort to America's elites. The Poles, Jews, Italians, they feared, couldn't possibly become *true* Americans.

Happily, the elites were wrong—dead wrong. Before too long, an America that had been "a nation of loosely connected islands," as historian Robert Wiebe called it, was becoming a more cohesive and unified whole. The building blocks of the civic life we take for granted today soon began falling into place. The medical profession standardized the curricula of the nation's medical schools. The practice of law, once open to anyone, was limited to those who had passed state bar exams. Teachers worked from a common curriculum that emphasized English and civics. Education became a transforming engine. The number of kids enrolled in high schools quadrupled from 1890 to 1910. At more rarefied levels, dozens of great research universities were formed.

A new order. The way America worked changed, too. Businesses were transformed from buccaneering, seat-of-the-pants outfits run by ragged eccentrics into professionally managed organizations. Factories were increasingly run according to the precepts of "scientific" management. The concept was pioneered by Frederick W. Taylor. His time-and-motion studies reduced each task to single steps, allowing managers to maximize production, even by unskilled laborers. Suddenly, the chaotic and unstable economy of the 19th century was a thing of the past.

Nowhere was change so pronounced as in the military. "We are a great nation," Theodore Roosevelt said in 1898, "and we are compelled, whether we will or not, to face the responsibilities that must be faced by all great nations." This was not just rhetoric. In February 1898, as Americans protested Spain's suppression of a revolt in Cuba, Assistant Secretary of the Navy Roosevelt ordered the Pacific fleet to stand ready to attack the Philippines if war came. It did, and before American forces could roust the Spaniards from Cuba, Admiral Dewey sailed into Manila Harbor and destroyed the Spanish fleet. To the surprise and delight of TR, the "splendid little war" sparked enthusiasm among Southerners and Northerners alike. Americans were suddenly possessed of a swaggering new confidence: They could project power far beyond their borders to achieve good ends.

That confidence swelled when Roosevelt, as president, won a treaty to let America build the Panama Canal. American engineers succeeded where the French had failed, bridging jungles and mountains with an elaborate system of interlocking channels; at the same time, Dr. Walter Reed conquered yellow fever. The lesson, taught in textbooks for years after, was simple—and breathtaking: American expertise could make the world a better place.

But the world was an increasingly perilous place, too. No sooner had the Panama Canal opened, in August 1914, than Europe was plunged into

war—which leveraged its own kind of change. President Wilson national-
ized the railroads and the shipyards. Newspapers were censored. War critics
were jailed. In the meantime, Wilson raised a military of nearly 3 million
men, and Americans took pride in helping to win "the war to end wars."

After, America boomed economically. But still it declined to take up the
mantle of Britain, now exhausted by wartime costs and slaughter. At home
Americans disagreed furiously about Prohibition and, in the Scopes trial of
1925, science and religion. Mass immigration was ended in 1924, but the
melting pot kept bubbling. Millions of workers bought cars and fled the
teeming tenements on new highways. For a brief, shining moment,
Americans seemed freed from the workaday worries of the rest of the world.

So they were thoroughly unprepared for the shocks of the second third
of the century—worldwide depression and the rise of totalitarianism.
Between 1929 and 1933, the nation's economy shrank by nearly half; 1 in
4 workers was unemployed. Abroad, the wounds of World War I festered,
the result, Lenin's Soviet Russia in 1918, Mussolini's Fascist Italy in 1922,
Hitler's Nazi Germany in 1933.

Instead of dividing the nation, however, these shocks forged new
bonds of common purpose. Popular culture helped. Despite the Depression,
radio ownership doubled between 1929 and 1932. Americans went mad for
movies. In 1930, in a country of 130 million people, movie attendance hit 90
million a week. The big screen created the strongest popular culture since
Dickens and defined for the world a characteristic American style—breezy,
friendly, open, optimistic.

All the way. But war clouds soon gathered again. The Sudetenland, Austria,
Czechoslovakia—Nazi belligerence knew no bounds. Most Americans, however, were unmoved. It would require another president named Roosevelt to
change that. In June 1940, as France surrendered to Hitler and Britain prepared
for invasion, FDR started selling arms to Britain and boosted defense spending. Facing re-election, he took the politically risky steps of supporting a military draft, then dispatched 50 destroyers to Britain. Americans supported the
moves, and Roosevelt was re-elected. Almost immediately, he won more aid
for Britain. After Nazi forces attacked the Soviet Union in the summer of 1941,
Roosevelt sent arms to Moscow and blocked oil sales to Japan. Again,
Americans applauded: If it required war to stop totalitarianism, so be it.

Then came Pearl Harbor. "We are all in it together—all the way," FDR
said in his fireside chat, two days later. "Every single man, woman, and child
is a partner in the most tremendous undertaking in our American history."
Roosevelt built his war effort on cooperation between big government, big
business, big labor. America became "the arsenal of democracy," its industrial might churning out the awesome tools of victory: 7,333 ships, 299,000
aircraft, 634,000 jeeps, 88,000 tanks. The top-secret Manhattan Project,
which cost $2 billion—the nation's total economic production in 1940 was

$99 billion—produced the atomic bomb. The result was victory over Germany and Japan, confirming America's status as the world's dominant military and economic power.

Just as the first World War had, the war against the Axis powers wrought extraordinary change at home. Americans got used to working productively, and even creatively, in large organizations. Big business, big labor, and big government—with occasional friction—produced a bounteous economy, not another depression. Postwar America's "organization men" and "conformists" produced the baby boom, the habits of the burgeoning middle class reflected in the new universal culture of 1950s television. Church membership reached new highs. Crime fell to record lows. Confidence in major institutions surged. Americans were bound together by common experiences—the comprehensive high school, the military draft, large corporations, suburbia.

This was also Cold War America. In March 1946, Winston Churchill, now out of office, went to Fulton, Mo., with Harry Truman and proclaimed that, because of Joe Stalin, "an iron curtain" had fallen across Eastern Europe.

Americans responded boldly. The Truman Doctrine promised to protect all "free peoples of the world." The Marshall Plan provided vast economic aid to Europe. The NATO treaty of April 1949 was America's first peacetime military alliance. In June 1950, Truman sent troops to Korea to stop the Communist invasion. Defense spending increased, and stayed high for years. America was engaged in a "long, twilight struggle," John Kennedy said. And her people paid for it with high taxes for defense and foreign aid, a military draft, air-raid drills, and listening to Soviet threats of nuclear war over Berlin and Cuba. All that is taken for granted today, but in historic perspective it was extraordinary. "Only a society with enormous confidence in its achievements and in its future," as Henry Kissinger wrote later, "could have mustered the dedication and the resources to strive for a world order in which defeated enemies would be conciliated, stricken allies restored, and adversaries converted."

Doubts set in. It didn't last. Halfway around the globe, a commitment that started with just a few hundred Pentagon advisers escalated into a war with more than half a million American troops—a war that could not be won. Aides to Presidents Kennedy and Johnson had devised a military strategy in Vietnam that was incapable of working. Defense Secretary Robert McNamara scornfully dubbed it, "the social scientists' war."

It was a war many affluent Americans did not find important enough to draft their sons for. McNamara's draft system allowed college students to avoid service. Antiwar movements on elite campuses produced a generation of academics and professionals who regarded the United States and the Communists as morally equivalent. By 1968, many of the planners and supporters of the Vietnam War saw it as deeply immoral. They no longer believed, as the Roosevelts did, in American exceptionalism—the belief that this country was uniquely strong and uniquely good.

In other ways, the postwar system was breaking down. Congress had passed civil rights laws in response to the nonviolent movement led by Martin Luther King Jr. But black protesters called for violence in response to white oppression.

Big government produced not only war and riots, but also stagflation—high inflation and low economic growth. Big businesses grew less supple and creative, turning out gas guzzlers with "planned obsolescence." Big labor unions stagnated, then lost membership. And the cultural unity of postwar America was splintering. Families with two television sets and several radios no longer watched the same shows and listened to the same music. The universal popular culture of midcentury soon gave way to rival countercultures, many hostile to old values. Starting in the late 1960s, birth rates fell and divorce and births to unwed mothers rose: "the great disruption," as Francis Fukuyama calls it. Crime and welfare dependency tripled from 1965 to 1975.

As the elites lost confidence in America, the American people lost confidence in the elites. Richard Nixon's rhetorical appeals to "the silent majority" rallied only some Americans, and his cool pursuit of geopolitical advantage, the opening to China, and withdrawal from Vietnam failed to engage Americans' yearning for moral purpose, even before his own moral authority was destroyed by Watergate.

Foreign policy elites increasingly saw American strength as malevolent, and were pleased to see it reduced. This was symbolized by the 1977 treaty to relinquish the Panama Canal. Elites, guilty about how America obtained the canal, saw this as necessary to prevent violence in Panama. But most voters still felt pride in this great American achievement, and opposition to the treaty energized Ronald Reagan's nearly successful challenge of President Gerald Ford in 1976.

American pride sank even lower when Iran refused to release 52 Americans held hostage in the U.S. Embassy in November 1979. Under international law, this was an act of war. But for months President Jimmy Carter refused to use force and tried to negotiate, and his half-hearted seven-helicopter rescue attempt in April 1980 failed. Each Carter policy was approved in the polls. But in the end, voters wanted results. Carter was beaten soundly by Reagan, whose threats to use force resulted in the hostages' release just as he was sworn into office.

Reagan embodied the characteristic American style of the 1930s and 1940s movies in which he himself had been a star. He shared most Americans' pride in their country and rejected the guilt complex of the elites. His tax cuts led to two decades of solid economic growth and low inflation, interrupted by recession briefly in 1990-91. Complacent corporate executives were ousted by leveraged buyouts and directors seeking more profits. Big corporations were challenged by tiny start-ups: IBM was replaced as the major high-tech firm by Microsoft. American computers and high-tech—the latest manifestation of 20th-century Americans' scientific and technological expertise—led the world. The peacetime expansions of the 1980s and 1990s produced 40 million new jobs, while the sputtering economies of Europe and Asia produced virtually none. Ordinary Americans' incomes surged and widespread stock ownership resulted in a stock market boom and real gains in wealth for the masses.

Unmatched prowess. Abroad Reagan, despite scorn from the elites, pursued an assertive policy like Harry Truman's. He increased defense spending, sent American troops to Grenada, and supported anti-Communist forces in Central America and Afghanistan. The defense buildup and Reagan's Strategic Defense Initiative convinced Soviet leaders that they could never match the economic and technological prowess of the United States.

Like the two Roosevelts, Reagan insisted on proclaiming the superiority of the American system. In London in 1983, he predicted the demise of the Soviet Union. In Berlin in 1987, he demanded, "Mr. Gorbachev, tear down this wall." By October 1989 the wall was history. The Soviet empire soon followed.

Today, at century's end, America is unquestionably the world's dominant military, economic, and cultural superpower. This has been the work of the American people. The 76 million of 1900 are now the 273 million of 2000. The descendants of the immigrants who choked the slums in 1900 are now firmly interwoven into the American fabric. The descendants of the blacks who were excluded by segregation in 1900 now have full civil rights and are surging into the middle classes and upper ranks of society. The new immigrants from Latin America and East Asia who have arrived since the 1965 immigration reform are progressing as their counterparts did a century ago.

The American traditions of excellence fostered by the elite of the first third of the century and the characteristic American openness depicted in the popular culture of the second third of the century gave the American people the strength and the confidence to forge ahead in the last third of the century when so many in the elite lost confidence in their country. Sharing with Ronald Reagan the belief that this country is "a city on a hill," they have won through to absolute victory over totalitarianism, as Franklin Roosevelt promised, and have made this the American century that Henry Luce envisioned.

U.S. POPULATION:
1900: 75,994,575
2000: 273,482,000*

MEDIAN AGE:
1900: 22.9
2000: 35.7

URBAN VS RURAL:
1900: 40% urban, 60% rural
2000: 75% urban, 25% rural

BIRTHRATE:
1900: 32.3 births per thousand
2000: 14.2 births per thousand

IMMIGRANT POPULATION:
1900: 14.7 percent
2000: 7.9 percent

**BIGGEST SOURCE
OF IMMIGRANTS:**
1900: Austria-Hungary
2000: Mexico

NUMBER OF MILLIONAIRES:
1900: 3,000
2000: 3.5 million

AVERAGE INCOME:
1900: $8,620* a year
2000: $23,812 a year

**DEATHS FROM
INDUSTRIAL ACCIDENTS:**
1900: 35,000 a year
2000: 6,100 a year

AVERAGE WORK WEEK
1900: 60 hours
2000: 44 hours

**CITY WITH THE MOST
MILLIONAIRES PER CAPITA:**
1900: Buffalo
2000: Seattle

**POPULATION OF
LOS ANGELES:**
1900: 102,479
2000: 3.8 million

CIGARETTES PRODUCED:
1900: 4 billion
2000: 720 billion

DAILY NEWSPAPERS:
1900: 2,226
2000: 1,489

FARM POPULATION:
1900: 29,875,000
2000: 4,600,000

NUMBER OF FARMS:
1900: 5,740,000
2000: 2,191,510

DOW JONES INDUSTRIAL AVERAGE:
1900: 68.13
2000: 11,000

PATENTS GRANTED:
1900: 24,656
2000: 147,500

PASSENGER AUTOS REGISTERED IN U.S.:
1900: 8,000
2000: 130 million

HIGHWAY FATALITIES:
1900: 36 per 100 million miles
2000: 1.64 per 100 million miles

MILES OF PAVED ROAD:
1900: 10
2000: 4 million

CARS PRODUCED IN U.S.:
1900: 5,000
2000: 5.5 million

**ADULTS COMPLETING
HIGH SCHOOL:**
1900: 15 percent
2000: 83 percent

HOMES WITH ELECTRICITY:
1900: 8 percent
2000: 99.9 percent

PRICE OF A STAMP:
1900: 59 cents*
2000: 33 cents

**FEDERAL BUDGET
OUTLAY:**
1900: $10.3 billion*
2000: $1.7 trillion

DEFENSE EXPENDITURES:
1900: $4 billion*
2000: $268 billion

NATIONAL DEBT:
1900: $24.8 billion*
2000: $5 trillion

**PER CAPITA
NATIONAL DEBT:**
1900: $325*
2000: $23,276

VOTER TURNOUT:
1900: 73.7 percent
2000: 48.9 percent

BOOKS PUBLISHED:
1900: 6,356
2000: 65,800

**AVERAGE SIZE OF
HOUSEHOLD:**
1900: 4.76 persons
2000: 2.62 persons

BEER CONSUMPTION:
1900: 58.8 gallons per adult
2000: 31.6 gallons per adult

NUMBER OF BISON:
1900: 400
2000: 200,000

**LIFE EXPECTANCY
FOR MEN:**
1900: 46.3 years
2000: 73.6 years

**LIFE EXPECTANCY
FOR WOMEN:**
1900: 48.3 years
2000: 79.7 years

MOST POPULAR SONG:
1900: "Good-Bye Dolly Gray"
2000: "Believe"

DEATHS IN CHILDBIRTH:
1900: 9 per thousand
2000: 0.1 per thousand

CANCER DEATHS:
1900: 64 per 100,000
2000: 200 per 100,000

DIVORCED MEN:
1900: 0.3 percent
2000: 8.2 percent

DIVORCED WOMEN:
1900: 0.5 percent
2000: 10.3 percent

William Pfaff, International Herald Tribune, April 9, 2002

Paris. Ever since communism collapsed, the notion has been put about in Washington that the United States should exercise its unrivaled power as an empire. This is held to be the way to bring stability to international society and solve the problems of terrorism, rogue nations, weapons of mass destruction and so forth.

To some in Washington, empire seems a career opportunity. To the ordinary American, I suspect, it simply looks like trouble. Military "empire" the United States already has. In the narrow military dimension, it dominates the world. But this is not readily translated into political power. The Bush administration has until now been unable to do anything about the war in the Middle East, where the United States identifies two of its most important national interests: a strategic interest in oil and political interest in the security of Israel.

The administration has let an unchecked Israeli-Palestinian war do immense damage to the overall American position in the Middle East and cause much harm elsewhere.

The "imperial" solution would have been to dictate terms of a political settlement and enforce them, with military power if necessary, against one side or the other or against both sides.

Secretary of State Colin Powell's coming visit to the region does not promise an imperial solution. It promises ultimately unsuccessful efforts to get another cease-fire and to start negotiations anew, on terms that will fail.

Afghanistan is slipping backward because of Washington's reluctance to assume an "imperial" role there, assuming that the foreign and domestic political costs would be too high.

Advocates of American empire are usually seduced by the notion that Washington's imperial authority would be accepted as positive, and that the empire would therefore be consensual. This idea rests on the uninformed assumption that the United States is generally seen abroad as benevolent.

Powell should explain to the president that even in allied Europe, disposed for more than 50 years to think well of America, Washington's exercise of power is seen as a serious international problem.

American unilateralism, which mostly used to be a containable matter of congressional egos and petulance, has now been turned into a foreign policy by the Bush administration. This undermines the fragile structure of international law and convention built up during the last three centuries, to which the United States made important contributions.

International law, since the 17th century, has rested on two principles: national sovereignty and the legal equality of nations, both of which Washington ignores whenever convenient.

American political, economic and cultural influence is not generally stabilizing. It uproots stable structures, for good or for ill. It means to do so. The Bush administration is a crusading government. There seem to be many in the administration who are convinced that military force can impose desirable political solutions. They think that Ariel Sharon has been doing a good job. Brute force can solve political problems, but it usually creates others. A solution for Israel's problem would be to drive the Palestinians into neighboring countries. One doubts that this is the road to lasting peace in the Middle East.

The statesman Edmund Burke once remarked that no greater calamity can befall a nation than to break with its past. The American past has been the rule of law, constitutional order, a free press, suspicion of power politics, avoidance of foreign entanglements and even hostility to standing armies.

The country's one adventure into imperialism, in 1898, proved not very satisfactory, and 18 years after fighting a war to acquire the Philippines, Congress promised the islands independence.

The Cold War broke America from that past. For a long time one could think that when the Cold War ended the United States would return to its better past. It hasn't happened.

The proposals for empire offered today are not intellectually serious, but they are significant. The political class and bureaucracy have become addicted to international power. They want more. The question is whether the people will follow.

Robert Kagan, Washington Post, May 26, 2002

President Bush is making a noble effort to pull together the fraying alliance, but the fact is Europeans and Americans no longer share a common view of the world. On the all-important question of power—the utility of power, the morality of power—they have parted ways. Europeans believe they are moving beyond power into a self-contained world of laws and rules and transnational negotiation and cooperation. Europe itself has entered a post-historical paradise, the realization of Immanuel Kant's "Perpetual Peace." The United States, meanwhile, remains mired in history, exercising power in the anarchic Hobbesian world where international rules are unreliable and where security and the promotion of a liberal order still depend on the possession and use of military might. This is why, on major strategic and international questions today, Americans are from Mars and Europeans are from Venus: They agree on little and understand one another less and less. Why the divergent perspectives? They are not deeply rooted in national character. Two centuries ago American statesmen appealed to international law and disdained "power politics," while European statesmen spoke of *raison d'etat*. Europeans marched off to World War I believing in power and martial glory, while Americans talked of arbitration treaties. Now the roles have reversed.

Part of the reason is the enormous shift in the balance of power. The gap between the United States and Europe opened wide as a result of World War II and has grown wider in the past decade. America's unparalleled military strength has predictably given it a greater propensity to use force and a more confident belief in the moral legitimacy of power. Europe's relative weakness has produced an aversion to force as a tool of international relations. Europeans today, like Americans 200 years ago, seek a world where strength doesn't matter so much, where unilateral action by powerful nations is forbidden, where all nations regardless of their strength are protected by commonly agreed rules of behavior. For many Europeans, progress toward such a world is more important than eliminating the threat posed by Saddam Hussein.

For Americans, the Hobbesian world is not so frightening. Unilateralism is naturally more attractive to those with the capacity to act unilaterally. And international law constrains strong nations more than it does the weak. Because of the disparity of power, Americans and Europeans even view threats differently. A person armed only with a knife may decide that a bear prowling the forest is a tolerable danger—trying to kill the bear is riskier than lying low and hoping the bear never attacks. But a person with a rifle will likely make a different calculation: Why should he risk being mauled to death if he doesn't need to? Americans can imagine successfully invading Iraq and toppling Saddam, and therefore more than 70 percent of Americans favor such action, particularly after the experience of Sept. 11. Europeans, not surprisingly, find the prospect unimaginable and frightening.

But it is not just the power gap that divides Americans and Europeans today. Europe's relatively pacific strategic culture is also the product of its war-like past. The European Union is a monument to Europe's rejection of the old power politics. Who knows the dangers of *Machtpolitik* better than a French or German citizen? As the British diplomat Robert Cooper recently noted, Europe today lives in a "postmodern system" that does not rest on a balance of power but on "the rejection of force" and on "self-enforced rules of behavior." *Raison d'etat* has been "replaced by a moral consciousness."

American realists may scoff, but within the confines of Europe the brutal laws of power politics really have been repealed. Since World War II European society has been shaped not by the traditional exercise of power but by the unfolding of a geopolitical miracle: The German lion has lain down with the French lamb. The new Europe has succeeded not by balancing power but by transcending power. And now Europeans have become evangelists for their "postmodern" gospel of international relations. The application of the European miracle to the rest of the world has become Europe's new *mission civilisatrice*. If Germany can be tamed through gentle rapprochement, why not Iraq?

This has put Europeans and Americans on a collision course. Americans have not lived the European miracle. They have no experience of promoting ideals and order successfully without power. Their memory of the past 50 years is of a Cold War struggle that was eventually won by strength and determination, not by the spontaneous triumph of "moral consciousness." As good children of the Enlightenment, Americans believe in human perfectibility. But Americans from Donald Rumsfeld to Madeleine Albright also believe that global security and a liberal order depend on the United States—that "indispensable nation"—wielding its power in the dangerous, Hobbesian world that still flourishes, at least outside Europe. Especially after Sept. 11, most Americans remember Munich, not Maastricht.

The irony is that this transatlantic disagreement is the fruit of successful transatlantic policies. As Joschka Fischer and other Europeans admit, the United States made the "new Europe" possible—by leading the democracies to victory in World War II and the Cold War and by providing the solution to the age-old "German problem." Even today Europe's rejection of power politics ultimately depends on America's willingness to use force around the world against those who still do believe in power politics. Europe's Kantian order depends on the United States using power according to the old Hobbesian rules.

Most Europeans don't acknowledge the great paradox: that their passage into post-history has depended on the United States not making the same passage. Instead, they have come to view the United States simply as a rogue colossus, in many respects a bigger threat to the pacific ideals Europeans now cherish than Iraq or Iran. Americans, in turn, have come to view Europe as annoying, irrelevant, naive and ungrateful as it takes a free ride on American power. This is not just a family quarrel. If Americans and Europeans no longer agree on the utility and morality of power, then what remains to undergird their military alliance?

George W. Bush did not create these problems, and he alone won't solve them. Indeed, there is no sure cure for this transatlantic divergence. Those on both sides of the Atlantic who implore Europe to increase its military capabilities are right—though a Europe that has so little belief in power is unlikely to spend the money to get more of it. Those who ask Americans to show some generosity of spirit, what the Founders called "a decent respect for the opinion of mankind," are also right. The United States should honor multilateralism and the rule of law when it can, and try to build some international political capital for those times when unilateral action is unavoidable. But even if it does, will Europeans show the necessary tolerance for American power?

Whatever else we do, let's stop pretending that we agree. That pretense has done little for the alliance since the end of the Cold War than create more confusion, misunderstanding and anger. Better that we should face our differences head on. That is the necessary first step on the road to recovery.

William Pfaff, International Herald Tribune, August 1, 2002

Paris. A new metaphor has been introduced into the trans-Atlantic dialogue, portraying Europe as enjoying a "Kantian paradise" made possible by the United States' ordering of a Hobbesian world.

Europe, by virtue of its wartime and postwar experience, is said to have established "a post-historical paradise of peace and relative prosperity, the realization of Kant's 'perpetual peace.'" This benign achievement causes West Europeans to recoil from the use of force, and to see international problems generally as open to rational and negotiated solutions. My quotation, and the argument, are from Robert Kagan of the Carnegie Endowment in Washington, whose widely promoted views have been reprinted in a number of foreign journals.

Kagan goes on to say that Europeans can enjoy this happy condition because a sober and illusion-free United States patrols the frontiers, beyond which lies a Hobbesian world where lions and tigers roam and good intentions unaccompanied by power can prove fatal.

The Europeans are congratulated on having put their bad past behind them—while being reminded that it was American intervention in two world wars that rescued them, and American Cold War power that spared them Soviet domination.

They also are congratulated on wishing to deal with the conflicts and problems beyond Europe with dialogue and persuasion. One day, they are reassured, that might even be practical.

Meanwhile, international order is maintained by an unsentimental United States, too wise to indulge illusions about dialogue and compromise in dealing with thugs, dictators, rogue governments and terrorists.

Kagan was an early promoter, in 1996, of the proposition that as circumstances have placed the United States in a position of world hegemony, this "hegemony must be actively maintained, just as it was actively obtained . . . . Any lessening of that influence will allow others to play a larger part in shaping the world to suit *their* needs."

He collaborated then with William Kristol, the neoconservative advocate of American foreign policy unilateralism who has probably been the most important single outside influence on the George W. Bush administration.

In 2000, the two observed that American hegemony is not only to American benefit but that of the world, since the United States "does not pursue a narrow, selfish definition of its national interest . . . and infuses its foreign policy with an unusually high degree of morality."

This is not an argument to which all will assent. One can make a better argument that American policies today are frequently the cause of international disorder and destabilization, and that they are more often driven by domestic advantage than by altruism.

Currently, Washington is debating whether or not to attack or invade Iraq in order to overthrow and replace that country's unsavory government. This cannot possibly promote stability in the Middle East in the short term, or in the longer run, other than by resort to a forecast—which most specialists would classify as amateurish wishful thinking—that Saddam Hussein's overthrow would cause democratic governments to spring up in his country and throughout the region. Why? A second Washington debate is whether to make an unprovoked attack on Iran to destroy a nuclear power reactor being built there with Russian assistance, under inspection by the International Atomic Energy Agency, within the terms of the Nuclear Nonproliferation Treaty, of which Iran is a signatory. It is again impossible to interpret such an action as promoting international order, or to justify it other than by way of a highly speculative scenario of Iranian nuclear attack on a neighboring country or on the United States.

No other government in the world would support such an action, other than Israel's. Israel would do so not because it expected to be attacked by Iran but because it not unreasonably opposes any nuclear capacity in the hands of any Islamic government.

The Bush administration's policy of providing virtually unqualified support—out of essentially domestic political motives—to Israel's policies in the occupied territories and Gaza is a self-evident source of potential regional disorder, as every government in the Near and Middle East and the Maghreb, from Turkey to Morocco, has already advised Washington. The argument that the United States today protects international society from Hobbesian disorder is untrue. Washington acts as Kagan in 1996 urged it to act, to protect a hegemonic position that serves its political and economic interests, and its perceived security.

There is indeed a Hobbesian world out there. It is one in which the United States is a determined and self-interested player, not noticeably inhibited by its "unusually high degree" of national morality.

Cultural Diversity

Imperialism, nationalism, and racism have been at the root of much of the horrific violence and oppression in the last two hundred years. We have only to note the genocidal wars in Rwanda and the former Yugoslavia in the past decade to realize that ethnic and racial strife was not ended with the defeat of the Nazis in 1945. As a result, concepts such as "multiculturalism" and "cultural diversity" have arisen as an alternative to racial or ethnic bigotry. These terms, however, are quite fluid and mean different things to different people. For some, valuing diversity means respecting others differences; for others, it means that any cross-cultural value or moral judgments are out of bounds. In either case, the intent is to empathize with people from other cultures, recognizing and appreciating their uniqueness, while refraining from any qualitative judgments. While this certainly is a healthier form of intercultural contact than imperialist oppression or extermination, such assumptions may have unintended negative consequences. According to Thomas Sowell, the current prevailing meaning of "cultural diversity" will lead to cultural stagnation. He argues that certain cultures at certain times and in certain places were better than others in certain respects or better adapted to the situation of the times. It is these attributes, he claims, that advance not just that culture but also all human civilization. Thus, he attempts to redefine "cultural diversity" so that it both serves as a rejection of racist and nationalist assumptions of cultural superiority and as a useful model for intercultural relations.

---

1. How does Sowell define "cultural diversity"?

2. According to Sowell, what is the function of culture? To what extent should cultures be protected?

3. Do you think his redefinition of "cultural diversity" works? Why or why not?

Sowell, Thomas, "Cultural Diversity: A World View," *The American Enterprise* (May/June, 1991), pp. 44–5. Reprinted with permission from *The American Enterprise*, a magazine of politics, business, and culture. On the web at <<http://www.TAEmag.com>>.

Diversity

"Diversity" has become one of the most often used words of our time—and a word almost never defined. Diversity is invoked in discussions of everything from employment policy to curriculum reform and from entertainment to politics. Nor is the word merely a description of the long-known fact that the American population is made up of people from many countries, many races, and many cultural backgrounds. All that was well known long before the word "diversity" became an insistent part of our vocabulary, an invocation, an imperative, or a bludgeon in ideological conflicts.

The very motto of the country—*E Pluribus Unum*—recognizes the diversity of the American people. For generations, this diversity has been celebrated, whether in comedies like *Abie's Irish Rose* (the famous play featuring a Jewish boy and an Irish girl) or in patriotic speeches on the Fourth of July. Yet one senses something very different in today's crusades for "diversity"—certainly not a patriotic celebration of America and often a sweeping criticism of the United States, or even a condemnation of Western civilization as a whole.

At the very least, we need to separate the issue of the general importance of cultural diversity—not only in the United States but in the world at large—from the more specific, more parochial, and more ideological agendas which have become associated with that word in recent years. I would like to talk about the *worldwide* importance of cultural diversity over centuries of human history before returning to the narrower issues of our time.

The entire history of the human race, the rise of man from the caves, has been marked by transfers of cultural advances from one group to another and from one civilization to another. Paper and printing, for example, are today vital parts of Western civilization—but they originated in China centuries before they made their way to Europe. So did the magnetic compass, which made possible the great ages of exploration that put the Western Hemisphere in touch with the rest of mankind. Mathematical concepts likewise migrated from one culture to another: trigonometry from ancient Egypt, and the whole numbering system now used throughout the world originated among the Hindus of India, though Europeans called this system Arabic numerals because it was the Arabs who were the intermediaries through which these numbers reached medieval Europe. Indeed, much of the philosophy of ancient Greece first reached Western Europe in Arabic translations, which were then retranslated into Latin or into the vernacular languages of the West Europeans.

Much that became part of the culture of Western civilization originated *outside* that civilization, often in the Middle East or Asia. The game of chess came from India, gunpowder from China, and various mathematical concepts from the Islamic world, for example. The conquest of Spain by Moslems in the eighth century A.D. made Spain a center for the diffusion into Western Europe of the more advanced knowledge of the Mediterranean world and of the Orient in astronomy, medicine, optics, and geometry. The later rise of Western Europe to world preeminence in science and technology built upon these foundations, and then the science and technology of European civilization began to spread around the world, not only to European offshoot societies such as the United States or Australia but also to non-European cultures, of which Japan is perhaps the most striking example.

The historic sharing of cultural advances, until they became the common inheritance of the human race, implied much more than cultural diversity. It implied that some cultural features were not only different from others but *better* than others. The very fact that people—all people, whether Europeans, Africans, Asians, or others—have repeatedly chosen to abandon some feature of their own culture in order to replace it with something from another culture implies that the replacement served their purposes more effectively: Arabic numerals are not simply different from Roman numerals, they are *better* than Roman numerals. This is shown by their replacing Roman numerals in many countries whose own cultures derived from Rome, as well as in other countries whose respective numbering systems were likewise superseded by so-called Arabic numerals.

It is virtually inconceivable today that the distances in astronomy or the complexities of higher mathematics should be expressed in Roman numerals. Merely to express the year of American independence—MDCCLXXVI— requires more than twice as many Roman numerals as Arabic numerals. Moreover, Roman numerals offer more opportunities for errors, as the same digit may be either added or subtracted, depending on its place in the sequence. Roman numerals are good for numbering kings or Super Bowls, but they cannot match the efficiency of Arabic numerals in most mathematical operations—and that is, after all, why we have numbers at all. Cultural features do not exist merely as badges of "identity" to which we have some emotional attachment. They exist to meet the necessities and forward the purposes of human life. When they are surpassed by features of other cultures, they tend to fall by the wayside or to survive only as marginal curiosities, like Roman numerals today.

Not only concepts, information, products, and technologies transfer from one culture to another. The natural produce of the Earth does the same. Malaysia is the world's leading grower of rubber trees—but those trees are indigenous to Brazil. Most of the rice grown in Africa today originated in Asia, and its tobacco originated in the Western Hemisphere. Even a great wheat-exporting nation like Argentina once imported wheat, which was not an indigenous crop to that country. Cultural diversity, viewed internationally and historically, is not a static picture of differentness but a dynamic picture of competition in which what serves human purposes more effectively survives while what does not tends to decline or disappear.

Manuscript scrolls once preserved the precious records, knowledge, and thought of European or Middle Eastern cultures. But once paper and printing from China became known in these cultures, books were clearly far faster and cheaper to produce and drove scrolls virtually into extinction. Books were not simply different from scrolls; they were *better* than scrolls. The point that some cultural features are better than others must be insisted on today because so many among the intelligentsia either evade or deny this plain reality. The intelligentsia often use words like "perceptions" and "values" as they argue in effect that it is all a matter of how you choose to look at it.

They may have a point in such things as music, art, and literature from different cultures, but there are many human purposes common to peoples of all cultures. They want to live rather than die. for example. When Europeans first ventured into the arid interior of Australia, they often died of thirst or hunger in a land where the Australian aborigines had no trouble finding food or water. Within that particular setting, at least, the aboriginal culture enabled people to do what both aborigines and Europeans wanted to do—survive. A given culture may not be superior for all things in all settings, much less remain superior over time, but particular cultural features may nevertheless be clearly better for some purposes—not just different.

Why is there any such argument in the first place? Perhaps it is because we are still living in the long, grim shadow of the Nazi Holocaust and are understandably reluctant to label anything or anyone "superior" or "inferior." But we don't need to. We need only recognize that particular products, skills, technologies, agricultural crops, or intellectual concepts accomplish particular purposes better than their alternatives. It is not necessary to rank one whole culture over another in all things, much less to claim that they remain in that same ranking throughout history. They do not.

Clearly, cultural leadership in various fields has changed hands many times. China was far in advance of any country in Europe in a large number of fields for at least a thousand years and, as late as the sixteenth century, had the highest standard of living in the world. Equally clearly, China today is one of the poorer nations of the world and is having great difficulty trying to catch up to the technological level of Japan and the West, with no real hope of regaining its former world preeminence in the foreseeable future.

Similar rises and falls of nations and empires have been common over long stretches of human history—for example, the rise and fall of the Roman Empire, the "golden age" of medieval Spain and its decline to the level of one of the poorest nations in Europe today, the centuries-long triumphs of the Ottoman Empire—intellectually as well as on the battle-fields of Europe and the Middle East—and then its long decline to become known as "the sick man of Europe." Yet, while cultural leadership has changed hands many times, that leadership has been real at given times, and much of what was achieved in the process has contributed enormously to our well-being and opportunities today. Cultural competition is not a zero-sum game. It is what advances the human race.

If nations and civilizations differ in their effectiveness in different fields of endeavor, so do social groups. Here there is especially strong resistance to accepting the reality of different levels and kinds of skills, interests, habits, and orientations among different groups of people. One academic writer, for example, said that nineteenth-century Jewish immigrants to the United States were fortunate to arrive just as the garment industry in New York began to develop. I could not help thinking that Hank Aaron was similarly fortunate—that he often came to bat just as a home run was due to be hit. It might be possible to believe that these Jewish immigrants just happened to be in the right place at the right time if you restricted yourself to their history in the United States. But, again taking a world view, we find Jews prominent, often predominant, and usually prospering, in the apparel industry in medieval Spain, in the Ottoman Empire, in the Russian Empire, in Argentina, in Australia, and in Brazil. How surprised should we be to find them predominant in the same industry in America?

Other groups have also excelled in their own special occupations and industries. Indeed, virtually every group excels at something. Germans, for example, have been prominent as pioneers in the piano industry. American piano brands like Steinway and Schnabel, not to mention the Wurlitzer organ, are signs of the long prominence of Germans in this industry, where they produced the first pianos in colonial America. Germans also pioneered in piano-building in Czarist Russia, Australia, France, and England. Chinese immigrants have, at one period of history or another, run more than half the grocery stores in Kingston, Jamaica, and Panama City and conducted more than half of all retail trade in Malaysia, the Philippines, Vietnam, and Cambodia. Other groups have dominated retail trade in other parts of the world—the Gujaratis from India in East Africa and in Fiji or the Lebanese in parts of West Africa, for example.

Nothing has been more common than for particular groups—often a minority—to dominate particular occupations or industries. Seldom do they have any ability to keep out others—and certainly not to keep out the majority population. They are simply *better* at the particular skills required in that occupation or industry. Sometimes we can see why. When Italians have made wine in Italy for centuries, it is hardly surprising that they should become prominent among wine-makers in Argentina or in California's Napa Valley. Similarly, when Germans in Germany have been for centuries renowned for their beer-making, how surprised should we be that in Argentina they became as prominent among beer-makers as the Italians were among wine-makers? How surprised should we be that beer-making in the United States arose where there were concentrations of German immigrants—in Milwaukee and St. Louis, for example? Or that the leading beer producers to this day have German names like Anheuser-Busch or Coors, among many other German names?

Just as cultural leadership in a particular field is not permanent for nations or civilizations, neither is it permanent for given racial, ethnic, or religious groups. By the time the Jews were expelled from Spain in 1492, Europe had overtaken the Islamic world in medical science, so that Jewish physicians who sought refuge in the Ottoman Empire found themselves in great demand in that Moslem country. By the early sixteenth century, the sultan of the Ottoman Empire had on his palace medical staff 42 Jewish physicians and 21 Moslem physicians. With the passage of time, however, the source of the Jews' advantage—their knowledge of Western medicine—eroded as successive generations of Ottoman Jews lost contact with the West and its further progress. Christian minorities within the Ottoman Empire began to replace the Jews, not only in medicine but also in international trade and even in the theater, once dominated by Jews. The difference was that these Christian minorities—notably Greeks and Armenians—maintained their ties in Christian Europe and often sent their sons there to be educated. It was not race or ethnicity as such that was crucial but maintaining contacts with the ongoing progress of Western civilization. By contrast, the Ottoman Jews became a declining people in a declining empire. Many, if not most, were Sephardic Jews from Spain—once the elite of world Jewry. But by the time the state of Israel was formed in the twentieth century, those Sephardic Jews who had settled for centuries in the Islamic world now lagged painfully behind the Ashkenazic Jews of the Western world—notably in income and education. To get some idea what a historic reversal that has been in the relative positions of Sephardic Jews and Ashkenazic Jews, one need only note that Sephardic Jews in colonial America sometimes disinherited their own children for marrying Ashkenazic Jews.

Why do some groups, subgroups, nations, or whole civilizations excel in some particular fields rather than others? All too often, the answer to that question must be: Nobody really knows. It is an unanswered question largely because it is an *unasked* question. There is an uphill struggle merely to get acceptance of the fact that large differences exist among peoples, not just in specific skills in the narrow sense (computer science, basketball, or brewing beer) but more fundamentally in different interests, orientations, and values that determine which particular skills they seek to develop and with what degree of success. Merely to suggest that these internal cultural factors play a significant role in various economic, educational, or social outcomes is to invite charges of "blaming the victim." It is much more widely acceptable to blame surrounding social conditions or institutional policies.

But if we look at cultural diversity internationally and historically, there is a more basic question whether blame is the real issue. Surely, no human being should be blamed for the way his culture evolved for centuries before he was born. Blame has nothing to do with it. Another explanation that has had varying amounts of acceptance at different times and places is the biological or genetic theory of differences among peoples. I have argued *against* this theory in many places but will not take the time to go into these lengthy arguments here. A world view of cultural differences over the centuries undermines the genetic theory as well. Europeans and Chinese, for example, are clearly genetically different. Equally clearly, China was a more advanced civilization than Europe in many scientific, technological, and organizational ways for at least a thousand years. Yet over the past few centuries, Europe has moved ahead of China in many of these same ways. If those cultural differences were due to genes, how could these two races have changed positions so radically from one epoch in history to another?

All explanations of differences between groups can be broken down into heredity and environment. Yet a world view of the history of cultural diversity seems, on the surface at least, to deny both. One reason for this is that we have thought of environment too narrowly—as the immediate surrounding circumstances or differing institutional policies toward different groups. Environment in that narrow sense may explain some group differences, but the histories of many groups completely contradict that particular version of environment as an explanation. Let us take just two examples out of many which are available.

Jewish immigrants from Eastern Europe and Italian immigrants from southern Italy began arriving in the United States in large numbers at about the same time in the late nineteenth century, and their large-scale immigration also ended at the same time, when restrictive immigration laws were passed in the 1920s. The two groups arrived here in virtually the same economic condition—namely, destitute. They often lived in the same neighborhoods, and their children attended the same schools, sitting side by side in the same classrooms. Their environments—in the narrow sense in which the term is commonly used—were virtually identical. Yet their social histories in the United States have been very different.

Over the generations, both groups rose, but they rose at different rates, through different means, and in a very different mixture of occupations and industries. Even wealthy Jews and wealthy Italians tended to become rich in different sectors of the economy. The California wine industry, for example, is full of Italian names like Mondavi, Gallo, and Rossi, but the only prominent Jewish wine-maker—Manischewitz—makes an entirely different kind of wine, and no one would compare Jewish wine-makers with Italian wine-makers in the United States. When we look at Jews and Italians in the very different environmental setting of Argentina, we see the same general pattern of differences between them. The same is true if we look at the differences between Jews and Italians in Australia, or Canada, or Western Europe.

Jews are not Italians and Italians are not Jews. Anyone familiar with their very different histories over many centuries should not be surprised. Their fate in America was not determined solely by their surrounding social conditions in America or by how they were treated by American society. They were different before they got on the boats to cross the ocean, and those differences crossed the ocean with them.

We can take it a step further. Even among Ashkenazic Jews. those originating in Eastern Europe have had significantly different economic and social histories from those originating in Germanic Central Europe, including Austria as well as Germany itself. These differences have persisted among their descendants not only in New York and Chicago but as far away as Melbourne and Sydney. In Australia. Jews from Eastern Europe have tended to cluster in and around Melbourne, while Germanic Jews have settled in and around Sydney. They even have a saying among themselves that Melbourne is a cold city with warm Jews while Sydney is a warm city with cold Jews.

A second and very different example of persistent cultural differences involves immigrants from Japan. As everyone knows, many Japanese Americans were interned during World War II. What is less well known is that there is and has been an even larger Japanese population in Brazil than in the United States. These Japanese, incidentally, own approximately three-quarters as much land in Brazil as there is in Japan. (The Japanese almost certainly own more agricultural land in Brazil than in Japan.) In any event, very few Japanese in Brazil were interned during World War II. Moreover, the Japanese in Brazil were never subjected to the discrimination suffered by Japanese Americans in the decades before World War II.

Yet, during the war. Japanese Americans, overwhelmingly, remained loyal to the United States, and Japanese-American soldiers won more than their share of medals in combat. But in Brazil, the Japanese were overwhelmingly and even fanatically loyal *to Japan*. You cannot explain the difference by anything in the environment of the United States or the environment of Brazil. But if you know something about the history of those Japanese who settled in these two countries, you know that they were culturally different *in Japan, before* they ever got on the boats to take them across the Pacific Ocean—and they were still different decades later.

These two groups of immigrants left Japan during very different periods in the cultural evolution of Japan itself. A modern Japanese scholar has said: "If you want to see Japan of the Meiji era, go to the United States. If you want to see Japan of the Taisho era, go to Brazil." The Meiji era was a more cosmopolitan, pro-American era: the Taisho era was one of fanatical Japanese nationalism.

If the narrow concept of environment fails to explain many profound differences between groups and subgroups, it likewise fails to explain many very large differences in the economic and social performances of nations and civilizations. An eighteenth-century writer in Chile described that country's many natural advantages in climate, soil. and natural resources—and then asked in complete bewilderment why it was such a poverty-stricken country. That same question could be asked of many countries today. Conversely, we could ask why Japan and Switzerland are so prosperous when they are both almost totally lacking in natural resources. Both are rich in what economists call "human capital"—the skills of their people. No doubt there is a long and complicated history behind the different skill levels of different peoples and nations. The point here is that the immediate environment—whether social or geographic—is only part of the story.

Geography may well have a significant role in the history of peoples, but perhaps not simply by presenting them with more or less natural resources. Geography shapes or limits peoples opportunities for cultural interactions and the mutual development that comes out of that. Small, isolated islands in the sea have seldom been sources of new scientific advances or technological breakthroughs—regardless of where such islands were located and regardless of the race of the people on these islands. There are islands on land as well. Where soil fertile enough to support human life exists only in isolated patches, widely separated, there tend to be isolated cultures (often with different languages or dialects) in a culturally fragmented region. Isolated highlands often produce insular cultures, lagging in many ways behind the cultures of the lowlanders of the same race—whether we are talking about medieval Scotland, colonial Ceylon, or the contemporary Montagnards of Vietnam.

With geographical environments as with social environments, we are talking about long-run effects not simply the effects of immediate surroundings. When Scottish highlanders, for example, immigrated to North Carolina in colonial times, they had a very different history from that of Scottish lowlanders who settled in North Carolina. For one thing, the lowlanders spoke English while the highlanders spoke Gaelic—on into the nineteenth century. Obviously, speaking only Gaelic—in an English-speaking country—affects a group's whole economic and social progress.

Geographical conditions vary as radically in terms of how well they facilitate or impede large-scale cultural interactions as they do in their distribution of natural resources. We are not even close to being able to explain how all these geographical influences have operated throughout history. That too is an unanswered question largely because it is an unasked question—and it is an unasked question because many are seeking answers in terms of immediate social environment or are vehemently insistent that they have already found the answer in those terms.

How radically do geographic environments differ—not just in terms of tropical versus arctic climates but also in the very configuration of the land and how that helps or hinders large-scale interactions among peoples? Consider one statistic: Africa is more than twice the size of Europe, and yet Africa has a shorter coastline than Europe. That seems almost impossible. But the reason is that Europe's coastline is far more convoluted, with many harbors and inlets being formed all around the continent. Much of the coastline of Africa is smooth—which is to say, lacking in the harbors which make large-scale maritime trade possible by sheltering the ships at anchor from the rough waters of the open sea. Waterways of all sorts have played a major role in the evolution of cultures and nations around the world. Harbors on the sea are not the only waterways. Rivers are also very important. Virtually every major city on Earth is located either on a river or a harbor. Whether it is such great harbors as those in Sydney, Singapore, or San Francisco; or

London on the Thames, Paris on the Seine, or numerous other European cities on the Danube, waterways have been the lifeblood of urban centers for centuries. Only very recently has manmade, self-powered transportation like automobiles and airplanes made it possible to produce an exception to the rule like Los Angeles. (There is a Los Angeles River, but you don't have to be Moses to walk across it in the summertime.) New York has both a long and deep river and a huge sheltered harbor.

None of these geographical features in themselves create a great city or develop an urban culture. Human beings do that. But geography sets the limits within which people can operate—and in some places it sets those limits much wider than others. Returning to our comparison of the continents of Europe and Africa, we find that they differ as radically in rivers as they do in harbors. There are entire nations in Africa without a single navigable river—Libya and South Africa, for example. "Navigable" is the crucial word. Some African rivers are navigable only during the rainy season. Some are navigable only between numerous cataracts and waterfalls. Even the Zaire River, which is longer than any river in North America and carries a larger volume of water, has too many waterfalls, too close to the ocean for it to become a major artery of international commerce. Such commerce is facilitated in Europe not only by numerous navigable rivers but also by the fact that no spot on the continent, outside of Russia, is more than 500 miles from the sea. Many places in Africa are more than 500 miles from the sea, including the entire nation of Uganda.

Against this background, how surprised should we be to find that Europe is the most urbanized of all inhabited continents and Africa the least urbanized? Urbanization is not the be-all and end-all of life, but certainly an urban culture is bound to differ substantially from nonurban cultures, and the skills peculiar to an urban culture are far more likely to be found among groups from an urban civilization. (Conversely, an interesting history could be written about the failures of urbanized groups in agricultural settlements.)

Looking within Africa, the influence of geography seems equally clear. The most famous ancient civilization on the continent arose within a few miles on either side of Africa's longest navigable river, the Nile, and even today the two largest cities on the continent, Cairo and Alexandria, are on that river. The great West African kingdoms in the region served by the Niger River and the long-flourishing East African economy based around the great natural harbor on the island of Zanzibar are further evidences of the role of geography. Again, geography is not all-determining—the economy of Zanzibar has been ruined by government policy in recent decades—but nevertheless, geography is an important long-run influence on the shaping of cultures as well as in narrowly economic terms.

What are the implications of a world view of cultural diversity on the narrower issues being debated under that label in the United States today?

Although "diversity" is used in so many different ways in so many different contexts that it seems to mean all things to all people, there are a few themes which appear again and again. One of these broad themes is that diversity implies organized efforts at the preservation of cultural differences, perhaps governmental efforts, perhaps government subsidies to various programs run by the advocates of "diversity."

This approach raises questions as to what the purpose of culture is. If what is important about cultures is that they are emotionally symbolic, and if differentness is cherished for the sake of differentness, then this particular version of cultural "diversity" might make some sense. But cultures exist even in isolated societies where there are no other cultures around—where there is no one else and nothing else from which to be different. Cultures exist to serve the vital, practical requirements of human life—to structure a society so as to perpetuate the species, to pass on the hardearned knowledge and experience of generations past and centuries past to the young and inexperienced in order to spare the next generation the costly and dangerous process of learning everything all over again from scratch through trial and error—including fatal errors. Cultures exist so that people can know how to get food and put a roof over their head, how to cure the sick, how to cope with the death of loved ones, and how to get along with the living. Cultures are not bumper stickers. They are living, changing ways of doing all the things that have to be done in life.

Every culture discards over time the things which no longer do the job or which don't do the job as well as things borrowed from other cultures. Each individual does this, consciously or not, on a day-to-day basis. Languages take words from other languages, so that Spanish as spoken in Spain includes words taken from Arabic, and Spanish as spoken in Argentina has Italian words taken from the large Italian immigrant population there. People eat Kentucky Fried Chicken in Singapore and stay in Hilton Hotels in Cairo.

This is *not* what some of the advocates of "diversity" have in mind. They seem to want to preserve cultures in their purity, almost like butterflies preserved in amber. Decisions about change, if any, seem to be regarded as collective decisions, political decisions. But that is not how any cultures have arrived where they are. Individuals have decided for themselves how much of the old they wished to retain, how much of the new they found useful in their own lives. In this way, cultures have enriched each other in all the great civilizations of the world. In this way, great port cities and other crossroads of cultures have become centers of progress all across the planet. No culture has grown great in isolation—but a number of cultures have made historic and even astonishing advances when their isolation was ended, usually by events beyond their control.

Japan was a classic example in the nineteenth century, but a similar story could be told of Scotland in an earlier era, when a country where once even the nobility were illiterate became—within a short time, as history is measured—a country which produced world pioneers in field after field: David Hume in philosophy, Adam Smith in economics, Joseph Black in chemistry, Robert Adam in architecture, and James Watt, whose steam engine revolutionized modern industry and transport. In the process, the Scots lost their language but gained world preeminence in many fields. Then a whole society moved to higher standards of living than anyone ever dreamed of in their poverty-stricken past.

There were higher standards in other ways as well. As late as the eighteenth century, it was considered noteworthy that pedestrians in Edinburgh no longer had to be on the alert for sewage being thrown out the windows of people's homes or apartments. The more considerate Scots yelled a warning, but they threw out the sewage anyway. Perhaps it was worth losing a little of the indigenous culture to be rid of that problem.

Those who use the term "cultural diversity" to promote a multiplicity of segregated ethnic enclaves are doing an enormous harm to the people in those enclaves. However they live socially, the people in those enclaves are going to have to compete economically for a livelihood. Even if they were not disadvantaged before, they will be very disadvantaged if their competitors from the general population are free to tap the knowledge, skills, and analytical techniques which Western civilization has drawn from all the other civilizations of the world, while those in the enclaves are restricted to what exists in the subculture immediately around them.

We need also to recognize that many great thinkers of the past—whether in medicine or philosophy, science or economics—labored not simply to advance whatever particular group they happened to have come from but to advance the human race. Their legacies, whether cures for deadly diseases or dramatic increases in crop yields to fight the scourge of hunger, belong to all people—and all people need to claim that legacy, not seal themselves off in a dead-end of tribalism or in an emotional orgy of cultural vanity.

THINKING ACROSS CULTURES

1. If you had to come up with a one-word label for the twentieth century, what would that word be? Why? What other words did you consider and reject? Why?

2. To what extent are the events of the twentieth century the result of ideas and events in the late eighteenth and nineteenth centuries? Give a few examples.

3. What are some aspects of the relationship between Western and non-Western societies in the twentieth century? Compare this to the

relationship between West and non-West in the Age of Encounters and the Modern Era.

4. As the United States finds itself the sole super power at the beginning of the twenty-first century, what lessons might it draw from the past on how to exercise that power?

5. While knowledge of history does not allow one to predict the future, it does allow us to think in terms of possible outcomes. Based on the events and ideas of the twentieth century, what might we expect of the twenty-first?